The Circular Structure of Power

PHRONESIS

A series from Verso edited by
Ernesto Laclau and Chantal Mouffe

There is today wide agreement that the left-wing project is in crisis. New antagonisms have emerged – not only in advanced capitalist societies but also in the Eastern bloc and in the Third World – that require the reformulation of the socialist ideal in terms of an extension and deepening of democracy. However, serious disagreements exist as to the theoretical strategy needed to carry out such a task. There are those for whom the current critique of rationalism and universalism puts into jeopardy the very basis of the democratic project. Others argue that the critique of essentialism – a point of convergence of the most important trends in contemporary theory: post-structuralism, philosophy of language after the later Wittgenstein, post-Heideggerian hermeneutics – is the necessary condition for understanding the widening of the field of social struggles characteristic of the present stage of democratic politics. *Phronesis* clearly locates itself among the latter. Our objective is to establish a dialogue between these theoretical developments and left-wing politics. We believe that an anti-essentialist theoretical stand is the sine qua non of a new vision for the Left conceived in terms of a radical and plural democracy.

The Circular Structure of Power

Politics, Identity, Community

TORBEN BECH DYRBERG

London · New York

First published by Verso 1997

Verso
UK: 6 Meard Street, London W1V 3HR
USA: 180 Varick Street, New York NY 10014–4606

Verso is the imprint of New Left Books

ISBN 1–85984–846–X
ISBN 1–85984–152–X (pbk)

British Library Cataloguing in Publication Data
A catalogue record for this book is available from the British Library

Library of Congress Cataloging-in-Publication Data

Dyrberg, Torben Bech.
The Circular Structure of Power / Torben Bech Dyrberg.
p. cm. — (Phronesis)
Includes bibliographical references and index.
ISBN 1–85984–846–X. — ISBN 1–85984–152–X (pbk.)
1. Liberty. 2. Social control. I. Title. II. Series: Phronesis (London, England)
JC585.L133 1997
320'.01'1—dc20 96–10251
CIP

Typeset by Password Publishing, Norwich
Printed and bound in Great Britain by
Biddles Ltd Guildford and King's Lynn

Contents

Acknowledgements ix
Foreword by Chantal Mouffe x
Introduction 1

1 Power as an Influence Term and Decision Making 20
The Behaviourist Conception of Power as Causation 21
Power as an Influence Term I: Reason and Autonomy versus Causation and Power 30
Power as an Influence Term II: Indirect Influence and Anticipating Reactions 38

2 Power, Causality and Political Agency in the Community Power Debate 50
Decision Making and the 'Two Faces of Power' 51
The 'Third Face of Power': Lukes's Theory of Power 63
The Problem of Power and Structure in Lukes's Theory: Causality and Responsibility in Power Relations 70

3 Power, Identity and Political Authority: Foucault's Power Analytics 85
The Politics of Foucault's Power Analytics 85
Power as Ability: Dispensing with the Constituent Subject 88
The Circular Structure of Identity: Reflecting on Limits 93
The Circular Structure of Power: The Politics of Representation 99

The Political Authorization of Power: The Juridico-discursive Representation of Power and Disciplinary Power 105
Concluding Remarks: On Power and Politics 111

4 The Presuppositionless Conception of Power: Power as Negativity 116
Advancing a Presuppositionless Concept of Power 116
I The Discursive Structuring of Social Reality 118
The Logics of Difference and Equivalence 118
Overdetermination and Hegemonic Power Struggles 123
Overdetermination as a Kind of Causality 130
II Power as Negativity and Identity 132
Power as Negativity 132
The Constitution and Negation of Identity 136
Antagonism and the Imaginary Nature of Identity 145

5 Identity and the Politics of Subjective and Real Interests 156
The Great Gift of Real Interests 158
Lukes's and Connolly's Conceptualization of Real Interests 163
How do Real Interests (Re)present Themselves 170
The Relation between Real Interests and Power 173
Concluding Remarks: Real Interests and Autonomy 178

6 Democracy and the Politics of Interests and the Common Good 183

The Circular Structure of Power I: The Political and Politics 184

The Circular Structure of Power II: Political Representation 191
The Democratic Political Community and the Common Good 194
The Common Good I: The Political and the Social 200
The Common Good II: Individual Interests and the Public Interest 208
Value Pluralism and Liberal Democracy 221
Concluding Remarks on Hegemony and Democracy 234

Postscript on Conceptualizing Power 238
Power as Retroactive Causation 238
The Circular Structure of Ability and its Conceptualization 241
Order as Reality Effect 245
The Political Ordering of Power 249
Origin and Power: Is There a Will to Order? 252

Notes 257

Index 286

Figures
2.1 Power and responsibility 74
3.1 Ability and making a difference 97
3.2 Political authority, sovereignty and social control 110
4.1 Identity and negation 147

Sincerity!
Cultivate this virtue
and realize
the profound truth that
the manifest and hidden are one.

Morihei Ueshiba

Acknowledgements

Throughout the years it took me writing this book, I have benefited greatly from discussions with various people. First of all I would like to thank Ernesto Laclau without whom the present work would not have been possible. The stimulating intellectual environment in his seminars in the Department of Government, University of Essex, has been of inestimable importance. Also I would like to thank my parents, Kirsten and Oluf Dyrberg, as well as colleagues and friends: Assad Al-Shamlan, Henrik Bjørn Andersen, Benjamin Arditi, Henrik Paul Bang, Steven Bastow, William E. Connolly, Michael Freedon, Sue Golding, John G. Gunnell, Thomas Blom Hansen, Bob Jessop, Ami Moris, Hawa Rohany, Steen Salomonson, Charles E. Scott, Jens Peter Frølund Thomsen, Jacob Torfing and Jeremy Valentine.

Foreword

Chantal Mouffe

Power is a crucial category for political theory, yet it is a very elusive one. Attempts to define its nature have so far proved inconclusive and the very terms of the debate are still being contested. Is power derived from agency or from structure? Should it be seen as adhering to social systems or as a capacity to act? What does it mean to have or to exercise power?

Two main approaches to power are usually distinguished. The first, represented by the pluralist and elitist traditions, emphasizes the dimension of 'power over' and the existence of power struggles linked to conflicts of interest: the second, found in Talcott Parsons and Hannah Arendt, among others, stresses the collective capacity, the 'power to', and privileges the dimension of consensus.

In this book Torben Bech Dyrberg argues convincingly that both perspectives are inadequate and undertakes the formulation of an alternative approach. Taking the work of Michel Foucault as his starting point, his declared aim is to elaborate a non-derivative conception of power. This means envisaging power as coterminous with the constitution of identity and identification. Such a view can, in his view, be identified as 'postmodern' because it questions not only the transcendental objectivity of premodern views of the social order, but also the quasi-transcendental objectivity necessitated by the modern view. This postmodern conception of power should not be understood, though, as transcending modernity but rather as coming to terms with the modern condition of contingency, with the absence of ground, which was a characteristic of modernity since its inception. An important part of his argument is that this implies coming to terms with the political itself.

A non-derivative conceptualization of power needs to bring to the fore the immanence and irreducibility of power, which has to be envisaged in terms of negativity. This requires taking Foucault's power analytics a step further by showing how negativity plays a constitutive role in identity through identification. To do that, Dyrberg draws on recent developments in discourse analysis and Lacanian theory. Central to his analysis are the concepts of hegemony, antagonism and undecidability, which he mobilizes to show the imaginary nature of identity. According to such a perspective, every 'identity' is the result of a process of identification which always takes place within a complex set of power relations.

A central concern of the book is to bring to the fore the far-reaching consequences of such a conception of power for politics. Once power is no longer conceived as an external relation taking place between two pre-constituted identities but as shaping the identities themselves, democratic politics appears under a different light. Indeed, if relations of power are constitutive of the social, the main question of democratic politics cannot any more be how to eliminate power but, instead, how to constitute relations of power that are compatible with democratic values.

Another important consequence refers to the relations between power and legitimacy. The recognition of the purely constructed nature of social relations must find its complement in the purely pragmatic grounds of the claims to power legitimacy. This indicates that there is no unbridgeable gap between power and legitimacy – not obviously in the sense that all power would be automatically legitimate, but in the sense that: (a) if any power has been able to impose itself, it is because it has been recognized as legitimate in some quarters; and (b) if legitimacy is not based in an apprioristic ground, it is because it is based in some form of successful power.

This link between legitimacy and power is precisely what the model of 'deliberative democracy', currently in vogue, is unable to recognize, because it posits the possibility of a type of rational argumentation where power has been eliminated and where legitimacy is grounded on pure rationality. The deliberative democracy approach posits that political questions, in so far as they are of a moral nature, can be decided rationally. In its Habermasian version, the discourse-centred approach to ethics is presented as providing, through the exchange of arguments and counter-arguments the most suitable procedure for the universalization of interests and for the rational regulation of political questions. According to such a view, legitimacy in modern democratic societies is based on the conviction that the collective decision-making processes are arranged in such a way that they produce decisions which are the expression of an impartial standpoint which is equally in the interest of all.

Against this new avatar of the already long list of attempts to eliminate power by subordinating it to reason, Dyrberg rightly reminds us that power is an inescapable feature of human interaction, that it is ubiquitous, and that no identities can be formed independently of its effects. This is not to say that notions like democracy, the common good or public interest should be abandoned. They must instead be rethought in terms of what psychoanalysis helps us to envisage as an 'impossible good', that is, a good that exists as good only *so far* as we cannot reach it.

Introduction

Approaching the Problem of Power

'Power' is a complex and ambiguous term. Speaking of it, one is immediately struck by its contradictory status: ubiquitous and yet at once seemingly self-evident, it tends to suggest a whole host of meanings, ranging from the ability of individuals to achieve their goals despite resistance to the way in which a social order may be structured and reproduced. To clarify what the various theories of power typically revolve around, we can single out two main clusters of issues.

The first deals with the basis and nature of power. The central questions are typically whether power is anchored in and hence derived from agency or structure, and whether power as ability or capacity is a causal concept that somehow combines intentions and consequences. Often power is presented as an agency concept, focusing on the volitional or intentional aspects of social interaction. Power is located in the relations between individual or collective agents that either gain or lose power in their attempt to pursue their intentions or goals. Conversely, it can be understood as a mechanism or medium which binds together, or at least makes possible, the foundation of society, and which, as a consequence, appears to determine the broader forms of communal association.

The second issue deals with what might be termed the characteristics of power and focuses on what it means to have and to exercise power. This issue revolves around a number of more- or less-closely interrelated questions such as whether power, either as an agency or structural concept, is facilitative or prohibitive, productive or repressive, consensual or conflictual; whether power operates manifestly and/or latently; whether power relations are intentional or nonintentional, direct or indirect; and whether power should be conceptualized solely in terms of its exercise and/or in terms of resources and mechanisms which agents can draw upon when exercising power.

These two issues are themselves intertwined inasmuch as an identification of the basis and nature of power – sometimes referred to as the causal powers of agents and structures – leads directly into a characterization of power. Even though the two issues are connected, I am primarily interested in the first one because the problem of the basis and nature of power allows one to ask the pertinent question whether it is at all meaningful to conceptualize power in terms of derivation. This problem can be illustrated by a simple question, namely what it means to say that an individual, an organization or a party *has* power. This question touches, of course, on both of the two main issues, but it is the ontological problem of what it means to 'have' power which is fundamental for a theory of power. The first issue is in this respect prior to the second.

I do not, then, intend to go into detail about the various problems that arise in the attempt to provide an exhaustive characterization of power unless, that is, it is relevant to the main issue I am looking at, namely its basis and nature. Having said this, there are, generally speaking, two broad categories of characterizing power.

On the one side, we find a conception of power that is asymmetrical in that it stresses that power entails conflicts of vested interests, that power struggles are zero-sum games of winners and losers, that power, consequently, is 'power over'. This is because it secures compliance or control, or is a relation of dependence or a hierarchical relation of inequality. A view of power on these lines emphasizes that power by prohibiting, restricting, dominating, and so forth, establishes or maintains relations of superordination and subordination. Usually, but not always, this view goes hand in hand with agency conceptions of power for which power is located in agents' attempt to impose their will or interests on others despite their resistance. The pluralist and elitist traditions (which will be discussed in the second and third chapter) are typical examples of this approach to power.

On the other side, we have a symmetrical or communal conception of power that stresses that power is a collective capacity, a kind of community resource, which is more closely related to consensus than to conflict. In the case of conflicts we have a plus-sum game, meaning that everybody can gain, which in turn is based on the assumption that power, basically, is 'power to'. In this more benign view of power, phenomena such as conflict and domination that are associated with 'power over', are typically seen as parasitic upon, and as a perversion of, 'power to'. This approach stresses, when it is slanted towards an emancipatory interest, that superordination/subordination is not a 'necessary' feature of social relations (this position is defended, amongst others, by Benton and Isaacs). This approach can also be biased towards conservatism, as in the case of Parsons, where power, by depending upon the institutionalization of authority, is functional for the reproduction of the social order by facilitating social and systemic integration. In both cases, we find a view of power that locates it in collective action, systemic mechanisms or structures, and which underlines its productive nature.[1]

Power and the Structure/Agency Dualism

The aim of this book is not to go in depth into the intricate problems connected with the dualism between agency and structure, and how the various attempts to advance beyond this dualism are related to the conceptualization of power. My aim is more modest in this respect. I will focus on what I see as the basic assumptions that are built into the views of power – based as they usually are on agency and/or structure – in order to single out the central problems facing attempts to come to terms with the basis and nature of power. The general theme, which is the red thread running through the book, is to problematize the underlying assumption that implicitly or explicitly informs most theories of power, namely that power can be based on and thus derived from either agency or structure, as if these categories were not themselves somehow constituted by power.

The basic assumption of agency conceptions of power is that the relation between agent and structure has to be external. It is only by positing this relation as external that the dictum that individuals are by nature autonomous and rational can get off the ground. The external relation between agency and structure implies, in other words, that agency is internal to itself – that it is fully constituted, so to speak. The subject is viewed as constitutive, and this means, more concretely, that it is defined apart from, or as prior to, structure, which, again, is one of the main reasons why the latter is usually conceived in terms of external constraints on action.

Whilst agency conceptions are solidly rooted in the subject/object dualism, structural conceptions of power eliminate this dualism by getting rid of the subject. This is done by reducing the subject to subject positions within a structural totality, and this implies that the relation between subject position and structure must be internal. Practice is thus understood in terms of the rules and positions that govern it, and which the subject when 'acting' is a bearer of. This attack on the essentialism of the subject, as it is expressed in agency conceptions of power, slides, nevertheless, into an essentialism of the structure into which the subject is inserted. The reason is that the structural totality has to be internal to itself in order to be able to fully determine the subject. It is only to the extent to which it is capable of doing this that the subject can be reduced to subject position.

In these two diametrically opposed approaches which are mirror images of each other, we are faced with two forms of essentialism, namely those of the subject and object respectively. Since the mid-seventies, what has typically characterized the debates on the basis and nature of power has been to advance beyond this deadlock which characterizes the dualism of agency and structure. The aim has been to overcome what came to be seen as an outdated and sterile opposition between action and what constrained it. The discussions, in which Giddens is one of the most prominent figures, have focused on how agents are not only determined and restricted by structures, but also how these condition and facilitate agents by positioning them, thereby equipping them with the rules and resources, and hence the means to further their ends.

However, to re-stitch the gap between agency and structure by redefining the problem in terms of what constrains and what facilitates agency does not in the least undermine subject/object dualism.[2] The reason is that this dualism is not anchored in what is related to the characteristics of power, but is instead founded on the basis and nature of power. This means that power within agency and structural conceptions ultimately rests on the dictum of the constitutive subject and the constitutive structural totality respectively. It is this problem of essentialism one has to take issue with in order to challenge structure/agency dualism and the theories of power that are based on a reformulation of this dualism. The single most important task, then, is to scrutinize the often implicit assumptions that lie at the root of theories of power, namely that power is derived from either agency or structure, or a combination of the two that stresses that 'free will' is always circumscribed by the context in which agents operate. It is in this light that the dualism between agency and structure has to be situated.

Although the problem of agency and structure is a fairly recent debate in social and political theory it is, nevertheless, one that has a long tradition in Western intellectual history. Within political theory, political philosophy and democratic theory it is linked to the problem of the relationship between individual and community. In modernity it can be traced back to the tradition of social-contract theory from Hobbes onwards. The individual's faculty of will is, on the one hand, taken for granted, which is to say that it is prior to, and thus presupposed by, the contract. Or, to put it differently, contract *qua* contract presupposes that it is voluntarily entered by autonomous and rational individuals, otherwise it could not be legally and morally binding. Yet this constitutive subject can, on the other hand, only exist within the framework created by the contract (the social order), and this implies that the contract not only presupposes the constitutive subject, but also takes an active part in actually constituting it. The contract is, accordingly, the vehicle of what might be called the moment of undecidability which has played, and still plays, a decisive role – notably for the liberal tradition. It is, moreover, important for understanding the relationship between the subject and political power. The *raison d'être* of the contract has traditionally been to establish a firm ground for the monopolization of political power in the state whose legitimacy, in turn, is based upon consent.

What we find here is the first indication of a peculiar circularity that pertains to the structuring of power as well as the eclipse of politics. The subject is not only presupposed by the contract and hence by political power, it is also posed in this operation when political power posits the subject 'as it is'. Political power retroactively constructs the subject as a being whose autonomy and rationality antedates the political event of the entering of the contract. This construction plays a decisive role for political power whose source of legitimation lies in its own political construction of the pre-politically given subject. Again we find the ambiguity that pertains to modern discourses of power and politics, namely that, whilst the monopolization of political power plays a constitutive role for the social order, it also poses a threat to the subject, which is why it should be controlled and its scope restricted.[3]

It is this circularity in which politics posits its own presuppositions – or more precisely, it is this ultimately failed attempt to close the circle which triggers politics in the first place and keeps a space open for it – that smuggles an element of 'impurity' into the idea of the constitutive subject. At the same time, it builds an emancipatory vision of the end of politics into the discourses of political power, which characterizes modern political discourses – in particular, of course, its two main protagonists: liberalism and Marxism. We can thus say that in modernity political power is derogated to play merely a supplementary role, that it is located in, or in relation to, the state and that it is defined and legitimized in terms of its goal to maintain order. Hence the inability or unwillingness on the part of political modernity to play out the constitutive nature of political power.

It is this paradoxical relationship, in which political power posits its own presuppositions, that makes it important to challenge the dominant view, advocated by liberalism and the 'New Left', that political power is, and should remain, located in the state as the site of its legitimate exercise in order to protect civil society. This assumption – as it is advocated by, for example, Habermas, Held and Keane – inevitably assigns a schizophrenic role to political power, namely that it is a 'necessary evil'. It is necessary because it subjectifies the subject 'as it is' and, by extension, secures order; and it is evil in that it subjects, in the sense of encroaching upon, the autonomy and rationality of the subject. This predominantly negative, and in any case paradoxical, view of power as natural, necessary and repressive – as something that is inseparable from our freedom whilst also repressing it – can only be understood in the light of the modern attempt to monopolize political power in the state, and to domesticate it in terms of juridical and moral discourses. Foucault captures this understanding of political power when he says that '[p]ower makes men mad, and those who govern are blind; only those who keep their distance from power, who are in no way implicated in tyranny, shut up in their Cartesian poêle, their room, their meditations, only they can discover the truth.'[4]

Structure/agency dualism cannot be dealt with adequately in isolation from this paradoxical relationship between the subject and political power, nor can it be solved simply by giving way for an interaction between agency and structure. The problem does not disappear by arguing that structure instead of constraining action also facilitates it. The problem of the basis and nature of power – which can be approached as the problem of the extent to which it is warranted to conceptualize power in terms of derivation – cannot be solved by displacing the discussion to one that looks at the characteristics of power. Similarly, the relationship between the subject and political power – and, more broadly, the relationship between the individual and community – cannot be adequately dealt with by saying that the latter constrains and facilitates the former.

Instead, the crucial issue concerns the very objectivity of the categories of agency and structure, which is all-important for understanding the nature of power. The reason is that it is only in so far as agency and structure are objectively given – that is, given prior to the undecidability that pertains to politics and which politics cannot, accordingly, interfere with – that power can be conceptualized as being based on and, in turn, derived from these categories. As soon as this objectivity is problematized, as soon as it is questioned that power is based on, or caused by, something it cannot itself affect, the derivative status of power is itself cast into doubt.

The circular structuring of the relation between the subject and political power indicates, as already mentioned, that it is problematic to derive power from either agency or structure. Agency can only be fully constituted, be objectively given or internal to itself *vis-à-vis* a structure that posits it as presupposed, and which, accordingly, in this very act both constitutes it and subverts its internality to itself. This is the reason why a non-derivative conception of power cannot simply combine purposeful action and the structural means to sustain action. A theory of power has to address the fundamental question which this problematization of the 'causal powers' of either the subject or structure gives way for, namely what it actually means that the subject 'has' power.

A Non-Derivative Conceptualization of Power

As we begin to tease out the key issues involved in conceptualizing power and the traditions within political and social theory to which they adhere, a different theoretical approach becomes apparent. It is one intimately connected with political struggle and creativity; and yet, at the same time, one that commands no absolute ground or overarching authority. It is an approach that emphasizes that power is an irreducible relation or process; irreducible in the sense that it cannot be derived from anything above, beyond or pre-existing the very relations which constitute that process. Nor can power be derived from any form of social objectivity, such as free will or structural determination. It is this derivative notion of power that I challenge throughout, maintaining instead that power adheres to nothing but itself.

The irreducibility of power, I suggest further, must of necessity call for an approach that has a critical dimension; though not of course by virtue of claiming to exist in some manner 'outside' power, for this would lead us straight back to the point I am refuting, namely that of presupposing social objectivity. Rather, it calls for an approach that is critical in the sense of deconstructing the claims of such an objectivity, irrespective of whether it is cast in terms of the legitimate authority of political power or an emancipatory interest, or as structure or agency.

Irrespective of the fact that there is no agreement whatsoever as to how power should be defined, it could none the less be said that, in the most rudimentary sense, all notions of power entail 'ability'. One could go further and suggest that as power must be contextualized in some way in relation to the issue of the subject, then ability becomes a (if not the) defining characteristic of subjectivity. In short, we could say that the subject *has* power. And yet this form of 'having' – or alternatively, of 'not having' – raises a number of thorny issues, not the least of which deals with the question: how do we theorize or come to understand the very conditions within which ability is made possible, particularly when the concept of agency as such is being challenged?

This approach to power is one which addresses the metaphysically loaded conceptions of the subject whose ability is for the most part taken for granted, in the sense that it precedes the 'possession' or 'dispossession' of power. Inquiries into who has power, how they acquired it, and how much and under what circumstances are not fundamental to an understanding of ability, although they may no doubt be crucial in other contexts. They are necessarily secondary issues in a study of how ability is constituted, which is the proper subject matter for a theory of power that does not ground power in something outside itself. It is in this sense, then, that I propose to sketch the contours of a non-derivative conceptualization of power, which I believe is crucial for political theory, and which will be cast in terms of the constitution of identity.

As is well known, Michel Foucault went a long way towards addressing this question. My approach, however, whilst deeply indebted to his work, analyses in a substantively different way the claim that 'the subject has power'. I want to argue that this claim – and, more to the point, theorization of the very conditions of possibility from which this 'having' might emerge, take root or be maintained – requires a certain flirtation with a kind of transcendental logic. But, having said this, it must be emphasized that these conditions of possibility are not to be understood as simply 'there', that is, as simply 'awaiting recognition'; nor are they posed as somehow existing prior to power. Rather, these conditions, and the transcendentalism to which they point, must be understood against, or in terms of, the copula: ability *is* power.

There is no attempt here, in other words, to unveil some hidden condition; nor, on the other hand, is there a move to privilege or even accept a notion of power *as such*, if by this we mean that 'the real thing' can actually be found. Instead, I want to examine the very nub of the paradox that although power does not exist 'as such', it nevertheless 'makes a difference' – or, perhaps, it *is* difference, *that* which cannot be conceptualized proper.

In order to grasp this paradox, we must reconsider what the subject must be like in order to 'have' power and, therewith, ability. Indeed, we must reconsider, and in fact reject, the implicit assumption that in order to 'possess' (or not possess) power, there could ever be a subject existing prior to, or in some way apart from, that ability or power. But this also means that the very identity of the subject, as well as social and political constructs in general, cannot be taken for granted or reduced to the structural positionality of the subject *per se*. Rather, I am going to suggest that it must be studied in terms of an immanent process, that is, in the becoming of identity. It is to be able to grasp this moment of becoming, or this process in which identity is constructed, that the conceptualization of power has to be non-derivative. The reason is that in so far as power derives from something else, say, agency or structure, or a combination of the two, the moment of the becoming of identity cannot but presuppose what, in fact, needs scrutiny. The conceptualization of power cannot, in other words, presuppose the objectivity of the social (that the structuring of the social is grounded in, say, transcendental structures or the faculty of will), but has, on the contrary, to deconstruct what appears as given.

The attempt to outline this particular conception of power might at first appear as an odd and rather self-refuting undertaking, especially in light of the increasing stress on contextualism and relationalism that has characterized the intellectual history of the twentieth century. For, as has often been intoned, power is everywhere: in political relations, in economic relations, in gender relations, in juridical relations, regardless of how one chooses to define these relations. Given this, one might ask if it is not equally the case that there must be several conceptions of power on offer. One might even wish to reverse the problem and pose power as entailing a 'common core' to all those relations, something which *is* power stripped of all its contextual specificity – that is to posit a rock-bottom 'fact' of power.

I want to demur in both cases. There is no general form of power; nor, for that matter, is there an infinite set of particular types of power. I want to maintain, and notwithstanding these two cases, that power exists only in terms of a 'forgetting of its origins', that is, a forgetting of itself as 'pure' ability. The point is to draw attention to the nature of ability as the becoming of identity that, analytically speaking, is prior to its particular form and content. And more than that, I want to insist that it is only in terms of this 'forgetting' – or, to state it in a more affirmative manner, it is only in accepting a non-derivative concept of power – that one can begin to account for the variety of relations of political struggle, and indeed for the political itself in a non-reductionist way. The reason is, as already indicated, that in so far as power is based in social objectivity, such as agency or structure; and politics is conceived merely as a supplement to, say, an economic or social logic, then power and politics are deprived of their means of expression, so to speak. That is, by being reducible to other logics their specific nature cannot be accounted for.

The task I have set myself is not so much to advance yet another definition of power as to come to terms with the most important underlying problems facing its conceptualization, and to consider the consequences of these for political theory. Such an undertaking revolves, first of all, around what power as ability entails; this, analytically speaking, comes prior to the distributive question of 'who gets what, how, when and why?' This is not to suggest that this and similar questions are irrelevant, but rather that they – implicitly or explicitly – operate on the basis of ready-made assumptions as to the basis and nature of power as well as its characteristics. To make such assumptions is exactly what cannot be done here, and it is in this sense that we can speak of a non-derivative approach to the conceptualization of power. Such an approach could be termed a 'higher order' conception of power, because it focuses on how power as ability is constituted.

When we move from the higher-order to the lower-order level of analysis of power, we are confronted with various ways of making sense of its numerous characteristics: power is usually analysed as a causal mechanism, rooted in either agency or structure; it both generates and prevents conflicts and consensus; and its vehicle typically comprises interests striving to dominate others. When we set out to investigate what power is, we are always guided by specific research interests and prejudices (in the Gadamerian sense of 'prejudgements'). My approach is, of course, no exception. What I want to focus on is the relation between the higher-order and the lower-order level of analysis. The problem here is that we often make claims about what power is on the lower level which universalize a particular meaning and organization of power. Such a hegemonic enterprise is inherently reductionist, and it can be seen as a kind of mirror image of the prevailing assumption that power in general, and political power in particular, connotes repression in one way or another. That is, a higher-order level of analysing power looks at the ongoing processes of the constitution of identity into which particular strategies insert themselves in order to give these processes form and content. But these strategies at the lower-order level can never fill in, or fully domesticate, ability as such. There is, in other words, a constitutive or irreducible gap between the two levels, that is, between part and whole. In so far as this is not acknowledged, the conception of power becomes inevitably reductionist because the part is hegemonizing the whole, and its opposite, the whole is reduced to the part.

My aim in this book is to figure out what can be said about power at the higher-order level. The point is then to see how the higher-order structure of power conditions, and can be traced in, the lower-order structures. I am thus exclusively concerned with what can be said about the relation between the two levels, that is, how they are built into each other, and what this means for the constitution of identity. The higher-order structure of power is analysed as an immanent condition for the lower-order structuring of power. This assumption is, I believe, necessary to launch a non-derivative conception of power. The reason is that it holds the gap open between power 'as such' and the particular forms and contents of power, and this means that the latter cannot but be contingent upon the former. Such a conception of power holds that power at the lower level must, in order not to violate its non-derivative status, be in 'conformity' with the higher-order structure of power as 'the ability to make a difference'. It is in this respect I would hold that the approach to power is, and ought to be, non-derivative: we neither can nor should we make any assumptions as to what power as such is, which is another way of saying that it is and must remain an empty place. Or to put it differently, it is and must remain an unspecified and open-ended process of identification in which identity is becoming what it is. What I set out to establish is how this empty place of power as such, although it does not exist, nevertheless triggers effects. Hence that which *is not* is not simply absent, but is instead an 'absence incorporated', as it were. It is the stumbling block *within* ability around which the structuring of ability takes place. This is important for the later elaboration of power in terms of the collapse of the objectivity of the social, in a word, negativity. Laclau and Mouffe's discourse analysis is particularly important here, and will be discussed at length in Chapter 4.

Such an approach is, at the same time, a 'democratic' analysis of power in the sense that it is antithetic to the reductionism intrinsic to hegemonic attempts to impose the part on the whole, or particularity on universality. Foucault's critique of the axiom that power is inherently repressive is especially important here in that it demonstrates that the modern structuring of political power (the dichotomies pertaining to 'the juridico-discursive representation of power' between the political and the social, and power and autonomy/rationality) attains a kind of universal status. The empty place of power, the site of ability as such, is always 'present' as an ontological condition and possibility, which is why power cannot ever be exhaustively explained or definitively mastered by any political institution.

The task of this analysis of power is thus to show that various conceptions of power are based on this condition and draw on this possibility. This implies that power is the locus of contingency, meaning that any given structuring of power could always be different. This in turn shows the condition and possibility for democracy as a non-exclusive and non-hierarchizing order of things, which is another way of saying that it cannot be assumed a priori that democracy is simply a form of hegemony – of superordination and subordination. Laclau and Mouffe's term 'radical and plural democracy' captures this insight.[5]

Before sketching the contours of the arguments that will be advanced and worked through in the main body of the text, it is appropriate to situate the argument within the 'horizon' of modernity. Focusing on the triangle of politics-power-authority, we find modern political and social theory inaugurating a different structuring of the political authorization of power. It is one characterized primarily by a circular, as opposed to a derivative, logic. This is to say, it is one that rejects any form of external authority (be it God or a substantial conception of the common good) from which power might descend or be legitimated. In its place, modern political and social theory poses power in terms of human interaction itself. Here we find, then, a rethinking of the modern social order as one that is produced contingently, and yet one that is unable to mirror that contingency, and the particularity to which it refers, in the omnipotence and universality of divine providence. As a consequence of the absence of a transcendental realm uniting power and authority, the social has to ground its legitimacy on its own terms: that is, it has to structure itself. The solid legitimacy of the old social order, once granted by recourse to God, is thus transposed to a new social order whose power is imbricated within, and cast in terms of, a political structure which is, itself, never absolute or identical with itself. The political structure is, in other words, always already dislocated.

Clearly, this raises a problem. For we now find that the political structure represents both the locus for the authorization of power and legitimacy *and*, at the same time, the impossibility of fully uniting them. Left with no foundation, the objectivity of the social is suspended, and politics – no longer treated merely as a superstructural activity taking place within a social order – must now be conceptualized as that which is engaged in defining the very limits of that objectivity and, therewith, in constituting it. Hence the political embodies the moment of undecidability with respect to the objectivity of any given social order. This undecidability is, moreover, a moment that comes to light in the identity of the subject itself. For if we reject, as does modern social and political theory, an absolute or given status regarding the identity of a subject, we find that this identity is also established *vis-à-vis* structures of power and authority, and hence has to be understood as profoundly political. We are faced with the conclusion, then, that if one takes this circular structure of power and authority seriously, power itself has no a priori status. But we also face the claim that, as a consequence of entailing no essence or absolute ground, the most effective way to understand power is to approach it in terms of processes of identification, in the most politically undecidable sense of the term.

The Outline of the Book

The first two chapters deal with some of the more important contemporary discussions on the conception of power. They are juxtaposed in terms of, and against, the arguments presented in the Anglo-American 'community power debate' that prevailed roughly from the late 1950s through to the late 1970s. Unlike the discussions raised in the classical social-contract tradition, these debates are not primarily concerned with the possibility of establishing a social order. Nevertheless, they foreshadow a number of issues involved in the classical politics-power-authority triangle, among the most provocative being the question of the subject or that of social agency. Indeed, once the issue of the subject or agency comes under critical scrutiny, it becomes increasingly difficult to maintain the objectivity of the social order as one that, prior to the Enlightenment, would be 'guaranteed' by the regionalization of politics. In other words, it becomes increasingly difficult to pose politics as that which merely takes place in legislative and administrative apparatuses, whose purpose it is to make possible a fairly smooth transition from power to authority, that is, the attempt of political power strategies to become collectively binding.

Consequently, a double and intertwined movement or spiral is triggered as the community power debate develops. On the one hand, we find a politicization of social relations, which emphasizes, at least in part, that the undecidability inherent in the political structure of modern society cannot be domesticated by political institutions, regardless of whether they are representative, legislative or administrative. On the other hand, a corollary position cast in terms of the contextualization of power itself begins to emerge, which stresses that power is inherent in social relations, and that there are numerous and more- or less-subtle relations of power that can escape political representation or that are denied access to the established political arena. These two spirals – the politicization of social relations and the contextualization of power – lead to the conclusion that power and authority cannot be rigorously differentiated. As we will see, this slippage between power and authority means, at least in part, that the distinction between coercion and consensus becomes blurred as well.

The dictum of the autonomous and rational subject who could choose freely whether to engage in or abstain from decision making – a position the early pluralists maintained as *the* locus for exercising power – is, accordingly, also problematized. Radical critics of pluralism, notably Connolly and Lukes, argue instead that autonomy and rationality survive only in a vacuum, so to speak, and do so as an emancipatory interest. Yet, at the same time, the contextualization of power (particularly concerning its immanence in social relations and its constitutive role for identity) renders autonomy and rationality as both antithetic to power and unfeasible. As we will see, this double bind is precisely the conundrum Foucault addresses in his more thoroughgoing analysis of power.

Chapter 3 deals with Foucault's radical rethinking of power and its implications for political theory. We find that his radicalness emerges from the way in which he addresses the contextualization of power in relation to immanence. That power is immanent in social relations means – and this is decisive for advancing the non-derivative conception of power – that it cannot be derived from something prior to itself. In addition, the connection between the contextualization of power and the immanent nature of power becomes crucial for another reason: it allows one to question the objectivity of both the subject and the social order. Whereas within various agency conceptions of power autonomy is seen as a residual category connoting both an original identity and a kind of 'leftover' identity from that which is not structurally determined, Foucault tends to view autonomy in terms of the undecidability inherent in social and political constructs, all of which are engaged in power struggles. Hence the autonomous and rational subject or intersubjective order is neither given nor does it connote an essential ability, or even a possibility, to which emancipatory strategies must refer.

Implicit in the contextuality and immanence of power is the politicization of social relations; indeed, they are conditioned by power struggles. Foucault's point is not merely that certain interests are excluded from the political agenda or that there is a risk that consensus might be flawed by coercive means and thus not seem 'real'. Rather, it is to say that the power inherent in the representative political institutions, as well as in the institutional settings of modern society, is underpinned by the power of disciplinary and normalizing techniques. Moreover, it is also to say that these two techniques – these two forms of power that, until now, political theory has excluded from its domain – play a constitutive role for identity and the political authorization of power. By focusing on these two forms of power, incommensurable and yet at once supplementing each other, Foucault is able to point toward the variety of ways power is authorized. What we find with Foucault's analysis, then, is that the triangle of politics-power-authority is not simply located at the apex of the societal hierarchy (the state), but is to be found throughout the social order. Left with no a priori status, the analysis of power cannot be derivative. Instead, it has to be studied as coterminous with the constitution of identity and identification, and all that this might imply – not the least of which concerns the fundamental mechanisms at work in the very processes of forming that identity.

One way of understanding the community power debate and the Foucauldian analysis of power would be to situate them in terms of agency and the structural conceptualization of power, respectively. However, this is not the approach I have chosen. For, if we take the rejection of a derivative notion of power seriously and, therewith, the insistence that no absolute grounding for power can exist, it becomes far more fruitful to trace the tendency towards the growing contextualization of power, the immanence of power in social relations, and the concomitant politicization of social relations.

An understanding of power along these lines – that is, within the logic of a non-derivative conception – could be termed 'postmodern' because it questions: (1) the transcendental objectivity of premodern views of the social order; and (2) the quasi-transcendental objectivity required of the modern view. A postmodern approach cannot, arguably, do more than that. It neither transcends modernity nor stands modernity 'on its head', though it might be more appropriate to say that it places modernity firmly on its feet! For we have here a coming to terms with the modern condition of contingency itself: in terms of social constructs; in terms of undecidability; and in terms of the circularity pertaining to the politics-power-authority triangle. In short, this represents a coming to terms with the absence of a ground, or in a word, the political. And we find, given this absence, that politics is but a strategic power game concerned with constructing an authority retroactively or circularly *as if* it was already 'there', and in whose name that power can be invested and legitimized.

Given the immanent and ubiquitous nature of power, given also that it must be conceived in terms of identification, and given that politics plays a constitutive role for the identity of the subject as well as for the social order, the task in Chapter 4 is to advance a thorough understanding of the fundamental mechanisms at work in the formation of identity as an intrinsic feature of power. However, as we have seen, if one accepts the non-derivative approach, nothing can be a priori to power; for if power entails some a priori construct – identity included – the questioning of the objectivity of social reality would be invalidated and replaced by a new form of essentialism. And yet, how does power (and by extension, identity) exist in its 'absence' if there is to be no essentialized form? The only way to avoid this dilemma is to outline a conception of power that is itself antithetical to social objectivity but, at the same time, capable of accounting for the institution and subversion of that objectivity.

A conceptualization of power along these lines must be rethought in terms of negativity. This assertion is already implicit in Foucault's argument about the immanence and the irreducibility of power. That is, it is implicit in the argument concerning the impossibility of substantializing power, and therewith, the impossibility of accepting a fully constituted, 'fixed' or absolute identity (that is, one that is located 'beyond' or 'outside' power relations). What is required, in other words, is a rethinking of negativity in the light of the fact that power can best be seen as a 'complex strategical situation' which conditions the clashes between hostile forces. For negativity is, as Foucault might have said, a conceptualization at the limit: a political logic of inclusion and exclusion, of presence and absence; one that constitutes and subverts each reciprocally. This chapter attempts to flesh out these insights in much greater detail by drawing on the work of Laclau, Mouffe and Žižek, for whom negativity is precisely the limit of an impossibility – the impossibility of fully circumscribed identities or totalized social orders. Thus what these writers indicate is that negativity as the inherent stumbling block within identity is constitutive for identity inasmuch as it induces processes of identification and signification in the subject.

Power *is* this limit, the political moment of undecidability which, in confronting the subject, constitutes its identity. It subjects and subjectifies through objectification. Hence power as negativity does not mean that it is a 'negative force', a mere repressive mechanism. It is, instead, both productive and repressive: it throws the subject into possibilities of signification which it simply cannot master, but, precisely because of these possibilities, none the less sets up new conditions for their emergence, institutionalization, reproduction, or indeed destruction. It is from this viewpoint that the hegemonic strategies in which the subject inserts itself can be studied as attempts to change, and in that sense master, the social order. Hence it should also be noted that this aim of mastery is, ultimately, frustrated and that the condition and possibility of democracy are located precisely in this frustration, triggered as it is by undecidability and contingency, indicating that the order of things could always be different.

Chapter 5 teases out the implications of this kind of mastery by considering the politics of subjective versus real interests. Considered in the context of two important topics in political theory, that of the political representation of the subject and that of the social order, the impossibility of reaching the *real* interest of the subject is brought into focus; and, conversely, the point where the subject is autonomous or determined by itself and hence present for itself is put into question. The latter notion of the subject being present for itself must be rejected, it is argued, unless one is to remain caught up in a derivative understanding of power, wherein an emancipatory politics is assigned the task of excavating the remnants of a long-hidden autonomy, and thereby assumes its authority and/or legitimacy on that basis. The circular structure of power points in another direction: the *real* is always already instantiated retroactively in subjective interests as the possibility of doing things differently and better. Autonomy can thus be seen as a counterfactual possibility which indicates that any given social order could always be different. Autonomy itself is deprived of any substance, but it is nevertheless an idea toward which subjects can direct themselves. Autonomy thereby becomes a vehicle of the political imaginary that pinpoints the contingent and undecidable nature of social constructs.

The same type of argument is developed in the last chapter with respect to the politics of the common good and the articulation between individual interests and the public interest in a democracy. Such an undertaking requires, as a first move, coming to terms with the nature of political community and political authority, the relation between hegemony and democracy, as well as the relation between the political and politics. The purpose is to get an idea of the extent to which differences can coexist in a political community without destroying its structures of authority. That is, what is the acceptable scope for differences within a community; what are the conditions for laying down such criteria and when do differences become so paramount that they undermine the very community itself?

In the light of present-day politics, it might appear idealistic or even meaningless to speak of the common good and the public interest – the subject matter of the second part of the final chapter. The point is, however, that these terms are not only deeply ingrained in various democratic traditions concerned with political justice. They are, most importantly, I will argue, inherent in the political structure of Western democracies, where political authorities are assigned the task of making and implementing collectively binding decisions in the name of popular sovereignty. It is in this respect that the common good and the public interest are inescapable metaphors in politics. Their role, then, is not simply an ornamental one designed to make it easier to digest elite domination; that is to say, their function is not exhausted by saying that they are manipulative devices in hegemonic power struggles.

The common good and the public interest are neither a common denominator towards which every interest gravitates, nor a completely arbitrary imposition of the interests of the 'rulers'. These metaphors are, no doubt, legitimizing devices employed by hegemonic political strategies, but they are also means whereby a horizon of possibilities opens up which cannot be controlled by hegemonic strategies since it conditions them in the first place. It is here that we find the crucial difference between hegemony and democracy. Whereas the former is always a reshuffling of dominations, the latter stands as an ontological possibility and a critical principle, pointing towards a politics of non-hierarchy and inclusion. From a democratic perspective, this is what the common good and the public interest signify: the democratic practice of participating in institutional arrangements which accept differences. The legitimacy of this democratic principle depends upon its ability to be implanted retroactively in the social realm *as if* it was 'already there', as if there were something already existing to which strategies have to conform. Thus the circular structure of power and authority is at work here too: power is authorized in the name of an authority it has itself carved out.

Throughout the book, I have selected what I conceive to be the more problematic and intriguing issues in the debates on, and theories about, power. I have attempted to draw the most radical (and, in my view, the inevitable) consequences from this work in order to map out the contours of what I have labelled a non-derivative conception of power. This conception, as we now know, approaches the issue of power by directly addressing metaphysically loaded terms, like the subject and identity, rather than turning its back on them. Indeed, I go further than that: I aim to show why, when all is said and done, there is no other way to understand power itself, or to consider the radical consequences that arise from this comprehensive approach, than to plunge headlong into the metaphysical terrain of what power as ability means.

1

Power as an Influence Term and Decision Making

We will begin with a discussion of the behaviourist conceptualization of power, its relation to politics, and the arguments of its critics. We will consider, in particular, the 'community power debate' of the 1960s and 1970s. The reasons for returning to this debate are, first, that it has had a major impact on the understanding of power, and second, that it touches upon some of the most topical and contested issues confronting the conceptualization of power within political theory. These include the nature of political agency, the representation of interests, and the relation between political leaders and the citizenry.

The behaviourist approach to political theory was developed in the United States in the aftermath of the Second World War. In his commentary on the ideas and development of the study of political behaviour, Dahl draws attention to two aspects that characterize the behaviourist 'mood', namely methodological individualism and empiricism: political behaviour refers to 'the study of *individuals* rather than larger political units', and it seeks to understand 'all the phenomena of government in terms of the observed and observable behaviour of men', in order to bring the study of politics into line with modern empirical science.[1] In community power studies this approach was operationalized in terms of decision making: who made political decisions, and how influential or powerful were they? That is, was political decision making concentrated in the hands of a limited number of people (an elite) or was it dispersed throughout the political institutions? Although these questions are bound up with theories of democracy, the aim here is to focus on two closely related problems confronting the conceptualization of power.

The first issue concerns the behaviourists' adoption of the event-causation model which underpins the decision-making approach: that is, how events – understood as manifest conflicts of interests – produce causal consequences. The focus on discrete and observable events is individualistic in that it isolates changes in behaviour and locates power within these changes; it is empiricist in that it is only observable changes which can be traced to a decision that can count as power. However, as the debate develops, emphasis is increasingly put on the *context* in which power is exercised. From its location in discrete and observable events, a tendency emerges that sees power as a kind of structuring mechanism which need not always be observable. Thus conceived, the event-causation model is viewed as inadequate because it presents a reductionist picture of the way power works.

The second issue deals with the relation between power and politics, and focuses on the nature of agency, in particular political agency, and the form it takes in political power struggles *vis-à-vis* the representation of interests in the legitimate locations of politics. The point is that the growing contextualization of power goes hand in hand with a politicization of social relations, which renders it problematic to cling to the assumption that politics is confined to governmental bodies. In addition, it becomes problematic to view politics as an activity which, generally speaking, merely responds to demands and interests created outside the practice of politics in its legitimate locations. A key issue concerns the nature and scope of the representation of interests, and how agents become political agents by participating in political decision making in the public realm, or alternatively, do not attain the status of political agents due to their being denied access to the political agenda. The relation between power and politics indicates that political agency cannot be taken for granted, for example by reference to constitutional rights, but is, instead, marked by ongoing power struggles, where agents, interests and issues are either organized within or outside the political institutions.

The Behaviourist Conception of Power as Causation

Behaviourism endorses an agency conception of power in which the relation between power and the subject is external. This is not the place to consider in depth the issue of internal and external relations. It suffices to say that an internal relation determines the identity of the elements in the relation, whereas an external relation does not. The difference between internal and external relations is thus that identity in the former is relational, meaning that the relation is essential for identity, whilst it is atomistic in the latter, meaning that the relation is accidental *vis-à-vis* identity. It is in this sense that the relation between power and the subject in behaviourism is external, which is considered the *sine qua non* for conceiving power in terms of causation.

Although agents are caught up in power relations, which obviously affect them one way or another, there is none the less a residue that escapes the grip of power. This residue is autonomy or self-determination, which is equated with what agents 'really' are when they are not subdued in power relations. While mainstream behaviourists such as Dahl, Polsby and Wolfinger equate what agents really are with what they say they are, or with their stated policy preferences, radical behaviourists like Connolly and Lukes equate autonomy with an externalization of the relation between power and the subject, thereby emphasizing that the subject is not under the influence of external factors, that is, power. This idea of autonomy is posited as the regulative idea for contrary-to-fact arguments: how the subject would behave in the absence of others trying to influence it. The problems involved in this understanding of the relation between power and the subject are discussed in relation to real interests in Chapter 5. What is important for the present discussion is the idea that power is external to the subject and, by extension, that it is, basically, seen as repressive in the sense that it encroaches upon the subject.

These two aspects express an asymmetrical view of power as 'power over'. Whilst the exercise of power, according to behaviourism, encroaches upon agents' autonomy (it is power over another), it also presumes autonomy (the agents are not structurally determined). In any case, those who exercise power *could* have acted differently, and those over whom power was exercised *would* have behaved differently if it was not for this exercise of power (this is the criterion of significant affecting, which we will turn to in a moment). Self-determination is opposed to external determination that is equated with constraint, that delimits a space within which power can be exercised. All sorts of constraints can be thought of here, such as normative values and economic necessities. The blanket term is usually that of structure. One of the central questions facing this form of agency conception of power revolves around the relation between the form of causation pertaining to agents and that pertaining to structure. The aim of the present discussion is not to examine the agency/structure debate in depth but, instead, to focus on what is involved in asserting that power is a causal concept.

While Hobbes's and Weber's asymmetrical conceptions of power connote a means-end causal relation, stressing that power is both a causal and an intentional concept, the empiricist tradition to which behaviourism belongs abandons the last aspect and sees power solely as a causal concept, where the behaviour of one agent causes a change in the behaviour of another.[2] By eliminating intentionality and reason as causal factors, behaviourists construe power in mechanistic and atomistic terms of event causation. The consequence is a change in, or rather a restriction upon, the meaning of power as ability.[3]

The atomistic vision of 'man' and hence of power and causation is extended by Hume: 'All events seem entirely loose and separate. One event follows another, but we never can observe any tie between them. They seem *conjoined*, but never *connected*.'[4] The Humean legacy implies that power as a causal concept has to focus on discrete events that are separated from one another temporally and spatially, and that an observable change takes place in these. These two premisses are expressed in the view of power as involving 'significant affecting', and are located by isolating events and singling out relevant counterfactuals. The latter can, for behaviourism, only be divergences of behaviour which are expressed in manifest conflicts.[5] The idea of power is that *A* gets *B* to do something *B* would not otherwise have done: 'that *A* gets *B* to do something' is the event (which is most visible in cases of clashing interests), and 'otherwise' indicates: (1) conflict; and (2) a hypothetical claim about what *B* would 'have done' in the absence of *A*, which is thus the imposition of a contrary-to-fact conditional that cannot, by definition, be observable.[6]

The imposition of counterfactuals is necessary for the event-causation model, partly because power only exists when exercised, and partly because it is conceptualized in terms of significant affecting. This means that power is logically tied to events marked by conflicting interests, which excludes the possibility that power is operative in the absence of conflicts, which in turn is equated with consensus. The consequence of this refusal of contextualizing power is that it becomes difficult to grasp the relation between conflict and consensus, what consensus actually means, and how events are related to the order of things. This poses three interrelated problems.

First, to exercise power is to bring about a change; the next time power is exercised it is in the environment of this new state of affairs brought about by power struggles, which then produces yet another new situation, and so on *ad infinitum*. Each exercise of power is linked to the previous ones (as well as to anticipations of future ones) since an exercise of power takes place in a context brought about by antecedent exercises of power. However, behaviourism cuts itself off from the possibility of grasping this link between existing conditions (the outcome of preceding exercises of power which might be taken more or less for granted) and present exercises of power by considering power solely in terms of events. The concept of power becomes, consequently, reductionist because it succumbs to what Morriss has termed the 'exercise fallacy'[7]: it neglects the fact that existing conditions are sedimented forms of earlier exercises of power that cannot but be causally effective in producing new changes. If this was not the case, the exercising of power could have no consequences, whereupon it would not be a causal concept at all!

Second, the lack of contextualization presents a problem for the imposition of contrary-to-fact conditionals which counterpose the 'extraordinary' (the event) to the 'normal' state of affairs. The upshot of counterfactual reasoning is to render probable the way things would have been in the absence of the event in which power has been exercised. However, the exclusive focus on events, in which empirically discernible changes take place, prevents the study of power in relation to how things are 'normally' run – which is relegated to the realm of culture and hence not political – or what things would have been like in the absence of exercises of power. The problem is that while counterfactuals are necessary for showing that power is operative, they have to be ignored because they are not observable.[8] Counterfactual reasoning would, further, have to make the link the behaviourists wish to avoid, namely to previous exercises of power and how these have shaped the present state of affairs.

There is, finally, the problem of singling out *relevant* counterfactual standards against which the event in which power is exercised can be measured. Doing that would require linking events to the context in which they occur since they can only achieve significance *vis-à-vis* this context. This, in addition, calls for the need to differentiate between forms of influence or power, as well as between important and unimportant decisions, issues, agents and exercises of power. Behaviourism does neither because to do so would go beyond the confines of the event-causation model; it would also introduce a 'subjective' moment into the study of power which is not warranted by empirical data (that such occurs anyway, albeit covertly, will be clear from the discussions to follow).

When agency is defined apart from structure (because it is equated with external determination), structures necessarily play a constraining role on agency. Agency expresses autonomy, which becomes relativized when agents operate in rule-governed social settings. Relative autonomy thus attains the status of a residual notion mediating between internal and external determination. This account of agency and structure fits well into the empiricist conception of power. The paradigmatic model here is the mechanical idea of motion imported into the realm of social relations by Hobbes under the influence of Galilean mechanics, and further developed by Hume: bodies are naturally either at rest or at a constant velocity, meaning that a body does not move or change its course unless it is moved.[9] This means that when a change occurs in a body, it cannot but be under the influence of an external force. And likewise, in the absence of this force the body could not but behave otherwise, meaning that it would behave 'normally', that is, be determined by itself. Power is, within behaviourism, the name for such an external force which seemingly *conjoins* but does not *connect* bodies. This is why power has to be studied in terms of discrete happenings, events in which: (1) there is an explicit 'contact' or 'communication' between the one who exercises power and the one over whom power is exercised; (2) a counterfactual proof can be provided in order to demonstrate that a change has occurred; and (3) this change is externally induced rather than being the result of one's own 'free will'. These conditions are most clearly met in cases of overt conflicts, which are events of clashing preferences whose net result is a change in behaviour.

Although this approach can be seen as an agency conception of power, it is in fact irreconcilable with both structural and agency conceptions. It is obviously antithetic to the rationalism embodied in structuralist and realist views, which stress that exercises of power are *connected* even though they might not even seem *conjoined*. The reason is that power structures are constituted by internal power relations. Even a contextualization of power, which does not go so far as to look at power in terms of necessary relations, is unacceptable for behaviourism since that too would violate the model of event causation. It might be less obvious that the behaviourist approach cannot, properly speaking, be an agency conception either since it is entirely concerned with behaviour, which is not the same as agency. This is the reason why some writers, like Ball and Morriss, claim that behaviourism presents far too restricted a view of power, in that power as 'the ability to make a difference' cannot be grasped by the mechanical study of behaviour.

Power and causality are usually understood in terms of either agency or structure since the latter two terms function as the unifying and objective principles to which power as causation can be referred back. When power is treated as an agency concept, it connotes the ability of an agent to affect something; whereas causality is, especially within the behaviourist tradition, understood in terms of means and ends and, more specifically, as changes in behaviour. As a structural concept, power expresses the capacity of social forces to bring about consequences which are beyond the control of agents, whereupon it is these forces that make up the web of causal mechanisms. Hence, whilst power is the ability to make a difference, it is far from clear what ability and what the conditions for 'making' are. By not taking issue with these problems, the idea of power as causation presupposes what needs to be called into question, namely the nature of the relation between power and identity. As it stands, within behaviourism as well as in many other theories, identity is simply given as something objective, just as the societal realm in which power is exercised is, by and large, taken for granted.

A presuppositionless conceptualization of power should endeavour to avoid presuppositions like these, which slant theories of power towards objectivism – either voluntaristic or deterministic. This is not achieved simply by setting out to mediate the dualism of agency and structure by seeing how they are imbricated in each other.[10] The point is, rather, that the theorization of power cannot be confined within a continuum from agency to structure, since this would assume that power relies on a prior categorization of social reality whereby its alleged objectivity cannot be challenged. It is by breaking the link between power-agency and power-structure that it becomes feasible to make a breach in the seemingly symbiotic relationship between power and causation. Only in this manner will it be possible to advance a conceptualization of power which is not derivative in the sense that it hinges upon an already given objectivity.

The relevance of these considerations should be clear from the following discussion of how causality is conceived in relation to theories of power. An appropriate starting point is Lukes's comments in his comprehensive essay on power and authority:

> The absolutely basic common core to all conceptions of power is the notion of the bringing about of consequences, with no restrictions on what the consequences might be or what brings them about . . . [Power] is attributed to persons or collectivities or, sometimes, to systems or structures . . . To identify the power of an individual, or a class, or a social system, one must, consciously or unconsciously, have a theory of the nature – that is, the causal powers – of individuals, classes or social systems. In applying this basic notion to the understanding of social and political life, however, something further is required than the mere idea that persons, groups, or systems generate causal consequences: namely the idea that such consequences are nontrivial or significant in some way . . . A conception of power useful for understanding social relationships must incorporate a criterion of significance – that is, it must imply an answer to the question: What makes the consequences brought by *A* significant in such a way as to count as power?[11]

Here Lukes is putting forward three central claims. The first is that power is a causal concept: it links the intentions of those who 'possess' it to the consequences of these intentions being put into action. Power accounts, accordingly, for the 'bringing about of consequences'. This broad sense of the term corresponds to the definition of power as the ability to make a difference, which is often seen in volitional terms and hence understood as an agency concept. However, two other options are available if the causal factor in the 'bringing about of consequences' is located in the social system as either a community resource that agents draw upon, thereby strengthening the cohesiveness and controlled integration of a social order (Arendt and Parsons), or in the structures of social classes that determine subjects in asymmetrical ways (structural Marxism). This leads to the second claim: to differentiate between power and other types of action calls for the provision of criteria that single out power as a specific type of relation. Although this may seem trivial, it introduces the pertinent problem of how power can be differentiated from, say, influence, persuasion, authority, manipulation and domination. In the pluralist tradition (to which behaviourism belongs), power is usually seen as an influence term which covers a whole family of notions ranging from 'rational persuasion' to 'domination'.[12]

These two claims are interdependent. The reason is that when power accounts for the production of effects, it must be possible to identify it, thereby differentiating it from other phenomena. The understanding of power as the production of causal consequences that are significant in one way or another leads to the issue of counterfactuals, which raises two problems. First, given that power is an agency concept, a power relation implies that the agent *could* have acted differently and the recipient *would* have acted differently if power had not been exercised. This is why a certain degree of autonomy is presupposed for both elements of the power relation.[13] If the action of *A* affects *B*, it follows that *B* would have acted differently in the absence of *A*'s action. This would be a first criterion of significance, but one which is obviously insufficient since it merely indicates that a change has occurred. The second problem deals with one of the key topics in the debates between pluralists and elite theorists. This concerns the attempt to trace the production of an effect, that is, to establish a causal chain of events. This lies at the heart of the issue of differentiating between the influence terms. The problem is this: is *B* influenced by power if and only if it is feasible to account for the action(s) which affected *B*'s behaviour, that is, to the extent that it is possible to map out a causal sequence?

The third and final claim, and probably the most important one here, is that power is *attributed* to social entities, which is the reason for talking about power in terms of derivation. Lukes wants to identify the power *of* agents, systems or structures without first considering the issue of 'attribution'. This unquestioned presupposition implies that power theories focus upon *how* power is attributed to social entities, and it is here that the agency/structure problem finds its way into the discussion of power – namely whether power is derived from agency or structure. The reason this is problematic is that the nature of power as ability, and hence the nature of the subject, are not dealt with. By not scrutinizing what 'ability to make a difference is', it becomes impossible to pay attention to the historical changes in the structure of power, and hence the meaning of ability and, in turn, identity. It then becomes difficult, if not impossible, to come to terms with the relation between power and the subject: how identity is formed in political power struggles, that is, in the articulation of power and authority, and of individual and citizen. It is this issue that theories of power are usually reluctant to pose because it points at the essentially circular structure of power: that the *ability* to make a difference is itself constituted by the making of differences, meaning that power as ability poses itself as if it was presupposed. The dictum of the constitutive subject should be located in this posing as presupposed. It is in this light that the relation between ability and making a difference could be seen – where the circularity of power has, so to speak, been straightened out and turned into an external relation between subject and object or between agency and structure.

The problem of 'attribution' or 'derivation' can be illustrated by taking a look at pluralism. Although pluralism has argued against the existence of privileged centres of power, such as the monopolization of power by an elite or the dominant position of the bourgeoisie, it nevertheless treats power as derivative inasmuch as it derives, ultimately, from resources or 'base values'.[14] That is, power stems from something which is not itself power. Pluralism has, not surprisingly, been criticized by Marxists for neglecting the class struggle and the structural determinants of politics. In a critique of Lasswell and Kaplan, Poulantzas holds that the problem with pluralism 'is that (i) it succumbs to a voluntarist conception of the decision-making process, through disregarding the effectiveness of the structures . . . ; and (ii) it takes as a principle the "integrationist" conception of society, from which the concept of "participation" and decision making is derived.'[15] This critique is interesting in two respects. First, the latter point problematizes what pluralism takes for granted, namely the '"integrationist" conception of society', which is inseparable from the view that politics is confined within governmental bodies, which in turn are confined within an overall societal consensus on cultural values. This problematization takes the form of a critique of voluntarism – and this is the second point – which, in underestimating the efficacy of structures, is incapable of tracing power to its structural location: the class struggle.[16]

It should be obvious that here attention is being centred on the *ground* of power – how agents, systems or structures are 'attributed' power. Whereas for pluralism the unifying principle is behaviour, for Poulantzas it is the efficacy of structures. Yet the crucial questions of what it means to *have* and to *exercise* power are not addressed; or, rather, they are posed in a circular fashion by reference to base values and structural determinants, which are at one and the same time the medium and outcome of power. It goes for both of them that they attempt to confine this circularity within a derivative conception of power where values and structures determine the nature of causality as either links between events or as underlying mechanisms which exist independent of agents. The problem with this type of argument is that it cannot acknowledge the constitutive nature of power, since that would compel them to accept that its circular structure cannot be confined within a derivative approach without relying on the dogmas of either agency or structure. The reason why this essentialism does not work is, as already mentioned, that power defies every form of a priori grounding. Whether power is conceptualized in terms of agency or of structure does not change anything with regard to its derivative nature because the dictum of objectivity is not questioned; and it is exactly this dictum which cannot be presupposed on the higher-order level of analysis.

Power as an Influence Term I: Reason and Autonomy versus Causation and Power

There are two sets of problems connected with the assumption that power is a causal concept accounting for the production of significant consequences. The first deals with the nature of decision making in relation to consent and coercion by focusing on the limit case of power as 'rational persuasion' and 'dialogue between equals'. This throws light upon the problems of autonomy and causality and, in turn, on the idea that power is exercised within a continuum of consent and coercion. The second problem concerns whether power as causation is linked to effects that are intended, or whether it also includes those that are not. This issue is important in the course of differentiating between power and influence and in ascertaining what can count as 'significant affecting', that is, the production of causal effects.

What we have seen so far is that power is a causal concept. It is, as McFarland says, the very principle of social causation: power entails change, and this change is externally induced in behaviour *vis-à-vis* the event, whereby the agent does something it would not otherwise have done. This external relation between power and the subject finds its counterpart in the dictum of the constitutive subject (who is internal to itself, so to speak). It is typical of asymmetrical agency conceptions of power (power as a zero-sum game) – as opposed to the symmetrical theories outlined by, for instance, Arendt and Parsons – that change is operationalized in terms of conflict, and that conflict, in turn, is operationalized in terms of the clashes between vested interests. In situations of conflict between interests, consensus cannot prevail – which is why power is antithetic to consensus.

However, this statement needs immediate qualification, for society is not, according to the behaviourists/pluralists, torn asunder by power conflicts. The reason is that, although they would say that power relations exist everywhere in society, the types of power they investigate are those articulated within the legitimate locations of politics. To approach power and politics in this manner means that political power struggles take place within a normatively integrated society, whereby the political is 'superstructural' *vis-à-vis* the social or cultural 'base'. This is the framework for the analyses of power conducted by the pluralists, whose basic unit is the event – the scene of power struggles between conflicting interests whose eventual outcome is manifested in the making of a decision within a specific policy area.

By looking at pluralism and what the pluralists labelled, or rather stigmatized as elite theory, we can grasp the importance of power as a term of influence bearing on the way notions of intended/unintended effects and causality form an agency conception of power modelled on decision making. And, by extension, we can see how this conception of power presupposes a particular view of the relation between the political and the social. The relation between power and influence has been the subject of extended debate, which revolves around whether they should be treated as subcategories of each other, or whether it would be more appropriate to see them as different concepts.[17]

When power is seen as a form of influence it can be taken 'as being the most inclusive term, and, within this wider concept . . . [one can] distinguish two poles, the pole of "influence" and the pole of "domination".'[18] A similar approach is provided by Benn, who argues that 'it is more helpful to think of diverse uses of "power" and of associated words like "influence" as instances of different members of a family of concepts that do not all share any one particular characteristic but have various relations and resemblances by which they are recognizably kin.'[19] Thus power is a name for a web of interrelated notions; it is operationalized by posing two extreme limit cases. At one end of the spectrum figures 'rational persuasion', a situation in which *A* gets (causes) *B* to do what *A* wants (intends) by offering 'good reasons' rather than threatening *B* with sanctions in case of noncompliance. This form of influence is marked by consensus in that *B autonomously* accepts these reasons. At the other end lies some form of domination in which *A* secures the submission of *B* by actually coercing *B*. Thus power is exercised within a continuum of consent and coercion.[20]

Rational persuasion exhibits a kind of tautology: that the persuasion is rational means that it is internal to the subject because it is the subject itself who persuades itself. Consequently, this form of power (if it is a form of power at all) cannot really be accounted for in terms of causation which, as mentioned, presupposes external relations and hence some element of coercion. Because 'good reasons' are, by definition, accepted by the subject, they cannot be external factors encroaching upon the subject to get the subject to do what it would not otherwise have done since the subject is defined as autonomous and rational. Although the subject might be significantly affected by what it takes to be good reasons, the fact of being affected is not a causal consequence proper. Or if it is thus affected, it is in a round about manner: reason is internal to the (constitutive) subject, but in so far as the subject is affected, it must be because there is a clash between the internal and the external. That is to say, the subject has internalized norms, values, patterns of cognition and so on, which are, in fact, antithetic to it being autonomous and rational. Hence the subject is alienated: it carries something external within itself (the traces of a repressive power). When presented with good reasons, we witness a clash between this external dead weight within the self and what is truly internal, namely 'the peculiar coercion of the coercion free universal recognition'.[21]

The conclusion is that when power is viewed in terms of significant affecting within a continuum ranging from consent to coercion, or from rational persuasion to domination, these poles are implicitly – at least, within theories of power slanted towards empiricism – grounded in the dictum of the constitutive subject. This cannot, of course, be an empirical fact. It is, rather, a transcendental presupposition which the conception of power relies on or derives from, and which renders the latter meaningful as the ground of ability. This presupposition is, however, essentially unstable because its operationalizing device of significant affecting is torn between power and causation, on the one hand, and autonomy and reason, on the other:

coercion – external relation – determination by another – causation – significant affecting: power

---

consensus – internal relation – self-determination – reason – significant affecting: autonomy

There are two reasons why behaviourists cannot accept reason as a form of causation and hence as a form of power. The first most explicitly relates to the employment of event causation, which holds that a cause has to be identified or described independently of the effect. This is so because empiricism cannot accept a relation of necessity between particulars which are at most regularly conjoined and habitually 'experienced' as necessary. To hold reason as cause is to violate this empiricist dogma, since reason as the cause of an action and the action itself would invariably be implicated in each other. According to Clegg:

> The description of an action as a specific type of action and the statement of an intention as the cause of that action would invariably be implicated in each other because the intention-description would be the identification of the action as *that* type of action, rather than another. The cause and the effect would not be logically or conceptually distinct relations between 'things' but would be relations between a described action and the description applied to that action.[22]

In addition, reason, intention, belief and so on are not observable events – they cannot be properly classified as events at all; this, according to the behaviourists, disqualifies them as causal factors.[23] To claim that reason can be a cause would thus be to go beyond the event-causation model, and for two reasons. First, it would violate the implicit transcendentalist anchoring of empiricism which, as mentioned already, relies on the presupposition of the subject as *causa sui*. And second, it would form part of an argument that reason*ing, as a pragmatic endeavour,* is entangled in power relations and hence causally effective to some degree. This, in turn, would direct attention towards the sources of power, and the fact that these sources (broadly considered as the context within which power is exercised) condition, one way or another, the possibility for exercising power – that is, the subject's ability to act. This second point has particular bearing on discussion as to whether anticipating the reactions of those 'in power' can be seen as a form of power on their behalf, as well as on the attempts to soften the dualism of agency and structure, so as to allow the latter not only to constrain the former but also to facilitate it.

The second reason why behaviourism does not accept reason as cause has to do with the notion of the subject. Behaviourism runs into difficulties when it tries to work out the relation between power and autonomy: external and internal/self-determination are mutually exclusive, and this means that when a change occurs it is either externally induced (power), or the result of an 'internal conversion' (autonomy) which might be conceived in terms of 'rational persuasion'. The problem is addressed clearly by Lukes in his discussion of rational persuasion: as a form of significant affecting, it cannot but count as a form of power, but since the reasons are autonomously accepted by the recipient – which is, by definition, the case with *rational* persuasion – there are no divergences of interest and hence no conflict, whereupon it becomes impossible to provide a counterfactual standard against which the change can be measured. It becomes, in other words, impossible to substantiate the claim that the agent would have behaved otherwise in the absence of rational persuasion.[24]

In the absence of conflict, and hence power, the change has to be seen as self-induced even though it might be the intended effect of, and hence caused by, another agent and thereby an act of power. This indicates the antinomy between causality as a form of external determination, on the one hand, and autonomy and reason as a form of internal determination, on the other. Power is, when defined in terms of event causation, external to the autonomous subject, which is its own cause. This essentialist notion of the subject pervades the debates on the dualism of agency and structure, where it is expressed in the antinomy between power as causation and autonomy as the presupposition for power. This antinomy arises due to the difficulty of conceiving how change is brought about, which is the very subject matter for the analysis of power.

When power is the principle of social causation and hence the external determination of the subject, and when the subject is presumed to be internal to itself, then the fundamental problem consists in how subjects interact and how this interaction affects (changes) their identity. The crux is that the subject has to be fully constituted (determined by itself) in order to exercise power, whereas power cannot but be an external relation between subjects – what is more, a coercive relation because, by definition, it curtails the subject's autonomy. An important fact concerning the nature of power is thus laid down a priori, namely that power is equated with 'power over'. This assumption is inherent in the behaviourist premiss; and, moreover, it is virtually unquestioned in much of the literature extending far beyond behaviourism.

This 'repressive hypothesis' is coupled with another hypothesis that is slanted towards individualism and stands in the way of an understanding of community. The point is that the identity of the subject is at the same time antithetic to external pressure (power) whilst presupposing it, since power, one way or another, signals the 'essence' of autonomy, namely to be able to make a difference. The relationship between power and autonomy is thus almost schizophrenic: on the one hand, self-determination is antithetic to being determined externally; on the other, self-determination entails external determination of others. In short, self and other presuppose *and* antagonize each other.

This antinomy finds expression in the schism between consent and coercion *vis-à-vis* the community: because autonomy is the vehicle of both consent and coercion, the constitution of legitimate political authority is, within liberalism, marked by ambiguity, namely that this authority, while expressing the consent of the people, also represents a more or less explicit threat to them. Community is, according to this view, at once a necessity and a potential evil, because consent between individuals is only possible through a degree of coercion which, in turn, threatens them and hence the community.

The precarious relation between autonomy and power, which is one of both exclusion and conditioning, finds expression in: (1) a transcendental conception of reason which, instead of being constructed in the traditions of political discourses, is the expression of the self-determination of an equally transcendental subject; (2) an essentialism of the subject which serves to obscure both the way power as ability is constructed, and the understanding of how power, agency and structure articulate with one another; (3) a voluntaristic account of the dualism of agency and structure which takes the ontological distinction between agency and structure for granted, meaning that the identity of the subject, ultimately, is given independently of its structural locations; and finally (4) the mechanistic conception of power in terms of motion (pushes and pulls external to the bodies themselves) – typical of the empiricist tradition in which bodies are naturally either at rest or in a state of constant velocity.

The antinomy between autonomy and causation calls for a closer examination of rational persuasion as the limit case of power. If the limit is external to power, rational persuasion cannot itself be a form of power; whereas if it is internal, the opposite holds true. But in neither case can the limit be a limit proper since that term indicates both a 'here' and a 'beyond'. To conceive a limit is to conceive what is beyond it, and it is only by posing the beyond that the here can be identified. That is, a limit defines an 'inside' by excluding an 'outside', and it is itself neither. The limit is thus the point of undecidability, which is why the transcendentalist presupposition, mentioned above, is essentially untenable. As the limit idea of power, rational persuasion cannot but be ambiguously related to power. The reason is that it, on the one hand, connotes consent, as in the case of 'a dialogue between equals': power is absent, replaced by a form of influence characterized by autonomy and a commitment to 'truthful information' as opposed to 'manipulative persuasion'.[25] On the other hand, however, rational persuasion is also a form of power since it is a way of affecting someone in a significant manner, thus producing causal consequences.[26] This ambiguity requires clarification: how are autonomy and causation related in decision-making processes?

The ambiguous relation between rational persuasion and power stems from the contradictory attempt to bring together autonomy and causality. At the most rudimentary level, the crux is this: autonomy means self-determination, and if something is determined by itself, it cannot be caused by something else. In his discussion of whether rational persuasion is a form of power, Lukes acknowledges the ambiguous nature of the problem. 'I suspect', he says, 'that we are here in the presence of a fundamental (Kantian) antinomy between causality, on the one hand, and autonomy and reason, on the other. I see no way of resolving this antinomy: there are simply contradictory conceptual pressures at work.'[27] This is no doubt the case, which is probably why the insoluble dilemma has found a common-sense solution in the notion of *relative* autonomy, which simply mediates between the two poles in the antinomy, thereby establishing a continuity between agency and structure. It is necessary, however, to look at the conditions which bring about this antinomy.

The central question revolves around what is meant by rational persuasion. Can persuasion ever be motivated by reason alone, and what would that actually entail? Persuasion involves, however defined, a change of opinion. Were such a change to be entirely rational it would have to be algorithmic, whereupon there would be no room for autonomy. Seen in this light, rational persuasion, as the highest moment of self-determination, would slide into total determination, external to the self and to which the self would have to subscribe in order to act rationally. Rational persuasion is, accordingly, placed squarely between an either/or: between reason as the full realization of self-determination and reason as the equally full realization of an external necessity. The only way of solving this problem is to advance beyond the dichotomy between subjectivism and objectivism. One solution would be to view rational persuasion, and hence autonomy, as an insight into necessity, whereby self-determination is fully realized only when the self is entirely integrated into the whole, thus leaving no fissures between the identity of the subject and its positions. In this state of affairs there is no longer any difference between internal and external determination.

Another attempt to solve this problem would hold that since

rational persuasion is located at the point where subject and object merge – where they are transformed into their opposites – it cannot but be its own impossibility. For an argument to be fairly consistent, it must cut itself off from what it is not by excluding other possibilities. Hence there will inevitably be certain elements in a discourse that are related negatively to those outside it, since the very possibility of distinguishing between an inside and an outside presupposes a moment of closure and hence exclusion. The premiss of consistency thus rests on a prior act of exclusion that cannot itself be explained by reference to reason as such, which is exactly what clears a space for persuasion. The consistency of an argument is thus conditioned not by the argumentative 'force' alone (compare Habermas) but by the setting in which the argument situates itself and which 'allows' it to make sense. What counts as a good argument is, accordingly, conditioned by the limits to what is rational and reasonable; which is to say, that which conditions the rationality and reasonableness of an argument also undermines it. The point is that neither subject nor object ever manage to constitute themselves fully.

As the limit idea of decision making, rational persuasion is the point where the supposed highest moment of decidability is also the moment of undecidability due to the essential instability of the transcendental presupposition. It follows that decisions – rational persuasion included – are always marked by this disjunction; hence they cannot be algorithmic since algorithmicity presupposes what decisions deny, namely objectivity. This is pointed out by Derrida when he says that '[a] decision that didn't go through the ordeal of the undecidable would not be a free decision, it would only be the programmable application or unfolding of a calculable process.'[28] Decisions entail a moment of conversion in the Kuhnian sense: the transition from one paradigm to another is never entirely rational; thus a change of opinion can never be argued on the grounds of an internal, and hence necessary, development in reason alone. Laclau puts this succinctly when he says that if a 'decision *is not* algorithmic, in that case to decide implies . . . *creating* something which was not predetermined and, at the same time, cancelling out of existence possibilities which will not now be realized. Since the outcome of the situation is indeterminate . . . to choose a course of action implies an act of coercion with respect to other possible courses of action.'[29]

It is in this sense that decisions entail an irreducible moment of undecidability, which is what makes reasoning a constitutive feature of politics. Or to put it differently, it is this undecidability which makes politics a dimension of social life that cannot be reduced to the mere calculation of (individual) interests, or to a role as the medium for an underlying societal/cultural homogeneity of values. Reason is thus intertwined with power and pragmatically constructed in political discourses. It should be clear that consensus cannot be established without a moment of coercion (in the above sense of a conversion which is not solely 'caused' by the subject itself), just as autonomy cannot be brought about by eliminating power. The purity of reason, autonomy and consent are always marked by what undermines and constitutes them in the first place, which is to say that the self is never entirely itself, that is, internal to itself or constitutive. This is so not because internal determination is coupled with external determination – which would be to uphold the dualism of subject and object albeit in a modified version – but because the dualism dictating the terms for such a distinction is itself called into question.

Power as an Influence Term II: Indirect Influence and Anticipating Reactions

The second problem to be dealt with in relation to the view of power as significant affecting concerns the relation between power and influence. It has been argued that since power is the ability to make a difference, it has come to be seen as an influence term whose key elements are causality and intentionality. This is, of course, a rather undifferentiated view of power since there are various ways of achieving a future good (Hobbes), or enforcing one's will even against resistance (Weber). This has led to two ways of distinguishing between power and influence: in terms of intentionality as means-ends causality, or in the continuum of coercion and consent. Whereas power is, in Russell's words, 'the production of intended effects . . . [which] may be classified by the manner of influencing individuals',[30] influence is a broader notion that accounts for unintended consequences as well. A more elaborate approach along these lines is provided by Wrong, who incorporates resources in his definition of power. He says: '*Power is the capacity of some persons to produce intended and foreseen effects on others*'; thus '[p]ower is identical with intended and effective influence.'[31]

A definition of power in terms of intended effects is provided by McFarland, who takes power 'to mean intended influence (i.e. intended social causation): *C*'s behavior exercises *power* over *R*'s behavior if and only if *C*'s behavior causes changes in *R*'s behavior *that C intends*.'[32] Hence *A* has power over *B* if and only if *A*, first, is the significant causal factor accounting for the change in *B*'s behaviour, and second, this change is in accordance with *A*'s intentions. This does not rule out either unintended consequences of actions or those of anticipating reactions. What it does rule out, however, is the possibility that these phenomena can be seen as power. The reason is that they cannot be referred back to, or find their unifying principle in, the action initiated by an agent, which is to say that the intention of this agent is not the causal factor in bringing about changes. Hence McFarland aims at qualifying the behaviourist view of power by distinguishing between coincidence and cause,[33] where the criterion for this differentiation is the production of intended effects. By thus excluding coincidence as a form of power, he narrows down the behaviourist definition.

While power, according to these views, means '*intended* social causation', influence is a broader category, referring to 'social causation in general'.[34] Influence is a causal relation indicating that *A* causes a change in *B*'s behaviour. The production of such a change does not have to be intended, just as it can be both manifest and latent, or direct and indirect. This introduces a set of problems that are central to discussion of the decision-making approach to power and to the claim that power is a causal concept. It is, moreover, an issue which is related both to the idea that power is exercised within the continuum of consent and coercion, and to the dualism of agency and structure.

The notion of unintended influence or effects of actions calls attention to the problem of unawareness. *A* may get *B* to do something *B* would not have done in the absence of *A*, but this relation of influence is not necessarily obvious to either of them: *A* may be unaware of the influence it has over *B*, just as *B* may be unaware of being influenced by *A*. It then becomes 'difficult to establish the fact that there has been influence at all, and not merely a coincidence of decisions.'[35] When agents can influence each other and be influenced without knowing it, it becomes problematic to view influence in causal terms. This is so because the intention behind the effect cannot be identified with that which is required for establishing a causal relation. Moreover, it becomes impossible to make a clear-cut separation between 'rational' and 'manipulative' persuasion, since agents are not necessarily aware of what influences their opinions. Finally, the assertion that power involves 'significant affecting', which can be demonstrated through counterfactuals, becomes problematic because it is not always clear when and to what extent people are influenced and hence do something they would not otherwise have done.

The same holds true for the notions of indirect influence and anticipating reactions, which have been the key issues in the debates between pluralists and elite theorists. These notions are crucial for understanding how the pluralists depict the relation of representation between citizens and leaders. The point of contestation revolves around whether politics is an activity that goes on within the institutional sites of decision making in governmental bodies and in the sharing of power this enables, or whether politics has a broader societal scope which defines political agency through participation in power struggles, where agents address themselves to these institutional sites through the representation of interests. Pluralism assumes that modern Western democracies are polyarchies due to the existence of the political market where elites compete for votes, which prevents the concentration of power in the hands of an oligarchy.[36] Hence the contention that the relation between citizens and political leaders is marked by a high degree of openness and consensus, and that power is exercised and shared within a framework of legitimate authority which is not itself seen as politically contestable.

Dahl launches the idea that the politics of conflicting interests is the 'chaff' – that is, a kind of superstructure – which is based upon a widespread underlying consensus.[37] Thus the calculation of individual interests and their aggregation in the representative political institutions presupposes the integration of cultural values on a societal scale. The point is that Dahl implicitly recognizes that politics in its legitimate locations depends upon structures of authority in society. But because these structures cannot be grasped in terms of his episodic conception of power – the event revealing conflicting interests – they are categorized as 'social' rather than 'political'. The social is the realm of consensus and integration (or solidarity, to use the common social-democratic phraseology) which underpins the political. And correlatively, the primary role of politics seems to be to sustain the integrity of the social. Politics plays, in other words, the double and ambiguous role of 'bouncer' and 'midwife': it guards the social against excessive conflict and it turns up to resolve conflicts in order to restore the underlying consensus.[38] It should thus be clear that the conceptions of both power and the relation between the political and the social are intimately related. By reducing power to a matter of conflicts between vested interests, the political becomes, at the same time, impervious to the social. The subsequent contextualization of power and politics in the 'three faces of power' debate (which is discussed in the next chapter) addresses this problem, although with insufficient radicalness.

Seen in this light, political leaders will find it difficult to stave off voiced demands and interests, which in turn is the best guarantee for systemic integration. The voicing of demands and the raising of issues are voluntary acts inasmuch as individuals and groups freely decide whether it is more in their interest to raise a demand or to abstain from doing so. From this it follows that political inactivity and hence the renunciation of power sharing, are a matter of rational calculation rather than a consequence of a particular structuring of power; and by extension, that issues 'worth' debating *are* debated. Moreover, political inactivity is, claims Wolfinger, 'the common condition'; and, he continues, 'abstention from collective political action may be rational behaviour for any individual, since the likelihood that his own action will produce benefits to him is minimal.'[39]

Considering politics in volitional terms is congruent with the methodological individualism of behaviourism, where a community is viewed as the aggregation of individuals,[40] and where consensus, rather than being the result of the structuring of power sustained by defenders of the *status quo*, is 'the result of unguided molding of diverse attitudes'.[41] This individualistic consensus approach implies that agents are guided by nothing but the calculation of self-interest, and that every interest is able to manifest itself on the political agenda. This view of politics cannot but have an inherent reductionist bias since those issues that do not reach public consideration are, by definition, non-issues.

The linchpin of pluralist democracy is, as Debnam stresses,[42] the citizen-leader relationship. The medium through which this relationship is studied is governmental decision making, an approach pioneered by the classical elite theorists as part of their argument that power was concentrated in the hands of an elite who took all the important political decisions.[43] Since the vast majority of citizens are not engaged in decision making, the only way the pluralists can avoid the conclusion that power is shared by the few and not by the many is to urge, first, that political elites are competing with one another, and hence 'the opportunity for political action is kept open to the greater number',[44] and second, that the openness of elites and the consensus of the community are constitutionally guaranteed by universal suffrage, which gives the citizenry the possibility of exerting indirect influence over political leaders.

Both points are contested issues in the debates between pluralists and elite theorists, and they have both been modified by the neo-pluralists themselves. Although the elite theorists do not argue that elites are entirely closed, they do contend that they are more immune to outside pressures than the pluralists concede. They thereby question the claim that 'political action is kept open to the greater number', and that the issues reaching the political agenda do so in an unbiased fashion. They cast doubt on the weight given to the indirect influence of citizens over political leaders, which in turn touches upon a crucial issue in the conceptualization of power. This is whether power is best understood in relation to decisions over issues that have reached the political agenda, and should be studied according to the model of event causation (which entails the assumption that the processes of becoming a political issue is not bound up with power struggles); or whether a conceptualization of power is better off abandoning this presupposition, and instead studying how and why some issues attain political significance and others do not. Adopting the latter approach to the citizen-leader problem requires a contextualization of power that locates it in the mechanisms of inclusion in or exclusion from the political agenda.

The critique of the political predicament arising from behaviourism's pluralist assumptions concentrates on indirect influence and the anticipation of reactions, on the one hand, and on the nature of social inequalities – whether they are cumulative or dispersed – on the other. Both issues direct attention to the sources of power and the extent to which social inequality functions as a barrier to participation in politics, and hence as a barrier to political agency. If that is the case, it raises questions about the representability and hence the inclusiveness of the democratic institutions. These questions focus on the context in which power is exercised, and how this context is itself the outcome of power struggles.

These problems, which revolve around the degree, scope and possibility of participation in power sharing, are crucial for discussion of the nature of political agency since they concern the political representation of interests. The pluralists seem to have two reasons for asserting that inequalities are dispersed rather than concentrated, and that power is dissociated from indirect influence and anticipating reactions. One is that they defend the alleged polyarchical nature of modern liberal democracy. The other, which is more interesting in this context, is that the stress on decision making and event causation is not suited to coping with cumulative inequalities and the subtle and often informal channels of indirect influence, which would require a shift of attention away from isolated events towards the more enduring structures and inherent biases of organizations and institutions.

The main tenet of pluralism is that in Western democracies there is no single centre of power capable of dominating society; on the contrary, there are many centres, all of which compete for political power. Dahl takes the argument even further, contending that, since this is so in most American communities, it could be said that *nobody* runs them.[45] Here indirect influence and anticipating reactions play a crucial role in preventing political leaders abusing their power. Such assertions are intended to counter the claim advanced by the critics of pluralism that elites comprise fairly closed units, and that inequalities in the distribution of power (the resources that facilitate the exercise of power) tend to be cumulative, meaning that resourceful agents are better equipped to increase their power and their resources for exercising power than those who are deprived of resources. This is the pluralists' argument against looking at the sources of power-wielding, which would violate the event-causation model – and hence 'the canons, conventions, and assumptions of modern empirical science' – epitomized by the 'scientific outlook' of behaviourism.[46] It would thus be unwarranted to postulate the existence of a ruling elite by conflating the possession of presumed sources of power with being powerful.[47] The objection to investigating the sources of power is here brought to the point where they are eliminated altogether from consideration.

Since the pluralists hold that participation in decisions entails a sharing of power, it is mandatory for them to argue that although only a fragment of the population is actually engaged in political decision making, and thus in exercising power, the non-participating – and, in this respect, inactive – citizenry does, none the less, exert indirect influence over the politicians. The reason is that politicians are interested in re-election, and this is only possible if they adjust their preferences to those of the voters by anticipating their reactions to certain issues; otherwise voters would support other candidates.[48] Indirect influence is exercised in situations where there is no direct interaction between – in this case – citizens and leaders, and where the latter are guided by anticipating the responses of the former and adapting to their potential demands. It follows that political inactivity, far from being a threat to democracy, is, to a large extent, its guarantor because polyarchy is the best guarantee for system integration since power is used here to further 'collective goods'. Inactivity, then, reflects the absence of conflicts between vested interests, which in turn is seen as an expression of consensus and hence the absence of power.

It is here we encounter the problematic notion of indirect influence and the denial that anticipating reactions, with the exception of voting behaviour, can be a form of power.[49] The debates between the pluralists and their critics focus to a large extent on the pluralists' asymmetrical – and, in fact, inconsistent – treatment of indirect influence and anticipating reactions. That these phenomena are dealt with inconsistently is made clear by, for example, the claim that economic elites are incapable of influencing the decision-making process in governmental bodies, while the far less organized and less-educated lower-income groups are said to possess this capacity. The only argument offered in defence of this assertion is that the latter groups outnumber the former, and hence their votes carry more weight. Thus, despite the pluralists' objection to viewing power in terms of indirect influence and anticipating reactions, they do make one exception, namely voting behaviour. This argument is partly invalidated, however, by the generally very low turnout at elections in the USA, where a large proportion of the citizenry does not even make use of this rudimentary resource in order to take part in the sharing of power.[50] The groups that abstain from voting are primarily lower-status groups whose resources for exercising some form of influence are minimal. Why they should be better equipped than higher-strata groups to wield indirect influence – meaning that politicians are more responsive to the former than to the latter – has not been made clear even by the pluralists themselves.[51]

As Dahl himself points out in his discussion of the ambiguity of leadership, 'leaders do not merely *respond* to the preferences of constituents; leaders also *shape* preferences.'[52] He even provides evidence that the higher echelons of the business community in New Haven exerted power through the mayor, who acted in accordance with their interests by anticipating their reactions on 'important issues'.[53] This is not surprising, of course, on account of the concentration of powerful resources in the control of the business elite in comparison with the lower-strata groups, ethnic minorities, and so on, who do not make up a homogenous group with focused and articulated demands and interests. These groups are fissured by all sorts of cleavages, which provide plenty of scope for the manoeuvrings or strategic calculations of politicians and bureaucrats.[54] To claim that by representing the electorate politicians are responsive to it is somewhat hollow, or 'an article of faith' as Parenti puts it, because it is far from clear if there is, in fact, anything to respond to, what it is therefore that they do respond to, and what responding actually involves.[55]

Indirect influence operates in both directions; this has been emphasized by elite theory and more recently by the neo-pluralists. But the early Dahl also alludes to the fact when he says that 'one cannot measure influence so precisely . . . by appeal to direct evidence.'[56] In consequence, even the nonexistence of overt conflicts does not provide 'direct evidence' for the absence of more or less subtle forms of influence, which can never be entirely divorced from power and sanctions in the case of noncompliance. This, then, would be a situation in which power plays an active role in organizing consent – a conclusion pluralism cannot subscribe to, but one that it cannot, however, simply discard as unfeasible.

The role played by indirect influence implies that representation, far from being simply a response to whatever is conceived to be in the public interest, plays a part in its construction, something to which Dahl alludes when arguing that 'a political issue can hardly be said to exist unless and until it commands the attention of a significant segment of the political stratum', and that '[t]he beliefs of ordinary citizens become relevant only when professionals engage in an intensive appeal to the populace.'[57] Thus indirect influence and the anticipation of reactions are, on the one hand, excluded from the conception of power while, on the other, being incorporated into it in order to legitimate the view that decision making by elites cannot warrant elitist conclusions. It is in this context that the alleged widespread underlying consensus in the social realm constitutes an 'article of faith' which sustains what Poulantzas called the 'integrationist conception of society'.

The consequence of this understanding of the relation between the political and the social is that pluralism circumscribes discussion of how political agency is achieved; it is merely guaranteed constitutionally by universal suffrage. Whether agents make use of this power, and hence attain the status of political agents, is up to them – their own calculation of how best to spend their time – since no inherent bias exists in the relation between citizens and political leaders to hinder participation by the former in the sharing of power. The reason is that constitutional rights, by definition, render it untenable to judge anyone as powerless. The dispersion of elites and the democratic competition among them are seen as guarantors of society's representability as a universal sphere of political participation, which in turn underpins the legitimacy of the political authorities.

This is a rather restricted view of representation because it divorces the political from the social, and because it does not say anything about how and to what extent leaders are responsive and responsible to the citizenry. The result is a depoliticization of the way power legitimates itself through representation. This issue is brushed aside by reference to the fact that citizens are free to exercise indirect influence through the ballot box, and that nothing or no one is excluded from politics. A low degree of participation is either self-inflicted or the result of an insufficient mobilization of people for a given cause.[58] Abstention from participation in politics and the failure to mobilize a sufficient number of people cannot, according to pluralists, be caused by the way power is organized. For that would direct attention away from behaviour in decision making towards phenomena like indirect influence and anticipating reactions, and in turn to more durable structures of domination and subordination.

The asymmetrical treatment of indirect influence and anticipating reactions, as well as of the nature of inequality, illustrates how the circular structure of power operates in the pluralist conception. The analysis of power is curtailed in two respects. First, the ability to make a difference is narrowed down to a matter of decision making whose role is to provide a causal account for the change from one state of affairs to another, where this change is brought about by conflicts between vested interests. Second, to approach the problem in this way directs the analysis of power to its politically legitimate locations, whereby political authority is reduced to legitimate authority; and what does not fall under this latter heading is categorized as 'social' or 'cultural', and kept apart from the political.

The act of separating the political from the social, whilst at the same time turning the latter into the foundation of the former, implies that political power is basically legitimate as long as it does not violate the underlying consensus. And the only way to check this is to look for issues around which conflicts develop. But since conflicts do not go all the way down, so to speak, they cannot really shake what conditions them in the first place, namely the underlying consensus. Hence, by giving power a particular form and content, and by confining it within a particular structuration of the political and the social, pluralism presupposes what is in question, namely that citizens are able to exercise indirect influence over political leaders through the ballot box, that leaders in turn anticipate the preferences of the voters, and that inequalities are noncumulative. It is in this sense that 'the article of faith' is an ideological gesture whose vacuity papers over the gap between: (1) power as such (the ability to make a difference) and the specific construction of power in terms of causation, decision, interests, and the like; and (2) political authority as such (the allocation of values for a society) and the institutional settings of legitimate political authority.

The point is that pluralists do not allow for the possibility that political power, among other things, plays a role in fabricating a consensus that it then mirrors itself in. Instead, we are left with an 'untouchable' societal consensus which frames politics and offers a reductionist portrayal of power. The pluralists are, consequently, faced with the problem that they cannot really deny that indirect influence and anticipating reactions operate in both directions. First, there exists the indirect, and often informal, influence harnessed by resourceful groups with vested interests, who are obviously better equipped to influence the decision-making processes than groups lacking these resources, simply because the impact of their interests, decisions and actions is more profound than that of others. Second, there exists the kind of indirect influence favoured by pluralists, namely that politicians are supposedly responsive to the electorate inasmuch as they anticipate its reactions in order to get re-elected. However, this kind of indirect influence is open to question. The pluralists' contention that it restricts the manoeuvrability of elites, thereby preventing them from abusing their power, boils down to the shrewd idea that citizens and leaders are mutually committed to the legitimacy of the existing democratic political institutions, and that 'to reject the democratic creed is in effect to refuse to be an American.'[59] This is where the joker of the underlying consensus of common values appears in the *mise en scène*.

The elasticity of an argument like this is self-evident; and neither is Dahl able to substantiate it by recourse to his notion of power, which does not allow for incorporation of the anticipation of reactions into the theory of power.[60] To perceive voting behaviour as the only source of political power, and as the only form of behaviour where power can be studied in terms of anticipating reactions, is not only restrictive, but is also politically biased because it excludes other, more profound, sources of power. By focusing on decision making in governmental bodies, pluralists exclude from politics by definitional fiat all those issues that seldom or never reach the political agenda, and which then escape the analysis of power.

Dahl's argument about citizens' and leaders' commitment to the democratic creed has a twist to it since it can operate in both directions, in the same way that influence and anticipating reactions can. Even though everyone in a community expresses allegiance to a principle as meritorious as the democratic creed, it remains an empty phrase so long as it is not put into action, that is, interpreted or used in concrete cases. When such a principle is put to work it is inevitably going to connote something more specific, in this case deference to the manner in which politics is conducted. At this level there is plenty of room for political conflicts which, among other things, are concerned with how to interpret the democratic creed.[61] It is of little consolation to know that leaders, like the rest of the population, are bound by an accepted and unquestioned belief in the democratic creed, when it is the leaders themselves who take an active part in defining this creed, and hence what is considered to be the public interest. This is to say, the issues on the political agenda, and hence the legitimate scope for conflicts, are underpinned by the exclusion of what is seen as illegitimate. By not viewing this exclusion as political, the pluralists cannot see that the consensus expressed in the allegiance to such a belief has an inbuilt bias against that which tends to threaten it, namely those grievances which the 'political stratum' deems questionable because it is out of touch with the public interest.[62]

In so far as power as an influence term is bound up with indirect and unintended influence, as well as with anticipating reactions, it becomes increasingly inappropriate to view it as 'intended and effective influence' linked to clashes of interests involving explicit resistance. Constructing causal relations between manifest conflicts of power and resistance usually poses no major problems since the relation between intentions and consequences is fairly clear-cut. Hence the questions of significant affecting and counterfactuals are relatively easily dealt with. But this is not the case when it comes to anticipating reactions and unintended and indirect influence, because the assertion that consent means the absence of power cannot be upheld. This consequently calls for a re-evaluation of the notion of power, one that is able to take into account its subtlety and often disguised ways of operating. And this means that a number of underlying assertions about power should be questioned, such as whether power necessarily presupposes conflicts of interests, whether it lies within a continuum of consent and coercion, and whether it can be adequately explained only in terms of its exercise.

It is not surprising that the attempt by Bachrach and Baratz, and later Lukes, to radicalize a behaviourist conception of power by casting it in terms of social structuring touches upon these issues. In order to see how these fundamental problems come to the fore, at the same time heralding a crisis for behaviourism, it is necessary to probe more deeply into the conceptualization of power within the behaviourist tradition to which the above mentioned three authors are heirs.

2
Power, Causality and Political Agency in the Community Power Debate

The entire debate on the 'three faces of power' is framed by the following assumptions: (i) the subject matter of politics is power; (ii) power can be fully comprehended in terms of its exercise; (iii) the exercise of power is an event which can be analysed in terms of decision making; (iv) events and decisions can be defined in terms of conflicts between vested interests; (v) conflicting interests are addressed to representative political institutions; (vi) these institutions represent society inclusively in the sense that they reflect a widespread underlying consensus; and (vii) political power is defined in terms of 'power over' – that is, the attempt to enforce one's interests. However, the progression from decisions (Dahl, Merelman, Polsby and Wolfinger), to nondecisions (Bachrach, Baratz and Crenson), and further to no-decisions (Lukes) signals an ongoing contextualization of power which makes it more and more difficult to uphold these seven premisses. By the time we reach Lukes's concept of 'no-decision' we are bound to look for a type of power whose *raison d'être* is to hide itself by arresting conflict before it begins and to manipulate consensus.

The purpose of engaging in this debate is to make it clear that the relation between politics, power and conflicting interests is not one of necessity, but is instead a contingent articulation. Thus politics need not be defined in terms of power struggles, conceived as conflicts between vested interests. The focus thus shifts to the conceptualization of power and how it bears on the relation between the political and the social.

Decision Making and the 'Two Faces of Power'

Consensus is equated within behaviourism with the absence of conflict; and because conflict is seen in terms of clashing interests, where *A* tries to get *B* to do something *B* would not otherwise have done, consensus expresses self-determination, that is, people are free *from* external determination (notably political interference). According to this 'Newtonian' perspective, consensus connotes the normal state of affairs where bodies are naturally at rest. Seen in this light, it is thus up to the so-called 'neo-elitist' critics of behaviourism/pluralism to show that if a 'perpetual and unbreakable' consensus does not prevail, 'then there is some point in the process of forming opinions at which the one group will be seen to initiate and veto, while the rest merely respond. And we can only discover these points *by an examination of a series of concrete cases where key decisions are made*.'[1] To single out 'key decisions' does not present any major difficulties according to the pluralists, since important issues *are* issues around which conflicting interests prevail.

The alleged scientific nature of pluralism lies in its 'study of concrete, observable *behaviour*',[2] where decisions are made on issues which, in turn, provide empirical proof of the exercise of power. By linking power to decisions, Dahl's aim has been to give 'the most complete and objective history attainable as to what really happened in the course of each decision'. By tabulating 'successes' and 'defeats' for each participant involved in the making of decisions, an 'objective' picture would emerge of the overall distribution of power. The conclusion is that the 'participants with the greatest proportion of successes out of the total number of successes were then considered to be the most influential.'[3]

Bachrach and Baratz's critique of pluralism elaborates how indirect influence and anticipating reactions operate in relation to decision making as forms of power. As pointed out by Dahl, political leaders do not only respond to the preferences of citizens, they also take part in shaping them. Indirect influence and anticipating reactions are thus able, at least to some extent, to form the agenda where 'key decisions are made'. This calls into question what the pluralists see as unproblematic, namely the distinction between significant and insignificant issues, or between 'key' and 'routine' decisions. This problem is closely related to the criterion of power discussed in the previous chapter, that of 'significant affecting'. The pluralist method, which, according to Polsby,[4] consists of 'pre-selecting as issues for study those which are generally agreed to be significant', is biased, in the view of Bachrach and Baratz, because it specifies neither '*what* issues are "generally agreed to be significant" . . . [nor] how the researcher is to appraise the reliability of the agreement.'[5] The problem is then that 'by presupposing that in any community there are significant issues in the political arena, he [Polsby] takes for granted the very question which is in doubt. He accepts as issues what are reputed to be issues. As a result, his findings are foreordained.' The same critique is levelled against Dahl's notion of 'key political issues', which requires that 'the issue should involve actual disagreement in preferences among two or more groups.'[6]

Bachrach and Baratz's central idea is that the problem of power cannot be exhausted merely by concentrating on who gets their way in decision making, because such an approach is slanted towards individualism, which disregards the context in which exercises of power take place.[7] Because the pluralists do not look at how policies are implemented, their consequences and who they benefit, they are unable to provide 'objective criteria for distinguishing between "important" and "unimportant" issues arising in the political arena'.[8] By taking as significant those issues 'which are generally agreed to be significant', they exclude the possibility that leaders, by shaping preferences, can manipulate consensus. Since the pluralists cannot account for this possibility, the question of what makes up 'key political issues' cannot be read off from an apparent consensus, but is itself politically contestable.[9] It is in this connection that Bachrach and Baratz's plea for objectivity with regard to the differentiation between political issues on grounds of importance ought to be seen. Their crucial point is that they shift the emphasis from the exercise of power to the conditions for the emergence of conflicts, that is, to the sources of power wielding.

Whilst pluralists conceive power in terms of conflicts that cause changes in behaviour, Bachrach and Baratz adopt an institutional approach which, by giving full weight to indirect influence and the anticipation of reactions, aims both to understand consensus as the product of power, and to recognize that conflicts can be covert as well as overt. In doing so, they bring Schattschneider's theory of political organization and conflict into the power debate, in particular his notion of the mobilization of bias. Schattschneider's argument is that the characteristic feature of politics, leadership and organization is the institutional management of conflicts, and that this requires a selection, and hence a definition, of significant issues and political alternatives, which involves exercises of power.

This means that '[p]olitics deals with the domination and subordination of conflicts', which among other things involves setting the agenda for alternative options.[10] Control over conflicts is achieved by either displacing or substituting them (or alternatively, by resisting such action) or, still more effectively, by managing them before they begin. The management of conflicts is decisive for the cohesiveness of organizations and hence for their ability to reproduce themselves. 'All forms of political organization', Schattschneider concludes, 'have a bias in favor of the exploitation of some kinds of conflict and the suppression of others because organization is the mobilization of bias. Some issues are organized into politics while others are organized out.'[11]

This suggests, according to Crenson, that political organizations are always caught up in nondecision making, which 'impart[s] a degree of bias and unity to the political activities of a community'. Thus, 'a polity that is pluralistic in its decisionmaking can be unified in its non-decisionmaking'.[12] This is important with regard to what has been said about the nature of decisions and consensus as always procuring moments of coercion. It means that social and systemic integration is instituted through rule-following, whereby organizations generate forms of life with routines and rules which entail the exclusion of other forms. It is through this dimension of coercion, says Laclau, that 'the system of social organization can be seen as attempts to reduce the margin of undecidability, to make way for actions and decisions that are as coherent as possible.'[13]

It is against this background that Bachrach and Baratz contend that although power entails conflicts these need not be manifest. The consequence of this claim with regard to the so-called objective differentiation between significant and insignificant political issues is that the distinction 'cannot be made intelligible in the absence of an analysis of the "mobilization of bias" in the community; of the dominant values and the political institutions, myths, and rituals which tend to favor the vested interests of one or more groups, relative to others.' In conclusion, Bachrach and Baratz hold that 'any challenge to the predominant values or to the established "rules of the game" would constitute an "important' issue"; all else, unimportant.'[14] Thus power is inherent in the mobilization of bias because this form of indirect influence is the filter, so to speak, through which decisions over conflicting issues are channelled. By going behind decision making, by focusing on the organizational/institutional and societal context, this view implies that power is operative in preventing potential issues from crystallizing into open conflicts. This way of managing conflicts is, following Schattschneider, indeed the most effective manner of exercising power since it is easier to control than open conflicts.

Here we see the first move away from defining power in terms of clashing interests: power also plays the role of preventing potential conflicts from occurring, which implies that power is operative before actual conflicts. In so far as politics is defined in terms of power, it follows that politics, too, operates before actual conflicts. This move is important because it initiates a break with the presumed internal relation between power and politics, on the one hand, and conflicts of interests, on the other. Power is, however, still defined *vis-à-vis* conflicts but it is now ingrained in institutional settings; this means that it becomes more like a dispositional concept, that is, one which pays attention to conditions necessary for 'the ability to make a difference'. The general framework is, none the less, still the 'traditional' one which dichotomizes the political and the social – that is, change, rupture and conflict – and stability and consensus.

We thus have 'two faces of power'. The first is the pluralist assertion that 'power is exercised when *A* participates in the making of decisions that affect *B*.' The second, which enlarges the scope of power, emerges 'when *A* devotes his energies to creating or reinforcing social and political values and institutional practices that limit the scope of the political process to public consideration of only those issues which are comparatively innocuous to *A*.'[15] Bachrach and Baratz label this latter form of power 'nondecision'; it is connected with problems of consensus and conflict, and with distinguishing between events and nonevents, and action and inaction. The key point is Bachrach and Baratz's suggestion that the political comes 'before' the differentiation between events and nonevents, rather than being the 'result' of the differentiation, where events are located in the political and nonevents in the social. Instead of dichotomizing the political and the social by locating events in the political and nonevents in the social, Bachrach and Baratz enable the political to be viewed more as the terrain upon which the distinctions between events and nonevents arise.

A nondecision is, say Bachrach and Baratz, 'a decision that results in suppression or thwarting of a latent or manifest challenge to the values or interests of the decision-maker'.[16] It is a decision that prevents a latent or potential conflict from emerging, primarily with the purpose of maintaining the *status quo*. However, deciding not to decide *is* a form of decision making; or it is, in Bachrach and Baratz's words, 'the negative aspect of decision-making'.[17] There are two aspects to this form of nondecision, both of which – in contrast to the decision-making approach – prevent latent or potential issues from manifesting themselves. The first is to pigeonhole inquiries, proposals, petitions and the like, in order to avoid taking a decision which would be unpopular or otherwise prove troublesome. This would be one way of aiming to displace a conflict; another would be to co-opt those outside the organization, thus mitigating political cleavages through a substitution of issues. The second aspect of nondecisions has to do with anticipating the reactions of those in power. One can refrain from raising an issue either because the likelihood of a successful outcome is minimal, or because voicing it could lead to retaliation or be taken as an expression of disloyalty to the institution in question.[18] This can be read as the reverse of Dahl's argument that political leaders are responsive to citizens by way of anticipating their reactions and thereby adapting to their potential demands.

Exercising power by means of nondecisions is not, however, restricted to negative and indirect forms of decision making. The reason is that 'the mere existence of the "mobilization of bias"', say Bachrach and Baratz, 'is sufficient to prevent a latent issue from becoming a question for decision.'[19] This is the case when 'the dominant values, the accepted rules of the game, the existing power relations among groups, and the instruments of force, singly or in combination, effectively prevent certain grievances from developing into full-fledged issues which call for decision.' Although this form of power cannot be rigorously distinguished from the two aspects of nondecision making (since the mobilization of bias is operative in these as well), the emphasis given to this phenomenon suggests something more radical, namely that the bias inherent in every form of organization can function as a form of power. Moreover, it questions whether power can be studied adequately in terms of decisions involving manifest and/or latent issues, just as it problematizes the assertion that power necessarily implies overt or covert conflicts.

By studying power not only in terms of events/decisions but also in terms of nonevents/nondecisions, Bachrach and Baratz aim at contextualizing the events in which power is exercised; they do so by drawing attention to the role played by standing conditions in the possibility of exercising power. That is, they focus upon antecedent exercises of power which have become sedimented and which function as the framework and sources for the present exercise of power. These conditions for exercising power are not events that can be isolated from one another spatially and temporally,[20] but they are, none the less, causally effective with regard to issues destined for the political agenda. The contextualization of power thus has two consequences: one, the scope of conflict must be expanded to incorporate latent and potential conflicts which; two, casts doubt on the model of event causation.

The strength of this argument hinges, however, upon the notion of nondecision. The behaviourists were quick to condemn the term as a useless, or rather a redundant, neologism by construing it as a decision not to take a decision – which is, obviously, still a decision and therefore susceptible to the methodology of decision making and event causation. It is this problem in particular that has been stressed by pluralists in their criticism of the 'second face of power'. Discussions have primarily centred on the theoretical and methodological status of Bachrach and Baratz's argument that power can be exercised by thwarting a latent or potential issue. The pluralists maintain that there are insurmountable problems in identifying nondecisions empirically on the basis of the mobilization of bias. In his discussion of nondecisions, Polsby contends that although political systems necessarily limit the scope of issues to be decided upon – what he terms 'the conservatism of political agendas' – this does not present any problems for the pluralist approach. If systemic bias is to be analysed empirically it has to be studied in the ways it has actually been mobilized, and by whom; this involves examination of decision making, that is, by 'a discussion of those issues that are organized into politics'.[21] And, likewise, the only viable method of studying issues outside of politics is to focus on those that are 'desired by a significant number of actors in the community but not achieved'.[22] The problem is that the mobilization of bias – 'the dominant values, the accepted rules of the game' – may operate in such a way that 'a significant number of actors' simply abstain from voicing an issue, whereupon a conflict remains covert, meaning that it has 'not been recognized as "worthy" of public attention and controversy'.[23] It is by excluding this possibility that Bachrach and Baratz are able to claim that Polsby, and pluralists in general, are biased.

Even though nondecisions are understood as 'decisions to neglect'[24] or as a 'politics of prevention',[25] which are, contrary to the mobilization of bias, observable events, the main difference between decision making and nondecision making is that the latter contextualizes power by looking at 'how it is employed to sustain or modify the most fundamental aspects of political institutions and processes', and that 'political consensus is commonly shaped by *status quo* defenders, exercising their power resources, and operates to prevent challenges to their values and interests.'[26] Thus Bachrach and Baratz partly supersede the model of event causation: although they conceive power in relation to events where changes of behaviour take place, they do not study events in atomistic terms. On the contrary, for them power is exercised against the background of institutionally sustained mobilization of bias; or rather, this bias is embodied in exercises of power whose causal efficacy does not depend on decision making.

The criticism that pluralism is prejudiced has been rejected by the pluralists. They contend, first, that the mobilization of bias does not necessarily favour the *status quo*, but can equally work against the wishes of elites.[27] Second, and more importantly, when Bachrach and Baratz hold that power can be exercised in the absence of overt grievances, the notion of systemic bias becomes impossible to operationalize. The result is that some non-issues or nonevents are simply 'stipulated by outside observers without reference to the desires or activities of community residents'. The reason is that this research strategy cannot provide criteria for when a nonevent is significant and which nonevents are significant.[28] Advancing criteria of significance in terms of systemic bias is of little help here, or rather, it begs the question since this criterion cannot, according to the pluralists, be falsified. As a consequence, the whole enterprise 'becomes entirely a matter of taste, ideological preference, or prejudice'.[29]

Wolfinger offers a similar critique, arguing that nondecisions cannot be properly distinguished from 'apathy, laziness, pessimism, or lack of interest in politics' – all of which are examples of non-participation in politics, which is 'the common condition' of modern Western societies. Further, he claims that the identification of nondecisions rests on an idea of what one conceives as the 'ideal polity': the activities and the goals people *should* pursue.[30] Frey, in his more positive evaluation of the 'second face of power', holds that to depict a nondecision one must be able to discriminate between a failed attempt to exert influence and 'autonomous disinterest'.[31] Finally, Merelman criticizes the notion of mobilization of bias for holding that elites are capable of creating 'false consensus'. The problem is that such a claim cannot be falsified: both nonevents and unimportant conflicts point towards an elite controlling 'the dominant values' and 'the accepted rules of the game', just as important conflicts, by definition, point in the same direction.[32]

In their response to these criticisms, the defenders of the 'second face of power' point out that 'although the absence of conflict may be a nonevent, the prevention of conflict *is* an event.' It is, accordingly, 'subject to observation and analysis, and certainly to critical scrutiny'.[33] Hence neither the existence of elites nor that of false consensus are presupposed. The argument is that elites can prevent latent and potential conflicts from developing into major issues; in this way conflicts remain covert. The point is, as Frey notes, that the pluralists themselves allow for this possibility. Dahl, for instance, states that the 'old oligarchy' in New Haven was able to restrict the scope of conflicts by possessing 'that most indispensable of all characteristics in a dominant group – the sense, shared not only by themselves but by the populace, that their claim to govern was legitimate'.[34] The conclusion Frey draws from this 'picture of the relatively conflict-free, nondecisional system' is that 'the popular belief in the legitimacy of the elite's power was to a large extent inculcated by elite-controlled institutions.'[35] In his review of the debate, Hoffman argues a similar case: 'If consensus and elite rule can coexist, why can't a consensus be the creation of an elite? If there is no manifest conflict between rulers and ruled, then this surely must be deemed a possibility. It gives an added depth to what Lukes calls the two-dimensional argument about non-decision-making, for it suggests that a "shared belief system" which raises some issues for debate but suppresses others may itself be the product of elite rule.'[36] Even Wolfinger concedes that 'some examples of false consciousness are indisputable', and mentions as a case the Afro-Americans in the southern parts of the USA, whose 'reticence was due in part to repression' and manipulation.[37]

A nondecision requires that political grievances be put forward one way or another and then prevented from reaching the political arena. If that does not happen, there can be no event and no conflict, in which case, 'the presumption must be that there is consensus on the prevailing allocation of values.'[38] However, the key problem remains unsolved: namely how to discriminate between different forms of non-participation, ranging from nondecisions to 'autonomous disinterest', and constituting a scale from 'false' to 'genuine' consensus. This problem is inseparable from that of distinguishing between important and unimportant issues: when is an issue suppressed and when is it not pursued for one of a number of other reasons? And is it possible to differentiate these 'other reasons' – that is, the degree of consensus – from elements of coercion, given the mobilization of bias?

These problems are triggered by the incorporation of the notion of mobilization of bias into the conception of power. This leads to one of two possibilities: either systemic bias is restricted to the observable behaviour of managing and preventing embryonic conflicts, which, because it can then be assimilated to the behaviourist viewpoint, cannot but weaken the case of nondecision making; or – what seems to be the logical consequence of the notion – it cannot be so restricted, in which case even the absence of conflicts can be considered a result of power. However, the latter case would take us outside the behaviourist conception of power; for it would no longer be possible to conceive of power in terms of events (overt as well as covert conflicts) where *A* makes *B* do something *B* would not otherwise have done. Power could equally operate in such a way as to sustain what people normally do, whereby it would be meaningless to posit contrary-to-fact conditions. Hence the presence of an allegedly genuine consensus could not serve as an indicator of the absence of power. This, in turn, calls into question, one, the assumption that power is equated with 'power over', and two, the relation between this idea of power and that of autonomy as freedom from power.

Although Bachrach and Baratz criticize pluralism for linking power to decisions and overt conflicts, they do not break entirely with its basic assumption that power ought to be studied in terms of actual behaviour. They insist that, even in the case of the mobilization of bias, a challenge to the establishment must have been posed one way or another in order for power to be wielded. However, this assumption is far from being unambiguous since it is not clear how it is possible to distinguish between a latent or potential issue and an absent one. The problems involved here can be illustrated by the example of a nondecision given by Bachrach and Baratz:[39] A university professor is discontented with the ways certain things are run in his academic institution. He plans to criticize these at a faculty meeting, but when the moment arrives, he remains silent. A number of viable explanations are listed, all of which fall within the two aspects of negative decision making. Pushed to its logical conclusion, power as a nondecision takes place if and only if actual inactivity can be referred back to at least one individual who has 'consciously' acted (which can be done in solitude, as in the example) in a manner that somehow challenges the establishment.

There are two problems to note here, both of which point to an inconsistency in the 'second face of power'. First, in the example cited above, power has been exercised in the form of a nondecision.

Yet if the issue is not voiced at all, it remains a nonevent, with the conclusion that the situation is marked by consensus. However, it is also possible to draw the opposite conclusion, that the issue was not voiced due to the power of systemic bias: that the person anticipated that the reactions he would receive could be unfavourable to him, or that he had no chance of getting his proposals through anyway. If such suggestions are warranted, they show that anticipating reactions can reveal exercises of power in the absence of overt conflict, which in turn points to the importance of the sources of power.[40]

Second, if the bias of the system works in such a way that it forms people's identities to a greater or lesser degree, there is nothing to constrain actions or inactions arising from indirect influence of which agents may not be aware. This is true not only of the mobilization of bias, but also from Dahl's assertion that preferences can be shaped by elites. It reveals the arbitrariness of viewing power in terms of 'awareness', and of considering only those conflicts brought about by political leaders. Although the 'second face of power' initiates a decisive step beyond pluralism by contextualizing and enlarging the scope of power, which goes hand in hand with a politicization of social relations, it does nevertheless stop short of drawing the inevitable conclusion that inactivity and the absence of conflict can be the result of power. If that is the case, then the 'normal' state of affairs is imbued with power relations, which is to say that power is not only located in discrete events. Power is instead more like a conditioning factor for acting, which in turn renders it problematic to stick to the assumptions that power entails conflict and is repressive.

The exchanges between pluralists and their critics concerning the relation between conflict and consensus have concentrated on the need to find a way of establishing when issues and events that do not reach the political agenda are in any way significant and when they are simply absent – that is, when they are not even latent or potentially present. Thus Polsby asks: '*which* nonevents are to be regarded as most significant in the community[?] Surely not *all* of them. For every event . . . that occurs there must be an infinity of alternatives. Then which nonevents are to be regarded as significant?'[41] Whereas this question addresses the logical possibility of issues constituting relevant counterfactuals, Crenson's response to Polsby seems merely commonsensical and fails to get to the root of the problem. 'From the infinity of nonevents available,' he writes in his study of nondecisions in relation to air pollution, 'why should we pick those related to air pollution instead of those related to the prevention of elephant stampedes or the persecution of witches?'[42] The problem is that here Crenson presupposes what he was supposed to demonstrate, namely how one can differentiate between significant and insignificant issues. The same is true of Polsby, although for different reasons, namely that he assumes a dialogue between equals where power does not touch upon the voicing of issues, meaning that every issue has an equal claim to inclusion on the political agenda. This is where the premiss of the underlying consensus has the *de facto* function of screening out 'unacceptable' issues from the political agenda. If the selection of issues were a random enterprise, then those excluded from politics could not but be so as well, in which case Polsby would be right in asserting that the picking of certain non-issues rather than others would be a matter of the outside observer's 'prejudices'.

The point is, however, that the selection of issues by organizations, institutions, political parties and the like cannot be arbitrary since this would entail the disintegration of organization altogether. As Polsby has argued himself, political organizations always involve a moment of conservatism. If this means that there is an inertia with regard to what issues are discussed, how they are resolved, as well as who gets represented and whose views prevail in decision making, then neither the selection of issues nor the representation of agents can be arbitrary. The exclusion of non-issues and 'non-agents' cannot, accordingly, be arbitrary either, but has to involve some degree of systematicity. From this follows the possibility that significant issues and agents can be systematically excluded from the political agenda if they, for whatever reason, do not conform to the rules of the game.

The political would thus be understood in terms of decision making which is divorced from the issue of conflicts. This makes way for an understanding of politics in terms of the inclusion/exclusion of agents and the flow of issues into/from politics: that is, whether or not they reach the threshold of representation and hence become viewed as legitimate political agents and issues. Such mechanisms of selection are rooted in tradition, that is, in the 'normal' state of affairs. By thus moving out of the cul-de-sac, where it is impossible to assert the degree of importance attached to decisions, issues and agents, it becomes tenable to propose *relevant* counterfactuals with regard to exercises of power that do not presuppose event causation.

The exchange between Polsby and Crenson on the criteria for

differentiating between significant and insignificant issues shows the problems that face the event-causation model of power in singling out counterfactuals. When issues become such they are, by definition, important because a significant number of people regard them as worth debating, whereby unimportant issues are simply non-issues. This tautology, based partly on the atomistic and volitional conception of power, and partly on 'the integrationist conception of society', is a consequence of not contextualizing power and of not viewing politics in relation to society as such.[43] In so far as political institutions are assumed a priori to represent society inclusively, it becomes impossible to establish *relevant* counterfactuals since these cannot but be every conceivable would-be issue, whereupon the very criteria of relevance is lost. This is why we are faced with the sterile option: the differentiation between issues and non-issues is either what (some) people say it is or it is what an outside observer says it is. While the first solution cannot guard itself against the accusation of elite domination, the latter cannot avoid arbitrary 'ideological prejudice'. Avoidance of this impasse requires, first, a re-evaluation of the relation between the political and the social, and second, a contextualization of power which is capable of depicting relevant counterfactuals – how political institutions define certain issues as belonging to the political arena whilst precluding others, thereby distinguishing *de facto* between degrees of importance.

This is important for understanding the problem of anticipating reactions: because there is at least some degree of systematicity, inertia or bias involved in what gets accepted as issues, as well as in which decisions can be made, it follows that the anticipation of reactions plays a crucial role in policy making. Dahl's reference to the mayor's readiness to defer to the wishes of the business community in New Haven is one such example; others are provided by nondecision-making theorists, who argue that lower-status groups abstain from voicing issues because they perceive that the chances of their petitions being heard are minimal. Both examples show the inadequacy of conceptualizing power solely in terms of decision making in the legitimate political sites rather than in the political structuring of social relations in general. This approach cannot account for the contrary-to-fact conditionals brought to the fore by the often subtle mechanisms of anticipating reactions, which direct attention to the social context of exercising power and to the study of counterfactuals in relation to the inclusion/exclusion of issues, agents and the like. It should be clear that this alternative is not subjectivist in the sense of falling prey to 'ideological prejudice'. Rather, it goes beyond event causation by looking at how criteria of importance and the acceptability of issues are ingrained in the rules and routines of institutions, and shape the nature of conflicts and the consensus that might be reached. It is this aspect that Lukes's approach attempts to deal with.

The 'Third Face of Power': Lukes's Theory of Power

Lukes propounds his conception of power in *Power: A Radical View*. It embodies a 'three-dimensional view of power', which stands as a critique of what he refers to as the one- and two-dimensional views – the first and second faces of power. The understanding of power advances, according to Lukes, with Bachrach and Baratz's concept of nondecision, as it provides a more adequate picture of the various and often subtle ways power operates than is achieved by the pluralist approach. He none the less criticizes both for being behaviourist and subjectivist, because exercises of power in each are perceived solely in relation to decisions taken by agents. Lukes's three-dimensional view of power incorporates the first two dimensions with the addition of a third, namely that of 'no-decisions', which indicates that power does not necessarily stem from decisions. This 'third face of power' enables him to free his conception of power from behaviourism,[44] and to focus on the underlying social patterning which determines the capacity to act, that is, to wield power. The third aspect of power could, for want of a better term, be labelled systemic power, since it draws attention to the often disguised mechanisms of indirect influence inherent in social relations, of which agents are not necessarily aware.[45] Agents can be unaware of exercising power – a possibility that Bachrach and Baratz allow for too[46] – but they can also be unaware of power being exercised over them. In fact, it is not the case that agents are simply unaware, but rather that they are shaped by this form of power, which is akin to structural determination. It is important to see this form of power in relation to the dualism of agency and structure, which Lukes tries to mediate by further contextualizing power.

Lukes's conceptualization of power can best be understood as a radicalization of Bachrach and Baratz's use of the notion of the mobilization of bias. In deploying this notion one is, as mentioned, confronted with two options: systemic bias is either restricted to the field of nondecisions, to overt and covert conflicts, or it is expanded so as to account for even the absence of conflicts, in which case, consensus can be manipulated by power without the involved parties being aware of it. In opting for the latter, Lukes sets out to explore how 'the bias of the system is not sustained simply by a series of individually chosen acts, but also, most importantly, by the socially structured and culturally patterned behaviour of groups, and practices of institutions, which may indeed be manifested by individuals' inaction', that is, by nonevents and no-decisions.[47]

The radical corollary of Schattschneider's idea of managing conflicts even before they start is that power is not only exercised when an agent makes a decision, or when a decision suppresses a latent or potential issue, but also, and most importantly and effectively, when the very wants and desires of agents are influenced in such a way that they do not clash with those who wield power. It is with regard to this possibility of controlling conflicts before they begin that Lukes asks: 'is it not the supreme and most insidious exercise of power to prevent people, to whatever degree, from having grievances by shaping their perceptions, cognitions and preferences in such a way that they accept their role in the existing order of things . . .?'[48]

It should be clear, that while Lukes embraces the radical consequences of Bachrach and Baratz's nondecision-making theory and Schattschneider's mobilization of bias, he clings to the implicit premiss that power is 'power over'. That is to say, power is a kind of domination; or rather, the third dimension of power is a generalized and unsubjective manipulative power which assumes the character of a systemic power. The reason is that, in loosening the link between power and conflict while holding on to that between power and domination, we are left with a consensus that cannot be genuine but is instead manipulated. The assumption that consensus might be manipulated is, of course, radical compared to the dogma of pluralism, but it is none the less only a half-hearted attempt to advance beyond behaviourism. The two links are closely connected in the sense that a challenge to the first cannot avoid having consequences for the second: the presupposition that power is repressive hangs in thin air; compared to what is this power repressive? Lukes's answer is to invoke a hypothetical contrary-to-fact standard of genuine consensus based on full autonomy. This, however, introduces a series of problems, which we will return to shortly.

Lukes's idea of systemic power is, of course, unacceptable to the pluralists due to their insistence that observable conflicts are the only way of documenting the fact that exercises of power have taken place. This is so even though examples of systemic bias can be found in the works of pluralists themselves (compare Dahl and Wolfinger). By thus insisting on the visibility of conflicts as proof that power has been exercised, pluralists claim that the notion of the mobilization of bias falls prey to ideological prejudices. Lukes's response to this assertion is interesting because it throws light on his idea of systemic power. He concedes that there is a methodological problem involved in claiming that power has been wielded, notwithstanding a lack of evidence of overt and covert conflicts.[49] However, it is, in his opinion, illegitimate to 'move from a methodological difficulty to a substantive assertion' as the pluralists do when they argue that consensus implies the absence of power. 'To assume that the absence of grievance equals genuine consensus is simply to rule out the possibility of false or manipulated consensus by definitional fiat.'[50] He contends, moreover, that 'power is unique among social phenomena in its self-concealing tendency; in many situations, its observability correlates inversely with its effectiveness, which cannot, therefore, be measured only by techniques of direct observation.'[51]

The methodological problem arises because power as a causal concept, whose criterion is 'significant affecting', necessitates the depiction of a relevant counterfactual against which behaviour can be measured. In situations of observable conflict there are, seemingly, no problems in assessing when affecting is significant, since the criterion of significance is that a change in behaviour occurs: if *A* wants *B*, whose preference is *b*, to pursue *a*, and, presupposing that *A* can get its way with *B*, then *B* is going to alter its behaviour. *B* is thus significantly affected to the extent to which it pursues *a* instead of *b*, where the difference between *a* and *b*, *ceteris paribus*, constitutes the counterfactual proof that power has been exercised. In situations where there are no observable grievances, it becomes problematic to assert what *B* would have done in the absence of *A* because *B* accepts 'the existing order of things'.[52] An attempt must, accordingly, be made to demonstrate whether *B*'s compliance is manipulated, which involves reference to relevant *hypothetical* counterfactuals.

The nub of the problem is that if it is insufficient to analyse power merely in terms of clashes of interests because these are themselves manipulated by power, it becomes imperative to outline a counterfactual standard which stays clear of power, and hence becomes the expression *par excellence* of autonomy. Such a standard has to be hypothetical, or rather, a regulative idea since power as systemic bias pervades every social relation. To establish how this form of power operates in a context marked by consensus, it is necessary to counterpose agents' actual interests with those they would have in the imagined situation were they 'free to choose'. It follows that if the interests in the two situations differ, systemic power is operative. This is not surprising, given the ubiquity of this form of power. What it means is that the non-occurrence of conflicts, far from indicating genuine consensus, serves to paper over latent and/or potential conflicts which are repressed due to the fact that people may be unaware of certain issues they would pursue if they were free. And, conversely, in so far as agents might come to terms with the fact that their interests are shaped by systemic bias, the latent or potential conflicts would crystallize into open conflicts, just as non-issues would become issues.

It is important to note that Lukes maintains that power is, ultimately, connected with conflicting interests, factually or hypothetically. But these can remain latent and unrealized due to the existence of systemic power.[53] Autonomy is the backbone of the hypothetical counterfactual standard, which makes it possible to measure significant affecting despite the absence of conflict. It should thus be obvious that the notion of autonomy is, on the one hand, a vehicle of politicization, since it is held up against a consensus which may only be apparent inasmuch as it prevents latent issues from reaching the political agenda; whilst, on the other hand, it envisions a state of affairs in which power, and hence politics, is eliminated.

We are now in a position to look more closely at Lukes's definition of power. A qualified critique of the behaviourist approach of pluralism is provided by Bachrach and Baratz, although they too, according to Lukes, remain within an individualistic conception of power.[54] The problem with such an approach, and its episodic conception of power, is that it is unable to understand phenomena like the mobilization of bias, where power actively shapes the very preferences of individuals. Hence reference to individual actions cannot provide what Watkins has termed 'rock-bottom explanations' of social analysis. Furthermore, the atomistic focus on events makes it difficult to comprehend that the 'visible political activities of a community are more ordered and inhibited than an inspection of the activities alone would lead us to believe.'[55]

The last point stresses what the pluralists want to exclude from analysis, namely a capacity to wield power which is imbricated in the systemic features of social organization. Thus Wolfinger holds that 'defining power as a capacity to get one's way seems to lead to essentially unverifiable claims about potential power': that elites always manage to get their way. He then suggests that 'power is a relationship in which *A* gets *B* to do something that *B* would not otherwise do.'[56] Here Wolfinger confuses two aspects of power, namely the sources of power and its actual exercise. By rejecting the 'vehicle fallacy', he falls into the other trap, namely the 'exercise fallacy'.[57] If the choice was between 'unverifiable claims about potential power' and the atomistic and mechanistic model of event causation, it would obviously be unsatisfactory. However, this is far from being the case, since the possession of resources does not entail exercise of power: that is, the latter does not follow from the former – although it does not follow that the former can be excluded from a study of power. The necessity of focusing on the sources of power has been vindicated in the discussions of anticipating reactions and indirect influence, which even Dahl implicitly concedes are causally effective in bringing about consequences.

Lukes draws on the idea of capacity when he places at the centre of his theory the notion of interest, which is otherwise similar to the notions proposed by the first and second faces of power, and which he, moreover, holds to be 'predominant in contemporary political science'. He says: '*A* exercises power over *B* when *A* affects *B* in a manner contrary to *B*'s interests.'[58] Evoking the notion of interest in relation to power is an attempt to operationalize the concept of systemic power, and to draw attention to the fact that interests are not merely individual but take shape in a societal context. This last point stands as a critique of the pluralists' focus on actual policy preferences addressed to representative political institutions, which Lukes considers too narrow for analysing power. Hence the stress on interests is an attempt to widen the scope of power.[59]

Given that exercises of power may be disguised, agents are not necessarily aware of exercising power or having power exercised over them; it may not therefore be evident to either party that '*A* affects *B* in a manner contrary to *B*'s interests'. Moreover, when systemic power operates not only in a repressive fashion but also by shaping norms and preferences, it is possible that neither *A* nor *B* are aware of what their interests are. They are prone to misconceive them because what they take them to be has in part been determined by systemic power. In this situation, individual rationality tends to be undermined because the interests agents possess may not match those they would possess if they were not subjected to power, that is, if they were autonomous. It is this politicization of social relations (in fact, the plea for an extension of political participation), whereby the status of the wants and preferences of individuals are put into question, that urges Lukes to split the notion of interests into subjective and real interests. Whereas pluralism assumes that what agents take to be in their interests *are* their interests, for Lukes these constitute subjective interests.[60] Real interests, on the other hand, indicate what agents 'really' would pursue in the absence of power.

Lukes's purpose in introducing the notion of real interests is twofold. First, it enables him to argue his case for power as systemic bias by elaborating a counterfactual standard of autonomy, and thereby indicating the contours of significant affecting in the absence of both overt and covert conflicts. Second, it represents an emancipatory endeavour to (re-)create individual rationality. By making agents aware of the hidden mechanisms of power, Lukes foresees the merging of subjective and real interests. It is important to stress that real interests are not superimposed upon agents as is the case with the Marxist idea of objective interests, which are grounded in 'historical necessity' and which agents can either enact or fail to enact. Rather, real interests are, for Lukes, tied to 'hypothetical subjective preferences under conditions of relative autonomy'.[61] Thus Lukes's theory of power is behaviourist in the widest sense: what people prefer under these conditions is equal to their real interests, which is to say that power has not been exercised over them. This forms his argument against those who hold that his notion of power cannot be assessed empirically, and that the notion of real interests expresses an 'observer's assessment' that is independent of the actual formation of interests.

Nevertheless, one problem remains even when the relevant counterfactual condition of autonomy is in place. This problem was raised by Wolfinger in his critique of Bachrach and Baratz, but it applies equally as a critique of Lukes *avant la lettre*. In order to identify nondecisions, he says, one 'seems generally to come back to determining people's "real interests", as opposed to what they say they want or what they are trying to get through political action.'[62] The problem, then, is that even though one could advance 'a theory of political interests and rational behaviour' that was able to function as a counterfactual against which non-participation might be judged, there would be no way of assessing whether nonparticipation was the result of a nondecision or whether the theory was wrong. It thus follows that identifying 'nondecisions by means of a normative theory would be satisfactory only to those people who shared the ideological perspective from which the attribution of interests was made.'

The problems involved in invoking an external observer's viewpoint to assess real as opposed to subjective interests are indisputable. However, in rejecting the possibility that agents' interests are manipulated by power, the pluralists go to the other extreme of accepting as issues only those which are formulated by the political leaders, or more generally, those which do not challenge the 'Establishment'. The reason is, of course, that leaders are supposedly responsive to the citizenry, meaning that the political institutions represent society *in toto*.[63] This argument rests, as already mentioned, on the integrationist conception of society, wherein the political is at one and the same time isolated from the social whilst mirroring it adequately. It is this dubious assumption that enables pluralists to reject the idea of autonomy as real interests; this points to a cleavage in, and therefore a politicization of, political representation. Hence pluralism cannot avoid the charge that it is a theory which will prove 'satisfactory only to those people who [share] the ideological perspective from which the attribution of interests [is] made'.[64]

The problem of establishing the point at which autonomy is reached is a serious one, due to the systemic nature of the third face of power, which decrees that individual rationality cannot be set apart from the ideal of a rational society freed from the distorting effects of power – what Lukes calls 'an authentic assertion of autonomy', as is revealed in the traditions of democratic theory stemming from Rousseau and Mill.[65] The linking of 'authentic autonomy' to the elimination of power envisions the ideal of human emancipation, which can take the form of a 'dialogue between equals' or a 'non-distorted communication'. Thus there exists an affinity between Lukes's notion of real interests and Habermas's notion of emancipatory interests. Although this is not the place to engage in a comparative study of these notions, it should be noted that both argue that (real) interests are to be determined by the agents themselves by stipulating the contrary-to-fact conditional of a 'dialogue between equals';[66] and that this is made possible because the gap between the actual/subjective and the ideal/real is not unbridgeable. The latter exists latently in the former and is at once the means of detecting distortions in it. Thus Habermas says that 'we in every discourse reciprocally *presuppose* an ideal speech situation. The ideal speech situation is thereby characterized such that every consensus, which can be reached under its conditions, *per se* should count as a more true consensus.'[67]

The Problem of Power and Structure in Lukes's Theory: Causality and Responsibility in Power Relations

Having outlined Lukes's view of power, it is appropriate to engage with the problems raised by the third dimension of power: primarily, the relation between power and structure, which Lukes discusses in terms of responsibility and causation. Granted that power is a causal concept accounting for nontrivial effects, and that those who exercise power could have acted differently because they are relatively autonomous, it follows – not logically but by a 'wide intuitive appeal'(!) – that '[w]e want to know whom to hold responsible for the effects' of power.[68] This point is made more rigorously when Lukes contends that the purpose 'of locating power is to fix responsibility for consequences held to flow from the action, or inaction, of certain specifiable agents'.[69] Similarly, granted that agents have the ability to choose, Connolly suggests that 'there is a particularly intimate connection between alleging that *A* has power over *B* and concluding that *A* is properly held responsible to some degree for B's conduct or situation.'[70]

In arguing thus, Lukes and Connolly follow Mill's view that it is 'politically imperative to make demands upon men of power to hold them responsible for specific courses of events'.[71] The rationale behind this assertion is that historical occurrences are not a matter of fate; which is to say that they do not fall entirely outside the control of those who 'make' history. This is especially so when power is to a large extent wielded by elites, whose freedom to make decisions makes it imperative to attach political responsibility to events.[72] Mills's 'sociological definition of fate' has an affinity with structural determination, which is important here because it points to an antinomy between power and structure that is characteristic of agency conceptions of power.

The 'intuitive appeal' of linking power and responsibility in Lukes's and Connolly's analyses lies in the attempt to operationalize the notion of power – that is, to locate power within, and hence to identify the agencies responsible for, significant affecting. However, as mentioned, this is bound up with problems of verification because systemic power can operate independently of overt and covert conflicts. But to the extent to which it is tenable, first, to account for a situation in which agents have been affected in a nontrivial manner, and second, to place responsibility on certain actions or inactions, then a causal chain of events has been constructed. This is necessary in order to show that power has been exercised, to establish relevant hypothetical counterfactuals, and finally, to assert the identity of the agents involved in power relations.

The linking of power to autonomy, causation and responsibility raises two problems. The first concerns the relationship between awareness and unawareness, which is a question of whether power operates manifestly or anonymously. In dealing with this problem Lukes is primarily concerned with the question of unintended consequences of actions and inactions. The second concerns the levels of analysis, that is, the relation between power at the societal level and the power exercised by individual and collective agents. Both of these problems are bound up with Lukes's assumption that it is possible, and indeed mandatory, to place responsibility on exercises of power. The question is *how* and *when* it is feasible to hold agents responsible for wielding power when they are themselves shaped by it. It is in this context that the relation between power and structure should be seen.

The issue of unawareness in the exercise of power is one of the key problems in the decision-making approach, inasmuch as it touches upon what a decision is. Whereas the pluralists hold that both parties in a power relation are aware of power being exercised – due partly to their insistence that manifest conflicts are indicators of the existence of power, and partly to the fact that power is exercised through participation in decision making in legislative and administrative bodies – Bachrach and Baratz, for their part, argue that it is only necessary that at least one of the parties should be aware of it. This is where the problem of nondecisions arises. The existence of a covert conflict presupposes either that the agent who suppresses an issue is aware of doing so, in which case a nondecision is 'an *active decision* not to take action', a 'decision to neglect'.[73] But it can also be the case that those who wield power through nondecisions are not aware of the consequences of thwarting potential and latent issues. 'Simply supporting the established political process tends to have this effect', say Bachrach and Baratz, and from this they conclude that 'our main concern is not whether the defenders of the *status quo* use their power consciously, but rather if and how they exercise it and what effects it has on the political process and other actors within the system.'[74]

The problem with the second dimension of power is, according to Lukes, that whilst it insists that nondecisions are decisions, it also claims that agents do not necessarily 'use their power consciously'. This opens up a schism between decision making and the mobilization of bias: 'Decisions', says Lukes, 'are choices consciously and intentionally made by individuals between alternatives, whereas the bias of the system can be mobilized, recreated and reinforced in ways that are neither consciously chosen nor the intended result of particular individuals' choices.' It follows that 'an unconscious decision looks like a contradiction.'[75] Since power can be exercised and internalized unconsciously through systemic bias, Lukes divorces power and decision making by arguing that power can be operative even in the absence of conflicts and decisions – hence the notion of no-decision.

The notion of no-decision is touched upon in the exchange between Lukes and Bradshaw. The latter is of the opinion that 'we cannot legitimately conceive of an actor who possesses relevant information, or who is in a position to acquire that information (and aware of that), ever making a nondecision which is a *no*-decision, i.e. simply failing to make a decision.'[76] The agent has, on the contrary, made a decision not to act (a nondecision), but this is not necessarily taken formally, that is, registered. Agents may, for instance, be aware of the existence of political challenges and the fact that they prevent potential issues from being raised. But if it is not in the agents' interest to stop the activities they are engaged in and, moreover, if they do not see any viable alternatives to these, then their exercise of power can be the result of a tacit agreement not to put an issue on the agenda. Such a consensus is inseparable from systemic bias, which is the filter through which decisions are channelled. It can thus be argued that if Bradshaw wants to maintain the link between power and decision making, even in routine cases and in the absence of alternatives, he has to rule out the possibility of illegitimate unawareness in exercises of power. There is, then, either a decision to neglect or simply unawareness: it is possible to assign responsibility in the first case but not in the latter.[77]

In his reply to Bradshaw, Lukes sees this as a devaluation of the notion of decision, in that it embraces every form of action and inaction. His argument remains that power can be exercised without awareness of its consequences and in the absence of perceived alternatives; this does not, however, prevent one from assigning responsibility. He holds, moreover, that if Bradshaw wants to sustain the link between power and decision, he 'needs to show . . . that the absence of observable action necessarily *does* imply that a decision *was* taken'.[78] Lukes does not see any reason why the exercising of power should imply awareness of all its aspects. He lists three forms of unawareness: first, that of the real motives behind one's action (the 'standard Freudian case'); second, how others interpret it (the typical case for game theory); and third, and most importantly, the unawareness of the consequences of one's action.[79]

Lukes's argument is that to the extent that an exercise of power is 'unconsidered' or 'performed in ignorance of alternatives' it can be exempted from responsibility only if there are legitimate reasons for this being so. If this is not the case, however, no-decisions should be treated as hypothetically conscious acts of negligence – what he calls 'remediable ignorance'[80] – to which responsibility can and should be assigned. The question of responsibility and legitimacy in relation to conceptualizing power poses a serious problem for Lukes (as well as for Bradshaw and Connolly). Agents are seen as having the ability to exercise power only when they are relatively autonomous, that is, when they are not structurally determined but can choose among alternatives and can be held responsible for their choice. Because power is inseparable from responsibility within this analysis, the idea of legitimate unawareness becomes problematic. Legitimacy and responsibility seem, in fact, to be mutually exclusive in relation to exercises of power. The key question is whether agents – when acting or failing to act – either *are* or *should* be aware of possible alternatives, in which case they can be held responsible; or whether their lack of knowledge or information is excusable, in which case they cannot be held responsible. Since power presupposes – or rather expresses – autonomy, the question becomes whether or not agents' unawareness about their autonomy can be considered legitimate. This problem is further complicated by the fact that agents can be structurally determined, in which case their lack of autonomy means that they do not exercise power, and thus cannot be held responsible at all.

These problems give rise to three questions: Should a given action or inaction be regarded as structurally determined or the result of systemic power? If the latter is the case, is it then exercised consciously or unconsciously? And if it is unconscious, should it then be seen as legitimate or not? This shows that the problem of the relation between power and structure is made dependent upon an (implicit) ethical notion of autonomy whose ground is the constitutive subject, and whose 'model' seems to be the legitimate unawareness of exercising power which is *ipso facto*, and by way of the ethical imposition, exempted from counting as power and hence responsibility in the first place. This set of questions can be illustrated in the following way:

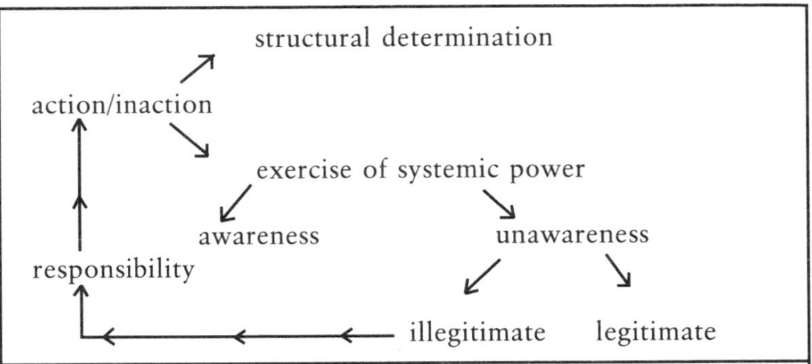

The arrows are not causal relations. Instead, they indicate that action/inaction *can be seen in terms of* either structural determination or exercises of social power. The latter can be seen in terms of either awareness or unawareness, and the latter can, again, be seen in terms of illegitimacy or legitimacy. In so far as the exercise of power is illigitimate it is, according to Lukes, possible and, indeed, mandatory to place responsibility on this action/inàction.

Fig. 2.1 *Power and responsibility*

The fundamental difficulty with Lukes's conception of third-dimensional power is that while it aims to supersede behaviourism by dissociating power from decisions, it insists at the same time on the juridical and moral endeavour of assigning responsibility to exercises of power. The nub of the problem is the feasibility of holding agents responsible for systemic effects of indirect influence which need not be the result of anybody's decisions and which are, moreover, exercised and internalized unconsciously. The affinity between systemic power and structural determination lies in the fact that both are intrinsic to social relations, where they operate as anonymous collective forces which are non-intentional. This should be seen as an extension of Lukes's critique of behaviourism and his aim to work out a 'dialectic of power and structure'. The notion of systemic power can be said to be successful in this respect because it blurs the differentiation between power and structure, whereby a rigorous distinction between internal and external determination – between agency and structure – cannot be maintained. Systemic power blots out the difference between conscious and unconscious exercises of power since they are present in each other, or presuppose one another; this makes it impossible to account for systemic power in terms of event causation.

The problem of counterfactuals should also be seen in this light. Lukes is justified in asserting that, given the difficulty of assessing when power has been exercised, it cannot be assumed that it has not been exercised. But he is not right in claiming that this problem is merely methodological.[81] It is more substantive because the nature of systemic power is such that, by partly obliterating the boundary between power and structure, it thoroughly blurs the extent to which agents are autonomous. This is, needless to say, serious, if not devastating, for an agency conception of power, which holds that agents' ability to exercise power depends upon their autonomy, and that this autonomy is antithetic to power. Lukes's view of relative autonomy cannot but be ambiguous because it is merely a common-sense residual, whose purpose is to mediate between external and internal determination, or what he refers to as 'external causes as against . . . internal reasons'.[82]

The ambiguity of the notion of relative autonomy renders his enterprise of assigning responsibility counterproductive because it is antithetic to the radical venture of outlining a theory of systemic power which plays a constitutive role for subjectivity. The reason is that to hold someone responsible for something implies that the agent's action must be treated as a sovereign choice, whereby agency becomes the causal principle *par excellence*. This is put succinctly by Dahl in his argument that in ethics and law 'the notion of responsibility rests on assumptions about strict causation.' 'In ethics the idea of moral responsibility involves', he continues, 'the paradoxical assumption that an individual should be held responsible for consequences only if he caused these consequences but was himself free not to have caused them. Thus the notion of responsibility implies that in some circumstances an individual's actions are simultaneously a cause and yet themselves uncaused.'[83]

It is this principle that Lukes's notion of systemic power subverts since agency is itself an effect of supra-individual forces, meaning that the 'self' of self-determination is just as much a determination by the 'other'. Hence the marriage between systemic power and responsibility is an uneasy one, to say the least, since they operate according to contradictory principles: while the former sees agency as an effect, the latter sees it as the cause. This must be seen as the inevitable consequence of transposing a legal discourse into the realm of the sociology of power. By imposing the former on the latter, Lukes cannot but take for granted what his analysis has otherwise called into question, namely the dictum of the constitutive subject, whose autonomy guarantees that it is its own cause. This paradox has repercussions on the methodological approach: while legal/moral discourses are inclined towards individualism, the sociology of power is slanted towards holism.

The third dimension of power as a kind of a societal manipulation and the dictum of the autonomous subject, which can be revealed by peeling off layers of third-dimensional power, indicates that Lukes operates on the assumption of an order/disorder dichotomy: the given state of affairs is, to a greater or lesser extent, marked by manipulation, false consensus, lack of autonomy, covert conflicts, a distorted consciousness and a distorted articulation of preferences and interests. This situation is a kind of systematized disorder, where the presence of power indicates the absence of a 'real' order characterized by rational persuasion, genuine consensus, autonomy, the absence of conflicts and alienation, and a free articulation of preferences. To conceive power along these lines is to see it as an external force and hence repressive *vis-à-vis* 'that' which would otherwise remain internal to itself, that is, autonomous. Thus power cannot but be derivative compared to 'that' to which it is 'attributed': the constitutive individual as the principle of order, an order which is 'there' before power – as in all forms of liberalism that take off from the presumption of the pre-political subject. A political consequence of the order/disorder dichotomy is the paradox of freedom, namely that one might be forced to be free. The idea here is that power can be used against power in order to restore 'that' which has been distorted by power. This is also Lukes's argument.[84]

Since the wielding of power is an expression of and presupposes autonomy, Lukes is faced with the dilemma of whether it is meaningful to hold agents responsible in situations where power is exercised in ignorance of its consequences. The question also arises as to whether it is meaningful to see the unconscious internalization of power as self-inflicted. These issues touch upon the extent to which it is reasonable to make use of notions like 'manipulated' or 'false' consensus, which are obviously important for Lukes's undertaking. In drawing conclusions from the idea of systemic power, a manipulated consensus can never be self-inflicted in the strict sense of the term, partly because the self can never be entirely itself, due to the very existence of this form of power, and because its real interest is autonomy. But the answer is far less conclusive when responsibility comes to play a constitutive role for power, that is, when the very idea 'of locating power is to fix responsibility'. The reason is that behind an agent who, unwillingly and without knowing it, gets caught up in manipulation lies a hypothetically autonomous agent who is the cause of its own actions, and who is the final arbiter as to whether it *should* be aware of power being exercised over it.

The question raised above, as to whether unawareness about one's autonomy can be considered legitimate, touches upon this problem. It may be objected that this question cannot be answered without reference to an actual situation. This is, of course, indisputable from a juridical point of view, which has to operate with the axiom of autonomous subjects who can be held responsible for their actions/inactions. However, the problem remains that there are two irreconcilable conceptual pressures at work in Lukes's analysis: that of systemic power and that of the juridical and ethical undertaking of attaching responsibility to actions and inactions. This antinomy is fostered by operating with two incommensurable types of explanation: a causal one which stresses significant affecting, and an intentional one which restricts the scope of power to cases of actual or hypothetical intended affecting.[85]

The introduction of responsibility into the analysis of power is an odd twist in the argument. It not only runs counter to the idea of systemic power, but also to the assumption that power is a causal concept accounting for significant affecting. An example given by Lukes himself illustrates this.[86] He considers 'the case of a drug company which allegedly exercises the most extreme power – of life and death – over members of the public by marketing a dangerous drug.' There is an obvious causal connection between the marketing of the drug and the 'life and death' of 'members of the public', meaning that they are significantly affected by the activities of the company. Relevant counterfactuals are easily depicted simply by comparing those who took the drug with those who did not. This, then, would count as an obvious case of power according to Lukes's earlier statement about causality and significant affecting. However, the invocation that the *raison d'être* 'of locating power is to fix responsibility' harbours this endeavour. From this it follows that the drug company has exercised power if and only if it either *was* or *should have been* aware of the consequences of its actions. But if it can be acquitted of both indictments, the charge of having exercised power is withdrawn. This is the case when Lukes elaborates on his example by asking whether cigarette companies exercised 'power over the public before it was even supposed that cigarette smoking might be harmful? Surely not.'[87] The reason is, of course, that they neither *were* nor *could have been* aware of the harmful consequences of smoking.

In arguing thus Lukes falls short of even the second face of power! In the example given by Bachrach and Baratz, of a university lecturer abstaining from voicing what he considered could be taken as a critique of the establishment, a potential conflict is thwarted by means of a nondecision. Why could this not be the case in Lukes's example too? And is it not possible to imagine a tacit or even an explicit agreement among the board members of, say, a tobacco company that they would have no interest whatsoever in investigating the health-damaging effects of smoking? Both possibilities would be obvious examples of nondecisions and hence acts of power. The question as to whether the company *should have been* aware of the health-damaging effects of their products is, curiously enough, not answered by Lukes, although the consequences to health of smoking tobacco have been known since 1881 when the first report on the topic was published in France by L'Académie Nationale de Médecine. This question is far from being a futile speculation of what agents ought to have done. It points instead to the context in which agents act. The growing emphasis today on environmental issues puts a greater strain on the products companies are marketing, which is to say that the extent of what they *should be* aware of has increased. In so far as they do not face such demands they must, following Lukes, be considered responsible for 'significantly affecting' the public. Lukes's discussion suggests that awareness, knowledge and taking responsibility are not immaculate conceptions but are, rather, discursively constructed in power struggles in which, say, tobacco companies are forced to be aware of the consequences of their products, and hence forced to take responsibility.

This discussion illustrates that our conceptions of knowledge and morals are bound up with power. Lukes's example of the tobacco company has a number of peculiar consequences with regard to the conceptualization of power: did tobacco companies suddenly begin to exercise power after 1881 when it was 'known' that tobacco was damaging to health? But then again, what does 'known' mean here? There can be all sorts of disagreements and power struggles over the validity of scientific and technocratic knowledge, which are at once intertwined with conflicting interests concerning results and, in turn, policy options. It seems that Lukes would agree that knowledge is caught up in power struggles between vested interests, and he thus appeals for 'the making of historical judgements about the locus of culturally determined limits to cognitive innovation'.[88]

Such a judgement is not merely a refinement of the analysis of power but is, rather, at its very centre since it delineates the limits between awareness and unawareness, and between legitimacy and illegitimacy. But this is not the whole story. The point is that it is not possible to avoid the conclusion that knowledge has itself become a 'culturally determined' matter. This has two consequences for the conceptualization of power. First, it blurs the distinction between causation and reason – between 'culturally determined limits' and 'cognitive innovation' – because the latter is bound up with the former, meaning that knowledge, rationality, rational persuasion, and the like, cannot be kept apart from power struggles. Second, seen in this light it becomes problematic to assume that power should be conceived in terms of domination which is external to rationality and autonomy. Hence the point is not merely that knowledge is caught up in power struggles, but that power is immanent in bodies of knowledge; in which case power assumes a productive role. These two points are crucial for grasping the relation between power and identity.

Both points are important for understanding what is at stake in Lukes's identification of power in terms of responsibility, a move that is detrimental to his power theory. To hold an agent responsible for an action presupposes that it has caused this action and hence exercised power. Alternatively, if the agent cannot be held responsible, it cannot be the cause of the action but is rather the effect of social forces it is not in control of, in which case it has not exercised power. But this being the case, the very idea of systemic power turns out to be a contradiction in terms! The reason is that when power qualifies as systemic, it escapes the control of agents because it assumes structural characteristics. But this cannot but be at odds with the idea that power is an attribute of agency whose autonomy is the originating causal principle of acting, which is to say that agency as the causal principle masters itself through its actions.

The ironic consequence is that Lukes's stress on responsibility inevitably leads him back to a position associated with an intentional conception of power and even with methodological individualism – which is, needless to say, at odds with systemic power. His analysis approaches Russell's definition of power as 'the production of intended effects'. It is only if consequences of actions can be referred back to the knowledge of those who initiated them that agents can be said to wield power, for it is only in this situation that they are in control of their actions, and hence the causal factor in bringing about effects. The modification Lukes adds to this view is merely the introduction of a hypothetical contrary-to-fact conditional of what agents *should* be aware of when acting or failing to act. Thus power can be the production of *un*intended effects but only inasmuch as the lack of intention or ignorance is 'remediable'. Otherwise 'talk of an exercise of power appears to lose all its point' since it is not possible to hold agents responsible for irremediable ignorance.[89]

In concluding this discussion, it is first of all important to draw attention to the antinomy in Lukes's theory between systemic power and the attribution of responsibility for power, which arises from his failure to clarify the nature of the relation between power/agency and structure. The problem is that whilst Lukes holds on to an agency conception of power, which dichotomizes power and structure, he also develops a view of power as essentially systemic – that is, possessing an affinity with structure. Although he pleads for 'a dialectic of power and structure', the two terms are nevertheless conceived as mutually exclusive since their identities are distinct from their interrelation. Hence it cannot be a dialectical relation, which would entail the opposite, that is, that the identities are constituted by their interrelation. Thus 'within a system characterised by total structural determinism, there would be no place for power', and power can, accordingly, only be understood as 'exercised within structurally determined limits', that is, within expanding and contracting opportunities and abilities to act. The problem is, then, to determine 'where structural determination ends and power and responsibility begin'.[90]

By posing the problem in this way Lukes confines himself within the zero-sum scale of external and internal determination, that is, structural determination which is inversely related to autonomy. Thus he is not in a position to draw the conclusion from his own argument concerning systemic bias that power is exercised *through* the web of structures rather than between its openings.[91] He holds that although 'agents operate within structurally determined limits, they none the less have a certain relative autonomy and could have acted differently', which is the very reason for operating with counterfactuals and attributing responsibility. This is, however, inconsistent with the notion of systemic power, which operates anonymously and is internalized unconsciously. In criticizing the individualistic 'behavioural focus' for being unable to come to terms with how '*potential issues* are kept out of politics', Lukes makes room for power being wielded 'through the operation of social forces and institutional practices'.[92] The point is that this inconsistency – triggered by the ethical and juridical injunction in the conceptualization of power – is necessary to avoid a blurring of the distinction between systemic power and structure to the point where they cannot be differentiated. Reaching this point would invalidate the assertion that power is an agency concept which accounts for significant affecting, whose *modus operandi* is event causation and the imposition of contrary-to-fact conditionals, and whose emancipatory hope is the fully autonomous subject that has externalized power.

It is at this point that Lukes's adherence to behaviourism runs into insurmountable problems: in so far as power does not entail decisions, but can be sustained by the mobilization of bias, the insistence on conflict as the proof of power being exercised has to be eliminated, which leaves his counterfactual validation of exercises of power in a vacuum. But, far from leading to a questioning of the assumption that power entails conflict, Lukes resorts to postulating the hypothetical counterfactual of real interests as expressing the autonomy of a subject which is not subjected to power. While thus transcending behaviourism, he remains, nevertheless, faithful to its basic idea of studying power in terms of significant affecting and events. The deficiency in Lukes's conception of power is that he inherits from behaviourism the model of 'power over', which is studied in terms of event causation and counterfactuals; this is obviously unsuitable for studying systemic power. This form of power is systemic precisely *because* it is a kind of power which does not induce people to do something they would not otherwise have done. Rather than viewing power in counterfactual terms, the notion of systemic power draws attention to the fact that power is embedded in rule-governed practices, that is, in what people *normally* do. This is why power and knowledge cannot be kept apart.

It should thus be clear that with the idea of systemic power Lukes reaches the limits of conceptualizing power in terms of agency, because this undertaking can only be safeguarded by virtue of introducing an inconsistency in the argument, which is at once the strength and the weakness of his enterprise. Having reached the limits of the agency conception of power, he is already beyond it; but this 'beyond' is marked by a lack of conceptual clarity concerning the nature of power and its relation to structure because the latter is unavoidably implemented in the former, and vice versa.

When Lukes contends that power might operate in the absence of conflicts due merely to the pressure of systemic bias, he transcends the behaviourist model of causality. The reason is that this model is geared towards dealing with events; thus when power is a nonevent (for example, standing conditions), it cannot be analysed causally except by transcending behaviourism. Since Lukes does not elaborate on the nature of the causal mechanisms that constitute 'social forces and institutional practices', his holistic account of power takes place in a vacuum. This has detrimental consequences for his overall attempt effectively to supersede behaviourism, since the only option is to fall back upon the behaviourist insistence on event causation, which he moulds in terms of responsibility and modifies by invoking references to hypothetical counterfactual events which could have taken place but did not.

One is thus led back to the cul-de-sac of assigning responsibility, which is the only way causal relations can be conceived within Lukes's theory.[93] This is so due to the lack of clarity concerning the relation between power and structure, and hence between the levels of, on the one side, individual and collective agents, and, on the other, society.[94] This problem is illustrated by his wavering between a holistic and a modified individualistic approach. His view of power is predominantly holistic when discussing systemic bias, whereas it tends towards individualism when trying to trace causal connections in power relations by fixing responsibility. The individualizing retreat is unavoidable since the societal level is an 'unguided moulding' of intentional as well as nonintentional power relations. Its system character consists solely in its anonymity which, in the last resort, has to be based on non-anonymity – the hypothetical presence of 'consciousness' – due to its constitutive link to agents. In this sense the individual is the very principle of order.

These are the consequences of a theory of power which, in the final instance, has nothing but autonomous agents as its basis. Lukes's problem in providing a causal explanation of power is inseparable from the disparity between derivative and pre-suppositionless conceptualizations of power. The formalism of his argument, in which power is expressed in the three types of decisions, is undermined, partly because power presupposes autonomous subjects as the unifying element that guarantees the causal principle of the agency conception of power, and partly because its effects are determined a priori as effecting those over whom power is exercised in a manner contrary to their (real) interests. These two aspects of the derivative conception of power are inseparable since both the emancipatory strategy of real interests, and the causal endeavour of placing responsibility on power, depend upon the autonomy of the agent through which the objectivity of social relations is grounded and the social order guaranteed.

Autonomy is meaningful only if it is possible to discriminate in a way that systemic power renders impossible, namely between 'consciousness' and 'unconsciousness'. It can thus be concluded that Lukes's theory of power draws on the most radical consequences of the decision-making approach by taking decisive steps beyond behaviourism, but that it constantly undermines its own arguments by not taking them to their logical conclusion. These inconsistencies place the theory squarely between a derivative and a pre-suppositionless understanding of power. Lukes's oscillation between these two approaches is probably most visible in his discussion of real interests – the cornerstone of his third dimension of power. Wolfinger was right to assert that this type of real-interest argument presupposes an 'outside observer', that is, a subject who is positioned outside the intricate network of power. Lukes's problem is that, according to his own argument, such a position cannot be occupied by a subject, since the subject *qua* subject is always 'contaminated' by power. By positing such a *place* from which emancipation can speak, where the self is identical with itself, Lukes's theory of power is inextricably caught up in a derivative conception of power, which poses an Archimedean point above the realm of power relations.

The lack of clarity concerning the two approaches to power calls for the development of a conception of power which does not discriminate a priori between power and structure, and thereby links power to either autonomous agents or objective structures. In that way it should be possible to transcend the dichotomy between power and knowledge/rationality, the equation of power with causation, and finally, the reduction of power to 'power over'. It is important to stress that the aim should not be to eliminate the notion of causality from the theorization of power. The problem is, rather, that when causality is a specific type of relation between elements whose identities are presupposed – when causality expresses a logic of identity – a presuppositionless approach cannot *ipso facto* assume causal relations between elements, since the upshot of this approach is to study power in terms of identification: how elements attain identity, and by extension, how causality is established. Foucault's power analytics, which we will now consider, marks an important step in the direction of advancing a presuppositionless approach to power cast in terms of identification, inasmuch as it scrutinizes a number of fundamental problems in the conceptualization of power such as autonomy, rationality and causality, as well as the relation between the political and the social.

3
Power, Identity and Political Authority: Foucault's Power Analytics

The Politics of Foucault's Power Analytics

Even though Foucault rarely engaged in direct dialogue with political theory, it would be quite mistaken to assume that his works are irrelevant for the study of politics. The fact that the problems he raises – for example, mental illness, sexuality – are rarely discussed within political theory, and that his style is considerably different from what is considered 'normal' within the study of politics, does not prevent his power analytics from addressing key issues in political theory. The contrast between the legitimate power/authority of the state (what Foucault terms 'the juridico-discursive representation of power') and the power of discipline and regulation indicates that the modern and, in particular, the liberal understanding of power and political authority suffers from acute deficiencies concerning the conception of power itself, and the relation between the political and the social.

From a political point of view, the major problem that Foucault's power analytics takes issue with concerns: (a) the reduction of power to a matter of domination, which can be grasped in terms of either its exercise or its possession – agency or structure; (b) the assumption that power is antithetic to the autonomy and rationality of the subject, and by extension, that power as domination is antithetic to knowledge as the quest for true non-coerced deliberation; and (c) the reduction of the political authorization of power, which articulates power and knowledge, to the legitimate authority of the state. These three issues are crucial for political theory in general and democratic theory in particular. Power is, from Hobbes onwards, typically conceived in terms of the desire to dominate – 'power over'; this is held at bay by a system of rights grounded in universal reason, which, again, is rooted in the axiom of the constitutive – that is, pre-political – subject. Rights thus guarantee individuals a certain amount of freedom *from* political power.

The relation between power and right has been the organizing matrix for liberal democratic theory as well as for the socialist recuperation or 'retrieval' of liberal democracy.[1] This approach to democratic theory is deeply entrenched in the three issues just mentioned: power, autonomy and subjectivity, and political authority. In so far as these issues are not addressed, we are bound to go on conceiving them in relation to the particular structure of the modern regime based on the sovereignty principle, which conveys a protective and, in fact, elitist view of democracy – by ostracizing the political from the social, and by isolating the citizenry from active involvement in politics.

By opposing power to autonomy, and the political to the social, theories of power make a number of assumptions about power. What Foucault's power analytics invites us to do is to scrutinize the underlying assumptions involved in discussing power. More concretely and, one might say, by way of 'provocation', he invites us to bracket the problem of the state (albeit temporarily) in order to create space to think about power unencumbered by the discourses of legitimate domination. The creation of such a space is necessary because it paves the way for an understanding of power that has been displaced from political theory due to the hegemony of the 'juridico-discursive representation of power', which has monopolized discourses on power. What Foucault thus aims to show is that power as it is conceptualized at the level of the regime does not exhaust power 'as such'. The point is not only to argue that power exists everywhere but, further, that the power relations existing throughout society do not necessarily conform to those which find expression at the level of the regime; and that, in so far as the former is conceived in terms of the latter, we are faced with a reductionist account of power. The point is, then, that the very conceptualization of power constitutes an inseparable part of power struggles: discourses *on* power are also discourses *of* power.[2]

Rather than approach at the level of the regime, we could embark upon our analysis by looking at the definition of power. Power is *ability per se* which cannot be logically linked to either domination or rights, that is, to a particular ontology or a normative theory of power. To reduce power to domination and to force it into universalized schemes of rights and obligations is a modern – and, more specifically, liberal – political strategy whose *raison d'être* lies in the principle of sovereignty. The political is identified with the state and public spaces, and is distinguished from the social, which is either a primordial or a residual category of that which is not (yet) political (typically the economy, culture, spheres of intimacy, and the like). It is in this light that Foucault's critique of the 'repressive hypothesis', 'globalizing discourses' and the 'constituent subject' should be seen.

Foucault's power analytics can be read as a kind of postmodern attempt to free the conceptualization of power from its modern straitjacket: the couplet of the repressive hypothesis of power and the globalizing discourses of rights, which is underpinned by the axiom of a pre-politically given subject. By not reducing political authority to legitimate authority in its centralized locations, Foucault paves the way for comprehending how power is politically authorized in all sorts of institutional settings where human beings are turned into subjects – institutions which cut across the distinctions between the political and the social, and the public and the private. The disciplining of the subject to be 'docile' and 'normal', and the ordering of society as a regulated entity, extend far beyond the institutional setting of legitimate state authority and repressive apparatuses of power.

In order to appreciate the importance of Foucault's power analytics for the study of politics, it is crucial to focus on the intimate articulation between power, subject/identity, knowledge and authority. The point is that the techniques of disciplining and regulation both trigger and embody power and knowledge, which mutually condition each other and form a constitutive part of the political authorization of power. In this scenario power cannot be understood as essentially repressive, just as politics cannot be grasped merely in the language of rights and obligations, consensus and coercion, legitimacy and illegitimacy, public and private, and the like.

By focusing on how power as ability is formed – how the identity of the subject and of the social order takes shape – Foucault launches what might be termed a presuppositionless conception of power and its political authorization. As a consequence of this approach, power and the political are viewed from the 'inside' and from 'below', and not from the 'outside' and from 'above'. What Foucault aims at is to study power and the political in the processes whereby they attain form and content, rather than to endow them a priori with form and content as if they were 'real' objects. Seen in this light power and the political are *in* the social as conditioning factors instead of being outside or above it, either determined by it or determining it:

> Between every point of a social body, between the members of a family, between a master and his pupil, between every one who knows and every one who does not, there exist relations of power which are not purely and simply a projection of the sovereign's great power over the individual; they are rather the concrete, changing soil in which the sovereign's power is grounded, the conditions which make it possible for it to function.[3]

Here Foucault is putting forward two claims: (a) the fact that power relations exist between every point of a social body means that power is located in differences between, say, social positions, and that difference as such does not necessarily entail a relation of domination or repression; and (b) the fact that relations of power are the soil in which sovereignty is rooted and conditioned means that the political authorization of power takes place throughout the social body, and that sovereignty cannot determine what conditions it in the first place.

This change of perspective has at least five consequences: (i) We move from conceptualizing power and politics in terms of determination and causation to a language of political potentials which condition but do not determine performance. (ii) As such a conditioning potential, it cannot be assumed a priori that power is endowed with either a particular form or content (among other things, this is an argument against the equation of power with 'power over', which is, rather, a specific codification of power). (iii) This move might – perhaps in a rather un-Foucauldian terminology – be termed an ontological turn in political theory which stresses the historical contingency of power relations and of social and political constructs. (iv) We move away from locating power and its political authorization at the level of the regime with its distinctions between, say, state and society and public and private, seeing it instead as an ongoing process taking place throughout the political system, understood as all those activities which concern the political authorization of power. And (v) we move from operationalizing democracy as merely a system of rights that protect and isolate the social from the political to a view where the political power of subjects can be used to assert individual autonomy and popular sovereignty.

Power as Ability: Dispensing with the Constituent Subject

The novelty and radicalness of Foucault's view of power is that he analyses it in terms of the *making* of the subject or the *becoming* of identity. Thus he does not operate with a priori assumptions as to what power and the subject are, and it is in this respect that we can speak of his power analytics as presuppositionless. It is in this light that one should understand his claim that we have 'to dispense with the constituent subject, to get rid of the subject itself, that's to say, to arrive at an analysis which can account for the constitution of the subject within a historical framework', and that '[p]ower in the substantive sense, "*le*" *pouvoir*, doesn't exist.'[4] A few reflections on the definition of power as ability will help situate what is at stake in this approach.

Etymologically, power means ability: to 'make a difference', which is the most basic definition of ability. It is basic inasmuch as it exists prior to the distinctions usually invoked in debates on power such as 'power to' and 'power over', and exercising and possessing power, as well as agency and structure. As the ability to make a difference, it is a secondary issue whether power ought to be conceived in either of these terms. What is important, however, is the implication in the assumption that power is defined as the ability to make a difference. This assumption actually sanctions a pleonasm because ability *is* 'making a difference', and because 'making' would be senseless if it did not entail 'difference'. 'The ability to make a difference' suggests that ability is embodied in an agent whose actions bring about changes, which are usually (since Machiavelli and Hobbes) analysed as causal consequences. It should thus be clear that defining power as making a difference raises the problem of how we go about conceptualizing ability: the agency of 'making' which is the vehicle of 'difference'. It is this problem that Foucault focuses on.

Here one could ask what this difference should be compared to? This 'what' has to be distinguished temporally and spatially from what the action, however defined, brings about; which is to say that power as the ability to make a difference is the limit between two situations. But what does it mean to assert that power should be conceived as a limit? If power was located in the 'making', one would typically be looking for abilities in agents and capacities in structures, the latter being a kind of resource functioning as a generative causal mechanism, which agents could draw upon when acting, that is, when effectuating a difference. 'Making', according to this view, would thus be prior to 'difference' as a cause to the latter's effect. Such a viewpoint is typically slanted towards a realist philosophy which attempts to detect the 'real' mechanisms beneath the surface manifestations of interacting agents. If, on the other hand, power was located in 'difference', one would typically be inclined to look at events thus dropping all references to abilities and capacities by simply focusing on overt behaviour. This is the empiricist or behaviourist model of event causation, where power is exhausted in its exercise: one event causes another which, accordingly, is its effect. It is not entirely correct to say that 'difference' takes priority over 'making', because the latter cannot be a feasible object for empirical study. Hence it is illegitimate to enquire into the possibility of possessing power, a power or a cause which may not be actualized, that is, brought into effect.

Foucault's conceptualization of power is located squarely between 'making' and 'difference'. Whilst the former suggests that power has to be conceptualized in terms of the innate capabilities of structures, which agents can make use of in order to bring about consequences, the latter assumes that agency can be conceived apart from structure, meaning that the relations between agency and structure, and between agents and events, are external. To define power in terms of either the internal relations of structures or the external relations between events is unsatisfactory because it presupposes what ought, in fact, to be questioned, namely that structure and agency can be conceived as fully constituted entities (entities with essentially given properties).

When 'making' is a process and the vehicle of 'difference', it follows that the agency embodying the 'ability to make a difference' is a metaphor for a becoming. Power is, accordingly, a name for becoming: the temporal limits between future, past and present, and the spatial limits between part and whole. Power as limit cannot ever be grasped or rendered law-abiding by institutions, meaning that both conceptualizations (knowledge) and institutions are *in* time – existing in or as processes of becoming. Foucault's power analytics is thus antithetic to the Kantian dualism of space and time, alias synchronic and diachronic analysis.[5] Power is the limit immanent in and constitutive of abilities and capacities; or, to put it differently, it is the name for the structuration of abilities and capacities. As a metaphor for becoming, difference and undecidability power perpetually avoids being stifled in a concept or in an institutional setting. In this sense, power is the name for *that* which constitutes identity but which in itself has no identity – the limit of language which, paraphrasing Wittgenstein, can only be shown.

The problem Foucault poses concerns the becoming of ability – ability as the limit as such – which is more fundamental than the problems of, say, who wields power, how and why – which does not, of course, mean that these questions are irrelevant.[6] The radicalness of Foucault's undertaking lies in his analyses of the temporal and spatial structuring of ability, which cannot, by definition, presuppose either agency or structure, or a combination between the two, since it is these very presuppositions that are under scrutiny. He sets out to question the dictum of the constitutive subject as the origin and causal principle of action, which is the axis around which the juridico-discursive representation of power revolves.

By conceiving power as becoming, Foucault asserts that power is immanent in the historical constitution of the subject and social relations in general. As the temporal and spatial limit, which is at one and the same time posed and presupposed by ability, power is the vehicle for contingency and undecidability, and hence the limit of social objectivity. As the limit, power marks the constitutive fissure of the identity of both the subject and social order, but it is at the same time *vis-à-vis* these limits that social entities position and identify themselves through modes of identification. The conceptualization of power in terms of the constitution of ability and identity should then proceed in terms of identification: how the subject becomes subject. This emphasis upon limits indicates the critical potential of Foucault's undertaking.[7]

The notion of the subject has, according to Foucault, a double meaning: 'subject to someone else by control and dependence, and tied to his own identity by a conscience or self-knowledge. Both meanings suggest a form of power which subjugates and makes subject to'.[8] This is not a doomsday vision of a power dominating everything and being internalized by the subject which, accordingly, becomes modelled in its image. A 'repressive hypothesis' like this would have to presuppose that power has an 'image' – that it is 'something' – which encroaches upon a self which would otherwise be identical with itself, either in an original state of autonomy or in the *telos* of a fully-fledged emancipation. By contrast, for Foucault, when power is located in the fissure within the self, power is the name for the non-identity within identity, or otherness within the self, which encourages processes of identification. The self cannot escape power because it cannot escape it(s)self in order to be identical with itself, which is conditioned by otherness.

As otherness within the self, power cannot be derived from capabilities, however defined, just as it cannot be something which either produces or represses something else. As limit or becoming, power has no positivity or substance and it is, as such, a name for *negativity*: not an 'anti-energy' concealing, refusing or blocking, but a name for *that* which cannot ever be fully brought under control, whether conceptually or by institutional devices. One of the major claims of Foucault's power analytics, pointing in the direction of understanding power as negativity, is that power cannot be a structure, institution or a kind of objectively given or specific ability. By emphasizing that power is immanent and ubiquitous, and that it is the ruptural and unbearable moment of nonidentity, Foucault states that power is 'the name that one attributes to a complex strategical situation'.[9] How is one to make sense of this statement?

A possible interpretation would be to see power in terms of the becoming of identity through identification, which always involves calculations and struggles ('strategical'), and as the peculiar vehicle of the becoming of an identity, which temporally and spatially positions itself by positing its presuppositions retroactively in order to ground itself ('strategical situation'). The temporal and spatial positing of identity *as if* it was presupposed, *as if* its identity was already 'there' before being posited in power struggles, is the 'complex strategical situation' Foucault names 'power'. The situation is complex since strategies have to be knitted together in time and space in order to be able to function as political poles of identification for the variety of heterogeneous demands and interests operating in hegemonic power struggles aiming at authorizing power politically. The complexity of time and space, furthermore, indicates that order is never either present or absent: the stress on limit and becoming indicates that order, stability and hierarchy cannot simply be contrasted with disorder, instability and anarchy. Because social orders exist *in* time and space, which mutually condition one another, ordering is, ontologically speaking, prior to order. In a complex strategical situation ordering poses order as presupposed, that is, as somehow given.

Seen in this light, one has to differentiate between power strategies and the complex strategical situation as such. The latter is an overall effect – a description of an absent societal totality, that is, a whole which is present in its effects only – that cannot exist without the former and which, while equipping this whole with form and content, also presupposes it. Foucault's intention is not just to provide an antidote to the repressive hypothesis by emphasizing the productive nature of power – that it is an ever-ongoing 'making of differences'. Rather, by distinguishing between the two 'levels', the aim is to outline a societal ontology which focuses on how order, identity and objectivity are constituted in processes of ordering, identification and objectification. Power strategies insert themselves in the complex strategical situation as the terrain which conditions them and which they at the same time 'make up'. Hence neither part is capable of determining the form and content of the other (which is why Foucault distances himself from both methodological individualism and holism). What we have here is a higher order conception of power which outlines the fundamental circular structure of power as the limit in time and space. On the lower order we find the myriad of power strategies whose form and content vary infinitely. Hence power is not a game one can choose to play or withdraw from, but is the very name of the game itself.

Foucault's distinction between strategy and strategical situation has implications for a conceptualization of political authority which is not coined in terms of legitimate domination. One ought to distinguish between political authority as a process characterizing the political structure (the political) and the activity of engaging in this process (politics). To act politically means to involve oneself in the political process which is always already 'there'. While politics has to presuppose the political, it provides it at the same time with form and content. To put it differently, political activity is only meaningful in so far as it presupposes the existence of political authority.

Foucault's nominalistic conception of power stresses the formal analogy among social relations: whenever they externalize each other in order to internalize 'their own' identity – thus identifying themselves by situating themselves *vis-à-vis* larger societal contexts in temporal and spatial terms – regardless of how, why and by what means this is done, we have a complex strategical situation and hence relations of power. We will now turn to what is involved in conceptualizing power as the becoming of identity, which paradoxically *becomes what it is*.

The Circular Structure of Identity: Reflecting on Limits

When power is conceived in terms of identification, the 'object' of power cannot but be the subject itself, that is, the becoming of the subject, which entails its objectification.[10] Power can be seen as the attempt to excavate the essence and hence the truth of the subject: its unknowable object, which requires that it is both 'subject to someone else' and tied to its 'own identity by a conscience'. It is in this sense that power as ability is constructed as the positing of 'its own' presuppositions: ability comprehends itself by carving out its 'itselfness', thus objectifying itself by retroactively presupposing that there is such a 'thing' as the 'itselfness' of the subject, which conditions its identity in the first place.

That power cannot be possessed points to the ontological impossibility of the subject grounding itself, or, what amounts to the same thing, the epistemological impossibility of conceptualizing power in 'the substantive sense', that is, as an object. It is this impossibility that triggers processes of identification in which the subject finds itself and does so with a practical understanding of the complex strategical situation into which it is inserted. Power cannot be fully grasped in terms of its exercise either, because that moment cannot but be transitory: the marker of a limit, a rupture which throws the subject into new situations. These, in turn, define and confine ability by positioning the subject; they provide, accordingly, new vehicles or resources for exercising power. To attempt to grasp power in terms of 'its' exercise or performance only is thus reductive because 'exercising power' poses *and* presupposes the network of power strategies. This network is an ontological capacity or a 'dispositional property' that conditions the positioning of subjects and hence the resources which might be used in the exercise of power.[11]

Because the subject is a historical construct its unity is contingent upon what Foucault terms 'the hostile engagement of forces'. There is no essential human nature to excavate, no universal emancipation to pursue and hence no alienation from a primordial purity and innocence. If the subject appears as nonidentical with itself, then alienation and the play of appearances are its only reality. If appearance is a mask, it is one that covers nothing but other appearances, which is why there is, strictly speaking, nothing to *un*cover. Unity can then only be thought of as an imaginary movement erected in power struggles. This unity is imaginary in that it bridges the unrepresentable gap between identity posed and identity presupposed, that is, between performance and semblance. The identity of the subject is thus not only imaginary but also a 'unity of domination'[12] which is immersed in hegemonic political strategies.

The hostile engagement of forces brought about in power struggles cannot be absorbed by an ideal continuity of history or neutralized by a political strategy of inclusion. Foucault terms the clash of forces an event, a rupture inscribed in the play of appearances, whose surface has no depth, underlying reality or necessity that it could be derived from or inserted within. An event is thus a void in the structure of identity and signification. It is, Foucault claims, 'not a decision, a treaty, a reign, or a battle, but the reversal of a relationship of forces, the usurpation of power, the appropriation of a vocabulary turned against those who had once used it, a feeble domination that poisons itself as it grows lax, the entry of a masked "other".'[13] As the effect of clashing forces, the event – the entry of the 'other' which is a ruptural or dislocatory moment – remains irreducible to its cause. Thus it becomes problematic to speak of power in terms of cause and effect because the relation between cause and effect is stitched. It is, moreover, incorporeal by virtue of its being a 'non-place': 'a pure distance, which indicates that the adversaries do not belong to a common space.' 'It is', Foucault continues, 'nothing but the space that divides them, the void through which they exchange their threatening gestures and speeches.'[14] The disintegration of 'a common space' is important in relation to the nature of power struggles, the politicization of social relations, and the lack of an essential communality around which the frontiers of social orders are structured.

Ability is the event, the non-place of the limit which, because it has always already transgressed itself, is a becoming; and the subject is a surface of inscription, an empty signifier, mapped out by power struggles – the politics of exclusions and inclusions. Politics is a matter of contestation, and 'to contest is', says Foucault, 'to proceed until one reaches the empty core where being achieves its limit and where the limit defines being.'[15] Identifications revolve around this empty core of non-identity, which they attempt to fill in order to define being. Political agents achieve identity by positioning themselves *vis-à-vis* their other, which is at one and the same time excluded and included. The pure distance towards the other provides the subject with an imaginary unity, a unity of domination and subjugation.[16] Politics can thus be seen as the activity of posing and presupposing limits, partly in relation to the societal whole, and partly in relation to a temporal continuity.

Ability *is* becoming, but one that defies being grasped in the causal language of resources and exercises of power because it is also the point of recurrence. The becoming of identity is not just a proliferation of differences, but also and at the same time a grounding of identity *as it is*. Processes of identification thus entail a duality of performance and semblance; this is vital for political representation, which both resembles and performs what it represents.[17] Hence both identification and representation are caught up in the politics of posing identity *as if* it was presupposed. This circularity is crucial for social entities which construe their identity in such a way that their politically contestable nature – their historical contingency – retreats in favour of a mythical grounding. This is the case with social-contract theories and, more generally, in the reduction of political authority to legitimate authority, expressing a no less mythical societal consensus brought about by an aggregation of preferences or by communitarian values. It is in this sense that the identity of social entities becomes the locus for what Foucault terms a 'fundamental reversal'.[18]

The notion of the fundamental reversal is decisive for grasping the definition of power as 'the ability to make a difference': identity is not just to make a difference but the *ability* to make a difference. Ability is retroactively construed as an originary causal and meaning-giving principle, a unity which is, however, in a constant process of becoming what it is. Haar puts it succinctly when he says:

> As the origin of values, and the origin also of every hierarchy of values, the Will to Power fixes the value of all values. But this origin cannot be reduced to a primordial unity, to any kind of identity, because it is nothing but a direction forever to be determined. On the other hand, this origin has and gives meaning only in retrospect – namely in and through the genealogical development that issues from it, and by which it is recognized.[19]

The point is that the unity of social entities (the subject or the sovereignty principle) are determined retroactively: the determination was 'there' before the direction – a 'there' which could not, however, be 'there' without a direction. It is here that the modern rationalistic fallacy of the reduction of political authority to legitimate authority shows itself: the subject is constitutive because its autonomy and rationality are construed as a primordial unity which predates, and is hence external to, the political moment of the institution of sovereignty. It then becomes the vehicle of legitimacy for political authority as legitimate domination by means of the myth of the social contract.

The stress upon the retroactive construction of meaning and the fundamental reversal are crucial for coming to terms with Foucault's argument against the idea of the repressive hypothesis, namely that power is something external that encroaches upon the subject from the 'outside'. In contrast to this legalistic conception of power, he emphasizes that power is internal to the subject by virtue of constituting it by disciplinary measures in various institutional settings. This appears to be a paradox: while the subject is inextricably caught up in the web of power relations shaping its very identity, it is also confronted with seemingly given or external structures controlling it. That is, power is creating 'the effect of an apparatus apart from the men themselves, whose structure orders, contains, and controls them.'[20] Far from seeing this apparent paradox as an issue left untouched by Foucault, which is what Mitchell argues, I would hold that it is, in fact, at the very centre of his power analytics. The point is that power as a temporal and spatial limit retroactively produces the 'reality effects' of both internalization and externalization – that is, power is itself nothing but the limit between these two processes – which is why it exhibits a peculiar circularity: it constructs reality (a structural effect) as if it was already 'there' as a 'fact' confronting subjects with an inescapable necessity.

Ability is itself a 'reality effect' which is immanent in making a difference, at once posed and presupposed, internal and external. It cannot be the vehicle of causation since it is at once cause and effect: ability is an effect which is transfigured as the cause. The process of transfiguration is that of the fundamental reversal: 'a direction forever to be determined' retroactively. Barthes's idea that denotation is the last connotation conveys the same idea: the last connotation provides functions, elements, conducts, sensations, pleasures, and so on, with a 'reading principle'. In making sense of this non-ordered myriad of things it turns them into an 'artificial' or 'fictitious' unity that can function as a causal principle which is distinct and thus external, spatially as well as temporally, from what it produces. Hence this last connotation, this last strategic move, has mutated itself into an imaginary cause which is, seemingly, beyond the power game itself that has to be revealed.

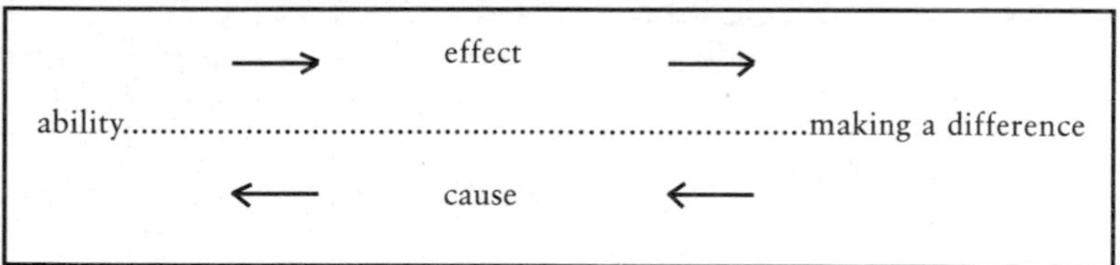

Fig. 3.1 *Ability and making a difference*

To understand power in terms of causation is to attempt to conceptualize and hence to arrest movement, that is, to control it by rendering it law-like. Foucault's point is that this endeavour is neither true nor false. Nor is it for that matter an ideological misconstruction. One might say, rather, that it is the epistemological aspect of the juridico-discursive representation of power which is inseparable from the institutional practices aiming at monopolizing political power in the state. His stress upon the intertwined nature of power and knowledge means that every attempt to endow power with a certain identity, form or manifestation cannot but be immanent in the power game itself, which is why discourses *on* power cannot but also be discourses *of* power.

The impossibility of grasping power 'as it is' *is* negativity, which is to say that negativity is a name for the seemingly endless attempts, and the frustration of each and every one of those attempts, to comprehend and ground ability – or, for that matter anything – 'as it is'. Power as the complex strategical situation means that power revolves around the impossibility of its having an 'origin', a 'basic nature' and certain 'manifestations'. Power as ability is constitutive since it cannot itself be grounded but grounds itself retroactively, which is to say that it revolves around the void in signification. Power is in a sense this void itself – limit, non-place or pure distance – which can only be traced through its effects.

Ability is, as this constitutive void where identity recoils into non-identity, the point where the individual finds itself *as it is*. However, this 'discovery' of the self-identical blind spot and originary causal principle cannot but be a construction of an imaginary unity resulting from identification. Hence the paradox that ability is a construction of something which has always been 'there' awaiting recognition, a discursive re-presentation of *that* which cannot present itself, but which is an ontological precondition. If this is an ideological process, the reason is not that it misrepresents reality but that the *constitution* of identity retroactively takes the form of its *excavation*: the fundamental reversal points to the imaginary objectification of becoming, which, by turning ability into a fictitious object – an essence construed as a key to the truth of oneself and the societal order – can serve as a pole of identification rooted in an unattainable mythical origin which can function as a ground for the subject.

Whilst 'ability' is part and parcel of 'making a difference', it is also seen, explicitly or implicitly, as its underlying cause whereby the latter transfigures itself as the effect of the former whose supposed unity is seen as the source of the meaningfulness of making a difference. By drawing attention to this fundamental reversal which shows the circular structure of power, Foucault takes issue with objectivism and the reductionism that goes with it. This is probably the reason why he did not launch a power *theory*, which, in his view, would be to assume a prior objectification.[21] Such an assumption would be inconsistent with the higher order approach to power as the ability to make a difference, which is part of the reason for labelling his approach presuppositionless.

I would claim that Foucault's higher order analysis of power as the ability to make a difference is conceived as an ontology of potentials that conditions, but cannot determine the more concrete lower order manifestations of power which, among other places, are shown in hegemonic power struggles. But this does not leave his power analytics in a vacuum: power is not simply a relation. It certainly is a relation, but one which entails a number of characteristics: the fundamental reversal between cause and effect, as well as the recoiling structuring of identity through identification, which in turn implies contingency and undecidability. It is on this level of analysis that we can talk about a presuppositionless approach to the problem of power: what can and what cannot be said about power 'in itself'. The question of whether power is basically 'power over', or 'power to' or 'who gets what when' is thus relegated to the lower order analysis which belongs to hegemonic power struggles. The higher order analysis, as it appears in Foucault's power analytics, should, I contend, be seen as an ontology of the social because it scrutinizes the constitutive features of what it means to act.

The Circular Structure of Power: The Politics of Representation

Foucault's conceptualization of power as negativity – the point of the fundamental reversal where non-identity recoils into identifications – is a contestation of the juridico-discursive representation of power which still dominates our view of power and politics. 'The essential role of the theory of right, from medieval times onwards,' Foucault writes, 'was to fix the legitimacy of power; that is the major problem around which the whole theory of right and sovereignty is organised.'[22] This model of power fosters a specific representation of the subject and its relation to 'royal power', namely the relation between a legitimate authority which reigns over the 'perpetuall and restlesse desire of Power after power' (Hobbes) and which in this sense possesses power, and a relatively autonomous and obedient subject (the citizen) who has exchanged its power for protection.[23]

The juridical or representational model of power holds that power: (a) emanates from autonomous individuals; (b) is transferred to the sovereign who thus possesses it; and then (c) is (re)turned to subjects in an alienated form which at once guarantees and threatens their identity as autonomous and rational. The relation between guarantee and threat is a rather uneasy one where power, regardless of whether it is defined in terms of sovereignty or emancipation, is placed squarely between internal and external determination. Power is a limitation upon autonomy, restricting the subject's ability to act; yet, or exactly for this reason, it preserves the idea of the constitutive subject, which in turn is to say that sovereignty and emancipation are the mirror images of each other.

'Power as a pure limit set on freedom is', says Foucault, 'at least in our society, the general form of its acceptability',[24] which requires a mediation between internal and external determination. The mythical nature of this mediation comes to the fore in the relation between autonomy and obedience. Obedience is distinguished from oppression by being voluntarily consented to. The linchpin of volition is the no less mythical construction of rationality which, in this context, is the medium forcing the subject to be free.[25] The result of this rational and autonomous consensus – this enforcement of freedom which retroactively establishes the political autonomy of the subject – is envisioned in the notion of relative autonomy. Its legal counterpart is that of balancing the relation between power and right, which is, basically, a question of establishing a trade-off between autonomy and obedience. By transforming itself into legitimate authority, which is matched by the consensus of the citizenry, power is able to contain its devious potentials – hence its acceptability.

The external relation between sovereign and subject rests on the assumption that their identities are given prior to the entering of the social contract. However, once this contract is established the relation has, paradoxically, always been 'there' awaiting recognition. This externality implies that power is rooted in a mythical *origin* and endowed with a basic *nature* and certain *manifestations*, and that the subject is equipped with a no less mythical human nature, which is epitomized in the immaculate conceptions of autonomy and rationality. The focus on externality and recognition, which accompany the dictum of given identities and which are operationalized in terms of causation, conveys a reductionist image of political power as a 'necessary evil'. Power, says Foucault in discussing the repressive hypothesis, 'acts in a uniform and comprehensive manner; it operates according to the simple and endlessly reproduced mechanisms of law, taboo, and censorship.'[26]

It is important to note that within this view, power is founded upon the subject's representation of itself as prior to power. However, even liberalism recognizes the undecidable relation between power and the subject: that power poses *and* presupposes this representation of the self for itself and for society. Power is located between an originary autonomy, where the subject as a human being has not yet turned into the subject as a citizen, and a relative autonomy, where the subject has become a subject by inserting itself into the social order. Power as ability is thus present *in itself* (autonomy as presupposed) but can only be present *for itself* by being re-presented (autonomy as posed). The point is that the 're' of representation cannot simply mirror what 'is', but performs the 'is' 'as it is', that is, as semblance.

The temporal and spatial nature of the politics of posing the presuppositions of the social order as the representation of order as such is particularly visible in social-contract theory, as well as in the legitimation of power more generally. The establishment of order presupposes what negates it, namely the state of nature. By entering the covenant, the structures of the legitimate political authority are retroactively construed as external to the subjects, which is why political representation, with its accompanying maxims of rights and obligations, arises as a problem to be dealt with. Legitimate authority has to be 'there' before identification, which obscures the fact that power plays an active role in shaping its own legitimacy, meaning that the latter is not independent of the former, just as the subject has to be 'there' before subjectification. The *raison d'être* of posing and presupposing authority as legitimate is to domesticate the circular structure of power by making it linear, and hence causal and controllable. Legitimation maintains the positing of presuppositions and thus the fixing and hierarchization of values, which is why it is basically a repressive power.

However, the hierarchization of values is not intrinsic to the higher order meaning of power as ability. Rather, it is a particular expression of the modern discourses of order, namely the reduction of political authority to legitimate authority and the operationalization of power as a causal concept, which can be controlled (conceptually and institutionally) by conceiving it in terms of an exchange relation of rights and obligations. The circular structure of power revolves around the becoming of what was, which gives meaning only in retrospect. The unity of the origin – *in casu* the autonomous subject as the locus for the legitimacy of the political authority – is, as mentioned, 'nothing but a direction forever to be determined'. This is why power as the limit between future-past-present and part-whole – of what is present and what is temporally and spatially out of reach because it is presupposed – conditions but cannot determine the concrete lower order structures of power.

It is this fundamental undecidability that the juridical model of power is based on, and which it tries to efface when claiming that power can be possessed and exercised lawfully. The point is, as Cousins and Hussain argue, that there is a 'homology between the jurisprudential approach to power and the epistemological approach to discourse'.[27] Power can, Foucault says, only be appropriated by reason if it is 'exercised in the form of the law' or 'in accordance with a fundamental lawfulness'.[28] His claim about the impossibility of possessing power is not merely ontological but epistemological as well. Hence the argument over the impossibility of submitting power to the law is also an argument against the feasibility of fully conceptualizing power and of grounding either the subject or the social order. The impossibility of possessing power is, furthermore, an argument against reducing power to 'power over': political power cannot be equated with domination and confined to the legitimate authority of the state and operationalized in terms of rights and obligations. Instead, it revolves around making a difference in a societal setting, however defined.

If power could be 'exercised in the form of the law', and if the political authorization of power took the form of legitimate domination, it would be possible to make a strict distinction, one, between legality, peace and stability on the one side, and illegality, war and instability on the other,[29] and two, between the political and the social. By contrast, Foucault argues that since contractual consensus can only define itself through the exclusion of oppression, this *ex*clusion cannot but be *in*cluded in its identity, and legality and peace cannot then be rigorously separated from illegality and war. Defining itself *vis-à-vis* this limit, legality cannot but be a particular strategy of oppression, just as peace is a strategy of waging war labelled politics.[30] Foucault's point in drawing attention to the never settled frontiers between war and peace is to stress that 'it is one of the essential traits of Western societies that the force relationships which for a long time had found expression in war . . . gradually became invested in the order of political power.'[31]

The aim is not to convey a cynical view of politics, but to emphasize that power and its political authorization cannot be squeezed into the dualisms of order/disorder, stability/change, consensus/conflict, and the like since power and politics are already presupposed by these dualisms. A social order cannot annihilate relations of force but aims instead to incorporate them into the edifice of legitimate authority. These forces are the irreducible underside of this authority, which cannot be assimilated to state power but which, none the less, underpin it. The point is that politics cannot be located solely in the state, and state power can only sustain itself on the basis of these ubiquitous power relations which map out the terrain for state action.

Laws, rights, juridical apparatuses, and so on, are thus far from being outside the grid of relations of force; instead they are codifications of this, meaning that they are crystallizations of the articulation of heterogeneous elements. This is put succinctly by Deleuze when he writes that, for Foucault: 'The law is neither a state of peace nor is it the result of a war which has been won: it is the very war itself, and the strategy of this war in action, just as power is not a possession acquired by the dominant classes but is an actual exercise of its strategy.'[32] When law is a way of waging war 'which permits the perpetual instigation of new dominations and the staging of meticulously repeated scenes of violence',[33] it is the mechanism segregating legality and illegality. This segregation conditions the endeavour of objectifying and unifying the law, which is itself a network constituted through the limits to what it is not. The relation between legality and illegality is, accordingly, one of ongoing transgressions and recodifications through violent hierarchizations.[34]

It is through the exclusion of illegalities that the imaginary unity and rationality of law can be established. This unity is imaginary rather than illusory because it is not an appearance hiding a more profound reality. It illustrates the circular structure of power, which finds expression in what Foucault calls the self-referring nature of sovereignty: 'What characterises the end of sovereignty, this common and general good, is in sum nothing other than submission to sovereignty. This means that the end of sovereignty is circular in that it comes down to the exercise of sovereignty itself.'[35] What is stated here is the quasi-tautology of law: that it must be obeyed because it is the embodiment of reason itself, that is, the rationality it itself has fostered and mirrors itself in. This 'must' – this 'peculiar coercion to non-coercive recognition' (Habermas) – is always already presupposed as that which renders law meaningful. The homogeneity of law can only be erected upon a prior exclusion of what is retroactively labelled illegal and which confirms the 'lawfulness' of law. Hence, law can only be comprehended at its limits, where it transgresses itself and turns into illegality. In other words, the illegal is constitutive for the legal by being excluded from it – an exclusion which retroactively constitutes legality as inherent in a complex strategical situation.

Sovereignty is not capable of ending the guerrilla warfare of power struggles. Rather, it can only sustain itself on the basis of, or by being a part of, this guerrilla warfare. The same holds true for what the law represses as illegal. The latter is at once functional for the law by forming targets and relays for exercises of power, yet it is also that which tends to subvert the unity of law, which is to say that resistance is an inherent dimension of power. If this was not the case, the relation between legality and illegality could be seen as a Hobbesian zero-sum game between a state of peace versus a state of nature. The external relation between them presupposes what the circular structure of power renders impossible, namely the ideality of fully constituted entities. What we have here is a representational model of power which identifies and controls power by modelling it in the image of legitimate domination through the principles of rights, obligations and consensus. This authorization of power is modelled on the fundamental reversal whereby power strategies attempt to efface their violent emergence by mirroring themselves in their own creation. This creation or becoming is externalized from – and thus appears to be located outside – the 'circle' of power, whereby it attains the mythological status of 'something' external: an origin and/or a *telos* which fills the void of non-identity or the impossibility of grounding. Thus the negativity of becoming assumes a positive existence through the duality of representation as performance and semblance.

The liberal view that power, politics and the state are 'necessary evils' should be seen in the light of the modern reduction of power to 'power over', and of politics to the legitimate domination of the state. The circular structure of power here performs the operation whereby the process in which power strategies erect an authority is at once a process in which the relation between cause and effect is reversed: the effect is constructed as a cause. Hence power is externalized in the very construction of authority in the sense that the latter appears to antedate the former – as something power has to represent in order to attain legitimacy. Evil connotes otherness *par excellence*, yet it is necessary in that otherness has to be incorporated into political authority, whose cohesiveness and legitimacy depends on the fact that it represents the subject as other than itself, and that the subject recognizes itself in the societal other, that is, in a re-presentation of itself as external to itself. Otherness is thus necessary to prevent the originary autonomy leading to excesses (the endemic danger of the state of nature, whether Hobbesian or Lockean); but it is also evil by virtue of the fact that it impinges upon this autonomy. This tension is thus located at the very heart of ability as essentially split, as a locus for undecidability. The point is that this tension indicates that the subject is, essentially, a political being – a being whose otherness the subject poses *and* presupposes in order to be what it is.

The Political Authorization of Power: The Juridico-discursive Representation of Power and Disciplinary Power

Power relations are, according to Foucault, neither part of an all-encompassing and homogenous 'great' power with a unique locus, as in Hobbes's *Leviathan*,[36] nor are they entirely fragmented and unable to coalesce into dominant strategies, which would be more in the spirit of pluralism. Thus it is not viable to dichotomize society into those who possess power and those who do not, just as it would be futile to assume that power is equally distributed. The argument about the impossibility of possessing power (the higher order conception of power) is prior to the question about its distribution (the lower order). This question is, in fact, badly posed inasmuch as it indicates either a contractual view of power modelled upon the autonomous and rational individual (the liberal tradition), or a structural view which assumes that power relations are underpinned by objective laws or generative causal mechanisms (typically the Marxist tradition). Common to both of these views is the conceptualization of power in terms of law, which finds expression in the discourses of either legitimate domination or historical laws of motion. It is characteristic of such a rationalistic approach that power is analysed according to a scheme of deduction – what Foucault terms 'the descending type of analysis'[37] – which, by locating power and politics in the state, analyses power from the 'outside' and from 'above'.

Foucault's focus on events and local contexts which cannot be fitted into a totality and deduced from a unitary rationality, and his rejection of 'the tyranny of globalizing discourses' – notably the juridico-discursive representation of power – lead him to advocate an '*ascending* analysis of power'.[38] That is, he does not locate power and politics solely in the state, but analyses power from the 'inside' and from 'below', taking its point of departure in the ubiquity of infinitesimal mechanisms of power. The aim is to grasp how the plethora of local power relations coalesce into general ones, whereby they become imbricated in various institutions through hegemonic practices. The relation between local and general strategies is characterized by the 'rule of double conditioning': local strategies cannot operate unless they are articulated with general strategies, just as general strategies cannot function if they are not rooted in local ones.[39] The relation between them is reciprocal with regard to conditioning and being conditioned: strategies are constantly (re)coded by the complex strategical situation, which cannot ever become 'a totality fully closed upon itself', but is a horizon which is immanent in practices. It should thus be clear that the study of political power cannot presuppose 'the regulated and legitimate forms of power in their central locations'[40] since state power is itself conditioned by, and conditioning of, the overall network of power relations.

There are three points here that are important for political analysis in general and democratic theory in particular. First, the ascending analysis undermines rights-based theories of power by emphasizing that power is, first of all, concerned with praxis (with making a difference) which is not logically tied to rights and obligations. This tie is a politically contingent construct forged by modern power strategies, notably liberalism. Second, the ascending analysis highlights the fact that the political authorization of power has a much broader scope than the juridico-discursive representation of power allows for. This is due to the latter's reduction of authority to legitimacy and its confinement of politics to the state, which isolates the political from the social and hence the citizenry from participating in politics. The point is that the legitimate authority of the state is immersed in the network of power strategies in which power is politically authorized on a continuous basis. And finally, the ascending analysis is cast in terms of (the rule of double) conditioning rather than in the deterministic language of cause and effect or agency and structure. From this it follows, one, that Foucault is speaking about power as a political potential which is related to ontology rather than performance, and two, that he gives full weight to the contingent nature of social and political constructs because the order of things could always be different.

The disciplinary and regulatory processes constituting the modern subject should be seen in the light of these three aspects of the ascending analysis of power. Foucault's argument is that these processes shape the subject as docile and responsible by subjectivating it through a multiplicity of micro-techniques which equip it with a 'conscience'. This sort of power cannot be grasped by the juridico-discursive representation of power because legitimate domination is but one type of power relation which, moreover, blurs 'the local cynicism of power' by representing the subject as autonomous, and the social order as more- or less-normatively integrated. By viewing power as 'becoming' Foucault avoids the sterile dualism of space and time – the synchronic and the diachronic – which assumes that integration, order and stability are dichotomized from disintegration, disorder and instability. His point is that the spatial is always temporal and hence contingent upon its historicity.

This critique of the Kantian dualism of space and time is crucial for appreciating the political importance of Foucault's power analytics. He aims to show the contingency of social relations by tracing the ubiquity of disciplinary and regulatory mechanisms within the setting of legitimate domination: how they become 'embodied in the state apparatus, in the formulation of the law, in the various social hegemonies'.[41] It is vital to note that disciplining and regulating are not antithetic to political power strategies. On the contrary, they should be seen as the primary means by which power is politically authorized, which is to say that they can be conceived as the 'practical underlabourer' of legitimate power. Foucault hereby advances an alternative to the predominant conception of the political authorization of power: one which does not, on the one hand, associate power with disintegration, the absence of order and instability, conceptualizing it in terms of 'power over' and locating it in conflicts of interests; and one which does not, on the other hand, associate authority with normative integration, order and stability, conceptualizing it in terms of legitimate domination and locating it in the pursuit of common interests and in expressions of consensus.

Foucault's points are not: (a) that sovereignty does not exist or that the model of legitimate authority is outdated or simply a fake, but rather that the juridico-discursive representation of power is only capable of operating on the background of the 'infra-law' of disciplinary and regulatory power with which it is articulated; (b) that humanism, autonomy and rationality are just a cover-up for disciplinary hierarchization, but rather that the latter fleshes out the conditions for the societal 'application' of the former; (c) that the individual is merely a fiction invented by bourgeois ideology, but rather that disciplinary and regulatory mechanisms fabricate the conditions in which the individual becomes a vehicle around which power produces its effects; and finally (d) that democracy and hence freedom and equality are illusions, but rather that the political authorization of power creates accountable and docile individuals who represent the real conditions, as opposed to the abstract claims of rights/obligations, autonomy/obedience and consensus/coercion. It can thus be said that power as legitimate domination is supplemented by power as discipline and regulation: the latter 'operationalizes' the former, but in a way that threatens its unity and basic assumptions. When the law is conditioned by and articulated with disciplinary and regulatory measures, law and discipline make up an inseparable whole, whereby the relation between them cannot but be necessary.

The power of legitimate authority would be ineffective were it not rooted in the infra-law of the political authorization of power which governs the actions of subjects on a continuous day-to-day basis in various institutional settings. Foucault talks about the 'colonization' of the law by disciplinary power, and the fact that power is 'exercised through, on the basis of, and by virtue of, this very heterogeneity between a public right of sovereignty and a polymorphous disciplinary mechanism.'[42] Egalitarian contractual relations underpinning the discourses of Western democracies cannot operate unless they are rooted in and articulated with the disciplinary and regulatory techniques that structure social relations. Legal rights and obligations are supplemented by disciplinary links; the explicit equality and symmetry of the law are supplemented by the inequalities and asymmetries of disciplinary mechanisms which are for the most part disguised; and the universal definition of the juridical subject is supplemented by the classification, normalization and hierarchization of individuals. It is in these ways that the intimate articulation between law and discipline takes shape.[43]

The articulation between juridical and disciplinary power is termed the governmentalization of both power relations and the state. It takes the form of an institutionalization of social relations, where power strategies become increasingly directed towards the state, or rather, they become the state. By being governed at the micro-level by standardized procedures, modes of regulation and norms, power relations tend to lose their specificity. They have, says Foucault, 'been progressively governmentalized, that is to say, elaborated, rationalized, and centralized in the form of or under the auspices of, state institutions.'[44] The state is caught up in ongoing processes of governmentalization that map out the terrain for political power struggles and the ways power is politically authorized. These processes play a crucial role in the structuring of the elusive boundaries between state and society, which is to say that governmentalization displaces the dualisms of state/society, public/private, coercion/consent.[45] These dualisms are the hegemonic effects of the political authorization of power strategies embodied in the juridico-discursive representation of power. Hence the terrain of politics is the political system as such, and cannot, accordingly, be reduced to an activity within its 'subsystem', that is, the regime. '[T]he State can only be understood in its survival and its limits on the basis of the general tactics of governmentality.'[46]

By stressing that both disciplinary/regulatory power and legitimate power become governmentalized, Foucault makes it possible to view the state as a strategic location in the political system – the terrain of power struggles which is at once an instrument and an outcome of these – which plays a crucial role in governing it, while at the same time being governed. This double aspect of governmentalization implies that while an increasing number of practices become part of the state, the state becomes more and more caught up in the struggles between various political forces, whereby it cannot be unified and possess a 'rigourous functionality'.[47] Just as power in the substantive sense does not exist, nor does the state. '[T]he State consists in the codification of a whole number of power relations which render its functioning possible', where power relations mean 'a more-or-less organised, hierarchical, co-ordinated cluster of relations'.[48] The state can be seen as a dispersed unity whose cohesion is precarious because it is erected in power struggles which define its limits within society.

The articulation between disciplinary and juridical power prevents the homogeneity of law and the unity of the state, both of which can be seen as operating in a continuum ranging from repression to regulation. Foucault tries to capture this articulation with what he terms the triangle of 'sovereignty-discipline-government', which is the nexus around which power is politically authorized.[49] Seen in this light it is a triple mistake to reduce political authority to legitimate domination: first, because power and politics are narrowed down to a concern with the state; second, because power and politics are seen as essentially repressive; and third, because the subject as citizen is merely a juridical subject.

It is on the basis of this rationalistic reduction that the dichotomies of state/society, public/private and coercion/consent are erected, which ostracize politics from tradition, that is, in the ways the subject conducts itself and others which are regulated by all sorts of institutional rules and routines. Thus, according to this view, politics is, or rather ought to be, confined within the state. Although this reduction is impossible, since the very differentiation between state and society is itself a (liberal) political strategy, it does none the less produce reality effects: the circularity of power entails that the limits are posed *as* presupposed, meaning that the limits transgress themselves by retroactively externalizing the entities they delimit. Power as limit creates, within the juridico-discursive representation, the structural effect that state and society are basically fixed realms whose identities are given before they are related. Thus power has to be deduced from and limited within its own effects, which are presented as its cause.

By contesting, one, the reduction of politics to the state, and two, the reduction of political authority to legitimate authority, Foucault is (implicitly) saying that the political authorization of power takes place in two 'spheres': in the sphere of legitimate domination, which concerns the problems of the political representation of interests with its focus on effectivity and legitimacy; and in the sphere of the disciplines and government, where power is embodied in regulative apparatuses, which focus on the individual and the population. The political institutions are located between, and serve to articulate, these two spheres which are, roughly speaking, associated with state and society respectively. The triangle of sovereignty-discipline-government is embodied in the political institutions, which are located in the public and quasi-public spheres. Figure 3.2 illustrates these points.[50]

Political theory traditionally conducts a descending analysis of power by focusing on the upper half of Figure 3.2: it studies power in its legitimate locations, and thus ignores the political dimensions of the various mechanisms of social control immanent in social relations. Foucault approaches power from the lower half of Figure 3.2 by studying how political authority operates on a daily basis in its nonlegitimate locations: the disciplinary and regulatory apparatuses. The political authorization of power taking place in these apparatuses prevents power from being grasped in a grand scheme of deduction. Instead, an ascending analysis is needed which supplements the descending analysis. It is in this light that Foucault's

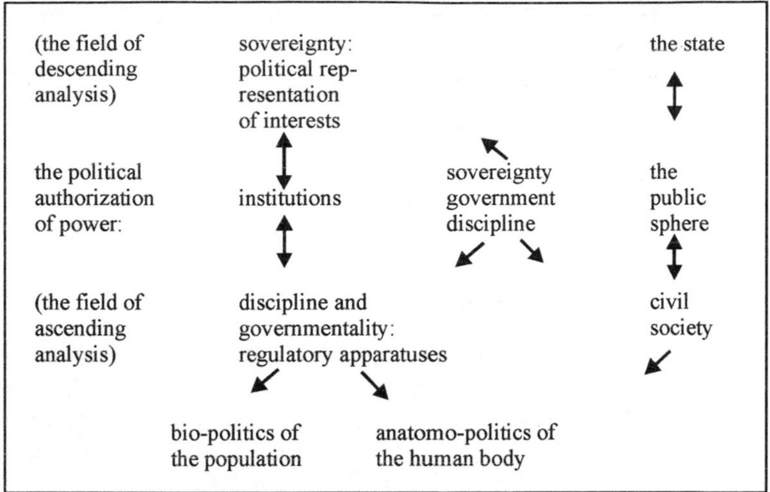

Fig. 3.2 *Political authority: sovereignty and social control*

proposal to 'eschew the model of Leviathan in the study of power' should be seen.[51] Institutions occupy a position between the legitimate framework of the political representation of interests, which is grounded in the juridical fictions of individual autonomy/rationality and popular sovereignty, and the regulatory apparatuses of social control in which stocks of knowledge are materialized. It is these administrative apparatuses that, in practical terms, sustain the regimes of legitimate domination.

Concluding Remarks: On Power and Politics

It has been argued that power is immanent in social relations and that the political authorization of power strategies are structuring wider and wider areas of social life at the micro-level on a day-to-day basis. Institutions – regardless of whether they are representative, disciplinary/regulatory or repressive – are never able to domesticate these processes. Rather, institutional complexes are inserted into the processes of political authorization of power, which are at once 'above' and 'below' these complexes, and which render every hegemonic regime contingent upon these ongoing operations. Political authority cannot then be reduced to, let alone be controlled by, discourses of legitimate authority.

Hegemonic regimes attempt, nevertheless, to perform this impossible task of reduction and domestication in order to possess power. The way this is done is by reducing political authority to the legitimate domination of the state, whereby politics becomes defined in terms of contractual relations between citizens and the state. The goal is to tame an otherwise uncontrollable power: what we end up with is a power which has managed to overcome itself – its restless desire to perpetuate itself in anarchic struggles – by entering into a contract with itself, and thus becoming the law itself. This type of political authorization of power is rational and legitimate in the grandiose sense that it is founded upon the contract, or in the more prosaic sense that it is the political representation of interests and their pragmatic trade-offs. The other side of the political authorization of power is not entrapped in globalizing discourses because it is, above all, practical and local: it is normalizing and physical by being fostered in alleged non-political sites such as the disciplinary and regulatory administrative apparatuses of power-knowledge. This type of power cannot be grasped in terms of the dualisms, such as rights/obligations, legitimacy/illegitimacy, consensus/coercion, and public/private which are usually evoked when analysing forms of regime.

One of the great advantages of Foucault's approach – which paves the way for advancing an understanding of power and political authority that is not cast in terms of the sovereignty principle and the constitutive subject – is that it undermines the dichotomization of the political and the social. As long as one clings on to this dichotomy either as an inescapable fact and/or as the great achievement of liberalism, one is bound to reproduce the predominant view in modern political and democratic theory: (a) that politics is, essentially, an administration of domination based on and reproducing a hierarchization of values (material as well as immaterial); (b) that power has to be defined as repressive in terms of a will to be subdued, and hence in relation to conflicts of interest, and thereby is defined as the subject matter of politics; and (c) that democracy, understood as individual autonomy and popular sovereignty, has to be operationalized exclusively in terms of a system of rights that above all is protective, that is, securing 'freedom from' 'power over'.

Foucault's radicalness lies in his approach to politics from the 'inside', meaning that the political is *in* the social instead of being located above it in the state, whose existence depends upon the inputs of economic resources and social support from the 'outside' (from what is outside the political sphere). It should be obvious that when political authority is immanent in the social it cannot but be ingrained in tradition. But just as politics cannot be stifled in contractual terms where its task is that of balancing effectivity and legitimacy, neither can it be identified in terms of *Gemeinschaft* or a communitarian essentialism, for which tradition is often depicted as a more- or less-homogenous and closed universe. Power and political authority do not reside in either conflicts of interests or normative integration, but are instead prior to this either/or.

Power is both productive and repressive, not simply by facilitating something while restricting something else, but because power and its political authorization are identifying and ordering a social realm. It is here that we can locate Foucault's idea of the fundamental reversal. A social realm is attuned to an imaginary unity, but this unity does not necessarily have to take the form of a rational myth emanating from a covenant that fixes a hierarchy of values. Things might work out differently: space and order are always contingent upon spatialization and ordering, not the other way around. Emphasis is thus put on ordering as ongoing processes in which given orders insert themselves. The point is that power and political authority are placed squarely between the dichotomies of order/disorder, stability/instability and hierarchy/anarchy. Again, we are not facing an either/or situation because power and authority are always already operating underneath or within these dichotomies that are set up by the juridico-discursive representation of power.

When power and its political authorization are *in* the social as a becoming that possesses neither an origin nor a *telos*, then this becoming is a point of recurrence that throws subjects into processes of identification whereby they become subjects. In this sense, power is the limit of identity that always transcends given identities, which are, accordingly, contingent upon their insertion in wider contexts. As the elusive point of recurrence, power is, in Lefort's terminology, an 'empty place' around which social orders structure themselves.[52] This is why power can only be rendered intelligible as 'the name that one attributes to a complex strategical situation', which simultaneously and reciprocally defines the situation, positions subjects, equips them with available resources, and throws them into games of signification.

It is in this light that one could situate Foucault's aim to study how 'human beings are made subjects'. The truth of the subject could be said to lie in its being human – a being which is 'there' before the subject becomes a subject, or a being which the subject poses as presupposed. The ultimate failure to reach this empty place of the subject before subjectification is the moment of rupture of negativity where the subject becomes what it is. The subject before subjectification – ability as an ontological potential before performance – and order before ordering are loci for the fundamental reversal characterizing the ideological impact of power strategies: their vacuity is their only means of functioning as nodal points for the endeavour of equipping social constructs with an imaginary unity, which is 'nothing but a direction forever to be determined'. Hence the emphasis on becoming as a contingent process or challenge which has no goal, and which does not excavate a hidden reality.

Notions like democracy, citizens rights, human rights, and real and public interests often function as nodal points in power struggles. Their vacuity does not mean that they are empty facades penetrated by and thus formed in the image of disciplinary power, which at times seems to be Foucault's point of view. Thus he states that the collectivization of sovereignty through struggles for democracy presupposes the institutionalization of discipline on a societal scale, that disciplinary measures become deeply rooted in the social nexus.[53] This is no doubt the case, and it was a recurrent theme in nineteenth-century liberalism, which feared that the extension of the franchise would eventually lead to a plebiscitarian democracy. The point is, however, that it does not exhaust the problem of political representation.

Democracy, rights, interests, and the like, are poles of identification in political power struggles, where they function as strategic signifiers around which political agency takes form. This is the reason why antagonistic interests are formed around them and, in turn, why the political institutions embodying them are relays for resistance, and hence loci for power struggles. It is in this light that one should see Foucault's argument that power ought to be conceptualized in terms of the undecidable and contingent processes of identification. What we are facing is an intricate articulation between political institutions, political agencies and political metaphors which changes the nature of each of them.

It is important to note that institutional rules and routines, political identity and political metaphors construct themselves through exclusion/inclusion, that is, through limitation, and that these limits retroactively construe the meaningfulness of these practices, identities and metaphors as 'given' points of orientation. It is here we witness the circular structure of power: that power as negativity is constitutive for identity, which is the non-objectifiable effect of clashing forces. By conceiving power as limit or becoming – as a direction which is, ultimately, undecidable and contingent –

Foucault makes way for an understanding of autonomy, democracy and political authority as volatile political projects that take shape in power struggles and cannot ever be guaranteed by political institutions: '"liberty" is what must be exercised.'[54] It is above all a practical political challenge pertaining to ability as becoming, and hence a challenge which is and has to be met everywhere and by everyone.

4
The Presuppositionless Conception of Power: Power as Negativity

Advancing a Presuppositionless Concept of Power

From the arguments so far advanced, it should be clear that Foucault's power analytics is better suited to deal with the growing contextualization of power, and the widening of the field of the political, than the agency models of power and politics, such as behaviourism/pluralism. Foucault argues that power cannot be regarded as a causal concept to be conceived in terms of agency and structure, and that politics cannot be confined within the legitimate sites of representative political institutions, but instead permeates the entire social realm. He sets out his alternative by undermining assumptions regarding the objectivity of the subject and power as something that can be attributed to the subject. Instead of presupposing either the faculty of will or the objectivity of structures, the relation between power and identity is studied as a process. That is why he analyses power in terms of identification which does not presuppose given identities. Foucault thereby advances a nominalistic and presuppositionless conceptualization of power that is both epistemologically and ontologically coterminous with power as 'the ability to make a difference'. Ability structures itself by enforcing limits which are both constitutive and subversive for identity, hence the emphasis on both subjectification and subjection. Power is here treated as synonymous with negativity: the constitutive fissures of social orders which preclude the full constitution of the subject's identity.

The Foucauldian approach is thus opposed to aprioristic conceptions of power. These operate on the basis of two assumptions. The first is that power is linked to social entities, meaning that it is a property of agents, structures or systems; the second is that it produces a priori determinate effects, such as controlled or normative integration, repression or ideological distortion. The only way in which a conceptualization of power along these lines can be bettered is to develop an argument in which power is neither derivative nor determinate, and the only way to conduct such an endeavour is to eschew both essentialism and reductionism.

In order to sustain the insights of Foucauldian power analytics, with its stress on the immanence of power, it is necessary to advance three aspects of power: that it is non-derivative, non-determinate and non-objective. Power is conceptualized in a presuppositionless fashion to the extent to which it exhibits these three aspects: (1) Power has no origin (such as the faculty of will) or structural setting, and thus is not an attribute of social entities. It is, instead, constitutive of identity broadly considered. (2) Power has no *telos* and consequently cannot be described a priori as either functional or dysfunctional for a social order; it is, rather, a conditioning factor. And (3) power is not, strictly speaking, part of a social order in the sense that it cannot be domesticated by it, thereby subverting its objectivity or preventing its full constitution. Power is thus conceived as negativity.

To perceive power in this way means, on the one hand, that it is immanent in the structuration of social reality, otherwise it could not be relationally constructed; on the other hand, it is outside the social realm by virtue of the fact that it constitutes and negates it. This has already been anticipated by Foucault's argument that power is the constitutive void in structures of signification, forcing limits upon the objectivity of both the subject and the social order. His nominalist conception of power is the most promising attempt to further a presuppositionless approach. By not assuming any prior objectification, power becomes the name for negativity; this is, for instance, shown in antagonistic struggles where the identities of the adversaries mutually negate each other, and thus do not belong to a common discursive space. The three aspects of the presuppositionless conceptualization of power entail that power as negativity plays a constitutive role for identity. In antagonistic power struggles the constitution and negation of identity are two sides of the same coin, which is why power is the vehicle of contingency. Substantiating these claims requires singling out those mechanisms which at once subvert the objectivity of social relations and play a constitutive role in shaping them. Against this background it should be possible to radicalize Foucauldian power analytics by maintaining its central arguments while overcoming the occasional oscillation between aprioristic and presuppositionless conceptions of power.

The most rigorous attempts to advance such an argument have been made by Laclau and Mouffe, and Žižek. The identity of social entities is established through articulatory practices ultimately triggered by antagonistic power struggles. The notion of articulation stresses that identity is formed relationally, and consequently that no locus beyond the discursive field of articulation, capable of fixing identity, can be provided.[1] The constitution, modification and subversion of identity that takes place in the articulation of various forces structures a social order in historically contingent ways. Two conclusions follow from the argument that identity is contextually determined and contingent upon its own structuring, and modified in power struggles: (1) the conditions of existence of identity cannot be essentially fixed structures and given capabilities that are left untouched by power struggles in which identity takes its form; and (2) since identity fully depends upon its conditions of existence, which are themselves contingent, its relationship with these conditions is a necessary one.[2]

I
The Discursive Structuring of Social Reality

The Logics of Difference and Equivalence

The relational nature of social and political practices implies that signification and identity entail difference, and that social formations can be seen as systems of differences established by posing limits to what they are not. Because the limit *qua* limit is neither interior nor exterior to an entity – because the 'here' is always defined *vis-à-vis* the 'beyond' – social entities cannot ever be fully constituted; or, what amounts to the same thing, structural closures and the fixity of identity, as well as the necessity that goes with it, are impossible. When necessity is the result of articulation, it is located in the relative closures effectuated by systematizing differences, which are the bases of hegemonic power struggles. Necessity is thus contingent upon the structuring of power (struggle, rule following, and so on), and is, as such, installed within the discursive terrain.

This terrain is structured by two reciprocal mechanisms, namely the logics of difference and equivalence.[3] The contours of differential relations have already been sketched by indicating that signification and identity entail difference, which can be illustrated in the following way: the identity of X_1 is construed through its difference from $X_2, X_3, \ldots X_n$. To claim that the identity of X_1 is differential rather than essential means that its difference from $X_2, X_3, \ldots X_n$ is part of X_1's identity. Thus other social entities are 'present' in X_1 as an 'absence', which is constitutive in that it determines X_1's identity by delimiting it from what it is not. The differential nature of identity and signification entails that the relations between social entities can never be either purely internal or external. If they could be, the delimitations among them would either be interiorized within the entities themselves or exteriorized. In both situations the essentialist principle of identity ($X = X$) would be retained, whereupon the limit could not be a limit proper.[4] By emphasizing the articulatory structuring of social entities, the dualism of internal and external relations is undermined because identity and signification exist in between interiority/presence and exteriority/absence. The discursive field is, as such, 'present' in each entity whose condition of existence depends upon this field, which is instantiated in each practice as its condition of existence.

A relation of equivalence is also a sort of differential relation in that it presupposes the differential character of identity. Yet its *modus operandi* is that whilst it presupposes differentiality it also undermines it. The differences between the elements which are constructed as equivalent are subverted, although not completely for, in that case, the elements would not be equivalent but identical. It is important to note two points here. First, subversion can take place because the social realm cannot fully constitute itself but rather, exists in the articulatory field of signification. When the structuring mechanisms are given by the logics of difference and equivalence, there is no ground beyond the discursive realm to prevent the collapse of structures. Second, equivalential relations imply that social entities are not merely given by virtue of their differences from one another, but also by virtue of *their* difference conceived as a whole (as a form of life with specific rules, resources, routines, and so on) – that is, from what they are not. Equivalential relations are thus established when articulatory practices institute themselves by posing something which is exterior to themselves.

Both aspects of equivalential relations are evident in the social-contract tradition of Hobbes and Locke. Although Hobbes aims at erecting a firm foundation for the social order, this foundation is, none the less, created mythologically and rhetorically by positing *Leviathan* as a common pole of identification and not as an emanation of God's will. It is the politically constructed nature of the necessity of *Leviathan* which renders it liable to 'negotiation', which is, of course, the springboard for the liberal tradition. By extension, to establish equivalential relations between subjects – relations which construct them as political subjects in the first place – implies that 'something' (a particular) within the social realm has been externalized and has established itself 'above' them (the universal) treating them as equal before the law.

The same basic mechanism is found in Freud's discussion of group psychology. Individuals identify themselves as belonging to a group by positing an 'external object', a leader with whom they can identify and hence confer authority upon: they 'have put one and the same object in the place of their ego ideal and have consequently identified themselves with one another in their ego.'[5] When individuals have 'identified themselves with one another' a chain of equivalence can be said to have been established between them, defining them as being part of a group. This, in turn, implies that a group, by virtue of being a group, has a structure of authority which is at one and the same time posed and presupposed. The logic of equivalence is, then, closely bound up with the circular structure of power and hence with the political structure of social orders.

It should be clear that the reciprocity between difference and equivalence accounts for the more- or less-precarious nature of structures of identification and social orders, as well as for the constitution of these orders in the first place. The logic of equivalence can be illustrated in the following way:

$$\frac{X_1 - X_2 - X_3 - \ldots - X_n}{Y}$$

What makes $X_1, X_2, X_3, \ldots X_n$ different from Y cannot be found by reference to their intrinsic characteristics, such as an underlying common denominator functioning as an objective reference point. Rather, their difference from Y cannot but be a strategic construct in which the exteriorization of Y produces the cohesion between $X_1, X_2, X_3, \ldots X_n$, which, accordingly, forms 'a "virtual order" of differences'.[6] The institutionalization of equivalential chains can thus account for the cohesion or integration between differential positions by framing them or providing them with a systemic character. Social orders are institutionalized and reproduced through processes of inclusion and exclusion, and it is at the point of intersection between them that hegemonic power struggles are located.[7] Power is, accordingly, immanent in the structuring of social orders because identity is formed through delimitation in the processes of inclusion and exclusion.

The intertwined logics of difference and equivalence can be illustrated by looking at how a racist discourse is currently taking shape in Denmark, a country that has not, hitherto, experienced racial conflicts on any great scale. The semi-populist right-wing Party of Progress (Fremskridtspartiet) has, since the mid 1980s, waged an increasingly aggressive propaganda campaign for 'Danishness', in line with the right-wing nationalist organization Danish Society (Den Danske Forening). The campaign is primarily directed against immigrant workers and refugees, who for the most part are Muslims; but Jewish culture has come under fire too. It is maintained that the increasing influx of Palestinians, Kurds and Iranians will, in the long run, outnumber Danes, thereby undermining Danish culture. The identity of these people is given as non-Danes, which not only means that they are not Danes but that they allegedly threaten Danish culture. The differences amongst these various peoples and cultures have been collapsed by establishing an equivalence between them: an image has been forged of them as intruders, troublemakers and welfare chisellers. An attempt has thus been made to undermine differential relations between Danes and these foreigners, and by extension those strategies aiming at their integration into Danish society.

To speak of Danishness is to pick up on a number of characteristics about Danes which are seen to be equivalential, characteristics which are meaningful only in relation to, and in terms of their difference from, say, being English, American or Swedish. To construct the national identity of a people – thereby establishing the people *as* a people – or to differentiate between cultures, nationalities, and so on, cannot in itself count as an expression of racism. The reason is, of course, that the mere existence of the logics of difference and equivalence, and hence of systems of differences, cannot account for antagonistic power struggles. The formation of collective identities does assuredly involve power, but to assert this cannot warrant the conclusion that the mere existence of systems of differences entails power conflicts. Racism, as a particular form of antagonistic power strategy, comes about when, as in this case, the

Party of Progress construes Danishness in relation to what the party sees as threatening it, that is, when Danishness becomes the mirror image of what it excludes. A great variety of daily phenomena, such as 'strange' music and clothing, 'smelly' food, the 'inhumane' prescriptions of halal and kosher slaughtering, an 'oppressive' religion (Islam), and 'exploitation' of the social-security system come together in an image of intruders and parasites who do not rightfully belong 'here'. That is, they are not part of 'us'.

The virtues of Danishness are thus built upon the vices of the excluded 'Other' which, by that very fact, is included in, or more precisely constitutive for, the identity of Danishness in the first place and which, moreover, gives this elusive strategy its sole cohesive force. However, far from being a weakness, the hollowness of this strategy may turn out to be its actual strength. Whether or not that is the case will, of course, depend upon the hegemonic success of the strategy, that is, whether it is capable of enforcing this friend/enemy relation between 'them' and 'us'. The extent to which this relation attains the status of an outlet for various kinds of social dissatisfaction and frustration triggered by, say, the high level of unemployment, especially among young people, their deteriorating chances of obtaining an education, and the running down of the social-security system will determine whether it becomes a pole of identification in political power struggles.

There is no doubt that the success of the Party of Progress in the elections in the late 1980s and early 1990s has, in part, resulted from its explicit hostility towards Muslim refugees. The idea of Danishness presents itself as an underlying fact: *that* which has always been *there* awaiting recognition, *that* which unites 'us' against 'them'. Hence the externalization of 'them' is crucial for establishing *our* identity, meaning that *we recognize ourselves* through this exclusion where *we discover what we were all along*. In positing our presuppositions – namely a given identity – we are thereby caught up in, or engaged in, a kind of reflexive movement. This 'fundamental reversal' constitutes the ideological cement of political strategies – what Lefort has termed the tautology of ideological discourse.[8] However, the alleged giveness of this identity, which typically revolves around the idea of culture as a unified and unifying ground,[9] cannot but be the result of its hegemonic construction. It is an effect presenting itself as a cause – the necessary fiction of representing something which is not present.

Power struggles come into existence when interpretations or forms of practice differ so much that they cannot be resolved within systems of differences (say, a hegemonic bloc) in which the subjects are positioned and with which they otherwise identify themselves. In situations like these, the rules prescribing what is appropriate cannot embrace certain forms of practice or interpretation, and thus a process of disintegration is triggered, opening a void between what come to be seen as irreconcilable forms of life. As a consequence, a reshuffling of structures of signification and identification takes place through processes of interiorization and exteriorization, effectuating new frontiers in social relations. The instability expressed in such situations varies from minor power struggles, in which the conflicting positions are relatively easily accommodated by the differential order of daily routines, to large-scale antagonisms.

The logics of difference and equivalence are crucial for coming to terms with the individuation and coherence of social orders, signification and identification, and these constructs are contingent upon the discursive structuring of social reality. In order to obtain a more accurate picture of how these logics are related to the problem of power, it is useful to look at the notion of overdetermination. This notion plays an important role in understanding, first, how local and general strategies are imbricated in one another; second, how the articulation of particularistic strategies brings about totalizing or societal effects; and third, how the contingent nature of social constructs takes shape. These three points concern the problems of hegemony, power and authority, and identity and identification respectively.

Overdetermination and Hegemonic Power Struggles

The notion of overdetermination, as it is employed by Althusser, is meant to account, first, for the unevenness in social relations, making domination and subordination inherent in them; second, for the irreducibility of the heterogeneity of social relations, which cannot, accordingly, be referred back to the social order as a ground; third, for the articulation between various practices and how they determine, and are determined by, political strategies; and finally, and as a consequence of the last two points, for the impossibility of univocality of the elements in the societal whole, which here is understood as equivalent to the discursive horizon. Hence the notion of overdetermination stresses that actions, far from being confined within structures, play an active role in shaping them, and over time become ossified in institutional routines, rule following and criteria of appropriateness.[10]

Althusser's notion of overdetermination describes the effects of the articulation of each practice on the horizon as a whole, as well as the effects of this horizon on each practice. Thus the overdetermination of practices reflects their condition of existence within the societal whole. As in the case of Foucault's 'rule of double conditioning', the local exists *as* the general, and conversely, the general is instantiated in the local.[11] Hence the part *is* the whole in the sense that it is conditioned by it, and this whole reflects itself in the part; which is to say that 'the Whole is always-already *part of itself*, comprised within its own elements.'[12] This does not mean that there is not a schism between part and whole. The hegemonic task of political strategies is to bridge this schism by transforming power strategies; this is achieved by incorporating them into structures of authority which serve a 'grounding' function.[13]

Overdetermination is bound up with the circular structure of power: power crystallizes authority, which represents the condition of existence for power, and is itself immanent in power. The point is not merely that political power strategies produce authority which, by becoming institutionally materialized, functions as the framework for exercising power. The point is also that the difference between power and authority is basically structural: authority is universalized power; it is a cluster of power relations which has occupied *the place of the political*, whereupon it has become the vehicle and symbol for the societal structuring of social relations. Political authority is, in other words, a power strategy which, by virtue of particularizing all other power strategies, attains a 'universal' status. Political authority attains this status because it is the overdetermined expression of power: the point of condensation where the particularity of power turns into its opposite by embodying universality.

Political authority can thus be seen as a power which has managed to universalize itself spatially and temporally. A political authority can legitimize itself by, for example, inventing a mythical origin – as in social-contract theory where authority is deduced from the proposition of autonomous and rational individuals. The linearity of this type of argument cannot, however, be upheld due to the overdetermined nature of political authority, which is stressed by the circular structure of power. The point is that the relation between political power and political authority is undecidable. The latter is not simply the effect of the former, which then constructs itself as the cause, political authority is both the outcome and the medium of power: it is an outcome of power struggles in the sense that it cannot be merely given, and it is a medium in so far as it is always already presupposed in political power struggles. So, perhaps it would be more correct to say that linearity is the consummation and successful legitimation of the circular structuring of power in much the same way as denotation is, as Barthes says, the last connotation.

Due to the heterogeneity and unevenness of systems of difference, the articulation between them is characterized by an uneven and combined development. The whole superimposes itself on each practice which, accordingly, is not autonomous but, on the contrary, is determined by the complexity of the whole (the complex strategical situation). When the whole is immanent in its effects, overdetermination becomes the mechanism which introduces the totality, understood as 'an ensemble of totalising effects in an open relational complex' which cannot ultimately be apprehended.[14] The totality is thus always present in its absence: it is a representation of an absence, the 'place' of inscription towards which political strategies direct themselves in order to speak in the name of society. It is, in other words, the locus for the authorization of power, meaning that the hegemonic task of political strategies is to occupy the empty place of the absent totality, which authorizes them to represent society as such.

The overdetermined character of the discursive structuring of social relations entails that systems of difference are 'present' in each other, which precludes their being present for themselves; thus the very mechanisms that constitute these systems also distort their univocality and fixity. Undecidability is, on this account, an ontological fact of social reality, which means that autonomy is a necessary feature of the complex determination of the whole whose openness and contestability at the same time turns it into a vehicle of contingency. To hold that the identities of systems and agents are shaped in processes of signification in which power is immanent makes it possible to speak about discursive constructs as signifiers, thus broadening this concept beyond its narrow linguistic use. The processes of signification, which are bound up with the logics of difference and equivalence, have two aspects: condensation/metaphor and displacement/metonymy.[15] Condensation arises when signifiers are fused into a single entity, which then embodies a variety of meanings. The process is characterized by a superimposition of signifiers in which one is replaced by another. The condensed signifier has a metaphorical effect which presupposes a regularity in the patterns of substitution, that is, a degree of sedimentation of those signifiers that are analogical. Hegemonic struggles can be seen in this light: their possibility lies in the fact that the meaning of signifiers cannot be fixed, and thus the task of political strategies becomes that of substituting one pattern of signification for another.

A signifier in which several elements have been condensed can be seen as a nodal point. By embodying a variety of meanings, nodal points are at once utterly ambiguous whilst also fixing the meaning of the signifying chain.[16] They can be regarded as empty signifiers whose vacuity makes them structural loci for the inscription of power strategies. Democratic rights often function as nodal points in power struggles. They are at once floating, empty and strategic signifiers around which political struggles are centred because they are the points towards which identification is directed. When a signifier becomes a nodal point, it makes a broad-based identification tenable, whereby it may be capable of hegemonizing broad segments of various groups. Yet this status also renders the signifier and hence the hegemonic project less homogeneous. It should be clear that this double aspect of nodal points is important for understanding the political struggles between power strategies whose success depends to a large extent upon their ambiguity.[17]

Displacement arises when signifiers substitute one another due to the proximity of their signification. The substitution is characterized by a transference of meaning from one signifier to another through chains of association. The transference of meaning is not analogous but contiguous: it is the process of associating some elements with each other, and hence dissociating them from others, that is decisive for establishing the coherence of political power strategies. Schmitt's emphasis on the friend/enemy relation, which he sees as a distinctively political relation, points in this direction: the identity of a people is established through chains of associations, where the ruled identify themselves with the rulers. Relations of contiguity can become sedimented through repetition and thus become analogical and sites of condensation and metaphor, just as they can break up existing structures of analogy, thereby dissolving nodal points.

Displacement plays a crucial role in the differential and equivalential logics embodied in the political institutions of the modern nation-state. The myth of the social contract, as mentioned, constitutes the subject as free and equal before the law. The rise and spread of the democratic imaginary, especially in the Western hemisphere, is to a large extent the history of the displacement of constitutional rights onto democratic and welfare rights. This development is part and parcel of the disintegration of traditional authoritarian structures (for example, clientelism and paternalism) and the expansion of public spaces which cover still more areas of social life, all of which show the importance of rights as nodal points in political struggles. What we witness here is a metonymical sliding of signification – of identifying and associating various forms of repression and fighting against them – which renders displacement more important in hegemonic struggles than metaphor since the latter indicates sedimentation which is the outcome of political struggles.

Struggles condensing a variety of elements entail a displacement of these in relation to other elements, since condensation can only occur when more than two elements have been displaced and fused into one. The nature of this element is an 'identity of opposites in a real unity'.[18] In a power struggle various relations of domination and subordination, comprising latent and manifest conflicts as well as antagonisms which have hitherto been displaced and repressed, find an outlet through the mechanisms of condensation and displacement by merging into a 'ruptural unity'.[19] Whilst a rupture is conditioned by and immanent in the logics of difference and equivalence, it cannot be an immanent part of identity or a differential moment in social relations, and it is, accordingly, 'outside'. The overdetermination of social relations means that they are constructed in processes of condensation and displacement whereby they cannot but be unevenly and hierarchically structured. Domination and subordination are thus far from being accidental or parasitic characteristics of social relations, as theories of universal emancipation would have it; they are instead constitutive traits of every hegemonic construction of power struggles.[20]

The more elements that are condensed in power struggles, the more dominant and central they are going to be in relation to the societal whole; thus other struggles become less dominant and are more easily absorbed into differential relations. This shows the importance of metonymy in power struggles. It also shows the importance both of the structural location of political institutions and of the institutions and organizations that take up a political role: that is, as loci for power struggles they condense a variety of conflicting interests. The hegemonic task of political strategies is that of associating a variety of manifest interests, as well as giving shape to latent interests which would otherwise be dispersed and suppressed because, amongst other reasons, they would *de facto* be excluded from the agenda in the political institutions. The success of hegemonic political strategies can be judged on their ability to substitute signifiers and stabilize new hegemonies, that is, to transform metonymy into metaphor.[21]

The overdetermination of social entities which, among other things, is expressed in equivalential relations, is crucial for the analysis of power in terms of negativity. If the discursive horizon was structured in an endless proliferation of differences – as in some postmodern scenarios that indulge in the end of 'grand narratives' and their replacement by pure particularism – the relation among signifiers would be one of coexistence, and the isomorphism between signifier and signified would have been retained. The consequence would be that the objectivity of social orders could not be put into question since the substitution/subversion of signifiers could not take place. The logic of the signifier, as it is presented by Laclau and Mouffe, and by Žižek, stresses not only the sliding of the signified under the signifier but also the destruction of the signified through this sliding. Whilst the coexistence of signifiers produces a dispersion of meaning, the aspect of substitution or equivalence (metaphor and metonymy) cancels out the specificity of identity and reveals negativity. This is why social reality institutes itself through the two mutually subversive logics of difference and equivalence which, nevertheless, presuppose one another.

The constitutive role played by these two logics implies that social entities exist in a permanent tension between positivity and negativity, which mutually subvert each other. Practices take place in this tension between the coexistence of signification and identification, and their substitution.[22] The emphasis on this tension is analogous to the intersection between inclusion and exclusion which, as mentioned in the discussion of decisions and nondecisions, is the location of power and politics. It is important to keep the distinction between positivity and negativity clear. Self-identity is never brought to completion in the former because signification involves difference. Neither is it fully constituted in the latter: not just because signification is differential but because a constitutive outside blocks the differential character of identity.[23] The identity of, say, a people is never entirely given. The reason is not that it is impossible to grasp this identity fully, since new aspects can always be added which modify the existing ones, but because it is threatened by 'aliens', 'intruders' or 'enemies'. But – and this is the point – it is precisely these aliens that form the reference point for attempts to hegemonize the identity of 'the people'.

The impossibility of consummating identity, regardless of whether we speak about elements or totalities, implies that 'the conception of "society" as [a] founding totality of its partial processes' becomes impossible. The same holds true for 'the object "society" as a rationally unified totality'. Hence, '"society" is not a valid object for discourse. There is no single underlying principle fixing – and constituting – the whole field of differences.'[24] The constitution of society is an imaginary grounding that fixes identity, whose imaginary nature is shown in the necessary fiction pertaining to politics: that the institutionalization of a social order entails a leap from power to authority. This leap covers the void between particularity and universality – the intangible object of representation[25] – that conditions politics in the first place, whilst politics at the same time attempts to erase it in order to reduce political authority to legitimate authority.

The constitutive void conditioning politics as a performative act plays a crucial role in hegemonic struggles, which are never capable of totalizing the societal horizon, whose contours remain intangible. Political agents operate within limits which define them in the first place, and therefore there will always be an 'outside' which at one and the same time constitutes and threatens them. The discussion of pluralism and its critics showed that these limits could take the form of nondecisions (Bachrach and Baratz) and no-decisions (Lukes), the function of which was to set the conditions whereby issues could reach the political agenda as well as be dealt with. Hence pluralist systems, which incorporate to a greater or lesser extent a wide variety of differences within their representative and administrative institutional settings, enforce limits which map out the space for representability and acceptability. These limits define and sustain the pluralist system by way of rules, resources, routines, and the like.

Contrariwise, even antagonistic political strategies, which polarize a context into two camps, operate within a horizon that defines the struggle in the first place. Such a horizon may be a professed allegiance to, say, democratic and human rights, which, although given different contents, serve as nodal points in political struggles because they map out the conditions for engaging in politics. But the horizon is also 'practical' in the sense of being made up of the rules, resources and routines that characterize the forms of life pertaining to political institutions that constitute the day-to-day basis of politics. Consequently, even in situations of extreme polarization, there is always a margin of a practical 'common ground'. This is so because that which is presupposed in a power struggle cannot at the same time be the object of it. To engage in a struggle is inseparable from being positioned, that is, from presupposing something. Struggles, accordingly, always have a constitutive blind spot: *that* which tries to escape the 'fate of contingency', that which pretends to stay clear of ambiguity and unfixity.[26]

Overdetermination as a Kind of Causality

Structures are not objective generative mechanisms, but are instead a dimension of the discursive structuring of social reality. The relation between structure and subject cannot, accordingly, be external, which is to say that it cannot be apprehended in terms of causation. We are, then, faced with an apparent paradox, namely that, while power produces effects and can be traced only through those effects, it is not, strictly speaking, causally effective. To address the problem of causality in relation to power requires that causation be viewed in terms of the discursive nature of social relations. This is where the notion of overdetermination comes in, to indicate that the relation between cause and effect is circular. The cause of an effect is given by the structuring of the whole, which exists in the part.[27]

Overdetermination can be conceived in terms of structural or metonymic causality, which holds that structure is interior to its effects.[28] This means, says Althusser, that 'the structure is immanent in its effects, a cause immanent in its effects in the Spinozist sense of the terms, that *the whole existence of the structure consists of its effects*, in short that the structure, which is merely a specific combination of its peculiar elements, is nothing outside its effects.'[29] The structural whole is, for Althusser, a founding totality of its elements, which corresponds to Spinoza's idea of eternity. Although Althusser's notion of structural causality expresses an essentialism of the totality which, in the final instance, eliminates structural dislocations and overdetermination, it is nevertheless possible to retain the notion of structural causality with the proviso that the totality never manages to entirely establish itself. It could instead be conceived of as a horizon of totalizing effects which institutes itself through articulatory practices.

Structural causality has an affinity with the logic of the signifier, which, as mentioned, involves not only the sliding of the signified under the signifier but also its substitution in this sliding. This means that power is coterminous with the logic of the signifier, and hence with the discursive structuring of social reality, because the unfixity and ambiguity of social entities imply the possibility of their subversion. The point is that 'the limit of the social must be given within the social itself as something subverting it, destroying its ambition to constitute a full presence.'[30] The limits of practices are given by the practices themselves when they subvert differential relations, and this is the reason why power exhibits a peculiar interiority and exteriority in relation to systems of difference: it is at once immanent in them, yet is also their limit and in that sense outside them.[31] The notion of structure indicates that a closure is enforced through limitations on practices by these practices themselves in the process of power struggles. The constitutive role of power in shaping structures implies that structures can be seen as the symptoms of negativity which institutional practices try to efface. Such attempts can only take place by enforcing limits and hence effectuating closures which reduce the margins of undecidability.

It appears to be a contradiction in terms to deny that power is causally effective whilst speaking about power *effects*. The point is, however, that power as the ability to make a difference is both cause and effect: ability is the cause of making a difference, but this effect also causes ability in the first place. If this were not the case, we would be back to the dictum of the constitutive subject. The point is, moreover, that cause and effect cannot be fully imbricated in each other since power is the spatial and temporal limit which poses and presupposes itself, which is why the essentialism of both element and totality disintegrates. The final point is that this 'itselfness' cannot be a substance; it is instead the 'pure distance' or the void within identity. There is thus a fissure between cause and effect, and power is the name for this impossibility of consummation. The 'cause' is, ultimately, the void in signification whose 'presence' cannot be grasped but only traced through its effects.

Derrida's notion of trace is useful here. When identity is blocked the subject is thrown back upon 'itself'. The nature of this circular movement is shown in the metonymic chain of various positions associated with those which have been negated. The association of subject positions is not prior to the actual negation. On the contrary, it is the negation which triggers the metonymic chain across already established differential and equivalential relations, thereby restructuring them. Hence the trace structure of power is immanent in social orders, which is why structures are metonymic chains whose moment of emergence is given in struggles, which prevents closures.[32] Even highly sedimented institutional settings exhibit elements of ambiguity, which are indexes of disseminated traces of power and the stumbling block to the politicization of the structuring of institutional organization.[33]

II
Power as Negativity and Identity

Power as Negativity

It has been argued that society is not able to institute itself as a closed order because it is itself the medium and locus of those logics of difference and equivalence in which overdetermination, and hence structural dislocations, play a constitutive and subversive role in the formation of identity. This second part of the chapter continues the discussion of how power is immanent in processes of identification. The aim is to further Foucault's power analytics by showing how negativity plays a constitutive role for identity through identification: the becoming of identity 'as it is', which in turn elucidates the circular structure of power. Approaching the problem of power in this way furthers the effort of outlining a presuppositionless conceptualization of power. This task requires a close reading of Laclau and Mouffe's notions of negativity and antagonism in order to see what is at stake in the constitution and disintegration of identity.[34]

A presuppositionless approach means: one, that power cannot a priori be given form and content (for example, that it is inseparable from conflict and is a zero-sum game, or that it fosters consensus and is a plus-sum game); and two, that it has to be viewed as coterminous with identification (the constitution of identity, that is, how 'the ability to make a difference' shapes itself). This does not mean, however, that all that can be said about power at this higher-order level of analysis is that it is simply a relation between subjects or social entities in general. Power as the ability to make a difference is, as we have seen in the discussion of Foucault's power analytics, a relation characterized by limitation, identification, contingency and fundamental reversal. These four characteristics are inherent in the circular structuring of power, and it is in this sense that we can talk about power as a complex strategical situation which is modelled around the notion of negativity.

Defining power as negativity, which in antagonistic power struggles takes the form of ruptural moments involving the blocking of identity, may at first seem at odds not only with the thrust of Foucault's work but, moreover, with the argument that power is constitutive for identity. The point is, however, that this is the only way to maintain the insights of his power analytics – whose *sine qua non* is to grasp power in terms of identification which, in turn, implies subjection and subjectification – whilst at the same time overcoming its ambiguities. To hold that power entails subjection and subjectification should not be seen as a pessimistic or cynical picture of what social life in general and political life in particular are all about. This is most likely Foucault's point as well. The link he saw between politics and domination was first of all directed against the juridico-discursive representation of power, but it was clearly not the model he preferred in his analysis of power. In any case, to hold that there is a necessary or logical connection between power, conflict, domination and politics is to misinterpret the nature of both the political and politics, and by extension to prevent an understanding of the potential of (radical) democracy.

The argument I wish to pursue here is that power as the ability to make a difference should be grasped not simply in terms of negativity but as *auto-negativity*. So far negativity has been conceived as the void in signification and identity which triggers processes of signification and identification. But there is something more at stake in this understanding of negativity, namely that power as pure or limitless possibility entails its own negation: in giving shape to the possible – in making decisions, nondecisions or no-decisions – we cannot but negate ability as such, that is, pure or limitless possibility. Power is thus auto-negativity: *that* which is always already the negation of itself, *that* which has no 'itselfness'. It has a virtual existence only as the trace of an impossibility, that is, as the recoiling structure or fundamental reversal in the order of things.

Is power, then, inherently repressive? The answer is that power is not repressive when seen in terms of limitless possibility; but when it establishes limits, it possesses a repressive dimension. These two aspects of power – the higher-order and the lower-order levels of analysis – indicate that the circular structure of power has a repressive dimension by virtue of shaping pure possibility as 'that' which was already 'there': the becoming of identity 'as it is'. To choose a direction entails a moment of coercion: for the subject that prefers *x* to *y* is not autonomous in the sense of being internally related to itself and externally related to the 'things' it chooses because it has 'extended' itself in, or identified itself with, those things. The subject is constituted by this decision, the decisions preceding it and those following it, which is to say that the subject exists in both time and space. Pure possibility, or power as such, is prior to whatever form and content these decisions take and hence to the repressive dimensions of power. We cannot, of course, ever encounter power or ability as such. What we are confronted with are endless varieties of practices, ranging from the force of a good argument to manipulation and blatant repression. The somewhat paradoxical point is, however, that we have to presuppose the presuppositionless idea of power as such in order to make sense of the contingency of social and political constructs, and hence the fact that the order of things could always be different.

Power shows its repressive side by forgetting, including/excluding, antagonizing, and so on. But to say this is by no means a concession to the 'repressive hypothesis'. There are three reasons for this. The first is that the argument does not hinge upon the dictum of the constitutive subject, which means that power is not determined by anything since it is nothing but pure possibility which is immanent in every practice. The second is that the particular form and content of the various repressive acts cannot be determined by power as negativity, which is immanent in and conditioning of power relations (the four aspects of the circular structure of power). The third is that the form and content of actions are contingent upon the complex strategical situation; that is to say, the latter can function as a contrary-to-fact standard which is the embodiment of pure possibility as a regulative idea of autonomy and radical democracy.

Power as auto-negativity is not only not at odds with Foucault's power analytics; it is, I believe, the most feasible way in which to outline a presuppositionless conceptualization of power. This notion of power cannot function as a foundation for the subject or the social order because it, by its very nature, defies any such attempt by being antithetic to the full constitution of identity. It then follows that power as auto-negativity, and the play of signification triggered by the blocking of identity in hegemonic struggles, fulfils the three criteria for advancing a presuppositionless conception of power: that power is non-derivative, non-determinate and non-objective. This is, furthermore, the basis for understanding the relation between power and authority, the political constitution of social orders and, finally, democracy.

The reason why power as auto-negativity is congruent with Foucault's power analytics can be illustrated by looking at his nominalist argument, which shows that hegemonic power struggles can be seen as being constructed in terms of the logic of equivalence. The more extended the equivalential chain becomes, the more the differential positivity of its elements collapses, causing their identities to be determined primarily in confrontation with each other. The antagonistic strategies are not capable of possessing an independent identity since they are constituted as hostile mirror images of each other. Power in such a situation has no positive content, common denominator or ground from which it can be derived. To grasp power solely in terms of its productivity would imply seeing it simply as a relation that constituted identity in a proliferation of differences. This would make it impossible to come to terms with the *ability* to make a difference as the locus of the 'eternal recurrence' of negativity; this in turn would render the analysis of power unable to challenge the objectivity of social reality. Power could not then be a name for the becoming of ability, since becoming cannot be separated from the cancelling of possibilities.[35]

There is, once the notion of the constitutive subject is abandoned, no logical link between power as auto-negativity and power as 'basically anti-energy'. When, as Foucault has argued, there is no original subjectivity, energy or desire for power to set out to negate, his power analytics opens itself to the possibility that the 'core' of identity is auto-negativity. Identity is shaped through identification, which means that identity is thrown into the plays of signification that constitute it. It then becomes problematic to uphold a rigorous distinction between its productive and repressive aspects, power and resistance, and 'power to' and 'power over'. When power says 'no', resistance is forced to say 'no' to the negation (negating the negation), whereupon it is forced into a play of signification, which is what characterizes power struggles and gives them their unpredictable nature. In short, the subject is situated in the pure distance or the void opened up by negativity as the absence of a ground.

To conceptualize power in terms of negativity implies two things. First, the moment of negativity is that of unfixing or subverting identity. Since identity is relational, the subversion of one position cannot avoid having repercussions on other positions. The moment of unfixity does not preclude the possibility that the network of positions will become stabilized again, in which case the effects of power have become absorbed – although the processes of absorption can never be completed. Rather, power is displaced onto the processes in which political strategies attempt to hegemonize the social order, which bears the traces of power. This is shown in the impossibility of social entities fully constituting themselves. Second, this view of power addresses the question as to whether power has an explanatory status or whether it is itself to be explained. However, such an either/or solution is not entirely to the point.

The explanatory effect of power as such – that is, the explanation carried out at the higher-order level of analysis – is limited to the basic structure of power, which conditions but cannot determine the lower-order level of analysis. In the latter type of analysis, it is surely the case that power has to be explained because the form and content of power relations vary infinitely. It is here that we encounter two problems with the apprehension of power in the language of causation. First, when power is immanent in processes of identification it is as a kind of internal relation that is antithetic to causal relations, which are external relations between given identities. Second, the circular structure of power is obviously at odds with linear causality, which would, for example, hold that power is simply a relation that accounts for a difference.

To single out a cause is itself an act of power which, in antagonistic power struggles, is analogous to naming or identifying an adversary or an enemy. By pointing out that one thing rather than another was the cause of a particular event, one is engaged in the activity of structuring social relations, that is, choosing directions in a complex strategical situation. By identifying something as the cause, one simultaneously conducts a double operation. First, by linking an effect to a cause one establishes a temporal and spatial direction in social relations, meaning that one is engaged in the structuring of the social terrain in order to render it meaningful (from a particular point of view). Second, by identifying something as the cause, one equips this something with a capacity or causal power, which is to say that one constructs the nature or identity of this something. Both of these aspects are immanent in power as such inasmuch as, in the case of power as the ability to make a difference, ability is retroactively identified as the locus for the causal power. By making a difference, power links this cause to effects whereby the social terrain is provided with a 'reading principle' that renders it intelligible.

The Constitution and Negation of Identity

It has been argued that the coherence and integration of social entities are discursively constructed by the logics of difference and equivalence. It has, furthermore, been argued that power plays an ambiguous role in relation to identity: at once subversive yet constitutive; at once unfixing identity whilst also instituting new closures. The questions are how identity is negated and what happens in this process. In attempting to answer these questions it will be necessary to see how power interrupts structured patterns of rule-governed relations, that is, formal or informal ways of governing oneself and others. While the identity of agents is structured around the subject positions or roles that condition and define agency within a system defined by rules, identification points towards the manner in which the identity of agents is formed in the interpretation and articulation of roles, rules and routines.

Identity takes shape in processes of identification which are conditioned by subject positions whilst at the same time pointing beyond them. The identity of the subject cannot then be reduced to its positions within a structure, meaning that the subject is not simply a 'structural dope'. There are two reasons for this, which together indicate the pivotal role of identification. The first is that the discursive structuration of social reality entails that structural closures are ultimately inconceivable, which is to say that structural determination is itself indeterminate. And the second is that identification entails a 'beyond': it is because structures cannot determine a system as a closed totality that the subject is never entirely identical with itself and can never be fully absorbed by the system to which it 'belongs'. It is this constitutive incompleteness of identity that triggers the processes of identification in which the subject 'finds itself'.

Identity can be seen as a symbolic representation of positions, which is a performative act of constructing identity 'as it is'. The ambiguity between performance and semblance points not only to the impossibility of accounting for an objectively given reality, but signals also the contingent nature of identity. Identification is a performative act that allows various activities to take place within horizons of interpretations by providing them with some degree of coherence. Because horizons cannot be entirely grasped, identity remains ultimately an intangible goal for identification. The construction of identity through identifications can be seen as a hegemonic project because identity is never given, but is made up by the articulation of various elements which do not possess an internal coherence. Agency is never given but establishes itself provisionally in processes of interpretation and articulation; that is to say, agency can be understood as a vehicle of the circular structure of power which is both its cause and effect.

The problem of negativity revolves around the relations between subject position, identification and identity. This can be illustrated by looking at rule following and the conflicts that the violation of rules might give rise to. When rule following is a matrix of practices whose authority is, ultimately, open to interpretation, following rules cannot but be an ongoing process of articulation and interpretation of the rules themselves. Hence the question of when and how they are violated is inevitably a matter of interpretation too. The question is whether the authoritative sanction imposed on those who allegedly defy the rules counts as an exercise of power. In answering this question it will be necessary to consider what is at stake in interpreting rules and in the identifications related to these interpretations.

Hobbes's discussion of punishment forms a starting point in the effort to answer these questions. Every subject, by entering the covenant, confers authority upon the sovereign, whose actions, consequently, originate in the subjects and should, according to this authorization view of representation, be treated as if the subjects had performed them themselves. Those who disobey the laws are therefore the authors of their own punishment, which is to say that no wrong has been done to them. Hobbes says:

> By this Institution of a Common-wealth, every particular man is Author of all the Soveraigne doth; and consequently he that complaineth of injury from his Soveraigne, complaineth of that whereof he himselfe is Author; and therefore ought not to accuse any man but himselfe; no nor himselfe of injury; because to do injury to ones selfe, is impossible.[36]

It is because the status of being a subject is the cause and effect of the institution of sovereignty that disobedience has to be seen as a negation of the subject's status as a subject. When the subject negates the law it cannot but negate itself; thus the enforcement of the law negates the negation thereby confirming the identity of the subject.[37] One could say, in Freudian terms, that the Hobbesian scenario is one where the ego completely identifies itself with its ego ideal, thus the violation of the latter is *ipso facto* a violation of the ego. The differences between Hobbes and Freud are, of course, that identification for the latter can neither be complete nor coherent, and that there is nothing which hinders the subject in doing 'injury to ones selfe'.

The Hobbesian conception of punishment rests on two assumptions. The first is that the impossibility of doing injury to oneself suggests that the subject who has entered the covenant is a constitutive and unified subject characterized by autonomy and rationality. It is inconceivable that this subject could be torn between conflicting interpretations of rule following because the rules it has laid down in the sovereignty principle are unambiguous and make up a complete system. Hence the unity of sovereignty is matched by the unity of the subject. This leads to the second assumption, namely that entering the covenant institutes a social order, which is characterized by the ruled completely identifying themselves with the ruler (the subject mirrors itself in the sovereign, so to speak). The transformation of power into authority has been brought to completion, and the social order is a closed totality that fully incorporates its elements. The result of both assumptions is the establishment of a deterministic system in which position and identity are indistinguishable: the political identity of the subject is exhausted in the rules that define its positions in the system. This scenario entails, on the one hand, that the authorities' exercises of power inevitably have an integrative function and, on the other, that rules are unambiguous and hence not subject to negotiation. Both of these assumptions must be considered as antithetic to democracy.

Although the Hobbesian scenario excludes the possibility of conceptualizing power in terms of negativity, it does point to a tricky problem concerning the relation between identity and rules, which is decisive for understanding an important aspect of power struggles as well as when power is exercised. When an institution punishes a subject for insubordination, it does so according to a set of rules which define not only the institution but also the subject as a member of that institution, that is, its role. Hence the rules defining the subject position and the rules enforcing the sanctions belong to the same corpus of rules governing a particular system. But from this assertion it does not follow that sanctions against non-compliance, and the means of coercion enforcing them, by definition either sustain the integrity of a system (authority) or negate the identity of those who defy the rules (power). To advance such an either/or solution to the problem of power would be to presuppose what cannot in fact be presupposed: that the system is closed, that rules are unambiguous and hence not open to interpretation, and that there is no schism between position and identity. Having argued against these three presuppositions, it is now possible to consider the relation between sanctions and power from the vantage point of the openness of systems, the ambiguity of rules, and identification.

Granted the importance of identification in assessments of whether power has been exercised, it seems reasonable to claim that sanctions against non-compliance would count as power in all but two extreme situations. The first is where the subject who has broken a rule acknowledges that the violation of the rule was unjustified, and subsequently that the sanction is legitimate. What we have here is a Hobbesian scenario of total submission where the negation of the rule is itself negated, that is, where the sanction rectifies the identity of the subject rather than negating it. The opposite extreme – usually associated with theories of universal emancipation – is where the subject fully identifies itself with violating a rule. As in the former case, the subsequent sanctions cannot negate its identity because the subject does not identify itself with the rules defining its role, which is to say that the sanctions confirm the identity of the subject as the 'locus of great Refusal'.[38]

The Hobbesian case of total submission, as well as the one Foucault sarcastically terms the 'pure law of the revolutionary',[39] are not only of little practical interest; they are, more importantly, unviable descriptions of the relation between position and identity. By treating position and identity as synonymous, the former presupposes the closure of the system and the fixity of rules, whereas the latter, by conceiving position and identity as antithetic, portrays identity in voluntaristic terms as being somehow beyond the system of rules and hence as external to power. The consequence of this idealistic and emancipatory vision is that the social order is also seen as a closed and fully constituted totality, which makes it a mirror image of the deterministic and integrationist conception. The possibility of resistance is thus either ruled out or has attained an 'accidental' status.[40] By assuming that agents are capable of totally identifying themselves either with their position or with a 'subversive outside', both visions indulge in an objectivist characterization of social reality. Identification then becomes secondary to position and identity, as well as to structure and agency, and cannot play the role of explaining how identity is constructed in the face of diverging interpretations.

Assessing exercises of power in a non-objectivist manner requires giving primary attention to processes of identification and interpretation. When an agent stands accused of violating a rule, it is likely that a conflict of interpretation is going to take place as to whether the rule has actually been defied. This implies reaching a decision concerning the most appropriate interpretation of the rule itself, which in part depends upon resources, routines, comparison with previous cases, and the like. The situation is one in which the agent, on the one hand, identifies itself, to a greater or lesser extent, with the rules governing the particular system of which it is part, whilst, on the other hand, also identifying with the action allegedly violating these rules. The situation is, accordingly, characterized by a split identification on the part of the agent who has supposedly violated the rule.

To ask whether the agent has *in fact* violated the rule is to pose the wrong question because such a 'fact' can only be established through interpretation, which is inseparable from the power struggle between the two parties – or rather, it is the upshot of this struggle. The conclusion is that, in so far as the negotiated outcome is a decision maintaining that the agent did break the rule with the result that sanctions are imposed on the agent for non-compliance, those who rectify the rules exercise power over this agent by virtue of negating his/her identity. The agent's action is itself, according to this interpretation, an attempt to exercise power because it violates the rules. The power to impose the sanctions revolves around the ability to mobilize the bias of the system, which might include a variety of factors such as economic and legal resources, manipulation, rules, rhetoric, and so on. These factors are, needless to say, themselves cause and effect of power as the ability to act.

Those who hold that an action violates a set of rules interpret it as being incompatible with these rules, meaning that the action is unacceptable. Power struggles revolving around conflicting interpretations might trigger a politicization of the existing structure of political authority because they affect the nature of the system in question. Considering an action as a violation of a rule entails that this action is contrasted to the system of rules, which is to say that by crossing the boundaries of this system the *systemness* of the rules is, implicitly or explicitly, invoked. In other words, a chain of equivalence is established which defines the limits of what is acceptable. Politicization occurs when these equivalential chains are brought into effect, that is, when the system defends itself as a system. The result might take the form of authoritative sanctions against non-compliance because the role of the political authority in a system is, among other things, to safeguard the system by whatever means. It can thus be said that power struggles, by unfixing certain rules in a system, by definition operate within certain limits, whilst at the same time exposing these limits by modifying them.

What has been considered here are power struggles arising from conflicting interpretations concerning violations of rules, and whether authoritative sanctions can be considered exercises of power. It is, however, important to maintain that the existence of power struggles does not exhaust power as such. Hence it is perfectly possible to imagine that power relations exist in fairly stable systems of differences and are reproduced without major conflicts on a day-to-day basis. To follow a rule, to know how to go on, to stick to a routine, to do what is considered appropriate, and so on, all indicate that institutional sites exhibit more or less sedimented forms of life and are, to a greater or lesser extent, slanted towards a certain conservatism in the setting of agendas. The daily operations of making and implementing collectively binding decisions by political authorities are located in these 'normal' and often non-conflictual power relations. The power relations we find in these institutional sites are based on delimiting systems of practices from other systems by including/excluding types of actions, agents, rules, routines, resources, issues, and so on. The ability to make a difference within these systems is both the cause and effect of the systems themselves, which is to say that systems are both the medium and outcome of practices. It is in this light that the debates on decisions, nondecisions and no-decisions should be seen because these forms of decisions, in the end, refer to the systemness of rule following.

Consequently, we are able to conclude that the difference between power relations and power struggles is that in the former power is exercised in accordance with particular rules, routines and criteria of appropriateness, whereas in the latter these rules and so forth are called into question.[41] To put it another way, power relations exist, or power is exercised, in more- or less-stable differential systems, which might be hierarchically structured in terms of domination and subordination, because the very nature of a system entails adherence to particular rules and specific – and usually unequally distributed – access to resources. Hence power relations exist *vis-à-vis* limits, but this does not necessarily imply conflict. On the contrary, politics is, echoing Schattschneider, the management of conflict even before it starts. Power struggles arise when these limits are overstepped because such violations of the relative autonomy of systems shake them to a greater or lesser extent.

Power struggles do not take place in a vacuum. Even the pluralists' event-causation model presupposes, although often implicitly, a societal context marked by a widespread consensus that is taken for granted. Because power struggles take place *vis-à-vis* the limits of differential systems, they cannot but presuppose these systems as their context. A context is not, then, an unstructured terrain where everything is possible but, instead, the intersection between various systems of difference which is structured by differential and equivalential logics. What we have here is a complex strategical situation which, at one and the same time, is a condition for the emergence and displacement of power struggles. The point is that various systems might clash, their rules and routines might be broken and their resources might be threatened; but the point is also that these systems to some extent make up a common horizon which might displace power conflicts or bring them to an end through authoritative decisions.

To put the matter differently: when a power struggle concerns, say, the interpretation of rules or who should get what, when and how, this conflict presupposes (implicitly or explicitly) not only a particular context but also that this context (which can be made up of various systems) has a structure of authority which is capable of settling the conflict. This authority does not have to take the form of the legitimate authority associated with the sovereignty principle; it is just as much ingrained in practical rule following, routines and criteria of appropriateness, as well as disciplinary and repressive mechanisms which govern all sorts of institutions on a day-to-day basis. It should thus be clear that power strategies address themselves to political authorities and operate within their 'jurisdiction'. But, and this is decisive, this does not necessarily mean that power strategies identify themselves with these authorities in the sense that the presence of authority entails the absence of conflict. Authority does not have to rest on either legitimacy or efficiency. It is first of all practical in nature: it is the ability to make and implement collectively binding decisions, and hence to ensure that these are *de facto* accepted.

It is important to bear in mind that the identities of agents involved in power struggles are articulated and hence modified in this struggle. At least three possible scenarios can be outlined here. First, the conflicting parties might politicize the conflict by associating the issues around which the conflict started with a variety of other issues. What takes place here is a construction of equivalential relations where each issue is seen as part of a larger whole. The alleged violation of a rule, for instance, is not only seen as unjustified on the part of the accused but also as part of a systematic exclusion of certain – and, from its point of view, legitimate – demands or actions. Although the conflicting parties subscribe to the same rules, they interpret them so differently that the rules tend towards the status of empty strategic signifiers. If the power struggle escalates, a major cleavage in the institution or between institutions might be inevitable, and the situation will be characterized by a fairly clear-cut frontier between the parties. The situation is thus marked by an antagonism.

The second possibility differs from the first only in terms of the scope of power conflicts. Politics is among other things the management of conflict and if a conflict is stifled even before it emerges, the exercise of power does not develop into an antagonism. All kinds of means can be thought of here, such as the authorities' mere threat of coercion or of imposing sanctions, manipulation, biased information, co-optation and compromise. The result is a dilution or displacement of latent and possible confrontations, and in turn the re-establishment of a differential order, which does not allow the construction of equivalential relations and the politicization that accompanies them.

The final possibility is the one in which power relations between conflicting interpretations are channelled through institutional routines rather than violating them. The ambiguity of rules means that there is a more- or less-restricted space of negotiability within which interpretations of rules, routines and criteria of appropriateness can prevail. As long as these boundaries are not crossed, the differences of interpretations can be kept within the differential order of the system in question, whereupon its relative autonomy *vis-à-vis* other systems is sustained. The system is thus characterized by a fairly high degree of stability.

These three scenarios show that politicization is an inherent possibility in power struggles. The reason is not just the presence of conflicting interpretations, demands or interests but also the fact that conflicts direct themselves to the political authority. Politics is, in fact, not only the management of conflict but also of stability. The first means that politics is involved not only in strategies of politicization but also in those of depoliticization, which is to say that both the forging and the dismantling of equivalential chains embody a political moment. The second means that politics is not exclusively associated with change and conflict but is ingrained in the ordinary setting of social life.

When the identity of a subject is negated, this exercise of power cannot avoid having more or less far-reaching repercussions on the overall identity of the subject, due to the relational nature of subject positions, and by extension, the structuring of identification. That is, an exercise of power activates, by means of metonymic tracing, a number of subject positions into which identity is projected. This is especially so if what is negated is a metaphor representing the sedimentation of equivalential chains. Here power not only blocks a specific position but a whole ensemble of overdetermined positions, whereupon the act of power, as well as everything associated with it, become constructed as Otherness *par excellence*. The more a subject position achieves the status of being a pole of identification, condensing a variety of elements, the more likely it is that when this nodal point is threatened an antagonism is going to emerge which will politicize the situation and be difficult to manage. On the other hand, if a position is only weakly coded, it is possible that such a threat will not have the same effects but can be displaced and absorbed into the differential identity of the subject.

There is, however, no proportionality between the degree of overdetermination of subject positions, political issues, and so on, and the probability of an antagonism arising when these positions or issues are threatened. It can easily be imagined that the blocking of a weakly-coded subject position or the suppression of a seemingly marginal political issue could trigger an antagonism. This means that a position or an issue which does not have the status of a nodal point at the moment when it is negated may none the less be the stumbling block to political struggle. It is also possible to imagine that a previous action or event which at the time was not coded as an antagonism may later be so. The action or event which hitherto formed part of differential relations now becomes associated with other factors, and hence seen in another perspective, where it becomes a moment in equivalential relations confronting an opponent. These are two examples of the unpredictability of politicization caused by the fact that identity is formed in processes of identification and cannot ever be entirely fixed. When apparently non-sensitive issues or positions are negated, a metonymic process may be released whereby that which is negated becomes associated with a plurality of other phenomena. It is in this process of forging equivalential chains among otherwise dispersed elements that each element becomes overdetermined and placed within a larger whole, thus achieving a particular identity and hence provided with a specific reading principle.[42]

Antagonism and the Imaginary Nature of Identity

For Lukes, as we have seen, it was crucial to try to figure out whether agents are aware of exercising power or having power exercised over them, or whether they *should* be aware of it. Power as significant affecting was, ultimately, a question of placing responsibility on actions/inactions. For a presuppositionless conception of power, which revolves around negativity, the problems of awareness and responsibility are displaced. Power relations neither depend upon awareness or intentions nor on the possibility of placing responsibility. The reason is that power is constitutive for the subject's own representation in the first place, and, by extension, because representation embodies both semblance and performance; that is to say, by identifying or locating power relations one is, unavoidably, entangled in an interpretation which is part and parcel of a complex strategical situation. This is why discourses *on* power are also discourses *of* power.[43] It is important to note that an exercise of power in which identity is negated cannot be treated as a fact awaiting recognition: there is not first a negation of identity and then a representation of this action as a negation as if the knowing subject was exterior to power.[44]

To speak of negativity as the impossibility of social objectivity is to imply that the identities of the opposing parties can be seen as the effects of each other. The negation of identity and the negation of this negation are inseparable, meaning that there is no negation which is not also a negation of a negation. This is why power *is* resistance and vice versa: constructing an adversary or an enemy ('the Other') is not only a negation but a double negation, in that it is a negation of an agent's possibility of being what 'it is', which it is forced to exteriorize one way or the other.[45] From this assumption it follows that identity has only been negated if negativity is exteriorized, and hence constructed as *that* which negates the identity. Whether the subject is aware of exteriorizing negativity, what it is aware of when doing it, or how it constructs the Other as a re-presentation of its impossibility of 'being what it is' are of secondary importance.

It has been argued that negation of identity takes place only inasmuch as there is an identification with what has been negated. When we turn to antagonism, there is the further condition that *that* which has been negated is entangled in metonymic traces with other elements, thereby creating a frontier against the Other. Here the description cannot but become circular since what has been negated depends upon identification: to see an action as, say, exploitative is already to view it as a negation of identity. The nature of an action as a negation is 'caused' equally by the action and the construction of this action by the subject. Because every activity is discursively coded there is no such thing as an action 'in itself' which can be studied as an 'objective' event. Consequently, no clear distinction can be upheld between cause and effect because they recoil into one another: the construction of the Other is an 'effect' of the negation which hence 'causes' it; yet this construction also 'causes' the action to be construed as a negation. Causality is flawed, which is why power has to be grasped in terms of identification and the 'fundamental reversal' which invokes the circularity of the positing of presuppositions.

The problem of what has been negated, which is inseparable from what one negates, is important for coming to terms with the nature of power struggles, and hence with subjectivity as constituted in processes of identification. Negativity cannot be transparent, and this means that what negates a subject, what has been negated, and what the subject in turn negates are never entirely graspable. The non-transparency of power struggles is crucial for understanding the constitution of subjectivity. The more a negated identity is overdetermined, the less clear it becomes what is actually negated and what negates, and we move accordingly from a situation of denotation to one of connotation. For whilst the former indicates fixity and transparency of meaning, the latter does the opposite.[46] It follows that, in the case of antagonism, the construction of chains of equivalences has been augmented to such a degree that the position which negates and the position which is negated mutually subvert each other. Moreover, in this play of connotation the identities involved are engulfed by a plurality of meanings. What negates becomes a symbol of the negated position's non-being, and what is negated becomes a symbol of an imaginary fulfilment of identity – of 'being totally myself' or being 'a full presence for myself'.[47] This can be illustrated by means of Figure 4.1.

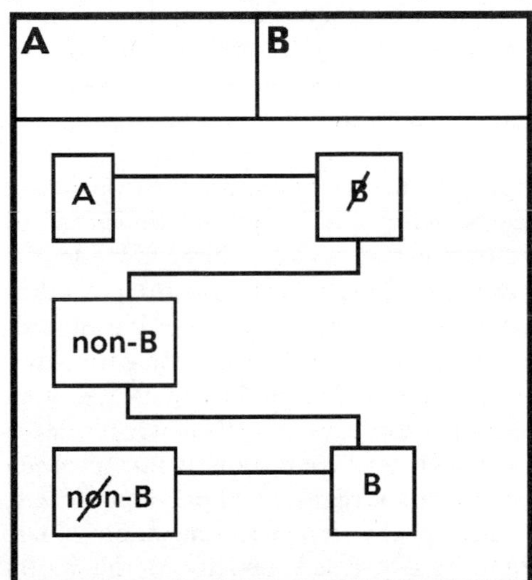

Fig. 4.1 *Identity and negation*

B is the negation of the negation of *B* itself ($\not B$), which is to say that *B* is always already prevented from being identical with itself. To speak of power as auto-negativity means that *B* is at once posed and presupposed. It is here that Foucault's idea of the fundamental reversal becomes relevant: *B* is both the outcome of *B*/ and 'that' which *B*/ 'really' is. What this means is that *B* is posited in power struggles as the truth of *B*/, namely 'that' which *B*/ 'really' is or would have been if its identity had not been negated. The point is that that which is the effect of power struggles (the realization of *B*) is retroactively construed as their real cause: it was because ***B*** could not be identical with itself that the antagonism could arise in the first place. The effect is, in other words, transfigured as the cause (the vertical line between $\not B$ and *B*). This operation cannot be grasped in terms of an ideological misrecognition or, for that matter, a cynical cover-up of what 'really' is at stake in the constitution of identity. Rather, we witness a fundamental undecidability here: *A* as *non-B* is at once that which blocks *B* *and* the externalization of the blocking of *B* (*B*/), whereby ***A*** becomes the symbolic representation, the metaphor, of *B*'s impossibility of being what it is (the principle of identity: *B* = *B*).

In an antagonism *A*'s negation of *B* leads to *B*'s construction of *A* as *non-B*, as *that* which blocks its identity. In this situation, it makes no sense to ask whether *A* 'really' blocks *B* or whether *B* 'makes it up' because there are no objective standards against which this 'really' can be measured. There are, as mentioned, only 'conversational' standards which are, of course, themselves entangled in power struggles. In any case, *A*'s identity is constructed hegemonically as the negation of *B*, whereby *B* can only posit ***A*** as *non-B* by transforming its own precarious identity into a full identity. It does this by externalizing the void in its identity which prevents it from being what it is, and naming it whereby 'being totally myself', is the mirror image of negativity. The fulfilment of identity is imaginary because it closes the discursive terrain in a recoiling movement: the externalization of the void is at the same time an internalization of identity, that is, its constitution and homogenization. This is so because a strategy that resists another does so by constructing a representation of *that* which defies symbolic representation: the Other. Negativity thus becomes positivated in the moment it encourages resistance, otherwise resistance would not be possible in the first place, meaning that an enemy could not be named.

The moment of naming is the moment of the imaginary

constitution of identity, of displacing and 'forgetting' negativity as if identity was given rather than being conditioned by negativity in the encounter with *A*. Forgetting, far from being a psychologistic imposition, is bound up with the positing of presuppositions, which is decisive for the ability of political strategies to position themselves in a complex strategical situation, and hence appear as strong poles of identification capable of engaging in power struggles. It should be clear that the imaginary constitution of identity is not an illusion if by that is meant a masking of the truth. Displacing and forgetting negativity is, rather, the condition that makes it possible for ability to make a difference (auto-negativity) and, by extension, for the subject to stage itself politically. The imaginary self is 'the effect of this misrecognition', which conditions its 'ontological consistency'.[48]

To be 'totally myself' connotes the imaginary fulfilment of identity, which consists in the attempt to displace negativity. The subject comes to terms with itself in this strategical situation into which it is placed – for instance, in hegemonic constellations whose cohesiveness is provided by the depiction of an enemy (racism might serve as an example here). It is in this process of externalizing negativity that the subject 'emerges' as the embodiment of the void, or as the cause and effect of this void, in the discursive structuring of social relations.[49] The paradox is that full identity is conditioned by negativity, meaning that what conditions identity also renders its consummation impossible. The relation between full identity and antagonism is, then, the impossibility of a relation, which is what defines the real in Lacanian psychoanalysis, namely 'a point of the immediate coincidence of the opposite poles: each of the poles passes immediately into its opposite, each is already in itself its own opposite.'[50] Auto-negativity should be seen in this light, which, as the higher-order structure of power, conditions identity in an undecidable manner. The reason is not only that power as such cannot determine the form and content of power relations, but also that these both pose and presuppose power as such.

An antagonism can never be transparent since each pole in the antagonistic relation destroys the other: each pole has transformed the other into an empty signifier, a metaphor signifying its own non-being. Antagonism is then characterized by a struggle between two equally imaginary constructions – non-being and full identity – which are the mirror images of each other. They reciprocally condition one another and are each other's strategic target, whilst at the same time collapsing into one another. Both the imaginary and the real can be traced through their effects in forming and subverting identity. These two processes cannot be separated: the imaginary is an effect of the real whilst at the same time attempting to domesticate it in order to fully constitute identity. *That* which aspires to master social reality is then itself unmasterable, and is part of the reason for the lack of transparency in social relations, which is most explicit in antagonistic power struggles.

In antagonisms the negated subject positions resist or negate that which negated them. But since that which is negated is an imaginary full identity, and that which negates is nothing but a symbol of the negated position's non-being (that which blocks this full identity), it follows that both that which negates (power) and that which negates the negation (resistance) tend to be empty signifiers because they are overdetermined effects of one another. This does not mean that people have no idea what they are doing when they resist power. It is, in the first place, an argument against the illusion of a unified subject and an equally unified and rational resistance. The non-transparency of power struggles is an argument against the vision of, say, a social class coming to terms with itself – becoming a class 'for itself' in the Lukácsian sense – realizing its objective interests by ridding itself of false consciousness, and consequently achieving a transparent and unified class-consciousness. It is also an argument against Lukes's and Connolly's vision of agents coming to terms with their real interests by eliminating power.[51]

Power is, in both of these emancipatory visions, seen as an alien dead weight imposing itself upon the subject which, in its absence, would be identical with itself and hence capable of self-determination. As a result, theories of human emancipation inherit the humanist and liberal dilemma of an essential autonomy which, however, is itself split because autonomy, on the one hand, is the locus of power whilst power, on the other, encroaches upon autonomy. This fissure entails that autonomy is not only substance but also subject, and this means that 'essence can appear only in so far as it is already external to itself'.[52] As the name for the ability to make a difference, power is 'already external to itself', that is, it has already negated itself in order to be what it is. Seen in this light, power struggles revolve around the externalization of the essence of identity, which is the very condition for posing identity as internal to itself. Whereas liberalism stages the schism between power and autonomy (compare the distinction between state and civil society and the tripartition of power), advocates of human emancipation and organic views of community (Habermas and some strands of communitarianism) envision a depoliticized world of transparency and autonomy, whose consequence is not only the elimination of power but also of autonomy itself.

It has been argued that power as auto-negativity entails repressive as well as productive aspects *vis-à-vis* the recoiling processes of externalization and internalization, which is why identity embodies aspects of both subjection and subjectification. When the subject is entangled in a power struggle and externalizes the impossibility of being what it is, it is carrying out a repressive act which at the same time establishes its identity. It follows that the subject cannot but internalize what it externalizes when it pinpoints an adversary or an enemy, which is to say that resistance is not possible without internalizing *that* which has been repressed. The unbearable void of negativity must be externalized, but this void returns *to* the subject and *via* the subject where it is represented as an external blocking of the subject's identity.

The problem with emancipatory strategies is that Otherness, rather than being an externalization of an always already blocked identity which is internalized, is conceived as an externality which is internalized (see fig. 4.2. in which the effect of emancipation ((that $B = B$)) is transfigured as the very cause of the possibility for detecting and fighting domination, that is, the internalization of the external). As a consequence we are presented with ideas such as the internalization of repression, which is often associated with ideological power. This inversion leaves unexplained not only how the subject was capable of constructing itself *qua* itself, in its 'sameness', but also how something which is external becomes internalized. The only solution is to resort to postulates of ideological distortion, false consciousness, alienation, and the like. But the relation between the Same and the Other cannot be made evident because the former is a unified, constituent subject, whereas the latter is a thing-like dead weight impinging on the former. The question of autonomy is usually posed in these terms: it is encroached upon by power which, as an external force, both impinges upon the subject *and* maintains the idea of a self which no power is powerful enough to eliminate because autonomy is conceived as the source of power.[53] By showing the essentially split nature of autonomy and by seeing power as the ability to make a difference, or rather as the limit between 'ability' and 'making a difference' – that is, by conceiving power as the name of this split – a presuppositionless conception of power transcends the impasse of both emancipatory and liberal strategies.

To illustrate what is at stake here we can draw an analogy between the notion of anxiety in Freud's later works and the conception of power as auto-negativity. Anxiety arises, according to Staten, 'when the self is threatened with the loss of those objects into which it has extended itself'.[54] The subject *is* only to the extent that it has 'extended itself' into objects; which does not mean that the subject is merely the sum of these extensions or identifications. It is at once something more and something less. It is more because, no matter how many identifications we can come up with, the subject as such cannot be grasped; and it is less because the subject is the 'fissure at the very centre of the structure', or the 'pure distance' between hostile forces.[55]

The point of drawing an analogy between power and anxiety is that anxiety is not the fear of (losing) this or that object, but of losing *that* into which the subject has extended itself, that is, its contextual belonging which accounts for its meaningful insertion into various discursive settings. Because the itselfness of the subject is not given beyond subjectivations but is the articulation of these subjectivations, what the subject 'fears' in anxiety is the loss of itself, and hence its sense of belonging. The 'object' of anxiety is, accordingly, negativity, that is, ability as such before it is given a direction. Since fear is connected to objects, the anxiety of losing oneself is, by definition, non-objectifiable in that it cannot be attached to any particular object. Or to put it the other way around, in anxiety the subject objectivates itself by distancing it(s)self from that into which it formerly inserted itself. We have here the appearance of the object, the thing, within the subject which prevents it from ever being totally itself.

When the subject is thrown back upon itself in power struggles its itselfness as non-being is shown. By extending itself into objects – by constituting itself in these extensions – and thus constituting itself within rule-governed contexts and within wider horizons of signification, the self endeavours to overcome the void of anxiety. It does this by externalizing this void; and the form this takes in power struggles is that the void is given the name of the Other. However, since the subject cannot but internalize what it externalizes, the void in identity and signification is displaced and given a direction. Freud's remarks are instructive here: 'it was anxiety which produced repression and not . . . repression which produced anxiety.' And, he continues, '[i]t is always the ego's attitude of anxiety which is the primary thing and which sets repression going.'[56] This illustrates that power or ability as such is an unbearable void, which is why it always has to be given a direction.

In power struggles the ability to make a difference is caught up in the repressive act of eliminating the Other. Hence, instead of arguing that power as repression is interiorized, the impossibility of being 'totally myself' is externalized and embodied in the representation of the Other as the positivation of negativity.

The political dimension of social practices can be viewed in the light of the play of displacements that make up complex strategical situations. Making and implementing decisions as well as, say, initiating, following and changing rules, routines and the like, are all attempts to master what cannot, ultimately, be mastered by giving the ability to make a difference a direction. However, the unmasterable (the undecidable and the contingent) is, by its very nature, inherent in every attempt to control one's surroundings and hence in performative acts in general. Practices can then be seen as symptom formations in the Freudian sense, which take place in order to prevent anxiety.[57] Being can thus be seen as a symptom in that it is a flight from non-being which entails displacement. Hence the positivation of negativity expresses a 'distortion' or 'misrecognition' which is not only unavoidable but also the upshot of strategic calculation and behaviour. This is why power and resistance can never form a 'direct' relationship, but are instead overdetermined effects of each other.

The relation between negativity and identity is both necessary and contingent: it is necessary because power is constitutive for identity, whilst this necessity at the same time renders its full constitution impossible. The productive/repressive nature of power shows itself in the effectuation of limits, which simultaneously show the finitude of identity *and* the possibility of transcending this finitude. While power relations revolve around the posing and presupposing of limits, power struggles revolve around the naming of the Other who poses identity as presupposed through the recoiling processes of identification. It is only by being limited, by being prevented 'from being totally myself', that the subject can project itself beyond finitude into an imaginary unity not only with itself but with the political community of which it is a member, thereby shaping and representing itself as an agent capable of acting.

In a power struggle, the negated identity and the desired identity recoil into one another. The identity which is negated is not merely a given identity but one which transforms itself into an imaginary identity still-to-be: an identity which is a pole of identification and which proliferates the subject's horizon, its temporally given space of representation. When an identity is negated the horizon into which it has projected itself is shown. The reason is, of course, that identity and its horizon (part and whole) are structured by the logic of equivalence. Hence the negation of the former is bound to produce effects on the latter to a greater or lesser extent. In power struggles two horizons confront each other, each of which constructs the other as *that* which prevents them from realizing their own identity (the repressive dimension of power). In this situation the antagonistic parties are thrown into a game of signification released by a metonymic chaining which proliferates their horizon (the productive dimension of power). Negativity has in this way a 'revelatory' effect by showing what Heidegger terms the *authenticity* of being, or what Kierkegaard calls 'the reality of freedom as possibility for the possible', or 'the anxious possibility of *being able*'.[58] That is, the being of the subject is revealed in the impossibility of its being what it is, which is to say that being collapses into nothingness. This triggers the possibility of an ideological 'misrecognition': in externalizing the void, the Other is represented as *that* which embodies the impossibility of presence (that I can be totally myself, so to speak), whereupon that which is negated turns into a positivity still-to-be which is none the less blocked.

It is important not to get the notion of transcendence wrong here. It does not signify a mediation between two antagonistic forces.[59] Rather it describes the development from the negation of identity to its imaginary fulfilment, which is mediated by the collapse of the positivity of the Other. Transcendence is the transposition not only of *B*'s identity from $\not{B}$ to *B*, but also of *A* to *non-B* (the naming of the adversary). The ideological illusion consists of a misrecognition of this process: transcendence is seen as an 'internal' development in *B*: from $\not{B}$ to *B*, indicating a process of dis-alienation, the 'discovery' of having suffered from, say, false consciousness and subsequently a 'discovering' of one's true self or real interests. *A* is seen as an external factor meaning that *A* as *non-B* is not a necessary moment in *B*'s identity. The problem lies, of course, in not taking into account the 'fundamental reversal' in the construction of identity: that *B*, in a power struggle, can only posit its identity by antagonizing *A*, and that this externalization of the Other is internalized in *B* where it takes the form of the positing of its presuppositions.

In facing negativity the subject projects its disintegrated and opaque identity into a full identity which it cannot be. What antagonizes the subject is simply the Otherness of this identity (although it has conditioned it), which is to say that the Other, no less than the negated subject, can be a full presence.[60] As a symbol of its non-being, the Other is nothing but an imaginary projection of the subject's own imaginary being, that is, of the impossibility of bringing its identity to completion. But since Otherness has itself conditioned the image of a full identity, this image is, in fact, the negation of the finite and precarious identity of subjects. Otherness re-presents itself in a seductive and ideological disguise, as a continuation and fulfilment of the development of the subject's finitude into self-presence, as if the development from $\not{B}$ to *B* was not mediated through *A* as *non-B*. It seems likely that this ideological disguise – or this 'strategic essentialism' to use Spivak's formulation – is an unavoidable illusion pertaining to power struggles where each party positions itself *vis-à-vis* the Other.

It does not matter whether the parties in a power struggle are aware of this mechanism because, rather than depending upon their representation, it stages representation. Moreover, even though subjects are aware of the ideological illusion of positing a full identity, such a positing is, none the less, essential for political strategies whose hegemonic success depends upon their ability to become poles of identification. Thus we have a situation where, in Žižek's words, 'they know that, in their activity, they are following an illusion, but still, they are doing it'.[61] Political agents have to act *as if* the fulfilment of identity – say, the elimination of repression and the realization of autonomy – was possible. That is, they have to pose it as the 'possibility of the possible' in order to transcend limits. But rather than merely facing the 'anxious possibility of *being able*', which would inevitably paralyse political strategies, hegemonic projects have to construct a space of representation in which the imaginary constitution of identity can be staged as if negativity could thereby itself be negated. Representation as performance and semblance is thus bound up with what has been termed the recoiling movement of power struggles in which the agents become what they are.[62]

5

Identity and the Politics of Subjective and Real Interests

The word 'interest' stems from the Latin *inter* + *esse*, which means between being. The subject exists fundamentally as an *inter-esse*: as a being who is concerned with its own being, which is not a substance but rather a projection in time and space. The subject thus exists as 'interested'. This is a necessary feature of being a subject, but it does not, of course, say anything about which interests the subject might pursue. The notion of interest has two meanings which are important for the present discussion: (1) that the subject strives to satisfy its needs, aspirations, and the like, as it conceives them; and (2) that interests indicate those needs which the subject 'has' regardless of whether or not it is aware of them. On this account it would be a reductionist error to conflate interests with explicitly stated needs, wants or preferences as behaviourism does. But it would also be erroneous, and equally reductionist, to 'substantialize' some interests, that is, to transform their contingent status into a necessary or objective one by, for example, deducing interests from social position.

The nature of interests as *inter-esse* implies that it would be a mistake to operate with an appearance-essence dichotomy. That is to say, subjective interests cannot be treated as a transparent medium for an essentially given identity, just as objective interests cannot be a transparent representation of an essential self. With the collapse of the appearance-essence dichotomy the couplet of subjective and objective interests cannot be sustained. However, this does not solve the problem of how the two aspects of interests – those we pursue and those we 'have' – are articulated. The decisions and the courses of action we pursue will always be surrounded by a greater or lesser degree of uncertainty: whether what we do is the right thing to do, whether we could do better or have done better, whether we could have predicted the outcome of events better than we actually did, whether what we did or are going to do actually prevented/will prevent what we really wanted/want. It is this unavoidable uncertainty which gives the notion of real interests its force.

To evaluate what is in someone's real interest, as opposed to what is in someone's subjective interest, is basically to pass a judgement about what one 'really' wants, or what one really ought to do in order to be true to oneself, as opposed to what one actually wants or does. The adjective 'real' connotes a possible course of action and does not, accordingly, hinge upon an elusive 'objectivity'. It points to a counterfactual possibility compared to the action which is either already chosen or is going to be chosen. The adjective 'real' thus circumscribes the field of subjective interests, or to put it differently, it maps out the range of options, that is, of possible courses of action and hence the horizon within which we 'go on'. When seen from this angle, the 'real' of real interests does not unveil an essential interest proper to the individual by virtue of, say, its social position or its specific situation. It is rather the marker of a limit which not only confines identity but also defines it. The real as such a limit of identity is thus the marker of undecidability, that is, of the contingency of our decisions.

But to assert that things can always be different from what they are simply because we have given up hope of excavating an Archimedean point which could fix the values of all values says, in fact, very little. What it does say, however, is that we are forced to make decisions and to pass judgements, and by extension that we should do it in the most reasonable manner conceivable. What it does not say is that we ought to abandon the notion of real interests simply because the 'real' cannot ultimately be founded. The 'loss' of a transcendentalist language, or what Lefort has called the 'markers of certainty', does not alter the fact that we are forced to make decisions and that, in doing so, we want them, somehow, to reflect what we 'really' want or are. The 'real' is a metaphor for contrary-to-fact possibilities and hence the limit to what 'is', which ultimately refers to power as the ability to make a difference. The real as the temporal and spatial limit might lead us to reflect upon the 'real' as 'that' which confines and defines our identity, 'that' which is beyond our selves, but which at the same time we can only detect within ourselves. In order to pursue this enquiry we will have to reintroduce (on the background of the two preceding chapters) the issue of real interests as theorized by Connolly and Lukes.

The Great Gift of Real Interests

Everybody experiences now and again something they afterwards have second thoughts about, and even regret having involved themselves in. Such an experience can be more or less painful, but it might give way to reflections about whether regretting is meaningful, and what it actually involves. For example, it might prevent further events of that kind by making one more sensitive to what one really wants and doesn't want. It is the question of this 'really' which Connolly's discussion of real interests focuses on. His definition goes roughly like this: if I am going to choose between a range of alternatives, my real interest would be the option I would go for if we imagine that, in the moment of choosing, I had already experienced all the available options and then decided on this particular one. By thus assuming that I had experienced what I was in fact going to experience, I would be in a position to undertake an informed and hence balanced judgement. The argument runs the other way as well: I may have doubts whether a decision I once made was the right one and, in order to figure that out, I would have to go back to the moment of taking the decision, bringing with me not only the experience I already had but on top of that, the hypothetical experience of a whole range of alternatives. This would again put me in a position to make a reasoned evaluation of whether it was best to do what I did or if I should have done something else.

Time is essential in Connolly's definition of real interests, which involves both an *ex ante* and an *ex post* aspect. The latter is imposed on the former under the auspices of a hypothetically assumed omniscient knowledge, which guarantees the rationality of the decision maker, *in casu*, the autonomy of the subject. It could, of course, be argued that these two aspects cannot be separated because they entail each other in that the former, in order to count as an assessment of real interests, presupposes the latter. But things are not that easy. In thinking about a bad experience it would not be nonsensical, or at least not unusual, to state two conflicting views: that I shouldn't have done it *and* that I wouldn't be without it because it taught me what I really wanted! After all, one learns by mistakes.

This conflict seems, at first, to confirm that the *ex ante* and the *ex post* evaluations cannot, or rather, *must* not be in conflict with each other. The problem is, however, that although the two assessments are interwoven, they *must* nevertheless be distinguished in order to make sense of real interests. To make this difference, and to hold that it must be non-conflictual, can be considered as ethical and indeed political injunctions, which are constitutive for the subject by providing at least a minimal guarantee of temporal cohesiveness in its identity.[1] The constitutive nature of politics implies that the identity of the subject cannot be given by virtue of its social position, but is instead constructed in processes of identification; and that real interests emerge in these processes rather than being ingrained in structures. The paradox of the *ex ante* and *ex post* argument is that real interests are *found* by directing oneself towards what one is already, where the 'is' represents an absence, or rather, a becoming of identity.

While the experience taught me something which I today regard as valuable, it also taught me that I shouldn't do it again, and perhaps that I shouldn't have done it at all. Thus, it is not difficult to imagine that I regret what I did while at the same time feeling that I wouldn't be without the experience: I am what I am today partly due to this experience in whose light I view subsequent events as well as those preceding it. It is this paradox that the ethical/political injunction seeks to overcome. Connolly deals with this problem by evoking an imagined fullness of the subject, envisioned in the state of omniscience, which is then retroactively imposed on the subject before the event that triggered this whole process. The gap between the *ex ante* and the *ex post* is thus bridged and the unity of the subject restored.[2]

Both anticipation and evaluation employ a counterfactual kind of reasoning: what would have happened if what actually did happen had not happened, and would the alternative be preferable? They are separated by a temporal distance, which is what makes the representation of the contrary-to-fact argument possible in the first place. This is why the ethical/political 'must' cannot have a solid foundation: it is an incision into a flow of decision making, a limit which establishes a before and an after. This limit is crucial for talking about real interests: it makes it possible to cut off certain options by following certain rules of conduct. It is, as such, a political intervention which installs an authority capable of indicating a direction to be followed – the authority being in this case the subject itself, or so it would seem.

The subject in authority cannot be the empirical subject, but is rather a projection that transcends its contextuality by directing the subject towards itself as it is before subjectification, that is, before it gets caught up in power relations. The subject before subjectification is the empty locus of authority. In this attempt to represent itself, the subject distances itself from itself by dragging itself to the point which delimits its being for itself from its being in itself. The imposition of a distance makes room for what Lukes's critics term the outside observer's judgement, which is, eventually, the political authority capable of acting in the name of society. The subject recognizes itself *vis-à-vis* this distancing embodied in the representation of counterfactual arguments, whereby it objectivates itself in order to scrutinize what it really is *vis-à-vis* its societal context.

Frank Capra's film *It's a Wonderful Life* (1946) illustrates the counterfactual reasoning brought to bear in Connolly's real interest argument centred around autonomy, knowledge and time. The story takes off at around 9.45 pm. when God receives several prayers from various people wanting him to help George Bailey (James Stewart). Time is short because one hour later George will be considering committing suicide by jumping from a bridge due to the desperate financial problems facing his company. The angel Clarence Oddbody is assigned the difficult task of preventing this from happening, and he has just one hour to get acquainted with George's life before coming to his rescue. On the other hand, time is no problem in heaven because God, as the very incarnation of the suspension of time, has absolute knowledge of what has happened as well as what is going to happen. (We might say that Capra's God is omnipotent in epistemological matters only. Otherwise the testing of Clarence makes no sense.) Shortly after meeting George a rescue plan takes shape when George claims that he wishes he had never been born. The wish is heard, and from now on George will experience his home town as it would be like if he had never existed. 'You'll see a lot of strange things from now on', says Clarence. 'You have been given a great gift George, a chance to see what the world would be like without you.'

The name of the town is Pottersville – taken from the capitalist villain Potter who controls it – and no longer Bedford Hills; the town has completely changed now, possessing a great number of night clubs and seedy bars; instead of Bailey Park, financed by George's company 'Bailey's Building and Loan', there is just a cemetery; and people are living in nasty shacks paying extortionate rents. George's younger brother Harry has died in a drowning accident at the age of nine because George was not there to save him as he actually did; and the death of Harry meant that he could not himself save a vast number of people from drowning in an episode during the Second World War. George meets his old boss Mr Gower who once owned a drugstore where George worked when he was a kid, but who is now a beggar after having spent twenty years in jail for poisoning Mrs Blain's son, which is what would have happened if George had not, as he had, prevented Mr Gower's mistake. He meets Mary who, instead of being his beautiful wife, is a reserved old maid; and his uncle Billy has spent the end of his life in an insane asylum instead of being his business partner.

George was given the great gift of experiencing, in the moment of the suspension of time, a grim look at a possible world marked by his absence. In this state he once again finds himself on the bridge in deep despair, praying for things to be back to normal. His prayer is heard and the rescue operation has thus been successful. In a state of euphoria he returns to his family and friends, who, in return for all his good deeds, help him out of the financial crisis. George has in this 'enlightened' moment decided what he really wants. His want is *real* because, in this moment of omniscient knowledge and hence autonomy, he has faced the consequences of an impossible option, namely the wish that he had never been born, which in turn prevents him from committing suicide. He has made that decision, which expresses his real interest, by directing himself towards what he is already, where the 'is' is a representation of an absent possible world. Clarence did not exaggerate: George was indeed given a great gift allotted to very few people, presumably. Although Connolly is more modest by not presupposing divine interference, he does assume the possibility of an autonomous and knowledgeable subject who, by means of suspending time, is able to throw off the veil of power once in a while in order to reach its real interests.

Before embarking upon a more thoroughgoing discussion of the notion of real interests, it is necessary to outline what is at stake in discussing the issue. First, it is an integral part of politics, where hegemonic power strategies aim at authorizing themselves, thus establishing a 'translation' between the *is* and the *ought* in order to confer upon themselves the ability and the right to act on behalf of society. It is, secondly, crucial for understanding what is involved in self-reflection, and how autonomy is related to subordination and oppression. The notion of real interests is thus important in two respects: it is a constitutive feature of the politics of representing interests, and it is a critical principle embodying emancipatory potentials.

The issue of real interests can be broached by focusing on the adjective 'real'. What makes some interests more real than others, and what does the 'real' of real interests signify – a correspondence between actual interests and 'reality' not as it is perceived, but as it *could* be perceived if the subject had more knowledge about its situation? Real interests are attached to the subject transcending itself: they lie between subjective and objective interests, understood respectively as peoples' actual interests and the interests they would have if they perceived their situation 'as it is'. Real interests are thus defined in contradistinction to, or rather as a limit on, what is objectively given regardless of whether that is will or structure.

My aim is to address the question of how real interests present themselves. This question is inseparable not only from politics and authority but also from power and how power plays a decisive role in shaping identity. I take this question to be more fundamental than plunging into a discussion of whether the notion of real interests should be abandoned either because agents are, axiomatically, considered the best judges of their own interests (whereby any talk about real interests is out of the question since it inevitably conveys totalitarian connotations) or because the notion hinges upon another axiom, namely that of the objectivity of structures, which agents somehow misrepresent, but into which they are capable of gaining insight – thereby overcoming alienation, false consciousness, and the like. The two ways of criticizing real interests are not that different, but they are typically proposed by two opposed camps: liberalism, which personifies social relations in order to escape the 'necessary evils' of politics; and new tendencies within Marxism, which are paralysed by the obvious linkage to totalitarianism, although they try to blur this by eliminating the essentialism in Marxism. However, the problem of real interests is neither solved nor does it disappear by turning one's back on it. The reason is, as mentioned above, that the real of real interests is a metaphor for the possibility of the possible and hence a limit to what is.

The reason the problem does not disappear is that it is not bound to the totalitarian phantasies of universal emancipation alone. There is nothing inherently totalitarian about real interests, which are, rather, an inherent feature of politics: taking care of oneself, caring for others, and acting on behalf of others, all of which are bound up with representation and legitimation. The claim that the individual is the best judge of his or her own interests has a strong ideological slant to it. Liberal ideologists would be the first to make this claim, while their political colleagues would not hesitate to violate it in governmental action if it was 'necessary'! Accusations of hypocrisy would not be of much use here. Rather, the discrepancy points to an essential feature of politics: not only the right to speak in the name of society but the necessity to do it – a necessity to uphold the social order, no matter what the cost. This is the reason why politics primarily has to do with the power of authority, that is, the making and implementing of collectively binding decisions. The conflicts which might arise in relation to these decisions then become patched up by ideological strategies seeking recourse to postulates about the real interests of the subjects. Thus the real of real interests points toward the horizon within which events and particular interests can be constructed as meaningful, which is decisive for authorizing power strategies.

Lukes's and Connolly's Conceptualization of Real Interests

Are real interests an impostorous construction whose reality is a sham, a seductive veil masking the hypocrisy of power strategies projected by those who 'know better' and are able to force their version of reality upon others? Those who argue along these lines would hold that individuals, by definition, are the best judges of their own interests, and that the lack of objectivity regarding the standard against which real interests should be measured presents a danger of abuse. The problem with these objections is that they do not question whether individuals can mistake their own interests. By assuming that individuals cannot make such a mistake, or that politics should proceed on the assumption (regardless of whether it is false or correct) that people know what their interests are, one assumes that interests are reduced to explicitly stated preferences and that power is reduced to explicit interpersonal relations.[3] It would thus be senseless to claim that people could be subordinated without being aware of it and without taking that fact into consideration when formulating their interests. That it might be difficult to detect power relations cannot, says Lukes, be a licence to 'move from a methodological difficulty to a substantive assertion. It does not follow that, just because it is difficult . . . to show that power has been exercised in a given situation, we can conclude that it has not.'[4] Such a conclusion is just as objectionable as the opposite assumption that people suffer from false consciousness caused by the inherent mechanisms of capitalist relations of production. We are in both cases presented with an aprioristic type of argument which begs the question of repression.

Whereas the subjectivism of individualism takes the faculty of will and hence individual autonomy as given, the objectivism of Marxism assumes that reality, as an objectively given order of laws, determines identity. Both install a moment of necessity in social and political interaction which functions as an ultimate source or reference point. To advance beyond such aprioristic and reductionist explanations one would have to move away from necessity towards the contingency of a reality which is only accessible through interpretations. This means that every form of reasoning, real interests included, is susceptible to negotiation and re-evaluation. Connolly's and Lukes's approach to real interests has the advantage of not presupposing a given relation between power and identity. Hence neither will nor structure can be uncontested starting points, which is to say that they are contingent upon the structuring of power relations. Although Connolly in his later works has gone much further in this direction, his argument about real interests is important for elucidating the relation between power and identity. It is in the light of this that I aim to see to what extent it is feasible to claim that people can be repressed without being aware of it. The task is to explain how power produces these effects and how some interests come to be interpreted as misconceived and, in turn, replaced by others which are more in accord with what the subject 'really' wants.

Lukes defines power in terms of clashing interests: '*A* exercises power over *B* when *A* affects *B* in a manner contrary to *B*'s interests'.[5] The pivotal role assigned to interests in this definition of power can be seen as an attempt to transcend behaviourism, for which power is defined in terms of explicit policy preferences. This approach is too narrow since it cannot account for the existence of a systemic dimension in power relations ('the third face of power'). This dimension entails that interests take shape in a societal context whereby they cannot be reduced to individual preferences; and by extension, that individuals are enrolled in power relations without necessarily being aware of it. Thus it may not be evident for either parties that '*A* affects *B* in a manner contrary to *B*'s interests'.

Systemic power is, moreover, not only repressive but also productive inasmuch as it shapes the norms and preferences of agents, which means that they may not even be aware of what their interests are. The contextualization and subtlety of power relations problematize the relation between power, interests and identity by pointing to two schisms. There is a potential schism between the interests agents actually have and the interests they would have if they were not dominated by power; the difference being that between autonomy and subordination. There is also a schism between the repressive and the productive aspects of power, which is not simply a matter of 'power over' and 'power to' but the fact that identity is to some extent shaped in power relations. The borderline between autonomy and subordination is consequently blurred. In order to cope with these two problems, Lukes splits the notion of interest into subjective and real interests, where the latter differs from the former by expressing the interests agents would have if they went through a process of autonomization.

Lukes's purpose in introducing the notion of real interests is twofold. First, it enables him to incorporate Schattschneider's argument about the mobilization of bias[6] within his view of power as systemic bias by elaborating a counterfactual standard of autonomy. This equips him with a tool for arguing his case that power significantly affects people even in the absence of overt and covert conflicts. The point is that if power had not been exercised, agents would have acted differently, and it is this *would have* which is at the root of the counterfactual standard. Second, it is an emancipatory attempt at re-creating individual rationality, which goes hand in hand with being autonomous. By making agents aware of the disguised mechanisms of power, Lukes foresees the merging of subjective and real interests through, for example, democratic participation. Thus real interests cannot be superimposed upon agents because there is no objective position from which this could be done. They express instead 'hypothetical subjective preferences under conditions of relative autonomy'.[7]

There is an affinity between Lukes's view of real interests and Habermas's idea of emancipatory interests. Both argue that real interests are to be determined by the agents themselves by proposing contrary-to-fact situations of rational persuasion or a dialogue between equals. This is made viable because there is no unbridgeable gap between the actual/subjective and the ideal/real. The latter exists latently in the former as its limit, which is the possibility *par excellence* for detecting therein traces of domination.[8] The hypothetical preferences made in a 'non-distorted communication' in which the autonomy of each participant is respected have, in order to be connected with the actual situation, to be 'relevant'. If this criterion can be met, Lukes has an argument against those who hold that his power theory cannot be assessed empirically, and that his conception of real interests expresses an 'observer's assessment' which is independent of the actual formation of interests. However, the problem remains of determining *when* the relevant counterfactual condition of autonomy is in place.[9]

Connolly suggests the following definition of real interests, which is shared by Lukes: 'Policy *x* is more in *A*'s real interest than policy *y* if *A*, were he to experience the results of both *x* and *y*, would choose *x* as the result he would rather have for himself.'[10] This statement raises two problems. First, to what extent is it feasible to claim that an agent is able to make a choice reflecting its real interests when the fact is that the agent, at the time of choosing, does not have any experience with the outcome of the decision? Second, we have to make a retrospective judgement as to whether a decision once made expressed an agent's real interests.

The first problem deals with the question of transparency. When Connolly says that 'were he to experience the results of both *x* and *y*' in the moment he was going to make the decision – if he knew the consequences of both decisions and then chose *x* – it would, seemingly, make sense to claim that this decision expressed his real interests, except that it would, in fact, render decision making meaningless![11] The problem is that power cannot but be involved in setting the choice between *x* and *y* , due to the contextualization of power, whereby there is no guarantee that *x* expresses the real interests of *A*. More importantly, there is no guarantee either that *A* even approaches his real interests by choosing *x* instead of *y* since it cannot be made evident that a dynamic is initiated which leads to the elimination of power. Although *x* represents what *A* 'would rather have for himself', *A* may not be 'himself', so to speak, because power has influenced *A*'s norms, habits, interests, and so forth.

The relation between power and identity is crucial here: *A is A* because of power; yet, for the same reason, *A is not A*! We are caught up in the paradox that by structuring the available options power becomes unavoidably embodied in real interests. Power is, consequently, not just an obstacle preventing the realization of real interests; it is also their indispensable condition of existence. This in turn means that power and autonomy cannot – not even within Connolly's and Lukes's own argument – be strictly separated. The relation between them is undecidable: power is externalized in order to achieve autonomy, yet in this process of externalization it cannot but be internalized in what is going to count as autonomy. The notion of real interests presupposes that power shapes identity *and* that it can be eliminated in order to achieve a truer identity. Power and autonomy are thus imbricated in each other whilst also repelling each other; or to put it differently, power forms both an internal and an external relation to the subject. This paradox is, in fact, a rather productive one because Connolly and Lukes, albeit implicitly, draw attention to the undecidability of power: that it is the temporal and spatial limit of identity, which at one and the same time defines and confines it by posing a 'here' and a 'beyond', and a 'before' and an 'after'.

The second problem concerns the retrospective judgement as to whether the decision an agent once made was in its real interests, or whether it would have been better to have chosen another option. Following Connolly, this is the choice between *x* and *y*. But this time the agent has already chosen and experienced *x*, and thus the choice is asymmetrical. The difference between the past choice and the present evaluation or interpretation of that choice (which is, of course, also a choice) lies in the agent's intermediate experience with at least one option, namely that of *x*. 'He' who has experienced *x* and 'he' who has yet to experience the results of *x* or *y* cannot be identical. To maintain the opposite would entail that agents could dispense with the intermediate experiences and the interpretations of them in order to reach an unprejudiced decision. But this is untenable since it would mean, basically, that experiences and interpretations did not influence agents, in which case, agency would have to be defined apart from social practices. This would be the idea of the constitutive subject which, on the one hand, is cast in doubt by Lukes and Connolly themselves due to their insistence that power partakes in the shaping of identity, whilst, on the other, it figures as the regulative idea of autonomy and rationality.

Connolly's definition of real interests hinges, none the less, on the assertion that 'he' who is going to choose (the *ex ante*) and 'he' who has experienced the consequences of the choice (the *ex post*) are essentially the same. To sustain this argument, the subject has to be conceived as possessing an essential identity which is present before power encroaches upon it and reduces it to a latent possibility; this requires careful interpretation to excavate. Because interpretations are *in* time, and because power among other things is the limit between *before* and *after*, the recourse to an essential identity would have to presuppose the collapse of time: letting the self return to itself in a recognition of that self presupposes that

that which poses the self as other than itself (power) is exteriorized. This assertion clashes with the argument that power constitutes identity, which is an argument that the subject *qua* subject is always already non-identical with itself. An inescapable void separates the *in itself* and the *for itself* of the subject – a void which cannot be filled by representation but is the condition for representing the subject in the first place, just as it is the condition for the subject's ability to recognize itself. It is this void which has been named auto-negativity.

The self's recognition of it(s)self is touched upon by Swanton, who is concerned with understanding the 'conditions which need to be satisfied in order for preferences expressed *after* experience of alternatives, to be privileged in an assessment of interests'.[12] This is the problem of stating *relevant* counterfactual situations, which concerns the tricky issue of identity and difference. She lists three conditions which deal with the question of identity and difference: (1) that the identity of an agent before the experience should be 'sufficiently integrated' with its identity after the experience; (2) that the agent must have a clear recollection of the past, which ought not to be 'distorted and coloured by the new perspective on life' acquired after the experience; and (3) that the evaluation of past and present situations 'must be made in a spirit of rational detachment'.[13] If these conditions – integration, memory and rationality – do not prevail the agent will not be able to make an adequate assessment of its real interests. That is, it will inevitably misrecognize what these 'really' are.

The question of the relevance of a particular counterfactual situation is inseparable from identity/difference and distance. Relevance indicates, on the one hand, a situation of autonomy where subjective interests coincide with real interests. This implies distance since it is, by definition, a situation which differs from the actual one. Yet on the other hand, if the counterfactual situation is too detached from the situation in which agents are actually choosing, it may not be relevant at all because it forms an entirely new and different situation. Hence the problem is not just to lay down the criteria of relevance and the extent to which they can be achieved, but also whether the relevant counterfactual situation can be relevant at all. This problem is raised by Connolly himself when he considers the paradox that the 'very process of preparing oneself to make the most reflective choice about one's interests affects the evidential status of the choice itself.'[14] Here the implicit stress on time undermines the assumption of an essential link between self-reflection and real interests. Connolly does not deny this: he sets it aside as 'certain elements of conjecture and speculation', whilst pleading for political toleration of 'those who, even after consulting our arguments and evidence, understand their own interests differently than we do'.[15]

Although toleration does not solve the problem, it is not an empty gesture because it is founded on 'reflective choice about one's interests' as an act of interpretation, which shows that the very process of getting to know oneself changes one(s)self. This change, or rather becoming, is our essential mode of being, and the term 'oneself' cannot but be the metaphorical effect covering the lack of an essential self, a lack which is inverted and assumes a positive existence by being represented as one's real interest. Thus real interests represent a becoming of identity, the limit between what one was and what one has become. We are hereby brought back to the relation between power and identity: the externalization of a power that is considered repressive, and the internalization of a power that is seen as rendering us capable of deciding ourselves. Recognition and misrecognition – returning to or going astray – should be seen in connection with the intricate relation between power and the subject which constructs identity in a recoiling movement of externalizing and internalizing power.

Recognition entails both identity and difference: the subject seems only to be able to recognize itself if its 'self' remains identical over time, that is, if it identifies itself with the metaphorical effect of the self. Yet recognition also entails distance, but a peculiar type of distance: one which overcomes itself because it undergoes increasing transparency: knowledge, rationality, autonomy and, in turn, emancipation. But these notions are nothing but metaphors for the circular nature of self-introspection: that the self represents itself or makes itself present again by posing its self as presupposed. The *raison d'être* of the performance of this positing lies in its semblance: that it poses the self *as if* it was presupposed. The essential self is thus an effect rather than an origin, but it is an effect which represents itself as an origin: as an object which can be excavated and, more importantly, as 'something' which we have to presuppose when we claim to act in an ethically correct manner. That is, we have to treat it as an end in itself and not as a means, meaning that we act as if it is the origin *par excellence* and not an effect of something more original. This circularity is visible in Connolly's and Lukes's treatment of autonomy, which sometimes plays the role of the regulative idea of the subject before subjectivation, whilst at other times it is more like a residual, which crops up when power retreats. Autonomy is both an origin and a residual which is envisioned in counterfactual reasoning where the latter (re)presents itself as the former.

How Do Real Interests (Re)present Themselves?

To advance an understanding of the relation between power and real interests that is capable of dealing with the paradox that power is imbricated in real interests *and* exteriorized from them requires a clarification of the relation between power and the structuring of identity and interests. Interests are established in power relations: a variety of elements are hegemonized into a particular configuration which constitutes the interest (temporally and spatially), and whose cohesiveness depends upon its capability of maintaining frontiers against its surroundings. Thus an interest takes form by delimiting itself from other interests, whereby *that* which is externalized cannot be absent but is included as traces in the identity of the interest. An interest is, accordingly, never identical with itself but exists in alienation from itself, just as the subject who is inscribed in strategies of interests, and takes an interest or is concerned, is never transparent. This means that interests have a blind spot which constitutes them while also escaping them. The *real* of real interests could be seen as this limit, at once here and beyond, which cannot be grasped since it is neither excluded nor included but exists as mere possibility. The real is thus coterminous with power as such: it is the nodal point of recurrence in every interest which signals the subject's attempt to become what it is.

The argument advanced here is that real interests are constructed in a recoiling movement out of power as pure possibility, which is to say that, in discussing real interests, we are engaged in a discussion about the very meaning of the ability to make a difference. Pure possibility is not the product of the articulation of power strategies, but neither is it simply given; it is, instead, at one and the same time both posed and presupposed; or it is constructed as a discovery of what was hitherto hidden. Real interests are, as such, 're-activations' of what was excluded; they mark a return of what was alienated. We have here 'an eternal recurrence of the same', that is, of ability as such, which, however, cannot but appear as yet another new metaphor. That is, we never reach the bottom line, ability 'as it is', because it is always already presupposed. What we do encounter when reflecting upon limits is their transgression, which opens up new possibilities and presents new stumbling blocks.

This moment of re-activation and de-alienation brought about in self-reflection, where the self returns to itself, cannot escape the circular movement of internalization and externalization which fosters alienation in the first place, whereby the re-*present*ation of the absent (the de-alienation or the bringing-into-the-present of the alienated) is in a sense a double alienation.[16] However, this double alienation or double negation (the exclusion of what was excluded) presents itself in the seductive guise of the return of the self, via itself as a knowledgeable agent, to itself. This would be the meaning of the rationalist idea of self-reflection as the imposition of a distance which overcomes itself. It is rationalistic inasmuch as it assumes that rationality is dichotomized from power, and that autonomy is 'acting according to a law discovered in an immutable Reason and given once and for all.'[17] This is the only way of making sure that the self actually returns to itself when engaging in self-reflection.

As a calling-forth of pure possibility, real interests are at once already there and yet to come: they are a construction of something new, yet a discovery of what is given. Real interests present themselves through this clash between future and past, which is the moment of interpretation and understanding. They can be seen in terms of an encounter with the reality into which the subject is inserted and finds itself. This encounter is not a confrontation with a given world whose externality is opposed to an essential self-determination. Encountering reality is rather an opening or a clearing, which is 'nothing but a direction forever to be determined'.[18] Reality thus conceived is the limit of experience: what the subject is and what it projects itself into, that is, what it is not yet. In the encounter with reality the subject is propelled towards a horizon of signification and into itself in a recoiling movement as *that* which was already *there*. It is in these processes of interpretation and identification that the subject becomes what it is. The *itselfness* of the subject is thus a becoming, whose direction is posed *as* presupposed.

Identity is becoming in processes of identification, which implies that the subject exists as a projection *in time* (between future and past), whereby its identity cannot only not be fixed; it is, more importantly, always already ahead of itself. As Heidegger argues:

> '*Dasein* ['being-there'] is never more than it factically is, for to its facticity its potentiality-for-Being belongs essentially. Yet as Being-possible, moreover, *Dasein* is never anything less; that is to say, it *is* existentially that which, in its potentiality-for-Being, it is *not yet*. Only because the Being

> of the 'there' receives its Constitution through understanding and through the character of understanding as projection, only because it *is* what it becomes (or alternatively, does not become), can it say to itself 'Become what you are', and say this with understanding.[19]

I have argued that Lukes's and Connolly's conception of real interests gets off the ground by collapsing time, which is the only way the self can be identical with itself. Real interests can only be discovered by forgetting one's projection into future and past, and thereby one is never present for oneself. Instead of seeing anamnesis as an ideological illusion, it would be more appropriate to conceive it as an essential structure of identity in which power is immanent. It is important to look at the problem of forgetting in order to understand the relation between power, identity and real interests. This is where Nietzsche's notion of the eternal return of the same becomes important. Real interests, as the interpretation of what one *really* is, are a positivation of the transgression of limits which confront the subject with new possibilities and which, in turn, structure power as such. They signal an encounter with what had hitherto been excluded, an outside, which is at once repressed *and* constitutive for an agent's identity. By encountering limits the subject is thrown into a game of signification that shakes its identity, which is why power is the limit that defines and confines identity.

The eternal return does not collapse time because it marks the structuring of time itself and hence of identity. The return teaches me that I was other that I am now: 'The revelation of the Eternal Return necessarily brings on the successive realizations of all possible identities.'[20] The revelation that I am capable of becoming innumerable others and that in the moment of this revelation I am the other of myself, will be forgotten, that is, repressed,[21] since it is the impossibility of identity which nevertheless constitutes it in the first place. This impossibility is auto-negativity, which prevents me from ever being identical with myself: in returning to oneself in self-reflection the I goes unavoidably astray because its itselfness cannot but be a positivation of negativity, that is, a metaphorical effect transvalued as a cause by the 'complex strategical situation'. In other words, in *re*cognizing and *re*turning to itself the subject always finds itself 'being-there', whereby it externalizes the anxiety that its 'itselfness' cannot be predicated since it is the void in symbolization. Hence identity establishes itself by forgetting and repressing other actually existing and/or potential identities, which is why power is constitutive for identity through identifications.[22]

The Relation between Real Interests and Power

We have seen that power as pure or limitless possibility entails its own negation: in giving shape to the possible we cannot but negate limitless possibility, which is why power is looked at in terms of auto-negativity – 'that' which is always already the negation of itself. It has a virtual existence only as a trace of undecidability which is located in the dislocated and recoiling structure in the order of things, which in turn accounts for the contingency of social relations.

Power is not repressive when seen as limitless possibility; but power relations have, by virtue of posing and presupposing limits, a repressive dimension, which simply means that something is included while something else is excluded. This means that in relation to identity, the recoiling structure of power shapes pure possibility as 'that' which was already 'there', which is posed as presupposed by 'the direction which is forever to be determined'. To determine the direction entails a moment of repression because the subject preferring x to y is not autonomous in the sense that it is externally related to the choice. It is, instead, constituted by this decision and the decisions preceding it, as well as those following it; which is to say that it is inserted, although never completely, in institutional settings with their specific structures. Pure possibility is, analytically speaking, prior to whatever form and content these decisions take, and hence prior to the repressive dimensions of power.

Power as such cannot be encountered. What the subject encounters in power relations (regardless of whether these are differential or antagonistic) are limits which confine and define its identity and role, and hence its ability to make a difference *vis-à-vis* institutional rules and routines. Power as such is disclosed in the openings and blockages of possibilities which, to a greater or lesser extent, reshuffle identity. By virtue of including/excluding practices, power relations constitute identity in terms of what is possible, appropriate or reasonable and what is not. In the moment of the disclosure of power as such some options, practices and identities which were hitherto excluded, find their way back into the 'realm of the possible'. This moment shows to a greater or lesser extent what Kierkegaard terms 'the anxious possibility of *being able*'.[23]

This moment of 'being able' revolves around the 'eternal return of the same' to which the subject diverts itself in order to 'become what it is', the point of presence which resists symbolization,[24] and which exposes the subject to possibilities. The point is, as Žižek puts it, 'that the Being in itself, when we try to grasp it "as it is", in its pure abstraction and indetermination, without further specification, reveals itself to be Nothingness.'[25] Ability as such and nothingness thus collapse into one another, and it is this nothingness within ability (auto-negativity) that triggers processes of identification as an escape from negativity. It is this ongoing displacement of negativity which forms the trace structure of power, which in turn is immanent in structures as dislocated.

The ways in which the subject projects itself into possibilities might be to call into presence previous acts of inclusion/exclusion where possible courses of action were negated. Here we enter the slippery terrain of what the possible courses of action in a given situation were. The reconstruction of previous complex strategical situations is, needless to say, interpreted in the light of the present situation. What counts for possible courses of action cannot be all those which were logically conceivable at the time, since that would extend the field of possibilities to the point where contrary-to-fact reasoning would be meaningless because it would violate the situatedness of identity, options, decisions, and the like. Hence the interpretation of what one's real interests were cannot proceed along these lines. But it would also be inadequate to restrict the possible courses of action to those which agents actually attempted to pursue albeit without success.[26] The reason is that agents may hesitate to voice issues which could be seen as somehow challenging the establishment (nondecisions), or not voice those that agents were not even aware of as alternatives (no-decisions).

Although it might be difficult to trace exercises of power, the calling into presence of the repression of previous possibilities is more than an exercise of remembrance. It is a representation of a chain of events – or it is a chaining of events – from the point of view of the subject trying to come to terms with itself. Whether a possible course of action was negated and whether this action was possible at all are, in fact, secondary for the constructing of real interests. The reason is that the *real* of real interests, as a projection of power, cannot have an objective reference point. The condition of existence for real interests is that reality establishes itself in a distortion of what it *really* is because it is always a displacement, externalization and repression of the moment of negativity.

The recoiling movement of power – that I constitute myself in the encounter of I as other than myself – cannot be transparent in the sense of being fully rational because 'it is inscribed in the very essence of the circular movement that the movement itself be forgotten.'[27] This circular structure of power is forgotten, and so are the alternative options which were, or might once have been, available. This means that reality, from being the limit showing the contingency of identity, inverts into something that is external to the subject that seemingly possesses an objectivity of its own which is 'there to be discovered'.[28] It is this 'discovery' that is labelled transparency: the return of the self to itself, which is, however, nothing but an inversion of negativity (a fundamental reversal) that is named autonomy, and whose vehicle is real interests. Real interests are those interpretations the subject holds in the encounter between itself and reality. Since it cannot hold on to anything in this encounter, real interests cannot but be a retroactive construction of reality 'as it is'.

The *real* of real interests is the trace of a rupture which cannot be endowed with an original meaning because this occurs as a subsequent rationalization that entails displacement. Far from invalidating all talk about real interests, the retroactive and imaginary construction of reality *as it is* is the very possibility of putting the notion of real interests to work. It is this constructed nature of reality which gives real interests their hidden and profound status as a privileged means to the truth of the self. The *real* of real interests remains blurred since it is conceived in the exercise of power, which effectuates the limits between the inclusion and exclusion of issues, agents, possibilities, and so on, and is a projection of this event. This event is characterized by a lack of transparency *vis-à-vis* whomever or whatever negated identity, that which has in fact been negated, and that which the negation of the negation actually negates. These issues are all open to interpretation, or rather, they spark off interpretation, and can, accordingly, only be settled through power struggles. It is through interpretation and struggle that the subject comes to terms with what it is, a process which at the same time conceals a change in its identity: the becoming of identity.

It is in the processes of interpretation that the subject poses not only itself but also reality as presupposed, which conceals the fact that the subject is a becoming or an event, in the Foucauldian sense of those terms, whose counterpart is reality as 'externally' given. The subject is the pure distance or non-place between various forces, the limit which is always already transgressed and which recoils into the opposite of itself.[29] Identity is thus in itself non-substantial, but in its endeavour to position itself the subject substantializes itself: it turns itself into an object, and between this object (the transparent subject) and the (empirical) subject there is an infinite distance which induces the imaginary constitution of the subject through interpretation. The *real* of real interests is the positing and overcoming of this distance, which is why it is intangible.

Power is immanent in action because action entails making a difference but how power is exercised is inseparable from how agents construct it. If construction meant recognition, power would depend upon, or be derived from, the subject's identity or awareness, whereupon it would be impossible to avoid the conclusion that one would not be repressed until one recognized it. For instance, if sanctions are imposed on somebody who violates a rule, that person may see that action as a repressive exercise of power whereas somebody else might not. A vicious circle would inevitably arise: has power only been wielded over those who actually perceive the situation as a blocking of their identity and react against it? And contrariwise, is power not wielded over the submissive person who accepts the situation? If such was the case, the conclusion would be that the less people are inclined to enter into a conflict, the less power has been exercised over them! That inactivity could be an outcome of power being exercised over one would thereby be unthinkable. Needless to say, such an argument glosses over the possibility that domination reduces the likelihood that people will put up resistance in the first place.[30] The point is not really whether power has been exercised, but *how* it is exercised and *how* it is received, both of which are matters of interpretation.

It is, in this context, important to stress that recognition cannot be a rational recollection of what 'really' happened, just as construction cannot be a performance guided by the subject's will. Power does not, as Foucault says, depend on the subject's own representations.[31] Identification is bound up with power, and the subject finds itself by tracing power through externalization/internalization, which in turn implies *re-cognition*. Cognition is itself caught up in power, and consequently there is no neutral or objective taxonomy which can account for the constitution of identity through limitations as well as whether an action negates identity. Limits and negations can only be detected through an analysis of how agents retroactively construct this action. The absence of conflict and resistance against the action cannot rule out the possibility that identity is negated. If it could, we would be back in the vicious circle where power would depend upon recognition instead of being immanent in it. Hence there is no logical link between awareness/unawareness and exercising power or being the recipient of the exercise of power.

Although power relations entail a moment of repression (located in inclusion/exclusion), they do not necessarily involve conflict and resistance. This is especially the case in so far as exercises of power do not violate the rules and routines of differential systems. But when these rules and routines are threatened, power relations are likely to spark off conflicts and resistance one way or another. Resistance might take the most diversified forms ranging from introjection to projection: from, say, depression to militancy. The exercise of power triggers effects, but there is no guarantee that these take the form of a 'direct' resistance against this exercise of power. Power struggles cannot ever be direct because they are overdetermined by the field of signification into which the subject is inserted and finds itself, which is to say that they always involve moments of displacement and condensation. By seeing an action as a repressive exercise of power, the subject externalizes what it construes as a blocking of its identity; that is, it projects the impossibility of being what it is, whereby it engages in a repressive act of resistance.[32] This is the meaning of power as limit: its productive/repressive nature where identity is established in confrontation with otherness, which is both externalized and internalized. Submissiveness might then be a displaced form of resistance, which, however, presupposes that this construction of identity can be traced back to a prior blocking of identity. If an adversary cannot be named in a power struggle, agents are left in a traumatic void which prevents them from performing the role of *political* agents.

Resistance cannot be distinguished from power since it negates what power negates. Resistance *is* power in that it is a negation of a negation. And for their part, power relations which negate identity will always be a double negation because by negating identity they negate what made this identity possible, namely the negation of its opposite. Ideology is immanent in this double negation because the 'second' negation retroactively calls forth the 'first' one: it is because the subject cannot be what it is that it resists power, a resistance which creates what it is.[33] Resistance is, accordingly, caught up in the circular structure of power, which is bound up with ideology because resistance, in order to be a strategy which is capable of functioning as a pole of identification, has to posit its identity as if it predated its adversary. Hence, to ask if the identity of the subject was *in fact* negated is to pose the wrong question because it presupposes an objectivity which was never 'there' in the first place.

Real interests are thus linked to power/resistance. It is this link that Foucault may have had in mind when saying that resistance is a showing of unactualized possibilities and hence a showing of the contingency of 'that which is'. It is because resistance is overdetermined by the discursive field that it discloses new directions. This is also clear from the way Connolly and Lukes argue their case for real interests through counterfactual reasoning, which points to the contestable nature of what was otherwise taken for granted, and which, moreover, entails the duality of representation, performance and semblance: the *creation* of the self as it *really* is. It follows that real interests cannot, *pace* the assertion of Connolly and Lukes, rely upon the regulative idea of the transparency of consciousness and the elimination of power. On the contrary, real interests cannot dispense with their condition of existence, that is, power. They show the fissures in social relations and serve as strategic guidelines for patching up an identity that is always precarious.

Concluding Remarks: Real Interests and Autonomy

I have argued that power as limit shapes identity through exclusion and inclusion; that this posits self-reflection as the recoiling movement of the return of the self to itself as other than itself; and that the construction of real interests emanates in power struggles, where the negation of identity throws the subject into a game of signification which triggers an unpredictable process of identification. The notion of real interests is, for these three reasons, a crucial feature of political life. The reasons are, first, that politics is an activity of governing oneself and others *vis-à-vis* societal contexts, which among other things involves the representation of interests; and second, that these contexts are liable to undergo changes which call for negotiation, interpretation and struggle. In conclusion I would like to offer some brief comments on how the politics of real-interest arguments are related to autonomy.

When *A* has to choose between *x* and *y* and chooses *x* 'as the result he would rather have for himself', the choice of *x* is marked not only by the excluded *y*, but also by the context which singled out *x* and *y* as available or appropriate options in the first place. This means that the 'he', for whom *x* and *y* were possible options, has excluded 'something' in 'himself' (namely 'that' which was expressed in *y*) which precludes that 'he' is ever entirely 'himself'. The reason is that the excluded *y* is included as an absence of *x*, that is, as the limit in *A*'s identity. Since *A*'s identity is always already limited, it is essentially open to rearticulation in various contexts. Contexts as complex strategical situations structured by the logics of difference and equivalence overdetermine policy options and patterns of identity. Two extremes might be cited here: options and identities are structured in terms of either differential relations or antagonistic relations.

Power is immanent in both types of relations. Thus power is exercised when, for instance, *A* and *B* face an alternative in which they prefer *x* and *y* respectively, and *A* succeeds in persuading *B* to go for *x* as well. Instead of trying to figure out whether persuasion is 'rational' or 'manipulatory' – that is, whether *B*'s compliance with *A* is autonomous or coerced – it is more relevant to distinguish whether the choice of *x* lies within or outside the range of acceptable options for *B*. If the former is the case, the decision is not antagonistic. Even *B*'s subordination to *A* cannot in itself count as an antagonistic relation in so far as *B*'s identity is constituted *vis-à-vis A* in a system of difference. It is only if the limits of acceptability are crossed that the decision might give way to an antagonism which is, accordingly, marked by the disintegration of differential relations.[34]

The choice of *x*, although it is within the range of acceptable options viewed in relation to the structure of *B*'s identity, may link up with other aspects of *A*'s ability to persuade and subordinate *B*, in which case *B* might construct these in a chain of equivalence confronting *A*. As a consequence, the choice of *x* may be conceived as antithetic to *y*, whereupon the former nonconflictual relation between *A* and *B* turns into an antagonistic one in which *A* wields power over *B*. Subordination has thus been transformed into a site of oppression. This metonymic chaining of events can account for the way seemingly insignificant issues can turn into pivotal ones when seen in broader contexts.[35]

The subject can get a glimpse of its real interests by tracing the ruptural moments where it is confronted with alternatives and where it has to make a decision which is, ultimately, undecidable. Since power exhibits a dimension of repression – the forgetful moment of externalization which is constitutive for identification – there is always going to be a schism between subjective and real interests because the former never completely manages to grasp the latter. Real interests exist latently in subjective interests, not as a presupposition about an ideal speech situation but as 'the anxious possibility of *being able*': as the limit of identity which shows the subversive and intriguing possibility of doing otherwise, and which renders identity contingent upon the *not yet*, the *yet to* become, and 'that' which was already 'there'. The detection of real interests is only feasible if this 'exterior' cannot be held at bay by forgetfulness or repression, but clashes with an existing structure of identity and hence with the existing structuring of practices and identities.

The subject is forced to be free, to enforce limits by projecting itself into the possible. This force – this peculiar necessity of subverting necessity – is a freedom without foundation. It is more basic than the liberal differentiation between 'positive' and 'negative' freedom which presupposes an already constituted subject. Hence this freedom can be characterized as an ontological potential that cannot ever be entirely domesticated by identifications, which is why structures are dislocated. Autonomy is not a specific state of affairs in which power has been eliminated. It is, instead, a challenge and a ruptural moment where the daily routines and structures of signification to a greater or lesser extent break up and are replaced by partially new ones. Autonomy is in this sense coterminous with power as pure possibility, which is the ontological potential for *making a difference*. The challenge of autonomy is not to choose between this or that but to direct oneself towards the moment of negativity, thus giving it a direction (auto-negativity). In doing so the subject is thrown into a game of signification where every grounding becomes uncertain and fades away. In securing a foothold, by making a decision, it slips once again into its daily routines where it finds itself 'as it is'.[36] This decision is a vehicle of the fundamental reversal where negativity assumes a positive existence whose form can be either specific institutional settings (a differential relation) or the naming of an adversary (an antagonistic relation) as if this 'Other' was simply an external determination blocking identity.

It can be said, then, that real interests indicate disclosure and undecidability, which are preconditions for autonomy. In directing oneself towards one's real interests and hence towards autonomy, one neither peels off layers of external determinations (which roughly corresponds to Connolly's and Lukes's project) nor plunges into a vacuous space of indeterminacy. Both options convey an essentialist idea of self-determination. When the *self* of self-determination and the *real* of real interests are themselves split, autonomy is always beyond itself, and in this sense it connotes transgression. This is why it embodies a critical potential which can be put to work in contrary-to-fact arguments.

It should be clear that, while Lukes and Connolly want to fix the meaning of autonomy by equating it with the elimination of power thus essentializing the contrary-to-fact conditional in terms of the constitutive subject, a Foucault-inspired vision of autonomy holds the place of the subject open by locating autonomy in power-resistance relations. Here autonomy is conceived as a challenge conditioned by the contingency of identity, which is to say that the contrary-to-fact conditional – the possibility of doing otherwise – cannot be essentialized but rather remains open. Autonomy is thereby a practice and a strategic calculation at the limits between the included and the excluded, which is why it cannot ever be controlled or simply guaranteed constitutionally by political institutions. The reason is that it is impossible to foreclose one's ontological potential.

This view of real interests is analytically sustainable because the suppression of alternative options does not imply their absence but instead their inclusion as lacks, which can be traced in power struggles, that is, in the clashes and displacements of power and resistance. The possibility of doing otherwise is thus causally effective in the sense that it has consequences for the actions or inactions of agents. The example given above, of how two people react towards authoritative sanctions imposed for violating rules, can be seen in this light. Their reactions present two directions where they exclude/include different options open to them. The one who apparently internalizes repression excludes the alternative of putting up resistance against those who impose the sanctions. Whether this exclusion is displaced and thus finds its way into other contexts where s/he exercises power depends upon how s/he has constructed his or her identity in this particular context. Inactivity cannot in itself be taken as a proof that oppressive power relations are either absent or internalized ('rational compliance' or 'false consciousness').

If it cannot be made evident that identity has been negated, there is no way of asserting that power has been exercised. But in so far as traces of resistance can be detected and somehow linked through metonymic chains to the sanctions, the claim is that this person has real interest in locating the traces of power/resistance relations, thereby directing him or herself towards the possibility of autonomy. By engaging oneself in such an undertaking, one is involved in an autonomization process by being confronted with the contingency of 'reality'. It should be kept in mind that the problem of what 'somehow linked' means cannot be a matter of detecting what 'objectively' happened by mapping out causal sequences, since objectivity (denotation) cannot but be 'the *last* of connotations' (Barthes) performed in the retroactive judgement where the subject interprets what it *is* or what *really* happened.

The problem is not so much how a particular action can be interpreted as an exercise of power, but rather how power relations are constructed as a resistance against other forms of power which bear its traces. This is decisive in coming to terms with one's real interests, which presupposes a metonymic form of causality in order to count for the way power and resistance are linked together. The point is that traces of power cannot be led back to an origin which determines them, since this origin is the void of negativity which cannot have either a fixed meaning or a *telos*. As a consequence, both empiricist and realist views of causation are inadequate. Neither is it the case that connections between particular relations of power and resistance appear so frequently that they can form the basis for a regularity principle, since power and resistance operate through condensations and displacements; nor is there any inherent necessity in actions which lead to certain outcomes (for example, since *A* is *A* it can cause *B*, or it is *A*'s '*A*-ness' which can cause *B*).

We are left with, or rather engulfed in, a metonymic causality that is contextually bound by structures of signification: displacements, condensations, recodifications and reversals. It is through these channels that we return to ourselves in order to become what we are. This becoming has no markers of certainty, but throws the subject into the anxious possibility of being able. The political ethics of real interests, and hence autonomy, would, on this account, be to hold the game of signification open by not hypostatizing the 'real'. That is, the real should be what it is, namely a limit whose transgression signals the autonomy of the subject, that is, its self-creation *vis-à-vis* dislocated structures.

6

Democracy and the Politics of Interests and the Common Good

Following on from the previous discussions of power and the constitution of identity, and in particular of the politics of subjective and real interests, the aim of this final chapter is to consider how we might come to terms with a notion such as the common good, and with the politics of individual interests and the public interest in a democracy. In my view, such an undertaking requires, firstly, conceptualizing political community and political authority, the relation between hegemony and democracy and, more generally, the nature of the political and politics. This might seem a round about way of approaching the discussion of the common good and the articulation of individual interests with the public interest. However, instead of broaching this topic directly, it will be more fruitful – indeed it is necessary – to situate it within a broader discussion of the ontology of the political and politics. This, I believe, is the key to grasping the issue in question.

The first sections open with a general discussion of the concepts of the political and politics in modernity, and then go on to consider the nature of political community and political authority, as well as the relation between hegemony and democracy. The purpose is to conceive of how it is possible – if it is possible – for widely differing, agonistic, and even antagonistic, power strategies and particular interests to 'coexist' in a political community without tearing it apart and destroying its structures of authority. That is, what are the limits, or the borderlines of inclusion and exclusion that define a political community, and what are the characteristics of the political authority that deals with this issue on a day-to-day basis? Or to put it another way, what is the acceptable scope for differences within a community, and when do these differences of opinions, values, interests, forms of life, and the like, reach the point when they question and undermine the very community itself? These questions are, needless to say, crucial to an understanding of the working of modern Western democracies, which exist in a world of globalization, regionalization, the decline of the nation-state, multiculturalism, and the hegemonic domination of political, bureaucratic and economic elites – to mention but a few of the decisive and divisive factors in present-day politics.

In this situation it might seem meaningless, anachronistic or hopelessly idealistic to speak of the common good and the public interest. The point is, however, not only that these terms are deeply ingrained in various democratic traditions concerned with political justice. They are, I will argue, inherent in the very political structure of Western democracies, where political authorities are assigned the task of making and implementing collectively binding decisions in the name of popular sovereignty. It is this fact of 'speaking in the name of society', to borrow Easton's phrase, that renders a term like the 'public interest', or similar metaphors, inescapable in politics. Hence their prescriptive or normative role is not a purely ornamental one designed to make it easier to digest elite domination, that is to say that their role is not exhausted by simply branding them manipulative devices in hegemonic power struggles. No doubt they are such devices, but they are also the means whereby a horizon of possibilities opens up – a horizon which cannot be controlled by any hegemonic strategy since it conditions strategic orientation in the first place. It is here that we discover a difference between hegemony and democracy. Whereas hegemony is always a reshuffling of dominations, democracy stands as a critical principle, or rather an ontology of potentials pointing towards a politics of non-hierarchy and inclusion. From a democratic perspective this is exactly what the common good and the public interest ought to signify: the mutual acceptance of differences in the political community.

The Circular Structure of Power I: The Political and Politics

The modern structuring of the political prevents political authority grounding and legitimizing itself by mirroring itself in the universality of either divine providence or its secular counterpart – whose most rigorous expression is Hobbes's *Leviathan*: 'that *Mortall God*, to which wee owe under the *Immortal God*, our peace and defence'.[1] *Leviathan* can be seen as a semi-secular attempt to recuperate this moment of political certainty by grounding the unity of political authority in the citizens' transfer of power to the sovereign. Given the impossibility of providing a transcendental universality, the problem of grounding society in itself is, from Hobbes onwards, dealt with as the problem of reducing political authority to legitimate authority – which is embodied in the nation-state and represents society inclusively.

The political is, from Hobbes onwards, dealt with as the very principle of order, and the 'agent' carrying out this task is embodied in the state. By locating the political principle of order in the state, the modern approach to the problem of political order focuses on the relationship between state and civil society, where the former dominates and depoliticizes the latter. It is in this context that we find the liberal dichotomization of state and civil society, which locates the political in the former and the social in the latter. The social order, as the embodiment of the common good established in the covenant, is the result of individuals' pursuit of their own interests in civil society. The cleavage between the social and the political, and between the individual and society, is thereby both sustained and mediated.

The modern state is instituted above society, which for that very reason is constituted as a levelled terrain in the sense that a formal equivalence is brought about between its heterogeneous elements. This finds expression first in civil and political rights, and later also in social rights. The political is, as Sartori points out, vertical rather than horizontal. It connotes domination over society, whereby it can no longer be seen as a communal activity fully imbricated in society as it is in the Aristotelian tradition.[2] The identity between the political and society thus disintegrates in modernity, where the former is located at the limit of the latter. The political is both inside and outside society: *inside* because society establishes itself in political acts of power struggle, and *outside* because these acts also expose social relations to universal criteria of legitimacy and regulations which are partly external to social contexts.

This view of the political as essentially repressive is closely bound up with the idea that power entails conflict and the suppression of will. The liberal version of the juridico-discursive representation of power portrays the political as derived from the autonomous and rational subject. Since this pre-political origin of the political is the locus for both consensus and coercion, the latter must be domesticated by the former without, however, eliminating it. The vehicle of this domestication is often idealized in social-contract theory, which locates the political in the state, and divorces the state from society. Thus the state = the political = conflict/domination, and this triangle is 'kept in place' by civil society = the social = consensus/sedimentation. Liberalism therefore has to strike a balance between the political and the social: whilst the former is constitutive for the latter, it must at the same time be subordinated to it by assuming the role of a supplement. To put it in the more figurative terms already used: the political is assigned the double and uneasy role of 'bouncer' and 'midwife'.

It is in this sense that the political is the principle of order; yet this principle is essentially split. The Janus-faced nature of the political stems from the role it is assigned, namely to mediate between a natural order of individuals' desires and a social order that regulates and represses this unruly state of nature. Since the individual's autonomy and rationality is located in the former, the political problem is that of inserting the individual into society without violating its autonomy and rationality (the 'midwife' function), whilst at the same time regulating, repressing and excluding those aspects of individual autonomy and rationality which represent a danger to the social order (the 'bouncer' function).

Here, politics is portrayed as being entirely dependent upon what is external to it, namely economic resources and social support. Politics is thus caught between efficiency (the economy, instrumental reason) and legitimacy (the social/culture, communicative reason), and its primary function is to balance these two demands which are often in conflict with each other.[3] This understanding of politics is rooted in the juridico-discursive representation of power whose constitutive features can be traced back to the two pillars of social-contract theory, rationality and autonomy; in present-day political theory these translate into instrumentalism and efficiency on the one hand, and ethics and legitimacy on the other. Politics is, within the dominant traditions of both liberalism and Marxism, conceived in terms of a repressive state power which shows itself in conflicts of interest. Hence power and politics are opposed to consensus and the social, where the latter is seen as the sedimentation of the political.

The modern relation between power and authority inaugurates what has been termed the circular structure of power. This is crucial for understanding the relation between the political, politics and society, namely that power strategies erect an authority in whose name they seek legitimation. The success of such an operation depends upon the extent to which a reversed causality can be established in which the effect (authority) somehow precedes its cause (power), and where this cause undertakes to fill out its effect, that is, to authorize itself. Politics is above all concerned with this *somehow*: with construing and cultivating something which is already 'there' (autonomy and rationality), which is to say that politics is located in the transgression of the particularity of power and the becoming of the universality of authority. This process takes place in two realms: in the juridico-discursive representation of power, focusing on the legitimacy of political power which is seen to be located in the state; and in the various institutional apparatuses, usually seen to be located in civil society, which regulate social interaction on a day-to-day basis.

It would, on this account, be a mistake to reduce political authority to legitimate authority, because the latter is a subcategory of the former, just as it would be a mistake to confine politics to the state, however defined. These tendencies are obviously closely connected. There are two reasons why this reductionism is problematic. The first has to do with the circular structure of power, namely that the attempt to establish a reversed relation of causality between power and authority cannot ever be brought to completion, meaning that the circle cannot be fully closed. There are always fissures in the structuring of political authority as legitimate authority because the latter cannot fully master the former which is its structural condition. Second, and by extension, political structure and political activity cannot be equated with the state and the practices taking place within it, or directed towards it, because the political authorization of power, as cogently argued by Foucault, takes place everywhere in society. Hence the existence of political authority is prior to the differentiation between state and civil society, itself a political strategy which is, moreover, codified juridically.

Political authority cannot, then, be equated with legitimate authority that is based on the consensus of its subjects – as is revealed in and represented by, say, the social contract – due to the Janus-faced nature of the political. It does not make sense to search for the lost origin where autonomous and rational individuals create the political by conferring their power on the sovereign. The reason is not that the contract is a myth, but rather that the role played by this myth as a legitimating device is displaced once we refuse the rationalistic fallacy eulogized by the sovereignty principle, and hence in the juridico-discursive representation of power, of reducing political authority to legitimate authority. We can put this somewhat differently by saying that the circularity involving power and authority is an overarching political structure that characterizes the political authorization of power, of which legitimate authority is part and by which it is conditioned. Seen in this light the social contract cannot be the constitutive moment of the political, but is instead part of the particular political structuring of the social which sets out to depoliticize it by presupposing what it itself poses, namely the pre-political ground of the political: the constitutive subject and, in turn, civil society.

To hold that power creates and is created by its own creation, or that power poses and presupposes authority, suggests that power strategies and power relations are always already conditioned by the existence of political authority as a historical a priori. The *raison d'être* of power strategies is to occupy the place of political authority so as to be able to make authoritative allocations of values for a society.[4] This place is empty, so to speak, meaning that it has neither form nor content a priori. It is none the less 'there' as a conditioning factor for political practice as the possibility to make and implement binding decisions, as well as symbolically as a horizon for what is possible and appropriate.

In both the liberal and the Marxist traditions politics is seen as an activity which is, ultimately and properly, confined within the state as the very site of the political. Here we are confronted with a restriction upon what is to count as politics, and we witness in particular a reduction of the political to a subsystem within society with a more- or less-specific location. Such a reduction is the first and decisive step in the construction of a hierarchy in which political power is confined, or rather confines itself, within structures of legitimate authority. The ultimate and proper reduction of the political to a subsystem within society is, besides being itself a political act, a normative imposition whose purpose is to prevent the politicization of social relations and the conflicts that may go with it. The point is, in other words, to immunize the principle of order from societal pressures, which in turn is why such a conception of the political is easily slanted towards elitism.

At this juncture, it is important to remember that the existence of political authority does not necessarily rest upon the two pillars of efficiency and value consensus. This is especially important for subsequent discussions of hegemony and democracy. In so far as political authority is reduced to the legitimate authority of the state, which is sustained by efficiency and consensus, it cannot but be fully imbricated in a hegemonic bloc. Two consequences follow. The first is that democracy is either antithetic to political authority or has to be defined in terms of competitive elitism. These two assertions are associated with emancipatory strategies and mainstream political science respectively. The second is that, by locating the political in the state, civil society is depoliticized in the sense that lay-actors are deprived of their 'political means of production' in the making of political authority. It is noteworthy that the debates on democracy within both left-wing and mainstream political science advocate this kind of protective democracy. The reason lies, I believe, in the largely unquestioned assumption, which is related to the repressive hypothesis of power, that the task of democracy is to secure 'freedom from' 'power over'.[5]

When the constitution of liberal democracy depends upon the political act of reducing the political to a subsystem confined within institutional and normative constraints that it itself creates, it follows that the political is a vehicle for a fundamental undecidability,[6] which is expressed in the liberal axiom that politics, or rather the political, is a 'necessary evil': it is necessary because it is the only place where power can turn into legitimate authority on a societal scale, and it is evil because even a legitimate political authority is not able to domesticate this place, which is why there is a permanent risk that it will exceed its limits and become coercive.[7] Although politics, within this scenario, has to be reduced to an activity uniting society without interfering in it, politics can never fully control what conditions it in the first place, namely the necessity of making authoritative allocations for a society.

Whereas the political is the place that renders society possible whilst at the same time tending to undermine the liberal and Marxist visions of an automatically regulated society, politics is the attempt and ultimate failure to ground society. Whereas the political can be seen as the field of possibility opened up by the dislocation of the ground of society,[8] politics is the structuring of this field. Whereas the structural location of the political implies that it is the place within a society from which society can be addressed in its entirety, politics is the activity of addressing. The ability to represent society, to act authoritatively in its name, is only possible from a place which is exterior to society. This place has a double role: it consists of representative and regulatory political institutions, and it is the point from which society structures itself; that is, where the articulation between its elements and their insertion into society, are redescribed.

The political has a structural and an institutional location, and the role of politics is to articulate these two locations. The political is, structurally speaking, the terrain whereon the articulation between particularity and universality takes place; that is, the terrain whereon social entities insert themselves in society.[9] In terms of its institutional location, the political is that sphere in society which holds the place of the political structure and in which hegemonic regimes are inscribed. Although neither the political structure nor politics can have a specific location in society, politics is the activity of linking oneself to the political institutions which hold the place of the political structure, and which are shaped by politics.[10] The undecidability of the political structure is also found at the institutional level, which is the *locus in quo* for power struggles: they play, on the one hand, an integrative function for society to the extent that they institutionalize, and are institutionalized in, representative and regulatory apparatuses; whilst these apparatuses, on the other hand, become new loci for power struggles, which might have the opposite effect. From this undecidability in the political principle of order it follows that the political structure is not able to determine politics, which is the activity of turning power strategies into bearers of the political structure in order to institutionalize them.

The impossibility of fully transforming power strategies into structures of authority entails that there is an ineradicable contradiction between the universal and the particular. Attempts to subsume the latter under the former lead unavoidably towards a particularization of the universal. The opposite holds true as well because the particular *qua* particular presupposes a societal context to which it has to refer in order to position and hence identify itself.[11] The particular and the universal cannot fully constitute themselves, nor can they exist independently of each other. They are distorted images of one another, which is why the place of the political embodies the undecidability between the particularity of power and the universality of authority. It is vital to grasp the nature of this place in order to understand the duality of political authority: whilst the latter is *a* part of society, it is also that part which is the key to all the other parts, meaning that it is *the* particular holding the place of the universal. Politics is the activity of giving that particular a content, and of holding the place of the universal so as to represent society inclusively.

A strategy along these lines is essentially political because it aims at grounding society by instituting a regime whose authority – in a democracy, that is – is assessable to public reasoning by virtue of the fact that it attempts to domesticate the place of the universal.

The point is that the circular structure of power and authority can only be brought to completion if representation is able to constitute what it represents. If this circular reasoning, which is the tautological *raison d'être* of the sovereignty principle,[12] succeeds, it is feasible to talk about society as a closed totality in which power and authority are united, and in which the state represents society inclusively. This is another way of saying that it has been possible for a power strategy to reduce political authority to legitimate authority and, moreover, that it has been possible to create a widespread societal homogeneity. Closure, unity and inclusivity are all phrases that point in the direction of a political vision, of eliminating politics. Both liberalism and Marxism typically share this vision because, for them, political power is the source of, or the expression of, the absence of the unity or the automatic self-regulation, of society, which is expressed in phenomena such as domination, repression, conflict and instability.

The Circular Structure of Power II: Political Representation

Society's representation of itself for itself cannot be a passive mirroring of a societal unity predating this act. The structural location of the political in the impossibility of society presenting itself for itself – an impossibility which is the locus of the political – assigns a paradoxical role to representation because it constitutes what it is addressing. The 're' of representation cannot refer to a ground that can be excavated, but marks instead what is literally absent, which is to say that representation is a performative act. Yet, the 're' also refers to something already existing whose identity precedes the moment of representation, whereby representation is an act of resemblance. Representation adds something to what is latently present but literally absent, and it is this bringing together of what is mutually exclusive that characterizes representation.[13]

The paradox of representation is bound up with the circular structure of power which, in its attempt to ground itself, has to present mythological juridical figures, such as the sovereignty of the individual and popular sovereignty, as if they were prior to their staging as representations in political action. The circularity of power and authority is straightened out, so to speak, which is to say that it presents itself as linear and causal. It should thus be clear that this attempt to dissolve the paradox of representation is closely related to the derivative conception of the political, that it derives from something external to itself. Such myths have played a constitutive role in modern political theory and practice because they aim to bridge the gap between power and authority in the political institutions, and more specifically, the schism between individual interests and the public interest. Representation thus presupposes the mythical and the fictitious in order to portray reality, which is to say that presence and immediacy presuppose absence and distance. Thus the public interest is not simply 'present' for society in the sense that it can be detected, inasmuch as we are sufficiently rational and detached from our own interests. It can only make an impact if society is reproduced within the political which, as an overarching structure, conditions the representation of contrary-to-fact regulatory principles that ought to be governing society.

Political representation plays a pivotal role in processes of identification by aiming to bridge the structural dislocations between individual and citizen, private and public, and society and state. By supplementing what it re-presents, political representation is caught up in the circular structure of power, that is, in the positing of the presuppositions of power. Power strategies aim to become embedded in institutional settings whose influence on social relations is channelled through relations of representation, and disciplinary and regulatory institutional networks which cut across the state/civil society distinction. In the crystallization of political authority, power strategies enforce a temporal and spatial distance in social relations whose legitimate expression is representation. Thus in the political authorization of power strategies, these strategies constitute themselves in a simultaneous process of distancing and an overcoming of this distance by representing what is absent. Representation is this process of evoking a distance and bringing together: a movement which inaugurates the presence of the political as an absence of an automatically self-regulated and homogeneous society, and hence a movement that calls forth political reasoning as a creative process of phronetic judgement.

By posing and presupposing what it represents, representation forges an image of society, which is why representation cannot simply copy reality. The gap between that which represents and that which is represented is constitutive for representation, and can neither be eradicated nor itself be represented. The gap can only be mediated in political processes of identification, where agents align themselves with publicly proposed schemes of interpretation which are able to articulate their specific interests within the loosely structured horizon of what is conceived as acceptable differences.

Thus representation can only exist if agents identify themselves with *that* which the representation endeavours to create and stage. Notions such as the common good and the public interest are typical examples here: they are able to function as political poles of identification because they position agents symbolically *vis-à-vis* societal contexts.

It is in the ineradicable difference between performance and semblance that we find the ideological moment, which can take the form of a rational myth whose function is to insert the particular within the universal thus bridging the schism between individual interests and the public interest. The ideological aspect of political power strategies is that of forging a unity between the particular and the universal, which is to say that politics aims to incorporate individual interests into the public interest in the name of the common good. Hence the rationale of politics lies in the ability to transcend particularity so as to represent universality. Interests must, in order to attain political significance, address themselves to wider societal contexts, whereby they are forced to transcend their particularity in order to become hegemonic. Politics is above all concerned with establishing authority relations, which, as mentioned, is the condition for making and implementing collectively binding decisions by creating poles of identification which can function as a common framework for political agents.[14]

It can be concluded that the impossibility of constituting society as a closed system, able to present itself for itself, assigns a peculiar role to the political. The political is the empty place of inscription, and politics is the activity of inscribing, that is, of acting in the name of the absent totality. One of the forms of this activity is representation which, exactly because it is structured around the constitutive gap between performance and semblance, involves imaginary and symbolic dimensions. This duality of representation implies that, in a democracy, the idea of universality (the absent whole) can and has to be retained even though its content changes.[15] This is only possible if the universal is present as an absence, whose structural location is the political, that is, the place from which society *in toto* can be addressed, well knowing that society as such is an impossible object that cannot, moreover, be controlled by political institutions.[16]

Against this background I would like to make three claims about political representation: (1) it articulates performance and semblance in which the hegemonic construction of a societal unity is posed *and* presupposed; (2) it aims to bridge the dislocations between individual and citizen, private and public, and society and state, as well as the political conflicts between individual and public interests, by articulating the particular with the universal; and (3) it is the vehicle for instituting a societal necessity which is thoroughly contingent, whereby politics covers attempts at both politicizing and depoliticizing social relations. The positing of presuppositions, the insertion of the particular into the universal, and the establishment of societal necessity, all point to the political constitution of society, to the fact that political power struggles are able to shape the horizons of society, which are represented in universal terms, but which, however, cannot but be contestable.

The Democratic Political Community and the Common Good

In order to appreciate what is at stake in discussing the politics of the common good and how individual interests are related to the public interest, it will be necessary to take a look at the notion of political community[17] because it is the community that embodies the common good. In broaching this discussion, we might say that a political community is marked by the logics of difference and equivalence, that is, by an articulation between diversity and regularity which delimits a particular discursive space. The crucial issue for a theory of democracy revolves around the possibility of deciding how various interests, values, world-views, and so on, which might be in conflict with one another can, none the less, coexist in a political community. It is this ordering principle of coexistence which is the subject matter of a political conception of the common good, however defined. To be more specific, the way we go about conceptualizing the common good in a democracy raises the thorny question of how it is possible to accept the autonomy of particular interests, rules, values, and so on, while at the same time preserving, and indeed extending, their 'ground' of articulation, that is, the ordering principle of coexistence.

In Chapter 4 we discussed the concept of antagonism and how it played a constitutive role in the processes of identity formation. We are now going to see how antagonism is related to the constitution of the political community. To approach this issue it will, in the first place, be necessary to discuss the relation between antagonism and context. The reason is that the political community, as a first approximation, can be seen as a context that is structured by the logics of difference and equivalence. Antagonism and context mutually constitute and subvert each other: it is the context that conditions and situates antagonism, but antagonism is also constitutive of context in the sense that it shapes, changes and undermines it. The context arises in the process of an antagonism between *A* and *B*. That is, in the process where *A* constructs various elements in a chain of equivalences which symbolizes the negation of *A*, its impossibility of being what it is: $\Sigma(b_1, b_2, \ldots b_n)/ B/$ non-*A*. *B* is a symbol of the negation of *A* (non-*A*), and *B* is a construct of the chain of equivalence between various elements: $\Sigma(b_1, b_2, \ldots b_n)$. Conversely, *B* might construct a similar chain of equivalences in which *A* symbolizes *B*'s impossibility of being what it is.

The context takes form in these processes. It is both the medium and outcome of the constructions of chains of equivalencies. It is a medium because these constructions do not take place in a vacuum. That is, they are always situated, and there is always some form of articulation with traditions, values, rules, commitments, social positions, and so on. Context is also outcome because it takes form, undergoes changes, and is subverted in these processes. To hold that context is both medium and outcome signals that time and space are closely intertwined. The reason is that in the construction of *A* and *B* as symbols of each other's impossibility of being what they are, a temporal dimension is evoked due to the circular structure of power, which is indicated by the fundamental reversal and the return of the blocked origin. The context is in this sense a time-space 'container': the context is a discursive space, and space *qua* space is articulated with temporality because the latter is contained in the former. That is, space is an organization or an ordering of time, and the opposite, time can only exist in so far as it is organized or ordered spatially. In so far as time is not spatially or discursively ordered it appears as a dislocation of space.[18]

The relation between antagonism and context is somewhat paradoxical: antagonism poses and presupposes context, but this constitution of the context, that conditions and situates the antagonism, points at the same time towards the possibility of dissolving it. The reason is that in the structuring of the context limits are necessarily established towards the environment, that is, other contexts. Thus in the very construction of an antagonism it cannot but establish its own limits, and therefore also its articulation with or insertion into other contexts, and this in turn might lead to its displacement and marginalization. What we have here, then, is that that which conditions hegemonic power struggles – the widening of the horizons for particular political strategies, that is, the structuring of a discursive space – also signals their contingent and more- or less-fragile nature. When an antagonism is articulated with other contexts it is, by definition, articulated with other time-space containers, and this might trigger dislocations; that is, the 'setting free' of temporality, possibility and freedom from their particular organization in other contexts.[19] The dislocatory event can be the result of antagonistic power struggles, but the opposite is also a possibility, as in the case when a dislocation renders new articulations possible and hence new possibilities of forging hegemonic blocs.

When a hegemonic agent endeavours to refer universality to itself, the particular identity of this agent tends to get somewhat blurred because it is itself an articulation of various elements. That is, the limits, and hence the identity of the hegemonic bloc, get more or less indistinct, and are contoured as a horizon of values, forms of life and ways of doing things through metonymic tracing (see Chapter 4) that are materialized in practical day-to-day rule following. This indistinctness of a hegemony is at once its condition of possibility and that which renders it contingent upon wider social contexts and dislocatory events, which is to say that hegemony is contingent upon this constitutive schism. A hegemony cannot ever be absolute because in the very process of trying to achieve this status it unavoidably undermines itself.

The impossibility of absolutizing a hegemony – its impossibility of establishing and maintaining rigorous limits to its environment – indicates that there is always a surplus of meaning that cannot be controlled by political institutions. This has important consequences for coming to terms with the relation between hegemony and democracy, and the nature of the political community. It is not possible to hegemonize a political community completely, and this means that the limits of the latter cannot ever be entirely clear-cut. Or to be more correct, to pin down distinct limits to its environment is only a possibility in extraordinary situations. The totalitarian regimes of the twentieth century testify to this fact: in their attempt to sustain themselves they cultivate an image of internal and external enemies, and this is done by disciplining and terrorizing society thus upholding a permanent state of emergency (that is, they attempt to render an extraordinary situation permanent).

It has been argued that the circular structure of power is immanent in social relations as a structuring principle that also characterizes the political authorization of power. Antagonism is a specific form of power struggles that can take place within the sphere (or jurisdiction) of a political authority. If that is the case, the antagonistic parties recognize the political authority as an authority, which means that they, for whatever reason, obey its decisions as collectively binding. What is important here is that contexts are both posed and presupposed by antagonism, and that they have more or less formalized structures of authority that perform a political role.

Antagonistic power struggles can take place between parties that accept these structures of political authority and hence the rules of the game, but the antagonistic parties can also struggle about the very structuring of the political authority itself, whereby the game metaphor does not hold. Often we will find a combination of these kinds of struggles, but regardless of the nature of the struggle, the antagonistic parties cannot but presuppose what they, in fact, partake in constructing, namely the political community and the political structures of authority. The larger the chains of equivalence that confront each other become, the more difficult it becomes to find a common ground or a point of convergence between them. This means that the possibility of the political authority displacing or marginalizing the antagonism becomes gradually more difficult. And by extension, the reference to the political authority by the antagonistic parties becomes more and more abstract, that is, symbolic.

The distinction between the political and the social is decisive for democratic politics. If we say that democracy is, or rather ought to be characterized by the political acceptance of differences we are, in effect, saying that the agenda of democratic politics consists of that which is a common concern for the political community. What is and what is not a common concern is, of course, itself a political question, but in so far as pluralism, and indeed value pluralism, is crucial for democracy, we are forced to make a distinction as to what is acceptable and what is not. The point is that the principle that guides this distinction must itself be political, which basically comes down to that it cannot be determined by what Rawls terms 'comprehensive doctrines', such as the communitarian idea of the normative integration of cultural values or the Habermasian idea of rational concensus. That is, the political idea of a common concern substitutes the search for a social or cultural common good.

The limits we set up to protect, widen and deepen the space of acceptable differences delineate the nature and scope of pluralism as a system, which is to say that it cannot be the task of democratic politics to judge all sorts of differences. When we are confronted with actions, practices or forms of life that do not fall within the broad framework of what is politically acceptable, these actions, practices, and so on, cease to be mere differences because, to a greater or lesser extent, they tend to threaten the pluralist system as such. To give an example: the death sentence on the British writer Salman Rushdie is not seen in differential terms. It is not an action on a par with other actions that make a difference within the discursive space of acceptable differences precisely because it violates the 'difference principle'. The reason is that the *fatwa*, by violating what 'we' conceive as politically acceptable, unavoidably evokes the plurality of acceptable differences as a system. It is this calling forth of the systematicity of differences which is constitutive of the 'we' and hence of the 'us/them' antagonism.

The violation of the system of acceptable political differences is, in other words, a violation of the constitutive metaphors of this system, that is, the nodal points of democracy, namely liberty and equality. It is crucial to keep in mind the contextual or limited nature of this antagonism: whilst the *fatwa* is a particular event that sparks off a more- or less-intuitive or explicit sense of the universality of the liberal democratic values, the democratic challenge consists amongst other things in *not* construing the *fatwa* in equivalential terms, that is, as a somewhat inherent or necessary aspect of Islamic identity. The reason is, of course, that this would warrant the exclusion of Muslims from democratic politics simply because they are Muslim, that is, identify themselves with a particular comprehensive doctrine.

In order to fight this form of racism it is important to notice two things. First, the political violence associated with, or exercised by, some forms of Islamic fundamentalism is neither a 'logical' consequence of Islam as such, nor is it the predominant form of Islam. Second, it is decisive for democratic politics to separate the political acceptance of differences and religious comprehensive doctrines. As long as the latter (regardless of whether they are Muslim, Jewish, Christian, or something else) are reasonable, in the sense that they accept and recognize each other as political agents, it will be undemocratic to exclude them from participation in the political community.

It is important to emphasize that terms such as 'politics of recognition', 'agonistic respect' and 'respectable moral disagreements'[20] represent (in the double sense of the term as performance and resemblance) a system of acceptable differences, and that this systematicity of differences is, and has to remain, fairly loose. It is a horizon of possibilities which is ordinarily experienced intuitively because we only occasionally experience the limits of the system as such. What happens when we do get confronted with limits is that we construct, implicitly or explicitly, chains of equivalences which call forth the system as such. The more- or less-evasive boundaries that usually mark out the horizons of acceptability, recognizability and public reasonableness are crucial for democratic politics. The reason is that the political authority in a democracy *cannot* and *must not* be in a position where it can fully control or monopolize the nodal points of liberty and equality, and hence the system. Democracy, as opposed to totalitarian or hierarchical regimes, is, in other words, an 'open society', because the limits it draws between acceptable/non-unacceptable are based on the principle of differentiality, and hence the possibility of the inclusion of various and even antagonistic comprehensive doctrines.

It might seem as if the democratic principle of the political acceptance of differences cannot be of much use since it is far from clear what acceptability actually means, just as it is unclear who is going to define it and according to which criteria. However – and in an analogy to a similar idea, namely that of the public interest – the indistinctness pertaining to this principle does not evoke some kind of subjectivism or solipsism: that acceptability is defined according to individual whims or, more appropriately, according to the interests of dominant elites. The idea of what politically acceptable differences are can only be made explicit in relational terms, that is, by contrasting it to what is unacceptable. We are hereby confronted with often very intricate and contentious ethico-political decisions. These decisions are ethical because they are concerned with what is right and wrong, and they are political because they deal with the authoritative allocation of values for a society.

A politically acceptable difference is an action, practice, value, utterance, rule or a form of life that is publicly reasonable *vis-à-vis* the ethico-political horizons of a political community. This definition is, admittedly, circular but it is an unavoidable circularity, and from a democratic point of view it is even decisive. The reason is that a 'linear' definition would hardly be able to avoid references to a substantial definition of the common good, where a number of virtues or base values would be defined as acceptable whilst others would be disqualified. But to undertake such an operation of inclusion/exclusion would, of course, itself count as an ethico-political decision, in consequence of which linearity 'curves', that is, it itself becomes circular. Two consequences follow: acceptability cannot be defined before it gets political as if the social or cultural realm was prior to or immune from the political; and democracy requires that the principle of the mutual acceptance of differences is a negotiated outcome and medium of public reasoning.

The Common Good I: The Political and the Social

The problem we are going to discuss now concerns whether the transmission from individual interests to the public interest is at all feasible in a modern political community given its irreducible value pluralism and lack of foundation – a lack that triggers the need to ground itself by naming 'that' which 'we' have in common. But is it possible to pinpoint a common denominator, and which role could it play if we knew what it was? These questions are especially acute for democratic theory. The reason is, of course, that the state has to legitimize itself in the name of popular sovereignty; but it is also significant that democratic theory is increasingly associated with anti-foundationalism and the contingency of community. Debates on the common good cannot but be marked by this postmodern trend, which renders it difficult to launch a politics of naming what we have in common, amongst other reasons because it is not at all clear who 'we' are, just as it is far from obvious who and what constitutes this we and how it is done.[21] To refer to some type of societal objectivity is not in vogue today, regardless of whether such an objectivity is cast in terms of deep-seated values shared by everybody or incontestable historical laws of motion that somehow translate into ethico-political maxims. Rather, we have to see the common good as a political metaphor which is brought about over long stretches of time in all kinds of power struggles where agents struggle for the political recognition of their identities, values, and so on, and that this metaphor operates as the medium and reference point for political practices and relations. A concept such as 'public reason', which is also a political metaphor that connotes impartiality and inclusivity, should be seen in this light.

The politics of individual interests and the public interest focuses on the schisms between interests as they are conceived by the political agents themselves and interests which pertain to society, that is, those which somehow 'express' the common good. It is uncontroversial to assert that individuals and groups pursue interests, but it is far from clear what it means for a political community, crisscrossed by all sorts of differences and antagonisms, to 'pursue' an interest and 'have' a common good. This impression is reinforced when we consider the difficulties we are up against when trying to reach agreement on various policies and the values they express. It is commonplace to assert that today we are unable to agree about virtually anything, which is why searching for and even debating the common good and the public interest are likely to be deemed futile or hopelessly idealistic. All conceptions of these terms are contestable, and appear more like rhetorical devices used by political elites to justify their particular interests.[22]

Viewing the matter in this perspective, we might be tempted to leave it at that and, instead, concentrate on the aggregation of interests as it is expressed in the principle of majority rule as outlined in the model of procedural democracy. This principle could form the guideline for a democracy as the closest approximation to the generalization of interests and the vision of a just society that we can achieve. This is basically Schumpeter's so-called realistic solution to the problem of the common good. Although his attack on 'classical' democratic theory might be seen as the definitive critique of its 'anachronistic illusions' concerning the political potentials of individuals – that their autonomy and rationality would be the best guarantee for detecting the common good – it should not be forgotten that Schumpeter himself, while discarding the idea of the common good, nevertheless puts forward five conditions which have to be fulfilled in order for his model of democracy as competitive elitism to get off the ground. There is no need to consider the detail of these conditions. What matters is that they revolve around a 'division of labour' between politicians, bureaucrats and voters which ensures that politics is restricted to party competition and to general law and policy making; that 'a well-trained bureaucracy' implements these laws and policies; and that the culture is marked by 'a large measure of tolerance for difference of opinion'.[23]

According to Schumpeter, 'the existence of a uniquely determined common good discernible to all' is not assessable by rational argument because we are dealing with 'irreducible differences of ultimate values'.[24] Hence there can be no agreement as to how we might define the common good, if it can be defined at all, and what use we could make of it even if we did manage to define it. It is, in short, an anachronistic concept which is, moreover, politically dangerous in a modern democracy. What we are dealing with here is a critique of a substantive definition of the common good as a common denominator or ground which is, *pace* Schumpeter, indisputable. Yet to speak meaningfully about a political community in the first place we do, unavoidably, make reference to something like the common good and the public interest. Schumpeter is no exception here although his terminology is, obviously, different. The point is that the five conditions underpinning his model of elitist democracy serve a similar function to the common good. These conditions occupy the place of the common good, which is, within his scenario, set apart from politics whilst at the same time conditioning it. That is, these conditions are simply treated as standing conditions which are not articulated with practical politics and political values. Thus understood, the common good puts restrictions upon what reaches the political agenda due to the division of labour between politicians, bureaucrats and voters, and a widespread acceptance concerning liberal values and the general direction in which policies should go.

The same type of argument is launched by the early Dahl, who also makes a sharp distinction between societal conditions and actual politics. In discussing the relation between what he calls 'the underlying consensus' and 'democratic politics', which is important for grasping the nature of the public interest, he says: 'what we ordinarily describe as democratic "politics" is merely the chaff. It is the surface manifestation, representing superficial conflicts. Prior to politics, beneath it, enveloping it, restricting it, conditioning it, is the underlying consensus on policy that usually exists in the society among a predominant portion of the politically active members.'[25] This statement is, of course, contentious, partly because the idea of 'the underlying consensus' is itself extremely slippery and hardly open to measure, let alone to negotiate, and partly because politics is confined within and derived from this consensus, which precludes the fact that politics has a role to play in its production.[26] It is in this way that politics is divorced from the social: it cannot be an activity *in* the social, but is instead associated with, or rather reduced to, conflicts of interests which are, however, confined within the framework of normative integration.[27]

This separation between politics and underlying conditions, as it is presented by Schumpeter and Dahl, is problematic because it leaves the relation between the political and the social unexplained. In order to overcome this problem it should be emphasized that the conditions for political activity are themselves the medium and outcome of this activity, just as the public sphere is not only the battleground on which conflicts are fought but also the outcome of these struggles which affect that ground and hence the rules of the game. This being the case, the public interest can be seen as the 'link' which articulates the standing conditions and various policies and power strategies. By stressing that this link is one of articulation rather than derivation, one concedes what today seems more obvious, namely that societal conditions are themselves political, which is to say that these conditions cannot escape the 'fate' of contingency. The political is, in this account, *in* the social as an ordering principle, which means that the social as the underlying framework of consensus cannot be prior to the political, or beneath it, enveloping it, restricting it or conditioning it. Three consequences follow from this account of the relation between the political and the social: (1) the political cannot be adequately conceptualized in terms of conflicting preferences and interests; (2) political power struggles cannot be adequately conceptualized in terms of the decision-making approach; and (3) a political conception of democracy cannot be adequately conceptualized in terms of procedural democracy.

Dahl's attempt to provide a ground for politics by deriving it from the underlying consensus is, however, interesting because it mirrors the hegemonic form of power struggles: that politics, by representing itself as legitimate and by displacing itself, poses the political authority as presupposed. Although this mirroring cannot represent anything beyond political power struggles, which implies that politics is more than a surface manifestation, the conception of politics turns full circle and reflects itself in the representation of the underlying consensus which it has itself engendered. In democratic theory after Schumpeter, political power is legitimized by procedural rules rather than by mirroring itself in the common good as a common denominator and aspiration for conflicting interests. To hold that political agents 'really' are committed to common values when they strip off their particular interests, that is, when they are rational and autonomous, is no doubt a falsehood. The problem remains none the less that democracy cannot – not even for Schumpeter and Dahl, as we have seen – sustain itself merely on procedural grounds. For both, the political needs to be supplemented by societal conditions and criteria which map out a framework of normative integration.

It is because the political cannot be reduced to conflicting preferences and interests that address themselves to the formal or legal institutional settings of politics that the political will always exceed given regime structures. And it is because democracy cannot be defended on procedural grounds alone, since these grounds are themselves in need of being grounded in political values,[28] that there inevitably is, and has to be, an articulation between the political and values whose means of expression is participation. Procedural democracy presupposes a strict separation between the political and the social, aggregation and integration, and the instrumental and the ethical. The political can only be dealt with instrumentally because it is reduced to a superstructural phenomenon of aggregating interests, which is conditioned by the 'pre-political' social base that is characterized by normative integration. Moreover, the procedural model is, in actual fact, biased in favour of an elitist view of democracy, either explicitly as in Schumpeter or implicitly as in Dahl, due to the stress on the aggregation of preferences and interests. The reason is, as we saw in the discussion of the debate on the three faces of power, that by taking the political out of the social, so to speak, it becomes impossible to see how political power struggles play an active role for the very structuring of preferences and interests, as well as for the possibility of getting access to influence the political agenda.

Certainly there has to be a framework within which political decisions are collectively binding if interests are to attain the status of public interest; but this is not the same as saying that those for whom the decisions are binding have to be normatively integrated. The public interest can be seen as the link between democratic decision making and its societal political conditions, and by extension, as the means of showing the framework of the political authority provided that this showing poses *and* presupposes the political authority. This proviso is decisive for a democracy and it is, as I have argued in the first two chapters, implicit in the criticisms levelled at the early pluralism of Dahl *et alii*. The arguments of Bachrach and Baratz, and especially Lukes, demonstrated that the underlying consensus could not be a ground which politics and power struggles are restricted or conditioned by. On the contrary, the development of the debate on the three faces of power made it clear that the ground itself becomes immersed in power struggles. Thus the solidity of the ground, and hence the derivation of power from legitimate authority, crumble *pari passu* with their politicization: instead of the two vertical levels – of superficial conflicts and an underlying consensus – we are faced with a politicized space whose horizons are, and have to remain, intangible.

That the ground of politics is itself political, and that public interest claims are negotiated outcomes of power struggles, are fundamental conditions for a democratic political authority. It is characteristic of this type of authority that the public interest cannot merely be conceived in terms of the responsiveness of those who represent to those who are represented, because that would undermine the duality of representation. To act on behalf of society implies something more than an expressed consensus and a constant or direct responsiveness, namely that 'there must be institutional arrangements for responsiveness', and that the relative autonomy of those who represent is cast in terms of their responsibility towards those they represent.[29] Instead of pointing to responsiveness to various forms of pressure and to consensus as a trade-off between dominant groups which pay lip-service to social or cultural values, responsibility and legitimacy involve a spatio-temporal distance from particularistic interests. It is this distance that is the locus for the public interest, which in turn reflects the spatial and temporal integration of a political community. Agents, in this respect, become political agents when they locate themselves in this spatio-temporal distance. That is, they become bearers of the political structure when they act on behalf of society.

Integration is not essentially normative, but points rather at the political articulation between part and whole, and future and past, which renders the 'capacity to speak in the name of society' possible.[30] This capacity that characterizes the political gives rise to three issues: (1) The relation between individual interests and the public interest is one of representation where the latter, one way or another, is bound to claim to represent the former in the name of public reason. (2) The medium in which this representation usually takes place is the public sphere, which at the same time is the medium that structures the articulation of interests. And (3) The public interest in a democracy is simultaneously the outcome of power struggles over vested interests and what is publicly reasonable, and the name in which these struggles and conflicting interpretations are fought.

The legitimacy of the political authority cannot be boiled down to consensus regardless of whether it expresses the absence of overt/covert conflicts or a commitment to particular values and ways of life. Rather, the question of legitimacy revolves around the political structure, which in a democracy is envisioned in the universality of the public sphere as a horizon of possible forms of rights and obligations grounded in the political community. This horizon is, for instance, shown in power struggles, which often employ contrary-to-fact reasoning by contrasting existing, and perhaps highly sedimented, power relations to alternatives. These alternatives, in turn, express a higher degree of autonomy and participation for the involved parties and, by extension, the inclusivity of political agents and the non-hierarchization between them.

The point of drawing attention to Schumpeter and the early Dahl is to show that the aggregation of interests as it is expressed in majority rule, and constitutionally underpinned by civil and political rights, cannot stand alone in a description of democracy. For both, the principle of aggregation is supplemented by the other principle of cultural or normative integration, and these two principles are located in, and govern, the political and the social respectively. Political authority is considered legitimate in so far as its two pillars are operative, namely the instrumental logic of rationality and effectivity pertaining to aggregation, and the communicative logic pertaining to normative integration. These two logics are seen as belonging to the political and the social respectively, which is why we are faced with a strict separation between the two realms. This approach is echoed in many left-wing theories of democracy today in that for them, democracy necessitates a clear-cut separation between state and civil society in order to protect civil society from the pressures of political power, which is seen as essentially repressive and located in the state.[31]

It should thus be clear that the public interest cannot be conceived as the sum of individual interests. The reason is that in order for interests to be aggregated, a principle of aggregation has to be instituted, and this principle cannot but be an equivalential standard sustained by a set of political rules and values which both express and constitute a common horizon within which interests, rules and values can be articulated and political participation can take place. This horizon is constituted by a systematization of differences which, usually over long time spans, delineates the limits between acceptable and unacceptable ethico-political differences. Aggregation and integration mutually condition each other, and should be seen in relation to this systematization of differences which in a democracy is continuously negotiated. Hence democracy cannot sustain itself on the basis of either procedural rules or by adherence to common values alone. Aggregation and integration are unthinkable without representative bodies which modify interests, and in turn constitute them as the boundaries of a political community, and hence what are seen as acceptable issues to be put on the political agenda.

Individual and public interests are articulated with each other, and it is this articulation which constitutes them. This means that individual interests cannot be treated as subjective facts as if they were given before entering the political arena. And the public interest cannot be equipped with an a priori content which is waiting to be revealed by autonomous and rational individuals capable of excavating the common good, just as it cannot be an arbitrary construction which is imposed on individual interests. Individual interests are public in the sense of representing supra-individual reference points,[32] and inversely, these reference points are produced in the articulation between various interests. The intangible horizon for political action, as well as the practical sense of what is publicly reasonable, are not only produced in the clashes of particular interests; it is at the same time also presupposed by these interests. The point is that the horizon, and hence the scope of the political authority, delineates the terrain for struggles by conditioning the formulation of interests as well as the procedures regulating their articulation.

The articulation between individual interests and the public interest, whose vehicle is the circular structure of power, implies that the public interest is both posed and presupposed in political action. The public interest can be said to be implanted retroactively in individual interests as the spatio-temporal medium and outcome of these interests. Politics is thereby an activity geared towards the maintenance and development of the frameworks of societal action, which in turn serve as reference points for the attempt by political strategies to legitimize themselves. The politics of aligning individual interests with the public interest is a hegemonic endeavour to define the former in terms of the latter, thus closing the gap between them by defining the rules of the game.

The impossibility of society closing this gap, and hence becoming an all-inclusive ground in whose name the political authority could settle irreconcilable conflicts, does not mean that political decisions cannot be made in the public interest. What it does mean is that the public interest is constructed argumentatively as the normative aspect of publicly assessable interpretations which validate what are rightful claims, issues and interests to be raised and pursued, as well as the procedure for settling conflicts. The role of the public interest is to maintain and further a common framework of various interests, and, against this background, to justify decisions in the case of disagreements.[33] This common framework is not based on a substantial conception of the common good but rather on mutual trust, which is what ultimately underpins political authority. When interests are qualified as public they connote inclusivity and universality *vis-à-vis* the political community, as opposed to individual interests which are particularistic by nature and perhaps mutually exclusive. Stress is thereby put on inclusion/exclusion, which is important for understanding the relation between hegemonic power strategies and the attempts to radicalize democracy by deepening and spreading the egalitarian imaginary to wider and wider segments of the political community.

The Common Good II: Individual Interests and the Public Interest

Interests can neither be equated with explicit preferences nor be deduced from the structural position of agents. Rather, interests take shape in the intersection between: (1) the political authorities and power strategies; (2) the political structure and political activity; and (3) representation as performance and semblance. This assumption implies that the power struggles between individual interests are conditioned by, and articulated with, the political structure as the ordering principle of a political community. A major task for democratic theory is to grasp how the articulation of interests is related to the common good and the public interest, and how strategies and policies trying to represent the public interest are conditioned by the political structure. Thus we have the three analytical levels of structure, institution and identity.

When interests take shape in relation to the articulation between structure, institution and identity, there cannot be an unbridgeable gap between individual interests and the public interest. They are, rather, partly imbricated in each other in the sense that they mutually constitute each other: interests are constituted in political processes in which various elements are articulated *vis-à-vis* the public sphere (or rather *vis-à-vis* the proliferation of public spaces), and hence to existing or proposed schemes of justification. Due to the fact that: (i) power strategies attempt to become authorized; (ii) politics is an activity which seeks to domesticate the political structure; and (iii) representation tries to perform what it resembles, individual interests can be 'incorporated' into the public interest, or to put it differently, they attempt to hegemonize the public interest by defining it; and inversely, the public interest is the negotiated outcome and medium of the hegemonic articulation between individual interests.

The movement from power to authority, and from political activity to the political structure, can be seen in the light of the duality of representation: individual interests are formed at a distance from the agents themselves by virtue of pointing beyond the bearer of the interest, that is, agents present themselves as political agents *vis-à-vis* that which transcends them, namely the engagement in the authoritative allocation of values for a society. The spatial metaphor of distance also entails temporality: short-term interests have to be balanced by a long-range view, and this requires a certain detachment from various forms of pressure, that is, a spatio-temporal distance which can be mediated through the public sphere via representation. It is only by evoking this distance that the political community can be integrated spatially as well as temporally. What is important here is the stress on the political nature of the long-range view of the public interest, namely that it is bound up with the power of authority in a paradoxical way. The public interest is, on the one hand, engendered by the inherent distance between political activity and the political structure, which finds expression in the clashes of hegemonic interests striving to speak in the name of society; whilst on the other hand, it is an outcome of these conflicts, whose expression is a minimization of this distance because it has attained the status of a 'societal necessity' by incorporating actual interests in a long-range view.

The incorporation of particularity under universality entails an ordering of time, which is an attempt to overcome dislocations so as to represent society as a coherent whole, where each element is a necessary part of that whole.[34] Weber's distinction between the ethics of intention and the ethics of responsibility illustrates this point as does Machiavelli's *raison d'état*. Political agents have to act according to the ethics of responsibility, meaning that they must be ready to do evil in order to prevent an even greater evil from occurring; or to put it in Machiavellian terms: 'a ruler who wishes to maintain his power must be prepared to act immorally when this becomes necessary.'[35] A political action is legitimized *ex ante* from an imagined point of view of the *ex post*: here political agents foster a temporal distance with the sole purpose of closing it afterwards. It is by means of this opening and closing of the spatio-temporal distance that they are able to create a discursive field that binds time and space within which they can carry out their tasks in a allegedly publicly responsible manner. Responsibility has an affinity with necessity in the sense that political agents perform the tasks they 'have' to perform. Responsibility can be seen as a kind of self-imposed necessity where the decisions, actions and strategies of political agents are represented as answers to events, situations, circumstances, developments, and so on, as if they were simply facts awaiting recognition and proper treatment, and not in part constituted by these very decisions, actions and strategies.

What we are faced with here is the attempt of political power strategies to hegemonize 'reality' by representing it 'as it is'. In so far as they are successful in this respect, an important condition is in place for the possibility that politics is seen as carried out in a responsible manner. Responsibility, necessity and similar seductive political metaphors aim at bridging dislocations, displacing or marginalizing antagonisms and conflicting interpretations over political issues. Responsibility as the representation of reality as it is, is a way of evoking spatio-temporal distance and proximity between political action and 'standing conditions'. This operation is intimately connected with the circular structure of power in a paradoxical way: representation tends to close the circle by making it linear or derivative, thus externalizing that which is represented from its representation by turning the former into something factual which the latter has to respond to. The important and somewhat paradoxical consequence is that political action is at one and the same time the vehicle of both politicization and depoliticization. What makes a political decision appear as responsible is its ability to forge an image of itself as necessary *vis-à-vis* the political community. However, the very condition of this self-imposed necessity is that a decision is taken and that this decision revolves around a moment of undecidability, which means that it cannot be read off, as it were, from a societal necessity. The moment of decision making is, instead, the moment of establishing necessity retroactively, which is to say that the political intervention poses a necessity as presupposed.[36]

The displacement of dislocations and antagonistic power struggles maps out the strategic field of what counts as the most expedient political metaphors to bridge the gap between political activity and the political structure. Reference to terms such as 'economic necessity', 'responsibility', 'liberty and equality', 'rights', and so on, are all devices for universalizing particular strategies, individual interests and forms of life and, as such, they attempt to align themselves with the public interest in order to occupy the place of the common good so as to appear acceptable and responsible. The overdetermined nature of these key metaphors renders them suitable to function as overarching reference points or poles of identification for a whole range of different, and even antagonistic, political strategies operating in the political community.

It goes without saying that power/knowledge strategies, and hence the disciplinary and regulatory mechanisms operating in every institutional setting, play a crucial role in establishing, subverting and reinventing necessity and reasonableness. This means that the political authorization of power: (1) extends far beyond the state as the site of legitimate authority; (2) is rooted in and conditioned by the political structure instead of in its legal locations; and, as a consequence thereof, (3) proceeds 'bottom-up' rather than 'top-down'.[37] These three points emphasize that individual and collective identity formations are eminently political processes, which is, as mentioned, the reason why the personal is political and vice versa.

Political strategies aim at reoccupying and rearticulating the predominant metaphors belonging to the political structure by giving them a particular content. The reason why the elusive term 'the public interest' is one of the prime means by which power strategies legitimize themselves is that it is a metaphor that evokes political values such as inclusivity, non-hierarchization, impartiality, justifiability, and the like, all of which point in the direction of creating a common framework within which policies are carried out. Agents direct themselves towards this egalitarian imaginary counterfactual situation not just to attain legitimacy but to inscribe themselves in the rules of the game, and thereby to achieve the status of political agents. However, as soon as the public interest lends its name to concrete policies it gets a particular form and content; consequently, the notion of the public interest has to remain elusive in order to attain political significance. Indeed, it cannot but remain elusive because it is both the outcome and medium of power struggles, which is another way of saying that it is articulated with the political structure.

The insubstantial nature of the common good, and hence the impossibility of ultimately fixing the public interest, far from being a threat to democracy, is its best guarantee. This requires, however, that democracy be conceived of as a differential system that allows for and requires constant processes of interpretation of rules, values and forms of life. The guiding principle for these interpretations has to be that the ultimate authority, and the horizon for collective action in the public sphere, lies in the mutual acceptance of political disagreement within reasonable limits. It is this acceptance, and the mutual trust that goes with it, which is the ethico-political bond of a democratic political community.

The public interest cannot be the sum of partial interests because it does not make sense to aggregate different, and even antagonistic, interests without a principle of integration. But neither can the public interest be the common denominator for these partial interests as if the differences between them were merely an appearance behind which we could excavate an essential unity (a substantial common good). What we can say is that the public interest connotes impartiality due to the absence of the domination of individual interests, and this suggests that it is a type of interest which every interest strives towards. It is, paradoxically, *that* which interests would have in common if they were able to renounce their particularity, although it is this particularity which constitutes their identity in the first place. This means that the qualifier 'public', strictly speaking, is a contradiction in terms: it is the point of recurrence which cannot be pinpointed; it is the limit of an interest which situates it in a larger context without which it could not exist or be what it is because identity poses and presupposes a spatial and temporal transcendence, yet it is also that which blocks the particularity of interests. The public interest lacks content but none the less supplies the particular with a content, and thus it is the ideological point *par excellence*: a signifier without a signified, and a place that cannot be occupied. The public interest is thus pure difference or differentiality as such, which is why it is both the outcome and medium of the articulation of individual interests. In other words, the public interest connotes inclusivity, but because inclusivity is unthinkable without what is excluded, the 'public' nature of the public interest cannot but be what Jameson in another context has termed a 'vanishing mediator'.

The primacy given to power struggles in the shaping of interests implies that they establish themselves by delimiting themselves from other particular interests. In the formation of hegemonic blocs, various interests are joined together in the attempt to make up the public interest, which is an articulatory process of both inclusion and exclusion. In this process of constituting interests there is always something which eludes and threatens them, and which at the same time constitutes them. In each struggle, and hence each interest, there is a surplus of meaning that constitutes the interest and situates it in wider contexts, whilst also defying attempts at being defined since definition entails fixity of identity and position, which takes the form of particularity. Hence dislocatory effects are, so to speak, inherent in the attempt by power strategies to become hegemonic. There are two reasons for this which revolve around the relation between political structure and political practice.

First, dislocations happen because the public interest as the 'occupant' of the empty place of the political structure cannot be reduced to an effect of the attempt by hegemonic strategies to fill it out. It is this irreducibility – or constitutive but vanishing distance between responsibility and necessity – which gives way for the three dimensions of dislocation, namely temporality, possibility and freedom. Second, and in continuation thereof, the public interest as the outcome of hegemonic struggles is constituted antagonistically to its cause, in the sense that the effect (the public interest and the democratic egalitarian imaginary that connotes inclusivity) is produced as the stumbling block of its cause (individual interests and the formation of hegemonic blocs). The reason is that no hegemony is able to master its conditions of possibility, namely the dislocated structure as the empty place of inscription. Or to put it in terms of representation: a hegemonic strategy is never capable of fully performing what it resembles.

The common good, as the nodal point of the articulation between interests, is the outcome of hegemonic struggles. But this outcome cannot be a full-fledged effect of these struggles due to the auto-negativity of power, which produces the common good as the inherent stumbling block to hegemonic power strategies. There is, accordingly, a fissure between cause and effect, which is why power as the ability to make a difference is located neither in the 'making' (cause) nor in the 'difference' (effect). Ability as such, which is the locus of auto-negativity, is the name of this fissure or this impossibility of being spatially and temporally ordered a priori, which means that it is the locus of dislocation, that is, temporality, possibility and freedom. A non-substantive conception of the common good thus holds that it revolves around the three dimensions of the dislocation of the political structure as the condition for the democratic logic of differentiality and inclusivity.

At this higher-order level of analysis the public interest cannot have a content and cannot, accordingly, be an interest proper. This is the reason why it is politically significant not only for those strategies which have attained a hegemonic position, but also for those resisting them which employ public interest arguments as a counterfactual possibility for criticizing inequalities. As soon as the public interest is given a content, that is, the moment it is embodied in a particular policy, its aura of universality tends to fade away and it emerges as yet another particular interest. The public interest can only come into existence by negating itself, but this does not, of course, say anything about the specific nature of the policies carried out in its name. Hence there is no reason for being agnostic with regard to being engaged in the struggles of defining the public interest. The reason why a political strategy tries to define (itself as) the public interest is, needless to say, that this is the only way in which it might succeed in becoming hegemonic. But this is not the whole story since strategies, in their attempt to achieve hegemony, have to inscribe themselves in, or become bearers of, the political structure, and this requires that they situate themselves in the field of articulation between particularity and universality. Their success depends upon their ability to universalize themselves so as to create a common horizon with which various forces can identify, while at the same time maintaining a distinct profile or identity. It should thus be clear that universality and particularity reciprocally condition each other, and that the latter, although it cannot ever occupy the place of universality, nevertheless has to address itself in terms of the universal.

Hegemonic struggles are characterized by individual interests striving to align themselves with the public interest, that is, to define it and hence the rules and conditions for acting politically. Such a definition involves a retroactive process which shows the circular structure of power, namely political power strategies aim at authorizing themselves: they represent what they construe, or they constitute what was already 'there' (the fundamental reversal between cause and effect) in the attempt to fulfil the task of the spatio-temporal integration of the political community.

It is, of course, impossible to provide guarantees against the risk that terms such as the 'common good' and the 'public interest' will be used as a foil for elite domination and strategies of social control. But it is important to note that this risk does not reside in the impossibility of providing these terms with a content a priori. On the contrary, this impossibility holds open a door to the possibility of radicalizing and pluralizing existing democracies. This possibility presupposes that the *means* as well as the *end* of the common good is the acceptance of differences and disagreement within limits that are defined and continuously modified or negotiated in the democratic process. This acceptance of differences must, in order to have a real impact, be present everywhere in the political community because a political authority can only sustain itself on the basis of what Foucault terms the 'rule of double conditioning': local and general strategies mutually condition each other.[38] The political status of local strategies and practices does not depend on their 'insertion' into antagonistic conflicts in the public sphere. Rather, they are political by virtue of being part of, constituting and reproducing the authoritative allocation of values in a political community, and this is not essentially bound up with antagonistic conflicts in the public sphere.

When the common good and the public interest function as metaphors of the empty place of power which political strategies attempt to circumscribe in order to become hegemonic, there is an obvious risk that these metaphors become loaded with hypocrisy, manipulation, fraud, lies, and so on. From a cynical point of view this is just what the public interest is: a strategic device to make it easier to digest elite domination and social control. But even if we accept this assumption, which is probably far more realistic than most of the prescriptive pleas for rational persuasion, toleration and autonomy, it nevertheless misses the point of public interest arguments. What is significant is not that the claims to speak on behalf of society are marked by domination, hypocrisy, and the like; the real issue concerns why and how political agents bother telling lies, acting as hypocrites and being deceptive. That is, why do political strategies need to universalize themselves one way or another in order to achieve political significance?

If, in trying to answer this question, one holds that politics is first of all about 'power over' which involves conflicts of vested interests, then one is not, I suspect, going to advance very far. The reason is that an explanation of politics in terms of the power to dominate cannot answer the question as to why political strategies have to distance themselves from their particularity and hence universalize themselves in order to achieve power. A typical elitist and mainstream liberal answer would be to beg the question by presupposing what needed to be explained in the first place, namely that political strategies must hide their real motives inasmuch as they are unlikely to meet approval. While this is no doubt the case, reference to manipulation is not, however, the whole story because it does not question the underlying premiss that the political is antithetic to the social, and that power is antithetic to freedom.

The point is not that manipulation has no role to play in politics, but that it has to be seen in relation to political structure and political practice. If the former is reduced to the state and the latter to 'power over', then the legitimation of political power boils down to the problem of how it is possible to dominate free individuals.[39] Legitimation here is reduced to a belief in legitimacy, and this belief has to be 'genuine' in the sense of not being contaminated by politics.[40] That is, it has to be rooted in the rational and autonomous individuals themselves (in civil society), which is to say that it cannot, or rather must not, be the product of elite domination (in the state). It is to underpin this assertion that the early Dahl proposes a strict separation between the political and the social: the legitimacy of the former is based in the underlying consensus that characterizes the latter. The separation between these two realms goes hand in hand with the conception of power in terms of decision making, which, among other things, distinguishes the subtle control mechanisms from the analysis of power that sustains democratic elite domination.

The critics of Dahl *et alii* have, as we have discussed in the first two chapters, attacked this conception of power, as well as the distinction between the political and the social. The radicalness of this critique resides in the broadening of the notion of power which, although still seen as essentially repressive, is expanded to capture the ways in which elite domination reproduces itself through nondecisions and no-decisions to produce its own basis of legitimacy. Although it provides an insight into the circular structure of power and authority, this critique does not challenge the reduction of political structure to the state, and politics to 'power over'. It is, consequently, not able to transcend the assumption that legitimacy concerns the relation between state and civil society, and that this in turn prevents political power from being understood as anything but elite domination, and that legitimacy can be anything but a successful foil for this domination. Hence even this radicalized version of behaviourism is not in a position to grasp the depth of what is at stake in public interest arguments.

To legitimize a policy in the name of the public interest is to forge a link between this policy and the political structure. This endeavour is not a matter of connecting the political conflicts of vested interests with an underlying consensus. It is, instead, a necessary condition for acting politically, that is, to be engaged in the authoritative allocation of values for a society. Lies, hypocrisy, fraud, and so on, are characteristic features of the relation between politics and the political due to the gap within the public interest between its claim to universality and its actual particularism which has to be covered over. The way in which such gaps are patched up range from the most fierce physical and psychological repression to the manipulation of biased information, and the more- or less-subtle institutionalized power/knowledge mechanisms of social control, such as surveillance, discipline and regulation.

The impossibility of ever bridging the gulf between universality and particularity would seem to indicate that the domination of individual interests, and the lies and hypocrisy that go with it, are unavoidable features of the relation between politics and the political. But here one should avoid the temptation to jump to the conclusion that this is simply the stuff politics is made of. The political agent, when trying to legitimize a policy in the name of the public interest, is a bearer of the political structure, and this means that a policy is judged in the light of criteria of inclusivity and non-hierarchy, which are, needless to say, antithetic to the domination of specific interests. Thus politics is basically the practice of minimizing the gaps in the public interest, which can be seen as a structural condition for acting politically, that is, to speak in the name of society. One of the ways of doing this, and hence of minimizing these gaps, is by way of lies and hypocrisy. It is in this light these 'darker sides' of political life should be seen, but it is also in this light that they can be exposed and criticized in the public sphere. Indeed, such a critique partakes in creating and shaping public spaces

The democratic politics of the articulation between individual interests and the public interest thus makes it possible to bring forth a deeper or broader ground of political agreement, while at the same time expressing the acceptance of disagreement and value pluralism. This possibility is rooted in the dislocated nature of the political structure, which entails that the public interest is contestable and hence subject to negotiation. When political strategies have to speak in the name of society, they cannot but appeal to a higher degree of inclusivity on the level of the political values and procedural rules that define the criteria and scope of membership of the political community. This is why particularism connotes exclusivity and hence potential domination. Whilst the political authority has to do with making and implementing collectively binding decisions, the political structure conditions the possibility of inclusivity and procedural agreement. This is why political institutions are contingent upon the political structure, which, as a kind of quasi-universality *vis-à-vis* the political community, makes it possible to advance counterfactual strategies.

That the public interest is, probably, *the* rhetorical device for getting one's way in politics does not, then, exhaust the definition of the public interest. It is equally the case that differences of opinion, interests, practices, norms and values have to make up a system that protects the mutual acceptance of differences. This principle is cultivated in civic traditions and operationalized in terms of civil, political and social rights. Immanent in this principle and hence in these traditions and rights is non-closure, non-hierarchy and non-exclusivity, which express differentiality as such. There are two important and closely connected points here.

First, democratic politics has to presuppose the possibility that differences have not yet achieved form and content, but are simply unspecified relations. This is not a claim that we can encounter differences that are not articulated into systems of differences. Rather, the point is that this presupposition of democratic politics holds a door open for counterfactual reasoning: that things could be different, which in turn links up with the arguments of contingency and undecidability. What is important here is that we are not forced to conceptualize political relations exclusively in terms of domination/subordination and conflict/consensus. Second, and by extension, differentiality as an ontological possibility distances itself from closure, hierarchy and exclusivity, which are contingent upon differentiality while at the same time violating it.

These two points draw attention to power as auto-negativity: by giving shape to the dislocated structure we negate it, because temporality, possibility and freedom as such become discursively ordered. As an ontological condition, differentiality is at once posed as a *telos* and presupposed as an origin, but it is a *telos* and an origin which exist as mere possibilities that cannot be causally effective. Hence while political agents are bearers of the political structure, they cannot be determined by it, which is why political decisions are marked by undecidability. The contestability and negotiability of public interest arguments reflect this moment of undecidability, while at the same time attempting to minimize it in order to create a temporal and spatial integration of the political community.

The common good in a democracy refers to this integration and hence to the articulation between structure, institution and identity in such a way that: (1) power is the empty place of inscription, which is expressed in the democratic political authority as both posed and presupposed by power strategies; (2) the institutional setting is marked by the acceptance of disagreement expressing inclusivity, negotiability and non-hierarchy; and (3) democratic practice is antithetic to elite domination by being a form of participation that gives real control over political decisions *in* the social. Seen against this background, the public interest is an interest geared towards realizing the common good. Although the former can be said to be related to the latter as a means to an end, the circular structure of power implies that the means also define the end or, to put it the other way around, that the end is also defined by the means that realize it. The point is, of course, that structure, institution and identity, by being articulated with each other, are also shaped *vis-à-vis* one another.

When Dahl says that '[o]ur common good . . . consists of the practices, arrangements, institutions, and processes that . . . promote the well-being of others', and that '[t]he opportunity to disagree about specific choices is the very reason for valuing the arrangements that make this opportunity possible',[41] the point is that the political structuring of a democratic authority is the acceptance of disagreement. In so far as we can accept these basic political values, we can set up a number of procedural rules for the democratic process which pin down the limits of acceptability, the nature and scope of disagreement, and the fundamental trust that this acceptance of disagreement fosters. A democratic political community must, constitutionally as well as in all sorts of institutionalized practices, sustain and further the acceptance of disagreement. Such a radicalization and pluralization of democracy requires, first, an acceptance of the autonomy of sub-political communities on the condition that they mutually accept each other as political agents, and second, an acceptance of the members' right to use the exit option without risking harassment.

The common good in a democratic political community ought to be a valuation of the civic traditions and institutional settlements which allow disagreement and gives equal consideration to various points of view within the limits of what is politically reasonable. That is, the democratic principle of inclusion/exclusion is that agents recognize and accept each other as *political* agents who can make a difference in the political community regardless of their moral, cultural or religious convictions. The reason why this is important is that interpretation, negotiation and participation are the only means of underpinning a democratic political authority. This means that they can only be positivated through practices governed by the egalitarian democratic imaginary which give way for procedural rules that make up the design of political institutions allowing for disagreement. Any policy that undermines these conditions is antithetic to the common good regardless of its degree of popular support. The common good does not, then, depend upon identification expressing value consensus but points, rather, at the limits to what is unacceptable, that is, to what would undermine and eventually destroy the democratic common good. The latter is thus defined negatively, that is, *vis-à-vis* these limits which, as mentioned already, evoke the systematicity of acceptability and reasonableness.

Seen in this light, the politics of the articulation between individual interests and the public interest ought to reflect undecidability and contingency both as an ontological condition and an ontological possibility; and bridge the description of the relation between the political structure and the political institution, on the one hand, and the prescription of political values and interests, on the other. The democratic common good connotes that the practical nature of participation and the legal nature of procedural rules should be articulated in such a way that the undecidability of political decisions is embodied in the constitutional and institutional setting of the political regime which is rooted in the political community. Hence, to judge whether a policy is in the public interest is to engage in a discussion on how it is articulated with the political structure of the community.

The impossibility of providing a neutral taxonomy, whereby we can measure whether a policy violates this structure, neither can nor should prevent us from being engaged in such a discussion. Everything is, of course, in the end a matter of interpretation; however, interpretation does not take place in a vacuum but, rather, in an always already structured whole which conditions it. In a democracy this whole is characterized by inclusivity, openness and non-hierarchy, and the prime task for a democratic common good is geared exactly towards maintaining and furthering this condition and possibility. It is this which is the subject matter of the common good, and hence the guideline for interpretations of what is and what is not in the public interest.

The relation between undecidability (practice) and dislocation (structure) signals the infinite options of contrary-to-fact situations, and hence that any agreement reached by political agents on political values and procedural rules, and enforced by the political authorities, could always be different. When we focus upon change we always give it a particular direction which cannot but be contingent upon the infinity of options of the possibility of 'being able'. The prime function of the common good is to keep this game going, to ensure that the ability to make a difference is 'real'. This means: (1) that power as such remains the empty place of inscription, and hence the locus of temporality, possibility and freedom; (2) that political institutions recognize the ultimate undecidability of decisions and hence make it possible to disagree; and (3) that there is a real possibility of participating in politics, that is, of effectively initiating and vetoing decisions at all levels in the political community. All of this requires that politics is an activity that takes place *in* the social and hence is not the prerogative of elites.

Value Pluralism and Liberal Democracy

It is, needless to say, important for democratic theory, regardless of whether it is slanted towards liberalism or communitarianism, to come to terms with the notion of community. What distinguishes these two strands of democratic theory is not whether there is a need for communal practices and fora,[42] but rather how the relation between the individual and community is conceptualized, and which role democratic politics plays, or should play, in relation to community. In light of the dividing lines between liberals and communitarians, the task for democratic theory and politics is often seen as that of performing a trade-off between the individual freedom of the atomistic or 'unencumbered' self and the cultural solidarity of the 'encumbered' self, pluralism and homogeneity, aggregating individual preferences and integrating communal interests and norms, voice and exit, 'thin' and 'thick' conceptions of the good, the right and the good, citizenship as a legal concept and citizenship as a concept of identification, procedural justice and substantive justice, and so on.

The idea is not to discuss these antinomies in detail. The reason is that the question of how the individual is related to the community cannot be of primary interest for political theory and democratic theory. It can only appear as an overriding concern in so far as it is presupposed that the political is derived from either the level of the individual or the community (or a combination of the two) as somehow given entities. But this is, of course, exactly what we cannot assume. As I have already argued, the political cannot be reduced to a supplementary appendix to a given order precisely because it constitutes order; and this in turn means that democratic politics cannot be reduced to a weather vane that swings between the above-mentioned antinomies. Seen from this perspective, one of the characteristic features of the liberalism/communitarianism debate is that it displaces the political and the possibility of democratic politics.

The disagreements between liberals and communitarians with regard to the relation between the individual and community lead to different conceptions of the political and the tasks of democratic politics. The political is typically, in modernity that is, conceived as a superstructural phenomenon that is located in the state and hence distinguished from the community or civil society. It is either an instrument whose basic role is to aggregate preferences formed outside political institutions, or a medium whose task is to further the normative integration of interests and values existing in the community. The problem with this alternative, and hence with one of the fundamental assumptions in the liberalism/communitarianism debate, lies in the reduction of the political to a community of either atomistic individuals or normatively integrated individuals. But if the political constitutes the community, that is, if the political is constitutive of order rather than being, one way or the other, derived from an already existing order (ideal, latent or actually present), and if, moreover, democracy presupposes an ontology of the political, then it follows that it is crucial for democratic politics to operate with a distinction between the political and the social which does not correspond to the state/civil society distinction. This means that a political conception of democracy and justice, has to be what Rawls terms a 'freestanding view', that is, independent in relation to comprehensive doctrines.

Thus conceived liberal democracy depends neither upon rational-agency models of an unencumbered self nor upon an agency model of an encumbered self that has internalized community norms. What it does require is a political structure in which citizens are free and equal, and where mutual recognition and acceptance of differences prevail. That is, an open society that delimits itself from totalitarian and hierarchical societies in which particular conceptions of the good have hegemonized the political authority, and hence endangered the conditions of public reasoning. Political liberalism thus understood forms a framework for the integrity and autonomy of various kinds of groups, communities and social movements. This means that the universal (rights and public reason) must be dissociated from the particular (regime form and the values, rules and interests that go with it), whilst it must at the same time be acknowledged that the universal is the product of and the medium for the particular.

If this requirement is not met, it will be difficult to hold that a political conception of justice could be free-standing and hence impartial with regard to the justification of different and even conflicting comprehensive doctrines. This would be problematic when we are dealing with social movements or communities whose values and forms of life, to a greater or lesser extent, differ from or are hostile towards the (liberal-democratic) majority culture. It would, accordingly, be problematic if democratic politics was endowed with an ideal of a substantive common good because such an ideal cannot but be antithetic to the politics of difference and pluralism, and hence with the political recognition and acceptance of the autonomy of, say, illiberal communities. Pluralism, or rather *reasonable* pluralism,[43] is a political value in itself that provides the best guarantee for individual and collective freedom and the rights that underpin it, which individuals and groups struggle to maintain and extend.

In order to defend a non-essentialist pluralism – which at the same time meets the challenges of multiculturalism and the politics of difference – it is imperative to stress that values cannot be led back to an underlying base value or a perfectionist ideal that revolves around either the constitutive rights of an unencumbered self or 'human nature', or a communitarian defence of cultural homogeneity or a substantive conception of the common good. A non-essentialist pluralism would draw attention to the insight that different conceptions of the good, and forms of life are not simply an appearance behind which we can discover a set of deep-seated values and norms that we all share, and which we can discover if we are able to put aside our particularistic interests and the 'superficial' power conflicts that are associated with pursuing them (compare Dahl's 'underlying consensus' as a pre-political condition for politics). Such an argument would have to assume that knowledge, freedom and order were given prior to politics as means to terminate political disagreement and power conflicts. This vision of the end of politics would have to presuppose the possibility, either in reality or as a regulative idea, of a dialogue in which consensus reached through rational persuasion had substituted power.[44]

If we say that plurality is constitutive and hence irreducible,[45] and that the task of democratic politics is to make and implement authoritative decisions that revolve around acceptable or reasonable differences in the political community, then at least two conclusions follow. First, it is not the case that we had better accept pluralism either because we are not yet, as a liberal might argue, so clear-sighted, rational and autonomous that we are able to find the common denominator in the midst of differences; or, as a communitarian perhaps would argue, because we are alienated in the sense that we have not yet come to terms with our historical or cultural heritage. Second, to further a non-essentialist pluralism, this pluralism has to stay clear of any particular comprehensive doctrine concerning the relation between the individual and the community, meaning that this value pluralism has to be formulated in strictly political terms. Thus conceived, pluralism expresses first of all the *political* value of liberal democracy which holds that those differences that can exist within the framework of public reason, as well as its institutional embodiment in the regime, is the common good we seek to widen and deepen.

The best way to do this is, first, to defend the (Rawlsian) principle that public reason should remain impartial with regard to the justification of reasonable comprehensive doctrines that exist and can exist within this framework; and second, to assert that democratic dialogue should be extended beyond the institutions of representative democracy. The latter is important because the political structuring of social relations and contexts cannot be reduced to, or monopolized by, any particular regime structure, and consequently, the way in which democratic dialogue is best sustained and advanced is to embody the principles of liberty and equality in actual everyday practices.[46] Both of these assumptions indicate the necessity of a bottom-up approach to politics and democracy which would stress that political authorities are rooted in the structuring of the political community.

Public reason, as one of the fundamental pillars of democratic politics, is formed by the articulation between values, interests, practices, and the like, that recognize not only each others right to exist, but also to make a difference in the political community. This articulation between politically reasonable agents revolves around the mutual political acceptance of differences. The political is both *above* the social and *in* the social, which is the reason why a political conception of justice has to argue that the *status* of rights must have priority over the good, whilst allowing that the good has priority in terms of the *origin* of rights.[47] This differentiation and prioritization is important because discourses of rights are to an increasing extent the medium and outcome of the political struggles for recognition of identity. To hold, as Rawls does, that rights ought to have priority over the good only makes sense when this priority is understood in terms of their status and not in terms of their historical origin. The latter is neither logically linked to the status we ascribe to rights nor with the possibility of effectively defending them. An unconditional defence of rights does not, then, depend upon a theory of the origin of rights because the latter cannot but be caught up in ideas of the good. The protection and furthering of rights are central to a political conception of justice, which is the reason why it has to be impartial with regard to the justification of comprehensive doctrines.

It should thus be clear that the borderline between the right and the good, and the political and the social, cannot be drawn rigorously. The same goes for the distinction between the anti-perfectionism of political liberalism, which holds that the political should be impartial with respect to the justification of the good, and the perfectionism advocated by communitarians and some liberals, which holds the opposite, that is, that the political is a medium for the protection and furthering of the common good. The reason is that rights can be seen as the political and legal transformation of the articulation between forms of life, ideas, strategies and interests that struggle for recognition and arise, take form and undergo changes over long stretches of time. Rights can thus be seen as the universalization of the common good or, alternatively, as the sedimentation and legal codification of the balance of forces in a democratic political community which is, and ought to remain, relatively immune to struggles between vested interests.

Struggles for civil, political and social rights should be seen in this perspective. Here emphasis is drawn to two closely related assumptions both of which sustain an idea of a radicalization and a pluralization of democracy. First, that rights, as the medium and outcome of political struggles for recognition, can only be sustained and extended in so far as people are willing and able to continuously fight for them. This is just another way of saying that regime structures are rooted in the political community, and that the scope of politics extends far beyond the juridico-discursive representation of power. Second, the political is, in a similar way, a temporal and spatial abstraction of the social, where the relation between the two levels is contingent. If this was not the case, the political could not have a specificity of its own, and it could not, accordingly, be free-standing. The political is at one and the same time constitutive of the social and its principle of articulation, that is, its structuring principle.

Political conflicts between comprehensive doctrines and the hegemonic blocs they in part constitute, over time shape (as indicated) the contours of a political conception of justice as well as the traditions of democratic politics. Politics is neither a mirror of social interaction nor entirely separated from it, and the same holds for the relation between the right and the good. This implies, among other things, that there is nothing that guarantees the compatibility of rights. Rights are, as Gray argues, 'often competing and conflictual in their implications for practice'.[48] That discourses of rights are the terrain in which agents struggle for the recognition of their values and interests implies that rights are the means for pursuing, revising or rejecting ideas of the good, as well as being ends in themselves that have priority over specific conceptions of the good.

What above all characterizes discourses of rights is that the political values of liberty and equality are articulated with what Lefort, following Tocqueville, has termed the 'democratic revolution'.[49] This articulation imposes upon rights claiming for agents a kind of universality *vis-à-vis* the political community. This implies at least three things. First, rights cannot be universal in the sense of being prior to the political community. On the contrary, they arise within, and are thus rooted in, this community, which is to say that they are – or rather, they have the potentials of becoming – the vehicles of democratic struggles of expanding and deepening liberty and equality. Second, rights cannot be the locus of neutrality if by that we mean that it is possible to find an 'Archimedian point' that is not contaminated by political power. Neutrality cannot but be circumscribed by the criteria of reasonableness that characterize a democratic political community in which rights are rooted and take form. This implies that neutrality of procedural rules only makes sense within limits that cannot themselves be neutral, because they are constituted and enforced by the substantive political value of popular sovereignty.[50] Third, the quasi-universality of rights implies that by engaging in these struggles agents situate themselves within public reason, because the very language of rights is, by definition, non-particularistic. In brief, discourses of rights can be seen as facilitating the criteria of reasonableness, that is, of the mutual acceptance of differences in the political regime and the political community.

The political values of liberty and equality are vehicles of a democratic logic which plays a subversive role *vis-à-vis* structures of domination whilst also being a horizon for democratic politics. These values cannot be given a specific content or be confined within specific locations apriorily, that is, independently of political interaction.[51] Instead, they express a civic tradition that articulates the institutional and the personal dimensions of politics and systematizes our intuitions about fairness, which can only be made explicit in political interaction that continuously revises the democratic values and the political institutions in which they are embodied. This implies that public reason embodies two principles. First, the rules and norms governing the political community as an all-inclusive aspect of political life are different from those governing the politics of organizations, groups, communities, and the like. Second, the rules of the political community have to aim at impartiality *vis-à-vis* the political dimension of these social contexts and the values and interests they express, otherwise value pluralism will be endangered.

The object of public reason is the democratic political community, and the nature of public reason is that it is a framework within which we conduct a political dialogue, well knowing that dialogues and conflicts inevitably lead to changes in this framework. Consequently, both the form and the content of this framework undergo changes over time.

An activity is, as mentioned, political if it is directed towards the authoritative allocation of values for a context, which can be either the entire political community or institutions, organizations, social movements, and so on. What distinguishes the latter from the former is not the nature of politics, but the limitations on the scope of collectively binding decisions. This distinction indicates that it would be dangerous for democratic politics if the specific interests and values constituting the politics of particular contexts were to hegemonize political authority in the political community. Such an attempt would undermine value pluralism as well as the democratic principle of self-determination and popular sovereignty. This is why the anti-perfectionist stance of political liberalism gives priority to the political over the social in the interest of the social, so to speak. It is crucial for the political to be free-standing in relation to comprehensive doctrines: it provides the best chances for the coexistence of, or for the 'overlapping consensus' between, incommensurable and even antagonistic values.[52]

Value pluralism is thus compatible with Rawls's reasonable pluralism, which goes hand in hand with 'partially' comprehensive doctrines that accept each other politically. A stronger claim could, in fact, be made that the distinction between the political and the social is the very condition for a democratic politics for whom value pluralism is decisive, because the political acceptance of differences is compatible with even antagonistic cultural differences.[53] The political authorization of power does not depend upon cultural homogeneity, which is to say that in order to accept individuals and groups as political agents we do not have to endorse their ideas of the good. Democratic politics thus conceived provides the best guarantee for self-determination and popular sovereignty and the rights that underpin it, which individuals and groups struggle to maintain and extend, whilst it at the same time allows for the possibility of collective processes of identification. That is, it does not rest upon an atomistic conception of the self or, for that matter, any other conception of selfhood.[54]

The political aspect of a decision depends upon its ability to articulate the limits of a context through mechanisms of inclusion and exclusion. This hegemonic logic, or this political function of systematizing differences,[55] is important for grasping the nature, scope and application of public reason. Rawls's political conception of justice could be seen as both the product of and the medium for the articulation between comprehensive doctrines. This indicates that his political conception of justice and democratic politics are posed as well as presupposed by social interaction. It does not seem plausible, then, that the political conception of justice can be entirely separated from ideas of the good, and from power struggles between these ideas. However, this does not imply that it is inconsistent to give priority to the right over the good when we talk about the status of the political conception of justice. It does not seem likely either that public reason is applicable only to the top echelons of political and judicial institutions. If public reason was, in fact, the prerogative of elites, it would only be among them that the overlapping consensus would have a real impact. This would go hand in hand with an elitist conception of democracy for whom elite autonomy is the meta-principle of democracy.[56]

Rawls's concept of the political seems to indicate that the political is: (1) an 'infrastructure' of all types of contexts that is not imbued with a particular goal, but which is instead a process of continuous goal seeking – an assumption that goes hand in hand with the concept of the political as an ontology of potentials; (2) the medium and outcome of articulations between comprehensive doctrines in time and space that form the civic traditions of the political community; and (3) the basis of democratic practices of public reason, and the political values that are associated with it, which have to have priority in relation to comprehensive doctrines that form part of social interaction.

If politics only entered the scene after the articulation of preferences in civil society, it would not be possible to hold that politics and political institutions play a constitutive role. Moreover, it would be impossible to distinguish between the overlapping consensus and a *modus vivendi* of interest compromises resulting from the aggregation of preferences. When politics is seen as a constitutive dimension of social relations the principle of public reason is applicable to democratic politics everywhere. The reason is that the qualification of reason as 'public' has to refer to the quality of reason and not to its institutional location, otherwise the notion of public reason would loose its critical and evaluative potential. Furthermore, an institutional definition of 'the public sphere' would be problematic, because historically it has been defined in relation to state and civil society and, moreover, because there is not *a* public sphere, but instead a variety of public spheres.

When we refer to public reason we refer to an aspect of collective action and a specific quality of reason. Political reasoning can fulfil the criteria of fairness *vis-à-vis* the limits constituting specific contexts. That these limits might be characterized by a high degree of perfectionism does not in itself undermine the principle of public reason. It only affects its scope of applicability, meaning that what is publicly reasonable in one context is not necessarily publicly reasonable in another. What this amounts to is that public reason cannot be divorced from the comprehensive doctrines that make up the various contexts. It is not, accordingly, possible to make a strict separation between anti-perfectionism and perfectionism, and public and private. Public reason is, in varying degrees, built into the structures of these contexts and reflected in the values, norms, rules and interests that govern them. Which is why it is intertwined with everyday democratic practices in which the personal and institutional dimensions of politics are articulated with each other.

The principle of public reason applies to democratic politics in each context, and the more they interact, the more the overarching context will have to abstract from the specific ideas of the good that govern each of them. This is why public reason has to be impartial *vis-à-vis* comprehensive doctrines in the political community. But since public reason is also defined in relation to these contexts, it is not able to divorce itself completely from these doctrines. The right cannot be isolated from the good, whereupon a full blown anti-perfectionism is not possible. It is not even desirable from a democratic point of view, because it would indicate that regime structures could be isolated from the political community. There is, rather, a continuum that goes from a high degree of anti-perfectionism – the hallmark of public reason given its premiss of fairness and its applicability to the political community as such – to lower degrees of anti-perfectionism that characterize democratic politics in social communities.[57]

Rawls's emphasis on reasonableness and common concern is important for the debate between liberals and communitarians because it undermines a number of basic, often implicit, assumptions in this debate. The points of contestation are not those between an unencumbered self and an encumbered self, just as the political is not a necessary evil which is predetermined to serve as either an instrument in the hands of powerful elites or a medium whose more benign aim is to realize the inherent social or cultural values of a community. By thus conceptualizing the political in a way that refuses to treat it as an appendix to either rational agency models or a communitarian insistence on cultural homogeneity, that is, by refusing to treat the political in derivative terms. Rawls paves the way for an alternative understanding of what it means to talk about the public interest.

Public interest arguments are usually coined in counterfactual terms as the interest individuals would pursue if they had full information, were acting benevolently or altruistic, and so on.[58] That is to say, power is opposed to knowledge, and individual rationality is opposed to collective (ir)rationality. It is these kinds of a priori assumptions Rawls is able to counter by shifting the terrain of the discussion away from economistic and sociologistic reductions of the political by approaching the political as a free-standing and constitutive dimension of social relations that has to attain priority over comprehensive doctrines when there is a conflict between the two. To strike a balance between political values we do not have to disregard our values and interests, which, in any case, would run contrary to the idea of the overlapping consensus. Hence we do not have to employ contrary-to-fact conditionals as to how we would behave if we had full information, were rational, disinterested, and so on. 'The veil of ignorance' assumes, in fact, the opposite.[59]

Alternatively, by arguing that the public interest is constituted politically, he advances the argument that individuals in the 'original position' operate behind a 'veil of ignorance', which is to say that they are prevented from getting access to full information and the bargaining power that goes with it. This implies that the original position, as a 'device of representation' for a democratic political community, is seen in terms of a political ontology of potentials that stresses performability within the constraints of the reasonable.

The latter is an overarching category in relation to the rational and the normative with regard to the nature of democratic political community.[60]

Two conclusions follow from this. First, the primacy given to either rational agents or cultural homogeneity is displaced in favour of a political ontology of potentials, and the latter is constitutive in the sense that it does not merely reflect an always already given (economic, social or for that matter religious) order. Instead, it revolves around creating and sustaining what March and Olsen call 'islands of imperfect and temporary organization in potentially inchoate political worlds'.[61] This ontology is, moreover, 'empty' in that there are no a priori goals built into the political, because it is, as mentioned, a continuous goal-seeking process. Second, power cannot, by inference, be equated with either the repressive image of 'power over' or the more benign or even emancipatory view of 'power to'. Instead, it seems more to the point to suggest that Rawls's idea of power finds expression in the two capacities that are foundational for his political conception of justice, namely the capacity for a sense of justice and the capacity for a sense for the good. These are worked out for the political and the social respectively and presuppose, in turn, a sense for a common concern.[62]

We can thus conclude that it is possible to defend a political community that pays allegiance to the political values of liberal democracy while also accepting the existence of incommensurable differences of values, rules, practices, and so on. This implies that the principle of reasonableness is laid down in the limits on arguments and practices that attempt to exclude interests, opinions, values and ways of life on the basis of, for example, social position, ethnicity, nationality, gender, sexuality and religion. What we get is a principle of mutual political acceptance within these limits.[63] This acceptance is neither based on nor can it be reduced to either an instrumental calculation, as in the model of procedural democracy that focuses on the aggregation of individual preferences or a normative integration, as in a substantive conception of the common good that stresses the formation of a collective identity. It is, instead, a *political* acceptance because it is conceived at the level of the political structure as the ordering principle of the political community.

It is because the political is both constitutive of social relations and functions as their structuring vehicle that it has to be articulated with democracy. One of the most pressing challenges facing democracy today is to reformulate the relation between universalism and particularism so as to make it possible in a democracy based on rights and a politics of difference for them to mutually reinforce each other, rather than being mutually exclusive. To face up to this challenge, democratic politics delimits a political space of mutual political acceptance whose limits are given by what is excluded from this space, namely those practices that exclude political agents on the basis of comprehensive doctrines that revolve around, for example, ethnicity, gender, religion, social position and sexuality.

When an individual acts politically within, say, a group or a social movement, it is confined within a more- or less-closed political structure of that particular context which is shaped and sustained by specific rule-governed practices and forms of life. The internal political structure of each context should be related to the overarching political structure in such a way that it, as a minimum, accepts the principle of the freedom of association, that is, the right to exit.[64] One can, in my opinion, require no more than that as the basis of mutual political acceptance between groups, communities, and so on. When we go inside a group the situation is somewhat different due to more- or less- marked differences between the political common good, which is closely related to the idea of public reason, and the specific ideas of the good, especially of non-democratic, groups. However, as long as the practices of groups do not violate the principle of the mutual acceptance of differences, they cannot be a common concern. That is why the persistence of a democratic political community should not rest on normative integration and a substantive conception of the common good.

There cannot be any *socially* defined common good nor, I would claim, is there any need of such a notion in democratic politics, because it would imply that particular social or cultural values would be the guiding principle for public reason and hence for a political conception of justice and democratic politics. This would, as Rawls argues, imply a violation of the principle that public reason ought to be impartial with regard to the justification of 'the good life', and such a violation could, in turn, only be implemented by means of repression, that is, by dominating other moral, philosophical and religious views.[65] However, this does not render the idea of the common good useless if, that is, it can be reformulated as the *political* value of democracy which revolves around a common concern and which signals openness and toleration *vis-à-vis* the limits of reasonable pluralism.[66]

These limits cannot, of course, be given once and for all but are, on the contrary, themselves politically contestable. They are the means and end of public reason, in consequence of which the latter points at the horizons of the political conception of the common good. The negotiable nature of the common good implies that it is vital to discuss the limits of acceptability and hence what reasonable pluralism is. These limits are themselves political constructs, and this means that what is considered reasonable is itself both the means and ends of a democratic dialogue that is characterized by mutual acceptance of differences. What is not negotiable in a democracy, however, are its two main principles, namely popular sovereignty and self-determination.[67]

A democratic regime operates, as does every other regime form, with criteria of inclusion and exclusion. But democracy is the only type of regime for whom the criteria of exclusion is based on the political principle of difference. This gives way for a *political* solidarity in the political community modelled upon the mutual recognition and acceptance of differences. It should thus be possible to defend a democratic political community that builds on civic traditions, endorses value pluralism and gives priority to the right over the good. This requires not only that public reason has to remain impartial with regard to the justification of the good, but also that it is applicable to democratic politics beyond the institutions of representative democracy. That is, it has to be solidly rooted in the civic traditions forming the political community.

It is important to note that this latter requirement does not imply that the democratic principle of mutual political acceptance of differences actually has to be applied in all sorts of context. There will, typically, be contexts (most likely, some ethnic and religious communities) that are hostile to this principle. By accepting their right to self-determination one also has to accept that whilst they internally might not be democratic, in the sense that they might not tolerate internal disagreement, they are, nevertheless, obliged to accept the autonomy of other communities. The latter further implies that it must be a democratic principle of an open and pluralist society – characterized by an overlapping membership of organizations, communities, social movements, and so on – that the members of these groups have an exit option.

Democracy is a challenge facing everyone, and this means that each and every individual is responsible for its persistence and development. The defence, furthering and deepening of democracy can never be stronger than the actual will of the members of the political community to fight for it, which is another way of saying that it cannot merely be guaranteed constitutionally, that is, at the regime level. Hence the importance of the tradition of citizenship for democratic theory, meaning that to create and sustain this will cannot be left to professional politicians and other elites without endangering the very roots of democracy. It is this insight Foucault alludes to when he says that '"liberty" is what must be exercised.' Self-determination and popular sovereignty make up an ethico-political challenge that face every individual, who, by taking up this challenge, defends not only his or her rights and dignity, but also the democratic political community which is the life-blood of preserving and extending the political values of democracy and the rights underpinning it.

Concluding Remarks on Hegemony and Democracy

In light of the preceding discussion, it could be argued that the term 'radical democracy' should be understood paradoxically: 'it is precisely *not* "radical" in the sense of pure, true democracy; its radical character implies, on the contrary, that we can save democracy only by *taking into account its own radical impossibility*.'[68] Radical and plural democracy concerns the ongoing process of seeking democratic goals within the structure of the political, and not the concrete attainment of goals within the political regime. Thus the radical imaginary of democracy cannot ever be fully realized in any given democracy, which is why radical and plural democracy is not, contrary to most liberal and Marxist understandings of democracy, a doctrine of 'reconciliation and mastery'. It has its ground in the political authority which has furthered not only totalitarianism, but also democratization as an open society that has tended to include more and more areas of social life, widening and deepening liberty and equality for everybody.

Radical and plural democracy would indeed require a hegemonic regime to provide it with both limitations through inclusion/exclusion and a particular identity. But this does not mean that democracy as such is a hegemonic project. Laclau and Mouffe express the difference between democracy and hegemony as follows:

> the logic of democracy cannot be sufficient for the formulation of any hegemonic project. This is because the logic of democracy is simply the equivalential displacement of the egalitarian imaginary to ever more extensive social relations, and, as such, it is only a logic of the elimination of relations of subordination and of inequalities.[69]

There is a discrepancy between the logic of democracy and a hegemonic project in that the latter situates itself in the former without ever being able to define or control it. The logic of democracy is within hegemonic practices because it originates in power struggles, but it is also above these practices as their horizon. A theory of radical and plural democracy must, consequently, operate on two analytical levels. On the one hand, we have the logic of democracy, which does not pertain to 'the positivity of the social'. That is to say, in itself it can neither attain a specific form nor be a causal factor in bringing about this 'positivity'. It is a quasi-transcendental political horizon of possibilities which conditions but does not determine political practices. This can be put to work, so to speak, as the 'free' variety available to agents in the political community, as opposed to the 'bounded' variety actually being used by the given regime. On the other hand, we have certain political practices which are in the social and which give the social a determinate form. These practices are constitutive in the sense that they cannot be determined by either overarching or underlying structures, that is, by a social objectivity.

Looking at the relationship between the logic of democracy and hegemonic project in this way has three consequences. First, as Laclau and Mouffe argue, it is the only means of sustaining the argument of the contingency of hegemonic regimes and the political structuring of social constructs in general. Second, it replaces the causal logic that characterizes the structure/agency dualism with the logic of conditioning potentials, which is incompatible with determinism and reductionism. And third, it sheds light on the nature of antagonism as showing the collapse of social objectivity, which is defined as belonging to the realm of hegemonic practices, and hence as conditioned by the political structure.

The 'upper' level of democratization as 'the egalitarian imaginary' is distinct from the 'lower' level of political practices in the same way that the structure of political authority is distinct from the regime structure. The existence of political authority is the very condition for both the regime and the political community, but it cannot determine the nature of any of them. In so far as the conceptualization of the political takes place on the lower level, one is inevitably caught up in the presupposition that the political systematization of differences, which revolves around decisions and hence inclusion/exclusion, necessarily implies antagonism, consent/coercion, rulers/ruled, elites/masses, and the like. It therefore becomes impossible to advance beyond the straitjacket of the modern dualisms and hence liberalism.

As long as the democratic imaginary is confined within a 'demo-elite perspective', it will remain the case: (1) that 'ordinary' citizens are ostracized from political participation; (2) that democratic institutions function as 'buffers' between state and civil society whose role is primarily protective; and (3) that political authority is reduced to legitimate domination whose role is to strike an uneasy balance between economistic and sociologistic models of aggregation/integration and instrumentalism/ethics. By conceptualizing the political and democratization as belonging to the upper level, it is possible to advance five arguments in line with those that shape the theory of radical and plural democracy:

1. The political is constitutive for and immanent in the social without being able to determine its concrete forms, which means that we move from a logic of determination and reduction to a logic of conditioning potentials and plurality.
2. These forms are historically contingent constructs that can never be permanently fixed or closed, which is to say that they are in constant processes of transformation.
3. The political is *in* the social, meaning that political authority stems from the structuring of the political community (the bottom-up approach), which is why politics cannot be confined to the state, just as authority cannot be reduced to legitimacy.
4. Political authority follows a logic of appropriateness, due to the undecidable nature of decisions (that is, that they have no ultimate ground) and the contingency of political institutions (that is, that they are conditioned by the political authority). It is in this respect that politics has firm ties to the concept of phronesis.
5. Emancipation need not be caught up in the sterile alternative between either a universalism that seeks to eliminate politics, or a doomsday vision that one form of oppression is bound to lead to another. A genuine contrary-to-fact possibility can be outlined that has not a priori excluded something and included something else.[70]

Coming to terms with these five points presupposes that both the political, and radical and plural democracy are analytically separated from the contingency of hegemonic projects. This is the only feasible way to sustain the argument about the contingency of the political structuring of the social, which underpins democracy as the articulation between self-determination and popular sovereignty.

Otherwise, we will unavoidably be confined within the typically modern inability to conceptualize the political due to its economistic and/or sociologistic reduction of the political, in consequence of which we are stuck with either a form of elitism which excludes lay actors from political participation, or a utopian universalism that refuses to think politically.

Postscript on Conceptualizing Power

Power as Retroactive Causation

Throughout this book I have tried to come to terms with the underlying presuppositions of the conceptions of power I have dealt with. Let us for a moment turn back to the etymological starting point for the discussion of power, namely that power is ability. Power means that we are able to do something, to make a difference: we *are* able or we *have* ability. The 'are' and 'have' appear as seductive metaphors not only because they seem self-evident, and hence as always already given presuppositions, but also because they invert a causal relationship. From at least Hobbes onwards power has been equated with cause. On the one hand, agents can produce effects because they 'have' power or 'are' powerful, but on the other, we can say that someone 'has' power or 'is' powerful only by looking at these effects. The issue at stake here is not whether power is located in something (will, structure, system) or whether it is located in effects (actions, practices, behaviour). The point is that the subject attains the status of the metaphor for the origin of these effects, and this means that it is the name of this 'something' in which power is located, which in turn is itself the vehicle of effects.[1]

What is at stake here is not only that the effect is perceived before its cause or that it is always open for discussion whether an effect can be led back to this or that cause. The point is rather that whilst power as ability cannot be a discursively valid object, it seems as if it has to be presupposed in order to make sense of what power is. In this respect, we can say that power is an extremely slippery notion characterized by its circularity. Power is an effect which, in order to circumscribe itself, poses itself as the fundamental causal principle. Power as the ability to make a difference doubles itself when the making of a difference presupposes an underlying ability that belongs to either agents, structures or systems from which effects can be derived. If, instead of deriving these effects from a hypostatized power as cause, we focus on the circularity of power, we will have to say that ability is immanent in difference, and that the ability to make a difference is a metaphorical, and indeed hegemonic, effect of power itself. Power is thus an effect whose cause is itself a retroactive effect of power.

Why is it so difficult to figure out what power is? Is it because it is everywhere and pretty well every relation can be a power relation, or is it because incommensurable theories stand in the way of reaching an understanding of what power really is? And what is this desire for power in the first place, including the desire to conceptualize or define it? We seem to reach out for what is unreachable, to attempt to control what always, in the final instance, escapes being fully grasped and brought under the control of juridical and political apparatuses. And consider this final instance: should we conceive power as the ability to do something, to make a difference – a will manifesting itself in spite of resistance, a structure determining that will, or a system or social order grounding both will and structure? Will, structure, system, or whatever other names we choose to play the role of overarching or last instances, always recede into the horizons of yet other and more profound or encompassing instances whenever they are stated. They are names employed to ground and define power in order to create a framework within which things make sense and identities can be positioned.

The search for grounding, defining and controlling power is perhaps in the end nothing but a desire to ground, define and control ourselves and others, and hence to reach out for ourselves *as we are*. The reason is that we have no other access to the subject than to trace its effects, well knowing that to speak of 'its' effects is to evoke the subject as a unitary causal principle. Here we find a paradox that pertains to the dimension of time. To order and locate effects is only possible if the subject is pointed out a priori as the causal agent bringing about effects – that it is somehow beyond or before these effects rather than being itself a name of these effects when they coagulate and become sites of dispositions. This operation is possible only by collapsing time because the subject takes the place of the origin rather than being seen in terms of an ongoing process of becoming *in* time. The paradox is that causation has to do away with the dimension of temporality in order to get temporality off the ground. That is, it has to presuppose a temporal distance between cause and effect in order to maintain the immunity of the causal agent, the subject. The articulation between time and causation implies, accordingly, a linear time with a beginning, an origin inaugurating temporality, which in turn summons an end, a *telos* that can take all sorts of forms: utopia, communism, the end of history, the vision of the end of politics, and so forth.

This paradox seems to be inherent in the attempt to understand power in terms of causation – the paradox being, of course, just one amongst several ways of reflecting upon the circular structure of power – that revolves around questions such as why and how things turn out the way they do, and who decides what, when and how. The debate on the three faces of power illustrates the problems of the triangle: subject, causation and time. The operationalizability and neatness of the behavioural focus on decision making as the causal vehicle of power (Dahl, *et alii*) is gradually blurred *pari passu* with the contextualization of power, and hence with the causal mechanisms. In this move towards context (standing conditions, asymmetrical power relations or structures), it no longer seems feasible to hold on to the axiom that the subject is placed outside the causal mechanisms. Bachrach and Baratz engaged in this kind of inquiry when envisaging the relationship between the self and power in their critique of behaviourism, which was radicalized by Lukes who did not take self-determination and consensus at face value, due to the possibility that they could have been brought about by forms of social power such as ideology, prejudice or manipulation that in part constitute the subject. Foucault as well as Laclau and Mouffe move beyond the strictures of an essentialism, *in casu* behaviourism and humanism, which either assume that interests are rooted in a will that is axiomatically presupposed, the rock-bottom fact from which a causal analysis of power takes its beginning, or envision that the self-identical subject can be reached as soon as the layers of repressive powers are peeled off (the issue addressed in the concern with detecting real interests in contrary-to-fact reasoning).

When we try to come to terms with the subtle ramifications of power in wider and wider contexts, something happens to the relationship between the activity of conceptualizing power and the object that is conceptualized. The latter can no longer be kept at a distance, in the sense that theory cannot be applied to a world whose objectivity is given by its externality *vis-à-vis* the subject. It never could, of course, but the emphasis on the contextualization of power has made this impossibility more visible by shattering the subject/object dualism, whereby theory and, more generally, knowledge cannot reasonably be considered neutral or objective either. Knowledge itself becomes politicized in the wake of the growing stress on context as a contingent construct imbued with power relations that condition processes of identification in which the subject finds itself. But problematizing terms such as distance, applicability, linear causation, and the like, does not automatically hand us over to a particular but crude image of a postmodern scenario of 'free play' where everything is possible, and where there is nothing but ongoing proliferations of differences that are never forced to return to what conditions them. To hold that the structure of power is essentially circular would make no sense in this scenario.

The situation is rather that when we take issue with these problems, we seem to be engulfed in an inescapable circular movement between the act of conceptualizing and what is conceptualized. When something is conceptualized it is turned into an object for recognition, which allegedly pre-exists the activity of recognizing and representing, otherwise this activity would not seem to make sense, at least not for a realist.[2] In this excavation of the object – which cannot but be its construction – in which knowledge and autonomy appear as external to power, we are unavoidably entangled in an objectification of ourselves, meaning that thought recoils in an objectification of itself. Hence the internality of the subject (will or autonomy) can no longer mirror itself in the externality of the world as an object (factual or structural). Power as causation is caught up in its own presuppositions which cannot accordingly be presupposed.

The Circular structure of Ability and Its Conceptualization

Ability – wilful, structural or systemic – is not an uncontaminated starting point, but is itself caught up in power struggles that revolve around its ground and the instigation of directions that always have to be decided or determined in the ongoing attempts to control identity. This ability, criss-crossed with aporias and contingencies, always loses track of itself whenever it attempts to position and identify itself *as it is*. But this is only half the story, as the discussion of Connolly's conceptualization of real interests attempts to illustrate, since ability cunningly returns as the organizing matrix and anchoring point for thinking power. Ability is not just a name, it is also a place, or it is, more accurately, a name of an amorphous, anonymous and unlocatable place which identification processes continuously have to posit and redefine as their presupposition in order to orientate, define and determine themselves. '[T]he origin is', says Foucault, 'that which is returning, the repetition towards which thought is moving, the return of that which has already always begun.'[3]

Here lie the great advantages of Foucault's power analytics and Laclau and Mouffe's discourse analysis, which do not just consist in a critique of value neutrality and essentialism, and an insistence upon the interdependence between theory and facts, epistemology and ontology. The crucial point lies, rather, in the circular movement that whilst the self cannot be prior to its objectifications, the latter do, none the less, construct something which accounts for or causes them. This 'something' can only be grasped as the name, or the place, of the self as presupposed through its positing of the objective world, whose externality and objectivity is mirrored in the self as internal to or identical with itself. What we are faced with here is the objectification of will or thought as an unthinkable and ungraspable substance, an unreachable object, within the subject itself which collapses the antinomy between subject and object whilst, at the same time, retaining the tension, breach or aporia that conditions movement and hence identification, ordering, and so on. It is this fundamental reversal in which the becoming of identity is conceived as emanating from the subject as the originary cause that lies at the centre of what Foucault termed the juridico-discursive representation of power. But the logic of this circular structure is not restricted to this representation of power that revolves around the constitutive subject. It is equally shown in deterministic or objectivistic discourses that posit given ontological conditions as epistemological presuppositions.

The circular positing of presuppositions that pertain to self, structure and system equips these and similar terms with an elusive reality-effect from which the derivative constructions of power and hence linear causal models take shape. The latter is thus founded upon circularity, or to put it differently, linearity is an attempt to straighten out circularity. Origin and *telos*, subject and object, are images of linearity, which is to say that these and similar metaphors cannot be foundational. It is in the attempt to advance an understanding of this essential circularity that power has to be defined at the limit, or rather as the limit, whose transgression takes the form of a recoiling movement in which ability establishes itself prior to its effects as a hollow reference point that hegemonic strategies try to fill out.

Power has to be analysed in terms of identifications by revolving around, whilst also questioning, aprioris: as the becoming of identity where substance *qua* substance poses the subject as always already given, what Žižek refers to as the subject before subjectivation.[4] This becoming of identity cannot but be self-referential in the sense that the self is the overarching reference point whilst also being constituted in this referring. It is a self-referentiality which is triggered by the impossibility of bringing the circular referring to completion, an impossibility which conditions the self. That is, an impossibility, or better, a constitutive negativity which *is* the subject.[5] This is the place of ability, and hence the origin and target for the hegemonic reversal of cause and effect, which means that hegemony always revolves around articulating time and space: future and past, part and whole.

But how do we go about conceptualizing power when it is not an object but more like a becoming: a self becoming itself. Power comes from everywhere and surely we cannot embrace everything with a concept, a master signifier, or an institutional device, which would somehow elevate our ability to understand the phenomenon and bring it under the sway of ethical maxims and the law. A commonsensical response to this objection could be to look at power as a family concept ranging from blatant repression to the fringes of rational persuasion. But what would have been gained by such an answer? Power would have another name, or rather other names, by being turned into an 'influence term', and the need for further theoretical inquiry would have been settled by this pluralizing device that seems justified in the light of the heterogeneity of power and the various ways we go about using that term. Still, it is not at all clear what power as an influence term means. All sorts of phenomena are lumped together because they have at least one thing in common, namely that something happens or a change occurs, and this change, which might in turn lead to other changes, has a cause. The problem is not that power is treated as a family concept or that it is categorized as an influence term. What does appear problematic, however, is the reluctance to deal with the fundamental question of what it implies to operationalize ability in the language of causation.

Is power a community resource or an ability connected with the social order and the individual respectively? In other words, is power ingrained in the construction and reproduction of the social order simply because order is the *conditio sine qua non* for being capable of acting in the first place, and particularly of acting in concert? Or is power identified with the ability to act that can take all sorts of forms, and which has been categorized in terms of 'power over' and 'power to', 'zero-sum' and 'plus-sum', from repression to persuasion? However, communitarian as well as individualistic approaches usually tend to beg the question as to what power is. The mistake lies in asserting that power *is*, that it is some-*thing* which can be pointed out: a resource, capacity or an ability, which either structures, social orders or individuals should be endowed with. By making such assumptions, one is already caught up in a conceptualization of power that has posed and thus fixed its presuppositions (a ground), which is exactly what one cannot do if these presuppositions are themselves to be called into question. That is to say, if the dialectics between posing and presupposing should be the focus of attention.

The point is not that of defining power – to get at the *real thing* – and then proceed to apply it to reality as if it existed independently of the discourses trying to come to terms with it. An approach on these lines would be futile. As we have seen, application is not a simple transmission from theory to reality; it is more like a construction of that reality, whose reality effect attempts to turn full circle by becoming a cause and hence a ground. We are thus thrown back to the inescapable circularity haunting the search for grounds and methodological principles, whether they lie in the theoretical construction or in the so-called external world. The positing of presuppositions is thus unavoidable. The point is, however, that the latter does not exist independently of the former. It does not assume a thing-like character from which everything else can be deduced if only it is interpreted 'correctly'.

What if the attempt to get at the real thing is itself power? This would not only imply that it is not beyond or before the power that tries to grasp it (the interdependence of theory and facts), but also that the very activity of reaching out for the real thing is power, where this act could be seen as an articulation between will and understanding. This would be Foucault's argument that power and knowledge are immanent in each other, which in turn implies that they are not immanent to something else that transcends power-knowledge, such as subject or object, because these concepts are rooted in the plane of immanence.[6] Seen in this light power would be the endeavour to delineate, circumscribe and consummate a space and a time within which things could be ordered, and in which a reality effect could be established, an effect presenting itself as the cause. That is, an ordering that could present itself as the unfolding of an order already there but only graspable in its unfolding, in its effects. The positing of presuppositions operates in this manner: the former construes the latter as its cause, from which it is derived, a derivation that presupposes itself in the sense that its operationalizability and success depend upon the instantiation of a spatial and temporal distance in which order becomes conceivable and can be detected. It is here we find the 'forgetting' of an always contaminated origin (that is, the subject only exists as a projection in time), because it only lives in its effects – effects which in turn produce its itselfness. But it is an origin, none the less, which survives in the self-referential suturing of identity and order.

Order as Reality Effect

The construction of reality effects requires this forgetting. A 'will to power' no doubt, but one which is not in control and does not stand aside or above the scenery of struggles. In other words, it does not reside above the political constellations and the judicial codifications of reality, although its primary means to render this reality legitimate consists of exactly that, namely distantiation and detachment, hence its plea for objectivity. However, to engage oneself in conceptualizing power is to be enrolled in political power struggles: to instigate limits, to position oneself and to be positioned, all of which necessarily changes oneself. One always finds oneself as already positioned and engulfed in the politics of living. Hence the search for limits and their transgression, which are the vehicles for becoming what one is; and this, in turn, means to be different because the forces that confine, constrain, orientate, position, liberate, spark off reflection, and so on, are the means for circumscribing and organizing identity and order. That is, they are more- or less-chaotic systematizations of chaos.

This attempt to bring about order cannot, then, be equated with the elevated stance of an autonomous and rationally detached observer who has thrown off his or her political garment in order to see things clearly. To be a rationally detached observer reflects the position of the subject of being at a distance, which is prior to and a condition for objectivity. The point is not simply that distance and objectivity are impossible. They are, of course, but the paradoxical virtue of this stance, and hence of the objective gaze, is that it systematizes and totalizes that which it observes and represents, whereupon it cannot after all be detached and least of all is it neutral. Perhaps we could say that whereas distance conditions objectivity the latter uses the former as a means to order part and whole, and future and past.

Autonomy and rationality are the irreducible opposites of power, which are posed or delineated by power strategies whilst also trying to escape their grip by virtue of being presupposed as given faculties, which power tries to grasp from the 'outside'. Hence the typical opposition between autonomy and power which paves the way for, or is an expression of, the 'repressive hypothesis'. Here we find an inescapable circularity that pertains to space and time which various conceptions of power, irrespective of whether they are rooted in agency or structure, try to make linear. The aim is, of course, to render power a causal concept that operates in accordance with 'the canons of science' which typically set out to turn reality into a substance that cannot present itself, but which is, none the less, 'out there' in its inert, mute and ungraspable presence waiting to be re-cognized and re-presented.

Again we see this reality effect which is a correspondence between reality and its conceptualization that renders the former intelligible and hence representable and even law-abiding. In this scenario, the rational has entangled and ordered reality in whose image it came into being. The alternative is not between realism and constructionism, both of which are equally inappropriate. It is in the undecidable relation between revealing and constructing that discourses establish their hegemonic identity, and in which they interpret and represent a reality that always escapes being fully captured intellectually as well as politically. The reason is not that reality is a substance that forever recedes when we try to comprehend it. The point is, rather, that it is the limit of the experience of objectivity which, nevertheless, is dressed up in an objectivity allegedly pertaining to its 'real' nature. A circular kind of reasoning, a conversion brought to bear in the search for stability and order, in short, for a ground. The limit of objectivity becomes itself the site of objectivity, or it contours a spatial and temporal horizon of objectivity, which is nothing but the positivation of negativity, that is, of the failure of fully capturing reality.

The representational way of thinking is a thinking of substances that cannot present themselves: *that* which is beyond our reach which we can term reality or ideality but which, functionally, comes down to pretty much the same thing. As long as we try to grasp power in terms of representation, we are bound to end up in a metaphysics of substances regardless of whether these are coined in terms of the ability of subjects, the necessity of structures, or the normative integration of systems. Power would in either case remain obscure, and the task of knowledge would be to unveil its mystical core. Such an unveiling could not but discover new veils, new representations of that which cannot itself be present. By following this path of linearity we would be led into an infinite regress which would, in the end, have to resort to postulates such as given conditions, abilities and facts in order to make sense. And then the whole process backwards: power deduced from these abilities and conditions, be they factual or structural. We would be back in a derivative understanding of power – empiricist, constructivist or realist – with its causal mechanisms, irrespective of whether these are statistical regularities or real mechanisms.

Linearity makes sense exactly because it stops short of going astray in infinite regress, or to use a more appropriate metaphor, before the line curves and looks back at itself, thereby distancing itself from itself which it inevitably does when it sees itself as a whole, that is, when it conceptualizes this whole as what it is. This is the moment that entices rationally detached objectivity – a speculative gaze no doubt, but no less objective. To see itself as a whole is only possible in so far as this whole is delimited, and it is this very act of imposing limits which is the moment of self-reference. This means that the self-referring whole is itself conditioned by, and is a particular structuring of, the articulation of power and knowledge. Due to its particularity it cannot but be one among other possible reading principles, which is to say that objectivity and contingency necessarily presuppose one another.

These temporal processes forwards and backwards, as well as the spatial processes between part and whole, are attempts to order time and space according to a linear causality. The behaviourist inclination to see power as an influence term delineates a space with causal chains mapped out in discrete temporal sequences making up, or rather containing events in order to account for a behaviour that is so visible that it cannot fail to escape the empiricist gaze (the actual decision), but whose contextual conditions or causes fade out of sight. In realist approaches, we are faced with a rationalist and determinist argument of generative causal mechanisms working their way up the intricate hierarchy of levels, from deep-seated structures to the actual agents.[7] The latter are bearers of a structural determination that springs from the causal power of things which, nevertheless, grows lax or, rather, confused and loses a good deal of its potency when it finally reaches its destination through the parallelogram of forces.

The dichotomies of democratic theories operate within a similar logic with their emphasis on legitimacy/illegitimacy and consensus/coercion, checks and balances, inclusions and exclusions, deduced in the name of the sovereignty of the people and the freedom of the individual, all of which is envisioned in notions such as the common good. And finally, lest we forget, there are the emancipatory ideals putting an end to all these intricacies by envisioning the elimination of power altogether in an attempt to reach genuine self-determination. They thus create a pure space, an origin recoiling in its *telos*, a space which has fully absorbed infinity, and hence frozen temporality. This is, needless to say, an inconceivable space, because space without time does not make sense except in a static and firmly grounded universe. This is the reason why emancipation cannot ever be what it claims to be, that is, transparent – a state where we finally would be able to become what we are.

The question is whether it is possible to imagine a form of causation that is not linear. This is important because the complacent recourse to linearity leaves the fundamental problem untouched, namely, what causes the identity which brings about causal effects. Instead of taking issue with this question, linear models discard it by presupposing ability (wilful, structural or systemic) as the causal factor, which is why they are stuck in a derivative understanding of power. But when it is the relation that constitutes identity then causation cannot presuppose identity, because it is contemporaneous with the processes of identification. Or more to the point, whilst identity is an effect of these processes the objectifying self-referentiality of the latter construe the former as their cause, that is, the object within themselves that has to be carved out in order to become what one is. This implies not only that causation is strategical through and through, but also that linearity curves in making up a terrain, a strategical situation.[8] This articulation between causation and identity expresses a kind of circularity which the notion of overdetermination tries to capture. It might be seen as a somewhat unwieldy or even nebulous metaphor for a causation whose linearity recoils in the positing of its own presuppositions.

It is here we encounter an undecidability between relation and identity, which indicates that identity is itself undecidable due to its relational structure. Relation and identity reciprocally pose and presuppose one another because the relation, by virtue of articulating identities, also constructs them as already given. It is this undecidability that renders realism and constructivism equally inappropriate. Both of them operate with a blind spot which has itself escaped the grip of power and from which power relations can be deduced. We could, of course, say that identity is relational, but since identity is by definition specific, relations must coagulate, as it were, and limits must be enforced between the clusters of identifications. Power is the name of this clustering, the strategical game of inclusion/exclusion, which is glued together with greater or lesser success by strategies, tactics, decisions, interests, circumstances, and so forth, all of which structure and institutionalize a terrain in which structures and institutions are created, persist and crumble, a terrain of forces that constrains and sets free. Hence Foucault's observation that 'power is not an institution, and not a structure; neither is it a certain strength we are endowed with; it is the name that one attributes to a complex strategical situation.'[9]

To study power strategically as the becoming of identity through processes of identification implies that, in giving shape to the possible, we cannot but negate ability as limitless possibility. Power as pure ability entails its own negation, it is auto-negativity: *that* which is always already the negation of itself, *that* which has no 'itselfness' but is an empty place. It has a virtual existence only as the trace of the circular structuring of the becoming of identity. Power as auto-negativity cannot be a foundational moment because it defies any such attempt by being antithetic to the full constitution of identity. Or what amounts to the same thing, it is an origin that keeps recurring in every strategical situation. It follows that power as auto-negativity is the only way to outline a presuppositionless approach to power: that power is non-derivative, non-determinate and non-objective.

The Political Ordering of Power

Political power in its various forms and institutional settings (representative, regulatory, repressive) relentlessly maps out and structures the social terrain in depth, although the former can never fully domesticate the latter. The reason is that the attempts to control identity are conditioned by that which, one way or another, evades domestication, and which can be termed resistance or subversive forces. The latter does not make up the irreducible substratum of a liberating energy, but is instead that which, while escaping the encircling manoeuvres of power strategies, is marked by these strategies as well as being their target. The subversive is, in other words, that which is excluded, and signals the limits of a social objectivity whose elimination would be a suffocating complacency, that is, the absence of politics. Power as auto-negativity, which shows itself in delimitation, cannot obey the law as if the latter was above the scenery of struggling forces instead of being part of the complex strategical situation.[10] The law cannot in its totality domesticate the social order, in whose name it operates, by interpreting itself in what it interprets and regulates.

Political power is not externally related to the social order, although it is particularly visible on its fringes as when it protects and provokes what appears sedimented and normal. By this means it shows the ultimate contestability of every order – a contestability shown every day with greater or lesser intensity. Power and politics are as such the loci for the truths, lies, openings, fissures and deficiencies in the social order that indicate the possibility of change, that things could be different, because necessity cannot anchor itself in anything except its own contingent construction. An ethical concern springs from these caesuras, sparked off by political power struggles and codified by the law, all of which revolve around the political authorization of power in which decisions have to be made, directions determined, and so forth.

The task of political authority would be to govern the strategical field of more or less unruly power relations by establishing some form of order. It would be a power encircled by itself, caught up in its own completion, and fully imbricated in the social order at every level. This authorization is not only legitimate in the grandiose sense that it finds its *raison d'être* in a mythical contract, or more prosaically, in the political representation of interests, and in their pragmatic trade-offs and cynical horse-trading. It is also normal and physical by virtue of being invested in all sorts of disciplinary and regulatory apparatuses. It is this duality of authority, with its descending paternal legitimacy formulated in terms of the juridico-discursive representation of power and its ascending maternal normality nurtured in all sorts of regulative apparatuses of social control, which attempts to govern the reproduction of the social order.

Here we find that the rationale for power in its juridico-discursive variant is coined in terms of a restriction on will ('power over'), whereas the power of discipline and regulation is ventured as the formation of will ('power to'). While the former portrays the political as the site where interests constituted outside the political institutions are represented, the latter is engaged in constructing and regulating wills that would otherwise be ungovernable. From here it would take but one step to conclude that the political supplements the social in that it completes it, although it is a 'dangerous supplement' as Derrida would say.[11] Political power would be the top-dressing, repressive by nature, securing that the formation of will does not go astray, lead to excesses or disturb order. Such a power contains all the seeds of becoming itself excessive, as when it encroaches upon civil society as the last vestige of uncorrupted individual freedom and communal bonds. This politics would have to be grasped in terms of submission and repression, at once parasitic yet inescapable. And civil society would be a residual category lumping together everything that is not caught up in the nitty-gritty business of politics. Autonomy and rationality would signal a flight or escape from politics as in both liberalism and Marxism for which politics has always been viewed from an illusory outside.

The emancipatory vision of democracy as well-ordered discussion fora of knowledgeable and reasonable participants in the public sphere is, of course, directed against power politics and the lies, manipulations, abuses, hypocrisy and secrecy that always surrounds it. Yet this vision, despite its occasional radicality, is blind towards that which in part conditions it, which is not necessarily publicly assessable, and which is not usually conceived as belonging to the political in the first place, namely the infrastructure of discipline, surveillance, normalization, regulation, and so on, from which the political authorization of power takes off. By not focusing on the formation of will as an essential part of the political structuring of the social order, this vision of democracy does not remain merely impotent for all practical purposes. In addition, its dichotomization of the political and the social is slanted towards elitism, partly because it takes upon itself the role of a fictitious observer seemingly above the scenery of struggling parties (a distance that vouches for its objectivity), and partly because the impetus for democracy and democratization is located in the top echelons of society instead of proceeding bottom up.

The restriction and formation of will are two sides of the same coin in the sense that will has to delimit itself or be delimited in order to be itself. In so far as autonomy is envisioned as the political overcoming of delimitation, it cannot but also overcome what conditions it in the first place, because self-referentiality requires delimitation. Power is both productive and repressive, not merely by facilitating something while restricting something else, but because it is coterminous with the hegemonic structuring of space and time. Power is a name for the construction of a spatial and temporal zone which, by virtue of being an ordering device, has to delimit itself in order to be identifiable. Both space and time recoil at their beginning and at their end, which is why linearity, causality and representation, when pushed to their extremes, collapse into their own empty images of the factual, ability or will, and system or structure. These are but names that designate various forms of social objectivity that serve as points of orientation, which are always transgressed and are thus contestable and subject to political reasoning.

Power is immanent in social relations not as their hidden and enigmatic substance, which requires being represented by a mediating subject, but as their limits – points of recurrence and stumbling blocks that throw subjects into games of signification and identification. Power is in this sense prior to the subject; or alternatively, power is the name for the political constitution of identity. This power, auto-negativity, is not anti-energy or repression – both of which would presuppose a constitutive subject – but *that* which evades substantialization, *that* which is too slippery to become fully institutionalized and rendered lawful although it is imbricated in institutions and laws and, indeed, constitutive for them. This non-substantial power, it seems, can only be rendered intelligible in terms such as 'the name that one attributes to a complex strategical situation', which simultaneously defines the situation, positions subjects, and throws them into the more- or less-hazardous terrain in which they find themselves. Thus power is the name for the limit of objectivity, ontologically as well as epistemologically, and it is only through this limit that we are capable of conceiving objectivity.

Origin and Power: Is There a Will to Order?

The representation of power as a causal mechanism is a tool to render power intelligible: a power to control power, a type of reasoning which is particularly visible in grand narratives such as social-contract theory, where linear causation curves to the point where it becomes tautological by presupposing what it construes, and vice versa. When linearity recoils in self-reflection it shows itself as hollow in the sense that it has no other foundation than its becoming, that is, in its being different from itself or, in a word, auto-negativity. By turning away from this abysmal opening, linearity becomes the site for an a priori, a dogmatism which allows for or, more correctly, requires that power is grasped in terms of derivation. That is, a power derived from that which allegedly precedes it: usually the subject or the structural whole, will or necessity. Linearity here is preserved for the sake of order and style. Foucault inverted perhaps: the cynicism of power is not only revealed in local settings where it is less legal, it also turns up in grand designs, because the transcendent concepts of these narratives cannot break away from their arbitrary closures and the names attributed to them, such as 'free will' or the 'will of the people'.

One of the most visible characteristics of the ruptural moment of modernity lies in the secularization of these arbitrary closures, whereupon the social order cannot simply mirror itself in what is infinitely beyond it, but is forced to construct itself. This change heralds the ubiquity of politics which is, amongst other things, also a democratic challenge which never allows, and even renders incomprehensible, a rationality and an autonomy situated outside its grip. Power is as such the limit of intelligibility and controllability, not because it is alien but because it is too familiar to be known. However, the difference is the same since knowledge *qua* knowledge turns its irreducible opposite, power, into an object, thereby also objectifying itself. Politics is the activity of enforcing, maintaining and challenging these limits of intelligibility and controllability, and the identities erected by them, *vis-à-vis* a 'constitutive outside'.[12]

What about these closures and limits then. Do they express a will to order and, if so, why, or alternatively, why do we have to presuppose such a will, and do we have to? If there is a will to order it would be a will to power that could not avoid being tautological, because will could not be in a position of exteriority to power. It would be a power to ground and control power, a necessity to establish and legitimate necessity. This is probably the reason why teleological theories and strategies have to reduce the origin to a primordial unity once given and never returning. This nostalgia in armour finds expression in, for example, the vision of the end of politics, the end of history, and so on. But when *telos* is crumbling because it has gone out of fashion, has become too compromised or cannot respond to new events, trends or problems, then its mirror image, the origin, loses its power, its ability to operate as a point of identification. That is, it cannot perform, it cannot be what it was, perhaps it can find no place to go. What this seems to imply is that when faced with the question of origins, we are always at a loss, because the answers we come up with are either arbitrary and hence dogmatic, or they are not answers at all. More precisely, we are confronted with the alternative of either postulating ability as the transcendent moment *par excellence* (will, structure, nature, God) from which everything else can be derived. Or we displace the question by exploding these metaphors in all directions, scattering them around and putting the pieces back again, saying that they were brought together in a contingent way, that they could, in other words, have been pieced together differently. The point here is that as soon as ontology and epistemology cannot be strictly separated we are deprived of the possibility of certainty, and this implies that we are caught up in circularity.

If we pursue this kind of reasoning, we take the first step toward reinscribing these transcending moments within the circular structure of power, where the origin is perpetually returning as 'that which must be thought and that which cannot be thought'.[13] That it must be and yet cannot be thought is the dilemma of having to conceptualize origin. But in taking up this task, we are facing the problem that conceptualization implies objectification, and that means to bring movement to a standstill. The very act of conceptualizing the origin is thus biased in favour of the axiom that origin is given as a primordial unity. Instead of asking why we search for the origin, we would perhaps do better to rephrase the question by asking what this search implies, what we are looking for when we look. By not accepting that origin is simply what is given, the search for it cannot be a search for its adequate conceptualization, because every attempt to conceptualize it is, by definition, inadequate. We have to remain pre-conceptual which is, of course, impossible, but at the least, we have to capture the origin in movement, in the flux of events, otherwise it could not be 'that which is returning, the repetition towards which thought is moving, the return of that which has already always begun.'

To proceed in this manner would indicate that the search for origin is the search for a perspective, a story to render events meaningful, to put them in context, in which case, the origin could not be a primordial unity possessing an identity. It would, instead, arrive after the *telos* as its projection, which underway transforms itself as its cause. To put it differently, *telos* would itself be a narrative that paves the way for the origin as that which always returns even when it comes for the first time, well knowing that there never is a first time. In so far as order hinges upon origin and is stretched out between origin and *telos*, both of which have to be reinvented along the way, which is the task of politics, then ordering is an ongoing process of becoming, which cannot but be the political constitution of order. If becoming cannot be thought, but nevertheless has to be thought, the reason is not that we have to transcend the circular structure of power in order to anchor it in an origin which is outside this circular movement. It is rather that movement, change, and the like, perpetually create something new that confronts us with the never-ending challenge of conceptualizing and coping with differences, and rapidly changing determinations in order to stop, or at least to slow down, 'the infinite speed with which they take shape and vanish'.[14]

If there is an ethics of power, it could be that of coping with, enduring or accepting difference, that is, the chaos of 'the infinite speed' or 'the multiplicity of impulses, the entire horizon of forces'.[15] The acceptance of difference cannot be equated with a self-pitying denial of the self or a renunciation of rigour. It is, on the contrary, an elevation of the self which at the same time overcomes itself, because the self-referring nature of this itselfness keeps returning as different, as stumbling-blocks and hence as challenges. The moment of auto-negativity is the moment of self as other, the self as created in the clash with otherness. We are faced with the possibility of accepting what seems inescapable: that the self cannot ever be entirely itself because power is primordial in the sense that as an origin it 'is nothing but a direction forever to be determined' and it 'has and gives meaning only in retrospect'.[16] It is this opening towards otherness – this negativity within oneself constituting the *one* of the *self*, that is, its identity – which finally prevents a firm positioning, a sharp frontier, condemnation, and so on. This is not a licence for shallow indifference, but for sincerity, a positioning which cares for its fragility – a questioning which requires answers to keep on questioning, an openness which requires closures to remain open, a sincerity which requires rigorous limitations to be alive.

Questioning, openness, sincerity: not a self-assertive arrogant self coupled with sickening confessional rites when it suddenly becomes less confident on being struck by anxiety. Between *it* and *self*, and *self* and *other*, there is an infinite distance punctuated by objectifications relentlessly trying to account for causal sequences in the name of autonomy, rationality and order, which attempt to reach the *one* of one-*self*, the self-same *vis-à-vis* otherness through processes of self-reference. The acceptance of otherness within oneself, whose irreducible opposite is the acceptance of the same in the other, is also the acceptance of this self as alive, as curious, as a becoming, oneself as familiar yet unknown. It is also a respect for directing oneself, a direction which has forever to be determined in the face of what is beyond, what is ungraspable.

We have two aspects of negativity here. One which is positioned against a concrete other, that is, one that positions itself by positivating the other, equipping it with an identity; and one which is held out in nothingness, transforming and mutating itself in the face of undecidability. The latter is, as Kierkegaard would say, the anxious possibility of being able, the fleeting moment that escapes incorporation and triggers positioning and positivation: hostile, self-assertive or caring. Hence the former aspect of negativity is the effect of the latter to the point where the concrete other, in its positivity, is the embodiment of an impossibility – of what one is not, cannot or will not be. Is the positivation of negativity or the objectification of otherness a representation of what cannot ever be there? No, inasmuch as representation presupposes linearity, causality and, most importantly, substance; yes, because the substantialization of otherness presupposes a mediating subject which is itself mediated (the subject as 'vanishing mediator') – a recoiling linearity. This subject is not the cause, but is itself the product of this positioning where it finds itself as its own cause, and hence as irreducible to this positioning: a deception no doubt, but apparently necessary, and thus with an evil slant to it because the ground is slippery. Hence the constitutive status of power and the inescapability of the ethico-political decisions. Decisions which, when taken, have already been made. This is not decisionism – the subject is the vehicle of this undecidability – but a touch of essentialism perhaps, although it is unavoidably strategic, elusive and seductive. In the face of otherness, linearity and determination do not vanish but recoil: space and time are not there beforehand but construct themselves at the limits, and as the limits, which attempt to order space and time by encapsulating them. It is in this way that one could see power as immanent in the subject, social relations and the social order.

Notes

Introduction

1. Cf. Steven Lukes, 'Power and Authority', in Tom Bottomore and Robert Nisbet (eds.), *A History of Sociological Analysis*, London: Heinemann 1978, pp. 635–9, and Steven Lukes, 'Introduction', in Steven Lukes (ed.), *Power*, Oxford: Basil Blackwell 1986.

2. Cf. Ernesto Laclau, 'Preface' in Slavoj Žižek, *The Sublime Object of Ideology*, London: Verso 1989, p. xv. See also Jacob Torfing, *New Theories on Discourse*, Oxford: Basil Blackwell 1997, ch. 6.

3. Cf. Steven Lukes, 'Power and Authority', p. 652.

4. Michel Foucault, *Power/Knowledge: Selected Interviews and other Writings 1972–1977*, New York: Pantheon Books 1980, p. 51.

5. Ernesto Laclau and Chantal Mouffe, *Hegemony and Socialist Strategy: Towards a Radical Democratic Politics*, London: Verso 1985, ch. 4.

Chapter 1 Power as an Influence Term and Decision Making

1. Robert A. Dahl, 'The Behavioural Approach in Political Science: Epitaph for a Monument to a Successful Protest', *American Political Science Review*, vol. 55, no. 4, 1961, pp. 766–7 (italics in original).

2. Cf. Steward R. Clegg, *Frameworks of Power*, London: Routledge & Kegan Paul 1989, pp. 41–2.

3. Cf. Terence Ball, 'Models of Power: Past and Present', *Journal of the Behavioural Sciences*, vol. 11, no. 3, 1975, pp. 214, 216.

4. The quote is taken from Brian Carr, *Metaphysics: An Introduction*, London: Macmillan Education 1987, p. 79. See also Terence Ball, 'Models of Power: Past and Present', pp. 123–214, 216; and Terence Ball, 'Power, Causation and Explanation', *Polity*, 1975, p. 195–6.

5. Jeffrey C. Isaac, 'Beyond the Three Faces of Power: A Realist Critique', *Polity*, 1987, p. 9; Steven Lukes, *Power: A Radical View*, London: Macmillan Education 1974, p. 41.

6. This view is propounded by Dahl in several of his writings. See, e.g., 'The Concept of Power', *Behavioural Science*, vol. 2, 1957, p. 204; *Modern Political Analysis*, 4th edn., Englewood Cliffs, NJ: Prentice Hall 1984, pp. 36–47; 'Power as the Control of Behaviour', in Steven Lukes (ed.), *Power*, Oxford: Basil Blackwell 1986, pp. 38, 40, 46–50, 54.

7. Peter Morriss, *Power: A Philosophical Analysis*, Manchester: Manchester University Press 1987, pp. 14–16.

8. Cf. Peter Morriss, 'Power in New Haven: a Reassessment of "Who Governs?"', *British Journal of Political Science*, vol. 2, 1972, p. 458.

9. Terence Ball, 'Models of Power: Past and Present', p. 215; Jeffrey Isaac, 'Beyond the Three Faces of Power: A Realist Critique', p. 8.

10. This will be discussed later in relation to Lukes and Giddens, who attempt to establish a continuity between agency and structure which, nevertheless, upholds the ontological difference between them.

11. Steven Lukes, 'Power and Authority', in Tom Bottomore and Robert Nisbeth (eds.), *A History of Sociological Analysis*, London: Heinemann 1978, pp. 634–5; see also Steven Lukes, *Power: A Radical View*, p. 26.

12. Cf. P. H. Partridge, 'Some Notes on the Concept of Power', *Political Studies*, vol. 11, no. 2, 1963; Terence Ball, 'Power', in D. Miller *et al.* (eds.), *Blackwell Encyclopedia of Political Thought*, Oxford: Basil Blackwell 1987, pp. 397–8; Stanley Benn, 'Power', in Paul Edwards (ed.), *Encyclopedia of Philosophy*, vol. 5–6, New York and London: Macmillan Publishers and The Free Press 1967, pp. 424–5; R. J. Mokken and F. N. Stokman, 'Power and Influence as Political Phenomena', in Brian Barry (ed.), *Power and Political Theory*, New York: John Wiley and Sons 1976. Talcott Parsons has criticized this view of power, which connotes 'the generalized capacity to attain ends or goals', because the lumping together of influence, coercion, etc., leads to conceptual diffuseness, 'thereby making it logically impossible to treat power as a *specific* mechanism.' ('Power and the Social System', in Steven Lukes (ed.), *Power*, pp. 94–5, 139–40.) A similar critique has been put forward by, among others, D. V. J. Bell, *Power, Influence and Authority*, New York: Oxford University Press 1975, pp.113–5; Hanna Fenichel Pitkin, *Wittgenstein and Justice*, Berkeley: University of California Press 1972, pp. 277–9; Peter Morriss, *Power: A Philosophical Analysis*, ch. 2.

13. Cf. Anthony Giddens, *Central Problems in Social Theory*, London: The Macmillan Press 1979, p. 91; Andrew S. McFarland, *Power and Leadership in Pluralist Systems*, Stanford: Stanford University Press 1969, p. 7; Herbert Simon, *Models of Man*, New York: John Wiley and Sons 1957, p. 66.

14. Harold D. Lasswell and Abraham Kaplan (*Power and Society*, New Haven: Yale University Press 1950, pp. 86–92) have outlined eight such values, namely power, respect, rectitude, affection, well-being, wealth, skill and enlightenment. A different typology of 'base values' is provided by Dahl, 'Power as the Control of Behaviour', pp. 44–6.

15. Nicos Poulantzas, *Political Power and Social Classes*, London: Verso 1978, p. 104.

16. Ibid., pp. 99–119.

17. The first view is the predominant one and is held by Harold D. Lasswell and Abraham Kaplan, *Power and Society*; Robert A. Dahl, *Modern Political Analysis*; Andrew S. McFarland, *Power and Leadership in Pluralist Systems*; and Herbert Simon, *Models of Man*. The second view is advanced by, e.g., R. J. Mokken and F. N. Stokman, 'Power and Influence as Political Phenomena' and D. V. J. Bell, *Power, Influence and Authority*.

18. P. H. Partridge, 'Some Notes on the Concept of Power', *Political Studies*, vol. 11, no. 2, 1963, p. 110.

19. Stanley Benn, 'Power', in Paul Edwards (ed.), *Encyclopedia of Philosophy*, pp. 424.

20. Harold D. Lasswell and Abraham Kaplan, *Power and Society*, New Haven: Yale University Press 1950, ch. 5.

21. Jürgen Habermas, 'Der Universalitätsanspruch der Hermeneutik', in Karl-Otto Apel *et al.*, *Hermeneutik und Ideologiekritik*, Frankfurt am Main 1971, p. 154.
22. Steward Clegg, *Frameworks of Power*, p. 43.
23. Terence Ball, 'Power, Causation and Explanation', p. 200.
24. Steven Lukes, *Power: A Radical View*, pp. 32–3.
25. Robert A. Dahl, *Modern Political Analysis*, pp. 39–40; see also Stanley Benn, 'Power', pp. 424–5.
26. Cf. Steven Lukes, *Power: A Radical View*, p. 33.
27. Ibid.
28. Jacques Derrida, 'Force of Law: The "Mystical Foundation of Authority"', in Drucilla Cornell *et al.* (eds.), *Deconstruction and the Possibility of Justice*, New York and London: Routledge 1992, p. 24.
29. Ernesto Laclau, *New Reflections on the Revolution of Our Time*, London: Verso 1990, p. 171.
30. Bertrand Russell, *Power: A New Social Analysis*, London: George Allen & Unwin 1938, p. 25.
31. Dennis H. Wrong, *Power: Its Forms, Bases, and Uses*, 2nd edn., Oxford: Basil Blackwell 1988, pp. 2, 4 (italics in original). See also Harold D. Lasswell and Abraham Kaplan, *Power and Society*, pp. 75–6; and P. H. Partridge, 'Some Notes on the Concept of Power', p. 111.
32. Andrew S. McFarland, *Power and Leadership in Pluralist Systems*, p. 13, see also pp. 6–7 (italics in original).
33. Jack Nagel, *The Descriptive Analysis of Power*, New Haven and London: Yale University Press 1975, p. 33.
34. Ibid., p. 13.
35. P. H. Partridge, 'Some Notes on the Concept of Power', p. 114.
36. The idea of elite competition is in debt to Schumpeter's 'realist' model of democracy. His critique of what he termed the classical model of democracy and his definition of a modern realist conception of democracy have had a major impact upon the pluralists (see, e.g., David Held, *Models of Democracy*, Cambridge: Polity Press 1987, ch. 6; Kenneth Newton, 'A Critique of the Pluralist Model', in *Acta Sociologica*, vol. 12, 1969, p. 211).
37. Robert A. Dahl, *A Preface to Democratic Theory*, Chicago: University of Chicago Press 1956, p. 132.
38. Dahl's conception of power and politics could be seen here as the 'agency version' of Parsons's structural functionalism where the role of power and politics is to sustain the system integration as well.
39. Raymond E. Wolfinger, 'Nondecisions and the Study of Local Politics', *American Political Science Review*, vol. 65, no. 4, 1971, 1071–2.
40. Cf. Geoffrey Debnam, 'Nondecisions and Power: The Two Faces of Bachrach and Baratz', *American Political Science Review*, vol. 69, no. 3, 1975, p. 895.
41. Peter Bachrach and Morton S. Baratz, 'Power and Its Two Faces Revisited: A Reply to Geoffrey Debnam', *American Political Science Review*, vol. 69, no. 3, 1975, p. 901.
42. Geoffrey Debnam, 'Nondecisions and Power: The Two Faces of Bachrach and Baratz', p. 891.
43. Cf. John Hoffman, *State, Power and Democracy*, Brighton: Wheatsheaf Books 1988, pp. 92–3.
44. Robert A. Dahl and Charles E. Lindblom, *Politics, Economics, and Welfare*, New York: Harper & Row 1953, p. 314.
45. See also Robert A. Dahl, *A Preface to Democratic Theory*, Chicago: University of Chicago Press 1956, pp. 133–4.

46. Robert A. Dahl, 'The Behavioural Approach in Political Science: Epitaph for a Monument to a Successful Protest', p. 767. Cf. also R. M. Merelman ('On the Neo-Elitist Critique of Community Power', in *American Political Science Review*, vol. 62, no. 2, 1968, p. 451, see also p. 453) for whom the elitists did not 'produce reliable conclusions which met the canons of science.'

47. Cf. R. M. Merelman, 'On the Neo-Elitist Critique of Community Power', p. 451; see also Nelson Polsby, 'How to Study Community Power: The Pluralist Alternative', *Journal of Politics*, vol. 22, 1960, p. 476; Nelson Polsby, *Community Power and Political Theory*, 2nd enl. edn., New Haven and London: Yale University Press 1980, p. 113.

48. Cf. William Kornhauser, '"Power Elite" or "Veto Groups"', in G. William Domhoff and Hoyt B. Ballard (eds.), *C. Wright Mills and 'The Power Elite'*, Boston: Beacon Press 1968, pp. 52–4.

49. It is important to keep in mind that the empiricist premiss of the behaviourists' idea of power requires 'communication' or 'contact' between agents, which is why indirect influence and anticipating reactions cannot count as forms of power. However, this argument is flawed by the behaviourists themselves in their account of the citizen-leader relationship.

50. Kenneth Newton, 'A Critique of the Pluralist Model', pp. 215, 217–8.

51. 'Almost all voting studies', says Newton in his argument that inequalities show cumulative tendencies ('A Critique of the Pluralist Model', p. 215), 'have found that the non-voter is least likely to have the political resources of money, education, status, political skills, political office and political confidence. That is why they are non-voters.' This indicates that there is a positive correlation between a low social position and a low degree of participation and hence power sharing. When the pluralists do not look at this problem it is due to their 'exercise fallacy', i.e., that power is conceptualized solely in terms of its exercise.

52. Robert A. Dahl, *Who Governs? Democracy and Power in an American City*, New Haven and London: Yale University Press 1961, p. 164, see also pp. 66, 89–90, 101–2. For a critical discussion of Dahl's notion of indirect influence in the context of an empirical study, see Matthew A. Crenson, *The Un-Politics of Air Pollution*, Baltimore and London: The Johns Hopkins University Press 1971, pp. 107–9, 179–80.

53. Robert A. Dahl, *Who Governs?*, pp. 137–8; see also Peter Morriss, 'Power in New Haven: a Reassessment of "Who Governs?"', pp. 463–4.

54. Cf. Geoffrey Debnam, 'Nondecisions and Power: The Two Faces of Bachrach and Baratz', p. 890.

55. Kenneth Newton, 'A Critique of the Pluralist Model', p. 220 and Michael Parenti, 'Power and Pluralism: A View from the Bottom', *The Journal of Politics*, vol. 32, no. 3, 1970, pp. 506, 519–20.

56. Robert A. Dahl, *Who Governs?*, p. 164.

57. Ibid., pp. 92, 324; see also Kenneth Newton, 'A Critique of the Pluralist Model', pp. 217, 220.

58. Cf. Michael Parenti, 'Power and Pluralism: A View from the Bottom', pp. 526–7.

59. Robert A. Dahl, *Who Governs?*, pp. 316–7.

60. Cf. Peter Morriss, 'Power in New Haven: a Reassessment of "Who Governs?"', p. 464.

61. Robert A. Dahl, *Who Governs?*, pp. 316, 318.

62. Cf. Michael Parenti, 'Power and Pluralism: A View from the Bottom', p. 529.

Chapter 2 Power, Causality and Political Agency in the Community Power Debate

1. Robert A. Dahl, 'A Critique of the Ruling Elite Model', in William G. Domhoff and Hoyt B. Ballard (eds.), *C. Wright Mills and the Power Elite*, Boston: Beacon Press 1968, p. 35.

2. Steven Lukes, *Power: A Radical View*, London: Macmillan Education 1974, p. 12.

3. Robert A. Dahl, *Who Governs? Democracy and Power in an American City*, New Haven and London 1961, p. 336. A somewhat similar argument is put forward by Lasswell and Kaplan in their definition of power as the 'participation in the making of decisions', where a decision is understood as 'a policy involving severe sanctions', with the proviso, however, that it is not always those officially 'in power' who make decisions. Harold D. Lasswell and Abraham Kaplan, *Power and Society*, New Haven: Yale University Press 1950, pp. 75, 74; Harold D. Lasswell *et al.*, 'The Elite Concept', in Peter Bachrach (ed.), *Political Elites in a Democracy*, New York: Atherton Press 1971, pp. 16–7.

4. Nelson Polsby, 'How to Study Community Power: The Pluralist Alternative', in *Journal of Politics*, vol. 22, 1960, p. 478; see also Nelson Polsby, *Community Power and Political Theory*, 2nd enl. edn., New Haven and London: Yale University Press 1980, pp. 95–6.

5. Peter Bachrach and Morton S. Baratz, *Power and Poverty. Theory and Practice*, New York: Oxford University Press 1970, p. 10.

6. Robert A. Dahl, 'A Critique of the Ruling Elite Model', p. 33; see also Robert A. Dahl, *Who Governs?*, p. 92. For a more detailed account of how to single out important or significant issues, see Nelson Polsby, *Community Power and Political Theory*, pp. 95–6; Andrew McFarland, *Power and Leadership in Pluralist Systems*, Stanford: Stanford University Press 1969, pp. 82–92.

7. Cf. Kenneth Newton, 'Community Politics and Decision Making: The American Experience and its Lessons', in Ken Young (ed.), *Essays on the Study of Urban Politics*, London: Croom Helm 1975, p. 17.

8. Peter Bachrach and Morton S. Baratz, 'Two Faces of Power', *American Political Science Review*, vol. 56, 1962, p. 948; see also Peter Morriss, 'Power in New Haven: a Reassessment of "Who Governs?"', in *British Journal of Political Science*, vol. 2, 1972, p. 460.

9. The critics of behaviourism/pluralism thus point, implicitly, at the circularity of political power and consensus: that the former legitimates itself by mirroring itself in the societal consensus it has itself fostered.

10. Elmer E. Schattschneider, *The Semi-Sovereign People: A Realist's view of Democracy in America*, New York: Holt, Reinhart & Winston 1960, p. 66, see also p. 71.

11. Ibid., p. 71.

12. Matthew A. Crenson, *The Un-Politics of Air Pollution*, Baltimore and London: The Johns Hopkins University Press 1971, pp. 178–9, see also p. 183. See also Louise Marcil-Lacoste, 'On the Subject of Rights: Pluralism, Plurality and Political Identity', in Chantal Mouffe (ed.), *Dimensions of Radical Democracy: Pluralism, Citizenship, Community*, London: Verso 1992, pp. 134–7.

13. Ernesto Laclau, *Reflections on the Revolution of Our Time*, London: Verso 1990, p. 172. See also Chantal Mouffe, *The Return of the Political*, London: Verso 1993, pp. 151–2.

14. Peter Bachrach and Morton S. Baratz, 'Two Faces of Power', p. 950; *Power and Poverty*, pp. 47–9.

15. Peter Bachrach and Morton S. Baratz, 'Two Faces of Power', p. 948.

16. Peter Bachrach and Morton S. Baratz, *Power and Poverty*, p. 44. See also Frey's interpretation of nondecisions and non-issues: 'A nondecision occurs when a choice among alternatives by one actor is either not perceived by him or, if perceived, is not made, and always, in either case, because of some exercise of power by another actor' (Frederick W. Frey, 'Comment: On Issues and Non-issues in the Study of Power', in *American Political Science Review*, vol. 65, no. 4, 1971, p. 1092). See, moreover, his discussion of different types of nondecisions/non-issues (ibid., pp.1093–4). For a pluralist critique, see Nelson Polsby, *Community Power and Political Theory*, p. 191ff.; R. M. Merelman, 'On the Neo-Elitist Critique of Community Power', in *American Political Science Review*, vol. 62, no. 2, 1968, pp. 453–60; Raymond E. Wolfinger, 'Nondecisions and the Study of Local Politics', in *American Political Science Review*, vol. 65, no. 4, 1971, pp. 1065–77.

17. Peter Bachrach and Morton S. Baratz, 'Decisions and Nondecisions: An Analytical Framework', in *American Political Science Review*, vol. 57, 1963, p. 641; see also Peter Morriss and Geraint Parry, 'When is a Decision not a Decision?', in Ivor Crewe (ed.), *British Political Sociology Yearbook, Vol. 1: Elites in Western Democracies*, London: Croom Helm 1974, pp. 322–31.

18. Peter Bachrach and Morton S. Baratz, *Power and Poverty*, pp. 8, 44–5; 'Two Faces of Power', p. 949. For a slightly different perspective on nondecision making in terms of more or less direct or indirect ways of exercising power, see Peter Bachrach and E. Bergman, *Power and Choice*, Massachusetts: Lexington Books 1973, pp. 7, 33; Peter Saunders, *Urban Politics, A Sociological Interpretation*, London: Hutchinson & Co. 1983, pp. 29–30.

19. Peter Bachrach and Morton S. Baratz, 'Decisions and Nondecisions: An Analytical Framework', p. 641; see also Peter Bachrach and Morton S. Baratz, *Power and Poverty*, p. 43.

20. Cf. Terence Ball, 'Models of Power: Past and Present', in *Journal of the Behavioural Sciences*, vol. 11, no. 3, 1975, pp. 217–8.

21. Nelson Polsby, *Community Power and Political Theory*, p. 190; see also R. M. Merelman, 'On the Neo-Elitist Critique of Community Power', pp. 456–7. A similar argument in this respect is presented by Morriss and Parry: 'To understand the power and the penetrability of any community it is better to replace blanket terms like 'nondecision' with a more precise analysis of the many different patterns decision making can take.' Peter Morriss and Geraint Parry, 'When is a Decision not a Decision?', p. 325.

22. Nelson Polsby, *Community Power and Political Theory*, p. 97.

23. Peter Bachrach and Morton S. Baratz, *Power and Poverty*, p. 49.

24. Allan Bradshaw, 'A Critique of Steven Lukes' "Power: A Radical View"', in *Sociology*, vol. 10, no. 1, 1976.

25. Michael Parenti, 'Power and Pluralism: A View from the Bottom', in *The Journal of Politics*, vol. 32, no. 3, 1970, pp. 521–2.

26. Peter Bachrach and Morton S. Baratz, 'Power and Its Two Faces Revisited: A Reply to Geoffrey Debnam', in *American Political Science Review*, vol. 69, no. 3, 1975, p. 901.

27. This is Dahl's assertion in *Who Governs?*. It has also been argued by R. M. Merelman, 'On the Neo-Elitist Critique of Community Power', pp. 453–4; Raymond E. Wolfinger, 'Nondecisions and the Study of Local Politics', p. 1077; Frederick W. Frey, 'Comment: On Issues and Nonissues in the Study of Power', p. 1092. This critique seems, however, a bit off target since Bachrach and Baratz themselves (*Power and Poverty*, p. 44) draw attention to the fact that the

mobilization of bias can benefit the majority, although emphasis is given to its conservative aspects.

28. Nelson Polsby, *Community Power and Political Theory*, p. 97.

29. Ibid., p. 191.

30. Raymond E. Wolfinger, 'Nondecisions and the Study of Local Politics', pp. 1071, 1077.

31. Frederick W. Frey, 'Comment: On Issues and Nonissues in the Study of Power', p. 1092, see also p. 1093.

32. R. M. Merelman, 'On the Neo-Elitist Critique of Community Power', pp. 453–4.

33. Peter Bachrach and E. Bergman, *Power and Choice*, p. 7.

34. Robert A. Dahl, *Who Governs?*, p. 17.

35. Frederick W. Frey, 'Comment: On Issues and Nonissues in the Study of Power', p. 1090.

36. John Hoffman, *State, Power and Democracy*, Brighton: Wheatsheaf Books 1988, p. 99.

37. Raymond E. Wolfinger, 'Nondecisions and the Study of Local Politics', p. 1077.

38. Peter Bachrach and Morton S. Baratz, *Power and Poverty*, p. 49, see also p. 50. This point is also stressed in their answer to Merelman: 'if a particular set of political beliefs was universally embraced in a given community, no one could tell whether the consensus was "false" or genuine.' Peter Bachrach and Morton S. Baratz, 'Letter to the Editor', in *American Political Science Review*, vol. 62, 1968, p. 1268.

39. Peter Bachrach and Morton S. Baratz, 'Two Faces of Power', p. 949; *Power and Poverty*, p. 8.

40. Cf. Jack Nagel, *The Descriptive Analysis of Power*, New Haven and London: Yale University Press 1975, p. 18.

41. Nelson Polsby, *Community Power and Political Theory*, p. 97.

42. Matthew A. Crenson, *The Un-Politics of Air Pollution*, p. 26.

43. Cf. Kenneth Newton, 'Community Politics and Decision Making: The American Experience and its Lessons', p. 6.

44. Lukes operates with a narrow and a wide sense of the term 'behavioural'. While the former refers to 'the study of overt and actual behaviour', the latter, which he himself endorses, 'is committed to the view that behaviour . . . provides evidence . . . for an *attribution* of the exercise of power.' Steven Lukes, *Power: A Radical View*, p. 24 (my emphasis).

45. The term 'systemic power' might be somewhat misleading since it usually connotes a form of power inherent in social systems which is dissociated from agents. Although this is not entirely so in the case of Lukes, it does indicate that his understanding of power comes close to attributing power to agents *and* to systems.

46. See, e.g., Peter Bachrach and Morton S. Baratz, *Power and Poverty*, p. 50.

47. Steven Lukes, *Power: A Radical View*, pp. 21–2. Wright Mills argues a similar case: 'We cannot today merely assume that in the last resort men must always be governed by their own consent. For among the means of power which now prevail is the power to manage and to manipulate the consent of men.' C. Wright Mills, in Irving Louis Horowitz (ed.), *Power, Politics and People. The Collected Essays of C. Wright Mills*, London: Oxford University Press 1970, p. 23.

48. Steven Lukes, *Power: A Radical View*, p. 24, see also p. 23. Cf., moreover, Geraint Parry, *Political Elites*, London: Unwin Hyman 1969, pp. 128–9.

49. See also Peter Bachrach and Morton S. Baratz, 'Power and Its Two Faces Revisited: A Reply to Geoffrey Debnam', p. 901.

50. Steven Lukes, *Power: A Radical View*, pp. 39, 24.

51. Steven Lukes, 'On the Relativity of Power', in S. Brown (ed.), *Philosophical Disputes in the Social Sciences*, Brighton: The Harvester Press 1979, pp. 270–1.

52. Steven Lukes, *Power: A Radical View*, p. 41.

53. Ibid., pp. 24–5. Lukes's critique of behaviourism is thus qualified in the same sense as Bachrach and Baratz's, although it goes further than theirs.

54. Ibid., p. 22.

55. Matthew A. Crenson, *The Un-Politics of Air Pollution*, p. 178.

56. Raymond E. Wolfinger, 'Nondecisions and the Study of Local Politics', p. 1079.

57. Cf. Peter Morriss, *Power: A Philosophical Analysis*, Manchester: Manchester University Press 1987, pp. 14–9.

58. Steven Lukes, *Essays in Social Theory*, Houndsmills: The Macmillan Press 1977, p. 6; *Power: A Radical View*, pp. 27, 34.

59. Cf. Steward Clegg, *The Theory of Power and Organization*, London: Routledge & Kegan Paul 1979, p. 55.

60. To 'maintain the opposite seems perverse' says Nelson Polsby, *Community Power and Political Theory*, p. 23.

61. Steven Lukes, 'Reply to Bradshaw', in *Sociology*, vol. 10, no. 1, 1976, p. 130.

62. Raymond E. Wolfinger, 'Nondecisions and the Study of Local Politics', pp. 1077–8.

63. Cf. Robert A. Dahl, *Who Governs?*, p. 92.

64. Raymond E. Wolfinger, 'Nondecisions and the Study of Local Politics', p. 1078.

65. Steven Lukes, 'Reply to Bradshaw', p. 129.

66. Cf. Jürgen Habermas, *Legitimation Crisis*, London: Heinemann 1976, pp. 111–7, see esp. p. 114.

67. Jürgen Habermas, 'Vorbereitende Bemerkungen zu einer Theorie der Kommunikativen Kompetens', in Jürgen Habermas and Niklas Luhman, *Theorie der Gesellschaft oder Sozialtechnologie – Was Leistet die Systemforschung?*, Frankfurt am Main: Suhrkamp Verlag 1971, p. 136, see also p. 122 (my translation). The German text runs like this: 'Die ideale Sprechsituation ist dadurch charakterisiert, dass jeder Konsensus, der unter ihren Bedingungen erzielt werden kann, per se als wahrer Konsensus gelten darf.'

68. Steven Lukes, 'Introduction', in Steven Lukes (ed.), *Power*, Oxford: Basil Blackwell 1986, p. 13.

69. Steven Lukes, *Power: A Radical View*, p. 56.

70. William E. Connolly, *The Terms of Political Discourse*, Lexington, Massachusetts: D. C. Heath and Co. 1974, p. 95, see also pp. 93–101.

71. C. Wright Mills, *The Causes of World War Three*, London: Secker and Warburg 1963, p. 100, see also his *Power, Politics and People*, pp. 24–5.

72. C. Wright Mills, *The Causes of World War Three*, 1959, pp. 12–5, 37–40.

73. Allan Bradshaw, 'A Critique of Steven Lukes' "Power: A Radical View"', p. 124.

74. Peter Bachrach and Morton S. Baratz, *Power and Poverty*, p. 50, see also Steven Lukes, 'Reply to Bradshaw', p. 130.

75. Steven Lukes, *Power: A Radical View*, pp. 21, 50; see also his 'Reply to Bradshaw', p. 130 and Peter Morriss and Geraint Parry, 'When is a Decision not a Decision?', pp. 324–5. The uses of the words 'intentionality' and

'consciously' (the latter being defined simply as the opposite of unawareness and, accordingly, different from the Freudian concept of the unconscious) are not without problems. It is not clear as to what decision makers should be aware of when making a decision, but it seems that they must at least be aware of making a choice among alternatives even if the chosen option is a matter of routine. This is, however, an ethical imposition which is off target here since it is exactly the presence of 'consciousness' which is called into question in the case of nondecision making whose context is the mobilization of bias. Thus is it an exercise of power when people: (1) know that they choose one solution rather than another; (2) cannot imagine alternatives to their 'chosen' solution; or (3) do not even think that there might be alternatives? All three options count as decisions in the widest sense of the term, but in the last one there is no awareness of alternatives; this has no bearing, of course, on the criterion of significant affecting.

76. Allan Bradshaw, 'A Critique of Steven Lukes' "Power: A Radical View"', p. 124.

77. Ibid., pp. 123–4,

78. Steven Lukes, 'Reply to Bradshaw', p. 130.

79. Steven Lukes, *Power: A Radical View*, p. 51; see also Torben Hviid Nielsen, *Samfund og Magt. Om Samfundstyper og Mennesketyper*, København: Akademisk Forlag 1988, pp. 163–4.

80. Steven Lukes, *Power: A Radical View*, p. 51.

81. Ibid., p. 39, see also p. 41; Steven Lukes, 'On the Relativity of Power', pp. 268–71.

82. Steven Lukes, 'On the Relativity of Power', p. 272. Lukes thus agrees with the behaviourists that reason cannot count as a causal factor. This has been discussed in relation to the problem of whether rational persuasion, as a form of significant affecting, also counts as a form of power. In his discussion of persuasion ('which is not a form of power'), Connolly argues that it is not possible to hold the one who persuades responsible since the one who is rationally persuaded is so by virtue of reason (William E. Connolly, *The Terms of Political Discourse*, p. 95, see also Steven Lukes, *Power: A Radical View*, pp. 32–3). The problem of internal and external determination with regard to autonomy is also important in relation to the discussion of real interests, which, as argued, express the preferences agents *would* have if they could decide freely, i.e., if determination was purely internal, or the self was entirely itself.

83. Robert A. Dahl, 'Cause and Effect in the Study of Politics', in Daniel Lerner (ed.), *Cause and Effect*, New York and London: The Free Press and Collier-Macmillan 1965, p. 88; see also Ernest Nagel, 'Types of Causal Explanation in Science', in Daniel Lerner, ibid., p. 17.

84. Cf. Steven Lukes, *Power: A Radical View*, p. 33.

85. Peter Saunders argues a similar case when criticizing Lukes for confusing two types of explanations in his analysis of power, namely causal and moral responsibility (*Urban Politics, A Sociological Interpretation*, p. 54).

86. Steven Lukes, *Power: A Radical View*, p. 51.

87. Ibid., p. 52.

88. Ibid.

89. Ibid., p. 51, see also p. 52; Peter Saunders, *Urban Politics, A Sociological Interpretation*, pp. 53–4.

90. Steven Lukes, *Essays in Social Theory*, p. 29; *Power: A Radical View*, pp. 54–5; *Essays in Social Theory*, pp. 7, 29; *Power: A Radical View*, p. 56.

91. Cf. Jeffrey C. Isaac, *Power and Marxist Theory: A Realist View*, Ithaca and London: Cornell University Press 1987, p. 36.

92. Steven Lukes, *Power: A Radical View*, p. 24.

93. Cf. Saunders's critique of Lukes for confusing causal and moral responsibility. It should be clear by now that this confusion is inevitable within his theory since causation can have no other means of expression. That is, in so far as causation was explained in terms of more- or less-enduring structures, he could not fully subscribe to an agency conception of power.

94. Allan Bradshaw, 'A Critique of Steven Lukes' "Power: A Radical View"', p. 126.

Chapter 3 Power, Identity and Political Authority: Foucault's Power Analytics

1. Cf. Frank Cunningham, *Democratic Theory and Socialism*, Cambridge: Cambridge University Press 1987, chs. 7, 8.

2. It is important to emphasize that what is criticized here is not discourses of rights as such. What Foucault takes issue with is that the ontology of power is grasped in terms of that particular power strategy labelled the 'juridico-discursive representation of power' which pertains to the sovereignty principle with its focus on rights and obligations. This critique is similar to that levelled against Lukes's attempt to understand power in terms of responsibility (cf. preceding chapter): the problems of understanding power in terms of right stand as a critique of: (a) the dictum of the constitutive subject; which is articulated with (b) the reduction of political authority to legitimate authority; which, again, is articulated with (c) the conception of power as a means-ends causation. These comments should be seen in relation to Foucault's statement that in politics we still haven't cut off the king's head.

3. Michel Foucault, 'The History of Sexuality', in Colin Gordon (ed.), *Power/Knowledge, Selected Interviews and Other Writings 1972–1977*, New York: Pantheon Books 1980, p. 187.

4. Michel Foucault, 'Truth and Power', in *Power/Knowledge*, p. 117; and Michel Foucault, 'The Confessions of the Flesh', in *Power/Knowledge*, p. 198. See also Peter Miller, *Domination and Power,* London and New York: Routledge & Kegan Paul 1987, p. 2.

5. The Kantian dualism of time and space is criticized by Anthony Giddens in, e.g., *A Contemporary Critique of Historical Materialism*, London: The Macmillan Press 1981, pp. 17, 29–34.

6. The point is that in posing these questions one has already, if only implicitly, presupposed what ability is. Foucault's way of addressing the problem of power is, among other places, touched upon in Michel Foucault, 'Intellectuals and Power', in Donald F. Bouchard (ed.), *Language, Counter-Memory, Practice*, Ithaca, New York: Cornell University Press 1977, pp. 212–4; Michel Foucault, 'Two Lectures', in *Power/Knowledge*, p. 92ff.; Michel Foucault, 'The Subject and Power', afterword in Hubert L. Drefus and Paul Rabinow, *Michel Foucault, Beyond Structuralism and Hermeneutics* Brighton: The Harvester Press 1982, pp. 216–7; and Michel Foucault, 'On Power', in Lawrence D. Kritzman (ed.), *Politics, Philosophy, Culture: Interviews and Other Writings of Michel Foucault 1977–1984*, London: Routledge & Kegan Paul, 1988, pp. 103–4.

7. Foucault claims that '[w]e have to move beyond the outside-inside alternative; we have to be at the frontiers. Criticism indeed consists of analysing and reflecting upon limits.' Michel Foucault, 'What is Enlightenment?', in Paul Rabinow (ed.), *The Foucault Reader*, Harmondsworth: Penguin Books 1984), p. 45. Foucault discusses the notion of limit in 'A Preface to Transgression' and 'The Father's "No"', *Language, Counter-Memory, Practice*. See also Charles

Lemert and Garth Gillan, *Michel Foucault, Social Theory and Transgression,* New York: Columbia University Press 1982, pp. 26–7, 63–70.

8. Michel Foucault, 'The Subject and Power', p. 212, see also p. 208.

9. Michel Foucault, *The History of Sexuality,* vol. 1, Harmondsworth: Penguin Books 1981, p. 93; see also Michel Foucault, 'The Subject and Power', p. 224.

10. Foucault mentions 'three modes of objectification which transform human beings into subjects': inquiries which are ascribed the status of sciences; dividing practices which consist of differentiating between, say, sanity and madness; and how the subject recognizes itself as a subject of sexuality. Michel Foucault, 'The Subject and Power', p. 208. See also Michel Foucault, *The Use of Pleasure, Volume Two of the History of Sexuality*, New York: Viking 1986, p. 4.

11. A somewhat similar approach in this respect is launched by Morriss in his critique of 'the exercise fallacy' and 'the vehicle fallacy': that the conceptualization of power can be reduced to either its actual exercise (e.g. behaviourism) or its resources (e.g. structuralism). 'So power, as a dispositional concept, is neither a *thing* (a resource or vehicle) nor an *event* (an exercise of power): it is a *capacity.*' Peter Morriss, *Power: A Philosophical Analysis*, Manchester: Manchester University Press 1987, p. 19, see also pp. 14–9.

12. Michel Foucault, 'Nietzsche, Genealogy, History', in *Language, Counter-Memory, Practice*, pp. 148–52; Gilles Deleuze, *Nietzsche and Philosophy,* London: The Athlone Press 1983, p. 40; Charles E. Scott, *The Language of Difference,* Atlantic Highlands, NJ: Humanities Press International 1987, pp. 93–6.

13. Michel Foucault, 'Nietzsche, Genealogy, History', p. 154. For a more elaborated discussion of the notion of event, see Michel Foucault, 'Theatrum Philosophicum', in *Language, Counter-Memory, Practice*, pp. 172–6. Scott discusses this latter essay in *The Language of Difference*, pp. 93–101. Foucault touches upon the notion of event and 'eventualization' in 'Questions of Method: an Interview with Michel Foucault', *Ideology & Consciousness*, no. 8, spring 1981, pp. 6–7. See, moreover, Barry Smart, *Michel Foucault,* Chichester: Ellis Horwood, and London: Tavistock 1985, pp. 54–60.

14. Michel Foucault, 'Nietzsche, Genealogy, History', p. 150. See also 'The Father's "No"', p. 173.

15. Michel Foucault, 'A Preface to Transgression', p. 36. See also his, 'The Political Technology of Individuals', in Luther H. Martin, *et al.* (eds.), *Technologies of the Self, A Seminar with Michel Foucault*, London: Tavistock Publications 1988, p. 146. The same point is raised in his discussion of reason and madness. Reason is constituted in the form of alienation since it, on the one hand, excludes madness from its domain whilst trying to domesticate it; yet, on the other hand, since reason can only define itself through the other, it has to define 'itself on the basis of this exclusion', meaning that the other is constitutive for the self. It is excluded yet included, which expresses a fundamental undecidability. See Karlis Racevskis, *Michel Foucault and the Subversion of Intellect*, Ithaca and London: Cornell University Press 1983, pp. 47–8. '*What is originative*', says Foucault, '*is the caesura that establishes the distance between reason and non-reason . . . hence we must speak of . . . this act of scission, of this distance set, of this void instituted between reason and what is not reason.*' Michel Foucault, *Madness and Civilization*, London: Tavistock Publications 1967, pp. ix–x.

16. Michel Foucault, 'Nietzsche, Genealogy, History', pp. 149–52.

17. See Wolfgang Iser, 'Representation: A Performative Act', in his *Prospecting: From Reader Response to Literary Anthropology*, Baltimore: The Johns Hopkins University Press 1989.

18. Michel Foucault, *The History of Sexuality*, pp. 155–6.

19. Michel Haar, 'Nietzsche and Metaphysical Language', in David B. Allison (ed.), *The New Nietzsche, Contemporary Styles of Interpretation* Cambridge, Massachusetts and London: The MIT Press 1985, p. 12.

20. Timothy Mitchell, 'The Limits of the State: Beyond Statist Approaches and Their Critics', in *American Political Science Review*, vol. 85, no. 1, 1991, p. 95.

21. Michel Foucault: 'The Subject and Power', p. 209. See also Michel Foucault, *The History of Sexuality,* vol. 1, p. 82. This is also the reason why his understanding of power cannot be given a 'real definition'. 'Power' does not, that is, correspond to a 'real' phenomenon whether that would be a certain ability agents are endowed with or an essential capacity about structures, which could be conceived in terms of generative causal mechanisms as in, for example, Bhaskar's transcendental realism.

22. Michel Foucault, 'Two Lectures', p. 95. See also *The History of Sexuality*, pt. 4, ch. 1; Mark Cousins and Athar Hussain, *Michel Foucault,* Houndsmills: Macmillan Education 1984, pp. 231–42; and Jeff Minson, *Genealogies of Morals*, Houndsmills: The Macmillan Press 1985, pp. 41–2.

23. See Michel Foucault's articles in *Power/Knowledge*, 'Two Lectures', pp. 88–108; 'Power and Strategies', pp. 140–1; and 'The History of Sexuality', p. 187. See also Michel Foucault, *The History of Sexuality*, pp. 87–9; and Karlis Racevskis, *Michel Foucault and the Subversion of Intellect*, pp. 91–5.

24. Michel Foucault, *The History of Sexuality*, p. 86.

25. The 'fundamental reversal' of autonomy is illustrated in social-contract theory: the forced choice of representing oneself as a responsible agent capable of choosing societal rules which already exist. Autonomy is thus not constitutive but is brought about as the retroactive effect of the choice itself. See Slavoj Žižek, *The Sublime Object of Ideology*, London: Verso 1989, pp. 165–6.

26. Michel Foucault, *The History of Sexuality*, pp. 84–5; see also 'Power and Strategies', pp. 139–40.

27. Mark Cousins and Athar Hussain, *Michel Foucault*, p. 232.

28. Michel Foucault, *The History of Sexuality*, p. 88; see also 'Two Lectures', p. 88.

29. Michel Foucault, 'Two Lectures', pp. 91, 95.

30. Ibid., pp. 105–6; and Michel Foucault, 'Truth and Power', p. 123.

31. Michel Foucault, *The History of Sexuality*, p. 102, see also p. 97. The reason for adopting military metaphors is, says Foucault, that there are only two models for analysing power: '(a) the one proposed by law (power as law, interdiction, institutions) and (b) the military or strategic model in terms of power relations.' His strategy is to adopt the latter in order to counter the former. Michel Foucault, 'Power and Sex', in *Politics, Philosophy, Culture*, p. 123. See also 'Two Lectures', p. 90; and 'Truth and Power', p. 123.

32. Gilles Deleuze, *Foucault*, Paris: Les Éditions de Minuit, 1986, p. 38 (my translation).

33. Michel Foucault, 'Nietzsche, Genealogy, History', p. 151.

34. This is again put succinctly by Deleuze when he argues that the 'law is always an arrangement of illegalisms, which it differentiates by formalising them.' Hence the 'law is a management of illegalisms' *(Foucault*, p. 37). Foucault discusses the topic of illegalities and law in *Discipline and Punish*, New York: Vintage Books 1979, pp. 82–9, and pt. IV, ch. 2. See also Slavoj Žižek, *For They Know Not What They Do*, London: Verso 1991, pp. 30, 32–3, 40–3, where he speaks of law as universalized crime.

35. Michel Foucault, 'Governmentality', in *Ideology & Consciousness*, no. 6, autumn 1979, p. 12.

36. Michel Foucault, 'Two Lectures', p. 97–8, 102; and *The History of Sexuality*, pp. 135–6.

37. Michel Foucault, 'Two Lectures', pp. 99–100. See also 'Nietzsche, Genealogy, History', p. 152.

38. Michel Foucault, 'Two Lectures', p. 99; and *The History of Sexuality*, p. 136.

39. Michel Foucault, *Discipline and Punish*, p. 27; 'Power and Strategies', p. 142; and *The History of Sexuality*, pp. 99–100.

40. Michel Foucault, 'Two Lectures', p. 96.

41. Michel Foucault, *The History of Sexuality*, p. 93.

42. Ibid., p. 106, see also p. 107; and *The History of Sexuality*, p. 144.

43. Michel Foucault, *Discipline and Punish*, pp. 222–3; and 'Two Lectures', pp. 105–6.

44. Michel Foucault, 'The Subject and Power', p. 224; see also 'Governmentality', pp. 20–1; and 'Truth and Power', pp. 122–3.

45. Barry Smart, 'The Politics of Truth and the Problem of Hegemony', in David Couzens Hoy (ed.), *Foucault, A Critical Reader*, Oxford: Basil Blackwell 1986, pp. 161–2.

46. Michel Foucault, 'Governmentality', *Ideology & Consciousness*, no. 6, 1979, p. 21.

47. Ibid., p. 20.

48. Michel Foucault, 'Truth and Power', p. 122; and 'The Confessions of the Flesh', p. 198. See also Timothy Mitchell, 'The Limits of the State: Beyond Statist Approaches and Their Critics'.

49. Michel Foucault, 'Governmentality', p. 19.

50. I'm grateful to Henrik Paul Bang who outlined this scheme at a seminar at Roskilde University in November 1992.

51. Michel Foucault, 'Two Lectures', p. 102.

52. Claude Lefort, John B. Thompson (ed.), *The Political Forms of Modern Society*, Cambridge: Polity Press 1986, p. 303.

53. Thus Foucault holds that the 'democratisation of sovereignty was fundamentally determined by and grounded in mechanisms of disciplinary coercion.' Michel Foucault, 'Two Lectures', p. 105, see also p. 106, and *Discipline and Punish*, pt. III, ch. 3.

54. Michel Foucault, 'Space, Knowledge, and Power', in *The Foucault Reader*, p. 245. See also 'The Subject and Power', pp. 221–2.

Chapter 4 The Presuppositionless Conception of Power: Power as Negativity

1. The notion of the discursive is, following Laclau and Mouffe, equivalent to social reality because the latter is relationally constructed through articulation.

2. The notions of articulation and contingency/necessity are, among other places, discussed in Ernesto Laclau and Chantal Mouffe, *Hegemony and Socialist Strategy: Towards a Radical Democratic Politics*, London: Verso 1985, pp. 105–14, and Ernesto Laclau, *Reflections on the Revolution of Our Time*, London: Verso 1990, pp. 18–26. Cf. also Foucault's assertion that the confrontation between power strategies (power/resistance) constitutes the identity of both, and that it is impossible to fix identity entirely.

3. Ernesto Laclau and Chantal Mouffe, *Hegemony and Socialist Strategy*, pp. 127–34.

4. Cf. the discussion of limits in Michel Foucault, 'A Preface to Transgression', in Michel Foucault, Donald F. Bouchard (ed.), *Language, Counter-Memory, Practice*, Ithaca, New York: Cornell University Press 1977.

5. Sigmund Freud, *Civilization, Society and Religion*, The Pelican Freud

Library, vol. 12, Harmondsworth: Pelican Books 1985, p. 147 (italics in original), see also pp. 152–3, 161–2, 167–8.

6. Anthony Giddens, *Central Problems in Social Theory*, London: The Macmillan Press 1979, p. 64.

7. This has already been discussed in the context of the community power debate. The notion of nondecisions draws attention to the fact that power is operative in the inclusion and exclusion of issues (and agents) on the political agenda. The sedimentation of patterns of inclusion and exclusion within institutional and organizational rule-governed practices expresses what Schattschneider termed 'the mobilization of bias'. A similar although less radical version of this topic is provided by Polsby's assertion of 'the conservatism of political agendas'.

8. Claude Lefort, John B. Thompson (ed.), The *Political Forms of Modern Society*, Cambridge: Polity Press 1986, pp. 202, 211.

9. The principle of fundamental cultural differences rather than biological differences is the hallmark of what Balibar terms 'neo-racism'. He says: '*culture can also function like a nature*, and it can in particular function as a way of locking individuals and groups a priori into a genealogy, into a determination that is immutable and intangible in origin.' 'The differentialist version states that *all* races (cultures) are lost (and thus human civilization) if they all come to swamp each other with their diversity, if the "order" which they constitute as distinct cultures dissipates, to be replaced by the entropy of a standardized "mass culture".' Etienne Balibar, in Etienne Balibar and Immanuel Wallerstein, *Race, Nation, Class: Ambiguities, Identities*, London: Verso 1991, pp. 22, 66. See also pp. 54–7, 215, 219–23.

10. Louis Althusser discusses overdetermination particularly in his *For Marx*, London: Verso, 1979: chs. 3, 6; and Louis Althusser and Etienne Balibar, *Reading Capital*, London: Verso 1979: pt. II, ch. 9. The notion of overdetermination is, however, flawed by Althusser's insistence on the economy as determining the structural whole in the last instance. The consequence is that he oscillates between structural causality, which he advocates, and the linear causality he rejects. For a critique of Althusser on this point, see Laclau and Mouffe, *Hegemony and Socialist Strategy*, pp. 97–105. These shortcomings are echoed in Foucault's power analytics, to the extent to which it leans towards viewing 'the order of power' as closed, i.e., as a ground which confines the scope of what he calls 'functional overdetermination'.

11. Cf. Michel Foucault, *The History of Sexuality*, pp. 99–100. The notion of overdetermination is thus directed against both methodological holism and individualism which hold, respectively, that the societal whole as a closed totality is ontologically different from its moments, and that it is nothing but the aggregate of these.

12. Slavoj Žižek, *For They Know Not What They Do*, London: Verso 1991, p. 46.

13. The problems of individual vs. public interests and subjective vs. real interests, which will be discussed in Chapters 5 and 6, are examples that illustrate this point.

14. Ernesto Laclau and Chantal Mouffe, *Hegemony and Socialist Strategy*, p. 103.

15. The notions of condensation and displacement were developed in Freudian psychoanalysis as tools for interpreting dreams, Sigmund Freud, *The Interpretation of Dreams*, The Pelican Freud Library, vol. 4, Harmondsworth: Pelican Books 1976, sects. A, B. Lacan has linked these notions to the linguistic categories of metaphor and metonymy, Jacques Lacan, *Écrits*, London: Tavistock Publications 1977, ch. 5. See also Anika Lemaire, *Jacques Lacan*, London and New York: Routledge & Kegan Paul 1977, pt. 7, chs. 17, 18; Anthony Wilden,

Speech and Language in Psychoanalysis, Baltimore and London: The Johns Hopkins University Press 1981, pp. 238–49; Kaja Silverman, *The Subject of Semiotics*, New York and Oxford: Oxford University Press 1983, ch. 3. Althusser has applied the notions of condensation and displacement in his discussion of overdetermination (*For Marx*, chs. 3, 6).

16. Freud used the notion of nodal point in relation to condensation of dream elements, see *The Interpretation of Dreams*, pp. 338, 456–7. It is also used by Laclau and Mouffe in order to account for how articulation partially fixes meaning, see *Hegemony and Socialist Strategy*, pp. 112–3. In his review of *Hegemony and Socialist Strategy*, Žižek says: 'The nodal points are points which structure floating elements in order to articulate and fix an ideological camp and in this manner its signification,' Slavoj Žižek, 'La Société N'Existe Pas', *L'Ane*, Oct.–Dec., 1985, p. 36 (author's translation).

17. Cf. the above example of the racist strategy construing 'Danishness' as a nodal point, which comprises a variety of heterogeneous elements.

18. Louis Althusser, *For Marx*, p. 211, 216.

19. Ibid., pp. 99, 100.

20. This does not, of course, entail that emancipation from particular structures of domination and subordination is impossible. The contingency of structures entails, on the contrary, that things could have been different, which is why autonomy is an immanent feature of the discursive structuring of social relations.

21. There is here a resemblance to Schattschneider's notion of the management of conflicts, which, amongst other things, deals with the displacement of conflicts even before they fully develop. 'Politics', he says, 'deals with the domination and subordination of conflicts', which means organizing issues in and out of the political arena. Elmer E. Schattschneider, *The Semi-Sovereign People: A Realist's view of Democracy in America*, New York: Holt, Reinhart & Winston 1960, p. 66.

22. Cf. Ernesto Laclau and Chantal Mouffe, *Hegemony and Socialist Strategy*, p. 129.

23. When the inclusion of some elements into a strategy, discourse or social order is coterminous with the exclusion of others and the latter makes up a constitutive outside, which forms what Derrida has termed the supplement which at one and the same time conditions and threatens an identity. Cf. Jacques Derrida, *Of Grammatology*, Baltimore and London: The Johns Hopkins University Press 1976, pt. II, ch. 2; Jacques Derrida, *Writing and Difference*, London: Routledge & Kegan Paul 1978, ch. 10; Jacques Derrida, *Dissemination*, Chicago: The University of Chicago Press 1981, ch. 9.

24. Ernesto Laclau and Chantal Mouffe, *Hegemony and Socialist Strategy*, pp. 95, 99, 111; see also Ernesto Laclau, 'Transformations of Advanced Industrial Societies and the Theory of the Subject', in Sakari Hanninen and Leena Paldan (eds.), *Rethinking Ideology*, Berlin: Argument-Verlag 1983, pp. 39–40; and Ernesto Laclau, *New Reflections on the Revolution of Our Time*, ch. 2.

25. 'As representation, however, arises out of the attempt to remove difference, what is to be removed appears to be something that does not have the nature of an object . . . It is intangible, and this fact cannot be concealed by any forms of representation – on the contrary, this intangibility inscribes itself into every form of representation.' Wolfgang Iser, 'Representation: A Performative Act', in his *Prospecting: From Reader Response to Literary Anthropology*, Baltimore: The Johns Hopkins University Press 1989, p. 242, see also pp. 245–6.

26. Derrida makes a similar point when asserting that 'the point of non-replacement is . . . the point of orientation of the entire system of signification,

the point where the fundamental signified is promised as the terminal-point of all references and conceals itself as that which would destroy at one blow the entire system of signs' (Jacques Derrida, *Of Grammatology*, p. 266). This 'point of orientation' is the nodal point, the empty core of 'the entire system'; *that* particular in which universality is embodied and where universality comes across itself in its opposite. As 'the fundamental signified' it is fully identical with itself, but this self-identity encounters itself as an absolute contradiction, which is why it has to conceal itself – that is, conceal that it is not *itself*. The notions of horizon and context are important for grasping the nature and scope of antagonistic power struggles because horizon and context are related to political authority. Derrida's 'point of orientation of the entire system of signification' is somewhat analogous to authority in politics. A political authority is not really obeyed for this or that reason – the usual type of explanation as to why people obey proceeds by striking a balance between effectiveness and legitimacy, which is another way of saying that the *raison d'être* of politics is found in economic rationality (instrumental reason) and social support arising in civil society (communicative reason) – but because it functions as 'the terminal point of all references' in practical politics on a day-to-day basis.

27. The contrast with the notion of multicausality should be evident. Although this notion states that the cause of an effect consists of more than one element, it not only preserves the principle of causal linearity, it also holds that the nature of the elements is not modified by their interaction. They preserve their differential identity because identity is specified apart from the relation which brings them together. The stress is thus on *interaction*, rather than on *articulation* which emphasizes the opposite.

28. Louis Althusser and Étienne Balibar, *Reading Capital*, pt. II, ch. 9; Jacques-Alain Miller, 'Suture (Elements of the Logic of the Signifier)', *Screen*, vol. 18, no. 4, 1977–78, pp. 32–4.

29. Louis Althusser and Étienne Balibar, *Reading Capital*, p. 189.

30. Ernesto Laclau and Chantal Mouffe, *Hegemony and Socialist Strategy*, p. 127.

31. Laclau and Mouffe's argument is similar to the one made in relation to universality and particularity. The closure of the Hobbesian social order rests on the premiss that the particular representing universality (the sovereign) stands above the order it represents. This exteriority is, however, invalidated because sovereignty is erected by the covenant, meaning that universality is embodied in its opposite, namely the particular, whereupon the schism between universality and particularity becomes situated *within* the social order. It is in this sense that limits are given within the social itself, destroying the possibility of a social order consummating itself. Cf. Claude Lefort, *The Political Forms of Modern Society*, pp. 191, 199–200.

32. See the chapters: 'Différance' and 'Signature Event Context' in Jacques Derrida, *Margins of Philosophy*, Brighton: The Harvester Press 1982; and Rodolphe Gasché, *The Tain of the Mirror*, Cambridge, Massachusetts: Harvard University Press 1986, pp. 186–94, 289–92.

33. A similar type of argument is presented by March and Olsen, who hold that the formation and articulation of interests are not prior or external to political institutions. See James G. March and Johan P. Olsen, *Rediscovering Institutions*, New York: The Free Press 1989.

34. See in particular Ernesto Laclau, 'Transformations of Advanced Industrial Societies and the Theory of the Subject'; Ernesto Laclau, 'Metaphor and Social Antagonism', in Gary Nelson and Lawrence Grossberg (eds.), *Marxism and Interpretation of Culture*, Basingstoke: Macmillan 1988; Ernesto Laclau,

Reflections on the Revolution of Our Time; and Ernesto Laclau and Chantal Mouffe, *Hegemony and Socialist Strategy*: esp. ch. 3.

35. Cf. the discussion of the two aspects of the logic of the signifier: the sliding of the signified under the signifier and the cancelling of the signified in this sliding.

36. Thomas Hobbes, *Leviathan*, Harmondsworth: Penguin Books 1968, p. 232; see also Hannah Fenichel Pitkin, *The Concept of Representation*, Berkeley and Los Angeles: University of California Press 1967, pp. 31–2.

37. The same type of argument can be found in two modern heirs of Hobbes, namely Carl Schmitt and Talcott Parsons. Schmitt's hostility towards liberal pluralism makes him advocate a notion of democracy which is modelled upon his understanding of what politics is basically all about, namely the friend/enemy relation. By externalizing the public enemy, a common space is created which is characterized by the homogeneity arising from the identification of the ruled with the rulers. In this totalitarian *führer* democracy there is no room for political disagreement, meaning that those who violate the societal homogeneity are the authors of their own punishment (see, e.g., Carl Schmitt, *Der Begriff des Politischen*, Berlin: Duncker & Humblot 1987). Parsons' view of power is, contrary to Schmitt's, consensual and not conflictual. By emphasizing that power is a mechanism of social integration, it attains the status of a system property which is linked to the furthering of collective goals. Power is thus legitimate by definition, and thus resistance to power shows a failure of integration, meaning that the power of authoritative decision-making units is not completely institutionalized. See, e.g., Talcott Parsons, 'Power and the Social System', in Steven Lukes (ed.), *Power*, Oxford: Basil Blackwell.

38. Michel Foucault, *The History of Sexuality*, vol. 1, Harmondsworth: Penguin Books 1984, p. 96.

39. Ibid.

40. To speak of the accidental status of resistance means that it is formed outside that which it resists, whose essential characteristics are not then affected by accidental events. Here one is situated in the dichotomous realm of internal and external relations, which haunts emancipatory discourses as well as the debates on structure and agency. By being confined within the pores of structures, agency is conceptualized in voluntaristic terms (just as resistance is seen in terms of a constitutive subject), which leaves the deterministic image of structures intact. The accidental can be contrasted with contingency which, by assuming the relational nature of identity, undermines the dichotomy between essence and accident, and hence between internal and external relations. Cf. Ernesto Laclau, *Reflections on the Revolution of Our Time*, pp. 18–22.

41. It should be kept in mind that it is not possible, strictly speaking, to make a rigorous distinction between applying a rule and questioning it, since the very practice of acting in accordance with rules, and hence applying them, defines and modifies these rules. The difference between power relations and power struggles cannot, then, be rigorous either.

42. This problem is pursued further in Chapter 5 which deals with the schisms between subjective and real interests.

43. The importance of this claim should not be underestimated. It stresses the impossibility of discourses somehow standing above what they interpret. The interpreter is not confronted with an 'external world' which is represented in discourses and then validated or invalidated by comparing them with 'reality' as if the latter could be represented in its factuality stripped of interpretations. Genealogy transcends the ideas of representation and linearity by searching not for the hidden unity of origins but for the lines of descent, whose unity is both posed and presupposed. Interpretation is, accordingly, actively involved in

shaping what is interpreted, and consequently truth cannot be a fixed point outside the reach of power, but is at one and the same time the outcome of power struggles *and* their point of orientation. Cf. Charles E. Scott, *The Language of Difference*, Atlantic Highlands, NJ: Humanities Press International 1987, pp. 106–11.

44. Cf. Michel Foucault, 'The History of Sexuality', p. 186, and 'Body/Power', p. 58; both in Michel Foucault, Colin Gordon (ed.), Power/Knowledge, *Selected Interviews and Other Writings 1972–1977*, New York: Pantheon Books 1980.

45. This can be seen as a preliminary indication of why resistance often connotes some form of grand vision of emancipation: by negating *that* which negates a subject, it becomes possible for it (once again) to complete its identity. Such an argument presupposes the proposition of the constitutive subject. It is Hobbes inverted!

46. Since literality and fixity of meaning are never achievable, denotation is, strictly speaking, impossible. The move from denotation to connotation is therefore used heuristically. In his discussion of the two concepts Barthes says: 'denotation is not the first meaning, but pretends to be so; under this illusion, it is ultimately no more than the *last* of the connotations (the one which seems both to establish and to close the reading).' Roland Barthes, *S/Z*, New York: Hill and Wang 1974, p. 9.

47. Ernesto Laclau and Chantal Mouffe, *Hegemony and Socialist Strategy*, p. 125.

48. Slavoj Žižek, *The Sublime Object of Ideology*, London: Verso 1989, p. 68, see also p. 193.

49. Cf. Ernesto Laclau, *Reflections on the Revolution of Our Time*, pp. 60–7; Slavoj Žižek, *The Sublime Object of Ideology*, pp. 173, 175, 178, 193, 195.

50. Slavoj Žižek, *The Sublime Object of Ideology*, p. 172.

51. Their arguments are, however, rather complex and deserve special attention because they throw light on the temporal dimension of identity *vis-à-vis* power. This is discussed in Chapter 5, on the politics of subjective and real interests.

52. Slavoj Žižek, *The Sublime Object of Ideology*, p. 226.

53. Cf. Michel Foucault, *The History of Sexuality*, pp. 81–7.

54. Henry Staten, *Wittgenstein and Derrida*, Oxford: Basil Blackwell 1985, p. 152.

55. Ernesto Laclau, preface to Slavoj Žižek, *The Sublime Object of Ideology*, p. xv, and Michel Foucault, 'Nietzsche, Genealogy, History', in Michel Foucault, Donald F. Bouchard (ed.), *Language, Counter-Memory, Practice*, p. 150. The subject for both writers is conceived as the limit which cannot ever be fully inserted in structures.

56. Sigmund Freud, *On Psychopathology*, The Pelican Freud Library, vol. 10, Harmondsworth: Pelican Books 1979, p. 263.

57. Sigmund Freud, *On Psychopathology*, pp. 284, 302.

58. Søren Kierkegaard, *Begrebet Angest*, København: Gyldendal 1962, pp. 71, 74. Kierkegaard discusses the concept of anxiety in relation to freedom in ch. 1, sect. 5. The question of authenticity in relation to anxiety is discussed by Martin Heidegger, *Being and Time*, Oxford: Basil Blackwell 1962, sect. 40. See also Martin Heidegger, 'What is Metaphysics?', in Martin Heidegger, David Farrell Krell (ed.), *Basic Writings*, New York: Harper & Row 1977. It should be stressed that the term 'authenticity' is not used here in an existentialist sense to connote an essentialism of the subject.

59. 'Antagonism does not admit *tertium quid*', say Laclau and Mouffe, because there is no common ground between the antagonistic forces which

could mediate between them (Ernesto Laclau and Chantal Mouffe, *Hegemony and Socialist Strategy*, p. 129, see also p. 126). A similar point is made by Schmitt in his discussion of the friend/enemy relation, which cannot be mitigated by a neutral third party (Carl Schmitt, *Der Begriff des Politischen*, pp. 27, 49–50). The impossibility of mediation does not mean that antagonistic struggles cannot be 'solved'. One way of doing it would be to eliminate the enemy, another would be to disintegrate chains of equivalences, which would open up to differential relations and hence a common horizon.

60. Ernesto Laclau, 'Metaphor and Social Antagonism', p. 256; Ernesto Laclau and Chantal Mouffe, *Hegemony and Socialist Strategy*, p. 125.

61. Slavoj Žižek, *The Sublime Object of Ideology*, p. 33.

62. Cf. Wolfgang Iser, 'Fictionalizing: The Anthropological Dimension of Literary Fictions', *New Literary History*, vol. 21, no. 4, 1990, p. 950.

Chapter 5 Identity and the Politics of Subjective and Real Interests

1. Weber's distinction between the ethics of intention and the ethics of responsibility can help illustrate this problem. The political subject, says Weber, has to act according to the ethics of responsibility: it must be ready to do evil in order to prevent an even greater evil from occurring. Politics legitimizes an action *ex ante* from the point of view of the *ex post*. This means that the political action fosters a temporal distance which it then closes. It is by means of this distance that a political strategy is able to create a horizon within which it can carry out its tasks in a 'responsible' manner. Max Weber, 'Politik als Beruf', in his *Gesammelte Politischen Schriften,* 4th edn., Tübingen: J.C.B. Mohr 1980, pp. 548–56.

2. William E. Connolly advanced his concept of real interest in two publications: 'On "Interests" in Politics' in *Politics and Society*, 2, 1972; and *The Terms of Political Discourse,* Lexington, Mass: D. C. Heath and Co 1974. It should be mentioned that in his later works, notably in *Political Theory and Modernity,* Oxford: Basil Blackwell 1988; and *Identity\Difference,* Ithaca and London: Cornell University Press 1991, he has advanced a critique of the essentialism of the subject, and hence the vision of restoring the unity of the subject. In light of this, he might be critical of his earlier writings on real interests. However, I still find his discussion of this subject 'thought-provoking', to use Lukes's phrase (Steven Lukes, *Power: A Radical View*, London: Macmillan 1974, p. 60).

3. For a critique of behaviourism see William E. Connolly, *The Terms of Political Discourse*, pp. 49–62.

4. Steven Lukes, *Power: A Radical View*, p. 39.

5. Steven Lukes, *Power: A Radical View*, pp. 27, 34, and his, 'Power and Structure', in *Essays in Social Theory*, Houndsmills: The Macmillan Press 1977, p. 6.

6. See Elmer E. Schattschneider, *The Semi-Sovereign People: A Realist's View of Democracy in America*, New York: Holt, Reinhart & Winston 1960, ch. 4.

7. Steven Lukes, 'Reply to Bradshaw', *Sociology*, vol. 10, 1976, p. 130. Lukes discusses democracy and participation in 'The New Democracy', *Essays in Social Theory*.

8. See Jürgen Habermas, *Legitimation Crisis*, London: Heinemann 1976, pp. 111–7. Elsewhere he says that 'we in every discourse reciprocally *presuppose* an ideal speech situation. The ideal speech situation is thereby characterized such that every consensus, which can be reached under its condition, *per se* should count as

a more true consensus. *The anticipation of the ideal speech situation* is a guarantee that we can connect an actually realized consensus with the true consensus.' 'Vorbereitende Bemerkungen zu einer Theorie der kommunikativen Kompetenz', in Jürgen Habermas and Niklas Luhman, *Theorie der Gesellschaft oder Sozialtechnologie – Was Leisted die Systemforschung?*, Frankfurt am Main: Surkamp Verlag 1971, p. 136 (my translation).

9. This point was already broached by Raymond E. Wolfinger in his critique of Bachrach and Baratz's discussion of nondecision making ('Nondecisions and the Study of Local Politics', *American Political Science Review*, vol. 65, no. 4, 1971, pp. 1077–8). What is important in this context is the nature of the 'observer's assessment'. The liberal image of the observer is, ultimately, that of the totalitarian party bureaucracy, which knows better than the individuals themselves what they want. However, this is on the whole a misleading picture, which Lukes himself seems to share, because it conceals the fact that the image of the observer is none other than that of the *political* assessment which is in a position of partial exteriority to the subjects. The point is that to speak in the name of society necessitates a temporal/spatial distantiation. Hence responsibility is prior to responsiveness (cf. Weber's ethics of responsibility). The aim of bridging the gap between the actual/subjective and the ideal/real by sketching *relevant* counterfactuals can thus be seen as an attempt to eliminate the 'necessary evil' of politics which exists in the schism between the two.

10. William E. Connolly, *The Terms of Political Discourse*, p. 64.

11. It would be meaningless because decision making revolves around undecidability and contingency, which condition the constitution of identity through processes of identification. The point is, however, that this description of real interests as the limit that gives shape to identity points to the fact that, in its own round about way, our real interest is to make decisions because this is the way we conduct ourselves and others. This in turn means that our real interest is to be part of an institutional setting which somehow 'reflects' or 'embodies' undecidability and contingency, and this, in turn, is an interest in widening and deepening democracy.

12. Christine Swanton, 'The Concept of Interest', *Political Theory*, vol. 8, no. 1, 1980, p. 93.

13. Ibid., pp. 93–5.

14. William E. Connolly, *The Terms of Political Discourse*, p. 72.

15. Ibid.

16. Slavoj Žižek, 'Beyond Discourse Analysis', in Ernesto Laclau, *New Reflections on the Revolution of Our Time*, London: Verso 1990, pp. 251–4.

17. Cornelius Castoriadis, 'Power, Politics, Autonomy', in his *Philosophy, Politics, Autonomy*, David Ames Curtis (ed.), Oxford: Oxford University Press 1991, p. 164.

18. Michel Haar, 'Nietzsche and Metaphysical Language', in David B. Allison (ed.), *The New Nietzsche, Contemporary Styles of Interpretation*, Cambridge, Massachusetts and London: The MIT Press 1985, p. 12.

19. Martin Heidegger, *Being and Time*, Oxford: Basil Blackwell 1990, pp. 185–6.

20. Pierre Klossowski, 'Nietzsche's Experience of the Eternal Return', in David B. Allison (ed.), *The New Nietzsche*, p. 108.

21. The relation between repression and anxiety is discussed by Sigmund Freud in 'Inhibitions, Symptoms and Anxiety', in *On Psychopathology*, Harmondsworth: Pelican Books 1979, pp. 237–315. His argument, as will be remembered from the previous chapter, is that it is anxiety that gives way to repression, and not the other way around.

22. Cf. the discussion on retroactive causality in Slavoj Žižek, *For They Know Not What They Do*, London: Verso 1991, pp. 201–3.

23. Søren Kierkegaard, *Begrebet Angest*, København: Gyldendal 1960, p. 74 (my translation). See also Ernesto Laclau, *New Reflections on the Revolution of Our Time*, p. 18.

24. See Wolfgang Iser, 'Representation: A Performative Act' in his *Prospecting: From Reader Response to Literary Anthropology*, Baltimore: The Johns Hopkins University Press 1989; and Slavoj Žižek, *The Sublime Object of Ideology*, London: Verso 1989, pp. 87–110. See, moreover, Jacques Derrida, 'Sending: On Representation', in Gayle L. Ormiston and Alan D. Schrift (eds.), *Transforming the Hermeneutic Context: From Nietzsche to Nancy*, New York: State University of New York Press 1990, pp. 117–8, 121–2.

25. Slavoj Žižek, *The Sublime Object of Ideology*, p. 172. See also his, *Le plus Sublime des Hystériques*, Paris: Point Hors Ligne 1988, p. 82.

26. See the exchange between Polsby and Crenson on the criteria for how and when issues reach/do not reach the political agenda: Matthew A. Crenson, *The Un-Politics of Air Pollution*, Baltimore and London: The Johns Hopkins University Press 1971, pp. 26–32; and Nelson Polsby, *Community Power and Political Theory*, 2nd enl. edn., New Haven and London: Yale University Press 1980, pp. 95–7. See also Ernesto Laclau, *New Reflections on the Revolution of Our Time*, p. 31.

27. Pierre Klossowski, 'Nietzsche's Experience of the Eternal Return', p. 110.

28. When *A* exercises power over *B*, *B* constructs *A* as *non-B*, as *that* which blocks its possibility of being what it is. The imaginary constitution of identity is located in the movement from the blocking of *B*'s identity to its reconstitution, as if the identity of *B* was just awaiting recognition. The *re* of recognition testifies to the void in identity as if identity could be (re)established without getting caught up in power relations, as if power was an external force encroaching upon it. It is in this sense that the circular structure of power produces what Mitchell has referred to as 'reality effects.' Timothy Mitchell, 'The Limits of the State: Beyond Statist Approaches and Their Critics', in *American Political Science Review*, vol. 85, no. 1, 1991, p. 95. Envisaging real interests is one way of inverting this moment of negativity, thereby attempting to fix identity in the recoiling movement of 'becoming what one is'.

29. The notion of pure distance, which Nietzsche employs when describing the relation between good and evil, indicates that it does not belong to 'being-there': it is not a distance between two given entities but their impossibility of maintaining a distinct identity altogether. See Michel Foucault, 'Nietzsche, Genealogy, History', in his *Language, Counter-Memory, Practice*, Donald F. Bouchard (ed.), New York: Cornell University Press, 1977: sects. 3, 4, 5.

30. This was one of the major points raised by Bachrach and Baratz in their critique of behaviourism and, moreover, a reason for studying power in terms of 'nondecisions'. See their two articles: 'Two Faces of Power', *American Political Science Review*, vol. 56, 1962; and 'Decisions and Nondecisions: An Analytical Framework', *American Political Science Review*, vol. 57, 1963. Lukes's contribution to this debate radicalizes the nondecision-making approach. Thus he asks: 'is it not the supreme and most insidious exercise of power to prevent people, to whatever degree, from having grievances by shaping their perceptions, cognitions and preferences in such a way that they accept their role in the existing order of things . . .? To assume that the absence of grievance equals

genuine consensus is simply to rule out the possibility of false or manipulated consensus by definitional fiat.' Steven Lukes, *Power: a Radical View*, p. 24.

31. See Michel Foucault, 'The History of Sexuality', in his *Power/Knowledge: Selected Interviews and Other Writings 1972–1977*, Colin Gordon (ed.), New York: Pantheon Press 1980, p. 186. He wants to show 'how power relations can materially penetrate the body in depth, without depending even on the mediation of the subject's own representations.' The point is that there is not first a negation of identity which presents itself as a mere fact, and then an interpretation of this fact which would be a mental representation of reality. The identity of the subject is constituted in the processes of interpreting the event, of representing it, which involves the duality of performance and semblance and, by extension, the posing of the identity of the subject as presupposed.

32. See Freud's discussion of the impact on adults of sexual traumas experienced in childhood, 'My Views on the Part Played by Sexuality in the Aetiology of the Neuroses', in *On Psychopathology*, Harmondsworth: Pelican Books 1979. There is no direct link between hysterical symptoms and 'repressed memories of childhood experiences'. Rather, 'between the symptoms and the childish impressions there were inserted the patient's *phantasies* (imaginary memories)'. (p. 75) Hence the important thing is not so much 'what sexual experiences a particular individual had had in his childhood, but rather of his reaction to those experiences – of whether he had reacted to them by "repression" or not.' (pp. 77–8) It should be clear that *reaction* is not a direct response to a past event, a 'pure' exercise of remembrance, which can be excavated and presented 'as it was'. It entails, instead, the formation of symptoms, which cannot but be a (distorted) representation of the event. In fact, event *qua* event cannot be represented since it is the fissure escaping the domestication by language and hence rationality. Distortion (which entails displacement and condensation) is thus the only way in which we recognize ourselves, which is to say that recognition is always a reconstruction. It is in this way that we always go astray when we 'return to ourselves'.

33. See Ernesto Laclau and Chantal Mouffe, *Hegemony and Socialist Strategy: Towards a Radical Democratic Politics*, London: Verso 1985, pp. 125, 129; and Slavoj Žižek, 'Beyond Discourse Analysis', pp. 251–4.

34. Ernesto Laclau and Chantal Mouffe, *Hegemony and Socialist Strategy*, pp. 127–31.

35. The relation between subordination and oppression is dealt with in Ernesto Laclau and Chantal Mouffe, *Hegemony and Socialist Strategy*, pp. 152–9.

36. The fundamental reversal pertaining to autonomy can, for example, be seen in social-contract theory: the forced choice of representing oneself as a responsible agent capable of choosing societal rules which already exist. Autonomy is thus not constitutive but is brought about as the retroactive effect of the choice itself in which power is immanent. See Slavoj Žižek, *The Sublime Object of Ideology*, pp. 165–6. The subject, as Rousseau would say, is only free inasmuch as it is bounded by the laws of its own making.

CHAPTER 6 DEMOCRACY AND THE POLITICS OF INTERESTS AND THE COMMON GOOD

1. Thomas Hobbes, *Leviathan*, Cambridge: Cambridge University Press 1991, p. 120. See also Carl Schmitt, *Der Leviathan*, Köln: Hohenheim Verlag 1982, pp. 79, 84.

2. Giovanni Sartori, 'What is "Politics"', *Political Theory*, vol. 1, no. 1,

1973, pp. 9–10. See also Hannah Arendt, *The Human Condition*, Chicago and London: The University of Chicago Press 1958, pp. 36–7; and Jürgen Habermas, *Theorie und Praxis*, 2nd edn., Neuwird am Rhein & Berlin: Hermann Luchterhand Verlag 1967, pp. 22–4.

3. See, e.g., the review of the development of Dahl's theory of democracy which amongst other things emphasizes this unsolved schism in his works. Richard W. Krouse, 'Polyarchy and Participation: The Changing Democratic Theory of Robert Dahl', *Polity,* vol. 14, no. 3, 1982, pp. 441–63.

4. Cf. David Easton, *The Political System*, 2nd edn., Chicago and London: The University of Chicago Press 1971, pp. 126–41.

5. Cf. Henrik Paul Bang and Torben Bech Dyrberg, 'The Political in the Social: An Ontological Turn of Political and Democratic Theory', *Working Paper*, Dept. of Social Sciences, Roskilde University 1993, pp. 6–16; and Henrik Paul Bang and Torben Bech Dyrberg, 'Hegemony and Democracy', *Working Paper*, Dept. of Economics, Politics and Public Administration, Aalborg University. 1993, pp. 4–15.

6. Undecidability stresses: (1) the impossibility of structural closure or the presence of a structural totality; (2) that the subject is neither internal nor external to the structure, but is constituted *vis-à-vis* it; (3) that decision is a contingent actualization of the possible (which presupposes context); (4) that ethico-political decisions presuppose this non-algorithmicity of decision, that is, the distance between structure as rules and resources and its actualization; and (5) that the subject is located in, or rather *is*, this distance between structure and decision. The concept of undecidability is discussed by Jacques Derrida, *Limited Inc.*, Evanston, Ill: Northwestern University Press 1988, pp. 116, 148; Jacques Derrida, 'Force of Law: The "Mystical Foundation of Authority"', in Drucilla Cornell *et al.* (eds.), *Deconstruction and the Possibility of Justice*, New York and London: Routledge 1992, pp. 24–6; Ernesto Laclau, *New Reflections on the Revolution of Our Time*, London: Verso 1990, pp. 29–38, 172–3; and Chantal Mouffe, *The Return of the Political*, London: Verso 1993, pp. 141, 144–7.

7. Lukes addresses this problem succinctly when he talks about 'the liberal project of both restraining the coercive power of government while claiming its authority to be based on consent and to promote the general interest.' Seen in this perspective the individual is constitutively split between its unruly desires (the state of nature) and its quest for order. That is, it is the locus of both coercion and consent. Steven Lukes, 'Power and Authority', in Tom Bottomore and Robert Nisbet (eds.), *A History of Sociological Analysis*, London: Heinemann 1978, p. 652.

8. Ernesto Laclau, *New Reflections on the Revolution of Our Time*, p. 56.

9. It is in this respect secondary whether 'society' connotes the nation-state or an international community. The point is that political agents have to operate, implicitly or explicitly, with assumptions about a societal whole.

10. We thus have three levels of analysis, namely structure, institution and practice, which must be taken into account when dealing with the articulation between individual and public interests on the one hand, and hegemony and democracy on the other. It is important to keep in mind that the term 'political institution' does not refer to the institutional *sites* of legitimate authority, but instead to those *practices* that revolve around allocating values authoritatively for a society.

11. Ernesto Laclau, 'Universalism, Particularism, and the Question of Identity', *October*, no. 61, 1992, pp. 87–8.

12. Michel Foucault, 'Governmentality', *Ideology & Consciousness*, no. 6, 1979, pp. 12–3.

13. Wolfgang Iser, 'Representation: A Performative Act', in his *Prospecting: From Reader Response to Literary Anthropology*, Baltimore: The John Hopkins University Press 1989, pp. 239, 241, 245–6; and Hanna Fenichel Pitkin, *The Concept of Representation*, Berkeley and Los Angeles: University of California Press 1967, pp. 8–9, 153–4. See also Ernesto Laclau, *New Reflections on the Revolution of Our Time*, pp. 38–9, 61–6, 231; Ernesto Laclau, 'Power and Representation', in Mark Poster (ed.), *Politics, Theory and Contemporary Culture*, New York 1993, pp. 277–96; Ernesto Laclau, 'Deconstruction, Pragmatism, Hegemony' in Chantal Mouffe (ed.), *Deconstruction and Pragmatism*, London: Routledge, 1997; and Ernesto Laclau and Chantal Mouffe, *Hegemony and Socialist Strategy: Towards a Radical Democratic Politics*, London: Verso 1985 pp. 119–21.

14. Richard Flathman, *The Public Interest*, New York: John Wiley & Sons 1966, pp. 50, 54–6.

15. Ernesto Laclau, 'Universalism, Particularism, and the Question of Identity', pp. 89–90.

16. Ernesto Laclau and Chantal Mouffe, *Hegemony and Socialist Strategy*, pp. 122–34; see also 'The Impossibility of Society', in Ernesto Laclau, *New Reflections on the Revolution of Our Time*, pp. 89–93.

17. In order to avoid misunderstandings it should be noted that the term 'political community' does not refer to a normatively integrated community, what Easton terms 'the *sense or feelings* of community'. By political community I follow Easton's definition that it is a community 'that shares a political structure' and a 'political division of labour' regardless of the degree of normative integration, value consensus, and so on. David Easton, *A Systems Analysis of Political Life*, New York: John Wiley & Sons Inc 1965, pp. 182–3.

18. Cf. Ernesto Laclau, *New Reflections on the Revolution of Our Time*, pp. 41–5. For a critique of the Kantian dualism of time and space, see Anthony Giddens, *Contemporary Critique of Historical Materialism*, London: Macmillan 1981, pp. 17, 29–34.

19. The three dimensions of dislocation are discussed in Ernesto Laclau, *New reflections on the Revolution of Our Time*, pp. 41–5.

20. The notion of 'respectable moral disagreements' stems from Amy Gutmann, 'Introduction', in Charles Taylor, *Multiculturalism and 'The Politics of Recognition*, Princeton: Princeton University Press 1992, pp. 21–4. See also Amy Gutmann, 'Justice Across the Spheres', in David Miller and Michael Walzer (eds.), *Pluralism, Justice, and Equality*, Oxford: Oxford University Press 1995, pp. 110–5. This notion differs from what I see as the basic characteristic of democracy, namely the mutual acceptance of differences which is not a moral concept, but a political one. Or more correctly, it is a political value that does not set out to judge the 'inherent' respectability/disrespectability of values, norms or forms of life of comprehensive doctrines. It merely requires that they accept each other as agents in the political community.

21. I discuss the political aspects of the discrepancy between 'demos' and 'ethnos' in the context of increasingly multicultural Western societies, in 'Which Liberalism, Whose Community?, *Working Papers*, no. 7, Centre for Theoretical Studies, University of Essex 1995.

22. Cf. Alf Ross, *Hvorfor Demokrati?*, København: Phillips Bogtryk 1967, p. 144.

23. Joseph A. Schumpeter, *Capitalism, Socialism and Democracy*, London:

George Allen & Unwin 1976, pp. 290–6. See also David Held, *Models of Democracy*, Cambridge: Blackwell 1987, pp. 170–7.

24. Joseph A. Schumpeter, *Capitalism, Socialism and Democracy*, pp. 252, 251.

25. Robert A. Dahl, *A Preface to Democratic Theory*, Chicago: Chicago University Press 1956, p. 132.

26. It will be remembered from the discussion of the three faces of power that Dahl amongst others had difficulties in maintaining that consensus could not be the result of elite domination, that is, nondecision making. See also David Held, *Models of Democracy*, pp. 198–9.

27. There is a close connection between this conception of politics and Dahl's advocacy of the decision-making approach to the study of power. It is because politics is a 'surface manifestation' of 'superficial conflicts' that it can be adequately grasped in terms of the power struggles between explicit policy preferences. The nondecision-making approach is a borderline case. It can be accommodated by the behaviourists in so far as it accepts the fundamental distinction between the political and the social, that is, between 'surface manifestations' and the 'underlying consensus'. But when nondecision making links up with 'the mobilization of bias', the structuring of beliefs, and the like, it disturbs this picture of the relation between the political and the social.

28. The point is, as argued by Gutmann and Thompson, that the procedural model of democracy presupposes the political value 'that the (reasonable) moral claims of *each* citizen deserve respect', which cannot, however, be generated from its own premisses. See Amy Gutmann and Dennis Thompson, 'Moral Disagreement in a Democracy', *Social Philosophy and Policy,* vol. 12, no. 1, 1995, pp. 92–9.

29. Hanna Fenichel Pitkin, *The Concept of Representation*, pp. 232–3; and John Plamenatz, *Democracy and Illusion*, London and New York: Longman 1973, p. 110.

30. David Easton, *A Framework for Political Analysis*, Englewood Cliffs: Prentice-Hall 1965, p. 54.

31. See, e.g., David Held, *Models of Democracy*, pp. 283–9; John Keane, 'Democracy and the Idea of the Left', in David McLennan and Sean Sayers (eds.), *Socialism and Democracy*, London: Macmillan 1991, pp. 8–9; David Held, 'Democracy: From City-States to a Cosmopolitan Order?', in David Held (ed.), *Prospects for Democracy*, Cambridge: Polity Press 1993, pp. 23–5. For a critique see, e.g., Ernesto Laclau, 'Negotiating the Paradoxes of Contemporary Politics, An Interview with Ernesto Laclau', *Angelaki*, 1:3, Oxford: Angelaki, pp. 45–6; and Henrik Paul Bang and Torben Bech Dyrberg, 'Hegemony and Democracy', pp. 2–11.

32. Virginia Held, *The Public Interest and Individual Interests*, New York and London: Basic Books 1970, pp. 29–32; 35–6.

33. Cf. Richard Flathman, *The Public Interest*, p. 38; and Virginia Held, *The Public Interest and Individual Interests*, pp. 186–9, 197. See also Chantal Mouffe, *The Return of the Political*, p. 50.

34. Ernesto Laclau, *New Reflections on the Revolution of Our Time*, pp. 41–2, 69.

35. See Max Weber, 'Politik als Beruf', in his *Gesammelte Politischen Schriften,* 4th edn., Tübingen: J.C.B. Mohr 1980, pp. 548–56; and Niccoló Machiavelli, *The Prince*, Cambridge: Cambridge University Press 1988, p. 55, see also p. 62.

36. Cf. Slavoj Žižek, *For They Know Not What They Do*, London: Verso 1991, pp. 188–3. The relation between decision, undecidability and politics is discussed by Ernesto Laclau, 'Deconstruction, Pragmatism, Hegemony'.

37. See, e.g., Michel Foucault, 'Two Lectures' and 'The History of Sexuality', in Michel Foucault, Colin Gordon(ed.), *Power/Knowledge: Selected Interviews and Other Writings 1972–1977*, New York: Pantheon Books 1980, pp. 92–109, 187–90.

38. Michel Foucault, *The History of Sexuality*, vol. 1, Harmondsworth: Penguin Books 1981, pp. 99–100.

39. It is this assumption, as we saw in Chapter 3, which characterizes the juridico-discursive representation of power where '[a]ll the modes of domination, submission, and subjugation are ultimately reduced to an effect of obedience.' Power has only an external grip on the individual, and this 'pure limit set on freedom is, at least in our society, the general form of its acceptability'. Michel Foucault, *The History of Sexuality,* vol. 1, pp. 85, 86.

40. Cf. David Beetham who criticizes both of these assumptions in his *The Legitimation of Power*, Houndmills: Macmillan 1991. The (Weberian) reduction of legitimacy to the belief in legitimacy, and the assumption of the externality between legitimacy and power are discussed in ch. 1 and pp. 60–3, 104, 107 respectively.

41. Robert A. Dahl, *Democracy and Its Critics*, New York and London: Yale University Press 1989, p. 307.

42. Cf. Will Kymlicka, 'Community', in Robert E. Goodin and Philip Pettit (eds.), *A Companion to Contemporary Political Philosophy*, Oxford: Blackwell 1993, p. 374.

43. Rawls distinguishes between what he calls 'the fact of pluralism' and 'reasonable pluralism'. Far from being a normative criteria, reasonableness indicates that agents mutually recognize and accept each other politically. John Rawls, *Political Liberalism*, New York: Columbia University Press 1993, pp. 36–8, 63–5.

44. The problems with such an argument is discussed in ibid. ch. 1, pp. 31–9.

45. Cf. Ernesto Laclau and Chantal Mouffe, *Hegemony and Socialist Strategy*, ch. 4; Chantal Mouffe, *The Return of the Political*, pp. 51–2, 136–7, 144–7; John Gray, 'Agonistic Liberalism', *Social Philosophy and Policy*, vol. 12, no. 1, 1995, pp. 116–21; I would claim that it is, moreover, at the very centre of Rawls's political liberalism.

46. A similar argument is put forward by Amy Gutmann and Dennis Thompson, 'Moral Disagreement in a Democracy', pp. 100–10.

47. Rawls makes a similar distinction between the presentation of the political conception of justice and how it is part of or derivable from comprehensive doctrines. John Rawls, *Political Liberalism*, p. 12.

48. John Gray, 'Agnostic Liberalism', *Social Philosophy and Policy*, vol. 12, no. 1, 1995, p. 120.

49. See, for example, Claude Lefort, *The Political Forms of Modern Society*, Cambridge: Polity 1986, pp. 302–4.

50. Cf. John Rawls, 'Reply to Habermas', *The Journal of Philosophy*, vol. 42, no. 3, 1995, pp. 173–5.

51. Cf. Ernesto Laclau and Chantal Mouffe, *Hegemony and Socialist Strategy*, ch. 4. See also James G. March and Johan P. Olsen, 'Institutional Perspectives on Political Institutions', paper presented at the IPSA Conference, Berlin, 1994, pp. 11–4, 17.

52. Rawls's concept of the overlapping consensus holds that it is neutral with regard to the justification of partially comprehensive doctrines, and that it is reasonable from the point of view of each of these doctrines to affirm this type of consensus, because it does not impinge upon their autonomy. More

precisely, it seems to be the best guarantee for self-determination and popular sovereignty. See John Rawls, *Political Liberalism*, pp. 134–6, 138–40, 150–1; John Rawls, 'Reply to Habermas', pp. 143.

53. Gray's defence of value pluralism runs into difficulties here, because he does not make this distinction between the political and the cultural. In his instructive criticism of the philosophical anthropology of the Enlightenment, which is modelled around the axioms of universal rationality and progress, he falls prey to another pitfall when he says that 'political allegiance . . . presupposes a common cultural identity', and 'that allegiance to a liberal form of life must always be a matter of cultural solidarity, not of universalizing rationality.' (Agnostic Liberalism', p. 128.) His 'political liberalism' is, in effect, placed uneasily between his insistence on cultural solidarity and his critique of universal rationality. The political is displaced because it is situated between the cultural and the rational, that is, between the normative integration of interests and the instrumental aggregation of preferences.

54. This is not, however, entirely correct in that we have to operate with the minimal assumption that the political person has the potentials for endorsing, revising and rejecting forms of life, political strategies, comprehensive doctrines, and the like. In any case, this ability is 'open' in the sense that it cannot determine any outcome. It is, I believe, best conceived as an ontology of potentials.

55. Ernesto Laclau, 'Subject of Politics, Politics of the Subject', *Differences: A Journal of Feminist Cultural Studies*, 7, 1, 1995, pp. 151–2; Torben Bech Dyrberg, 'Diskursanalyse als Postmoderne Politische Theorie', in Oliver Marchart (ed.), *Das Undarstellbare der Politic,* Wien: Turia & Kant 1997.

56. Cf. Eva Etzioni-Halevy, *The Elite Connection*, Cambridge: Polity Press 1993, pp. 101–21, 202–3. Rawls's idea of the application of public reason differs from the one I have proposed here, because, for him, it 'always applies to public and government officers in official forums . . . especially to the judiciary in its decisions.' John Rawls, *Political Liberalism*, pp. 252–3. See also his, 'Reply to Habermas', p. 140. The problem with this argument is that it conveys a rather restricted image of the valid range of public reason – an image which is closely connected with the underdeveloped emphasis on the political community or similar terms.

57. Cf. Torben Bech Dyrberg, 'Which Liberalism, Whose Community?', pp. 19–20.

58. To approach the issue of the public interest in terms of counterfactual reasoning is, amongst others, advanced by Charles Frankel and Walter Lippmann. The latter holds that 'the public interest may be presumed to be what men would choose if they saw clearly, thought rationally, acted disinterestedly and benevolently.' Walter Lippmann, *The Public Philosophy*, Boston: Little, p. 42. See also Felix E. Oppenheim, *Political Concepts: A Reconstruction*, Oxford: Basil Blackwell 1981, pp. 136–8. Cf. the critique of notions such as the common good and the public interest in so-called classical democratic theory put forward by Joseph Schumpeter, *Capitalism, Socialism, Democracy*, ch. 21.

59. John Rawls, *A Theory of Justice*, Oxford: Oxford University Press 1972, pp. 97, 136–42. See also John Rawls, *Political Liberalism*, pp. 24–7, 243–4, 305.

60. Cf. John Rawls, *Political Liberalism*, pp. 73–7, 203, 208–9.

61. James G. March and Johan P. Olsen, *Rediscovering Institutions*, New

York: The Free Press 1989, p. 16. See also James G. March and Johan P. Olsen, 'Institutional Perspectives on Political Institutions', paper presented at the IPSA Conference: Berlin 1994, p. 18.

62. John Rawls, 'Reply to Habermas', pp. 164, 167; *Theory of Justice*, p. 148.

63. Similar ideas are put forward by William E. Connolly's notion of 'agonistic respect', *Identity\Difference*, Ithaca and London: Cornell University Press 1992, pp. 13–4, 166; William A. Galston, *Liberal Purposes*, Cambridge: Cambridge University Press 1991, pp. 3–4; John Gray, 'Agonistic Liberalism', pp. 111–35; and Chantal Mouffe, *The Return of the Political*, p. 144–53.

64. This issue is discussed at length in the exchange between Kukathas and Kymlicka about individual and collective rights. Chandran Kukathas, 'Are There Any Cultural Rights?', *Political Theory*, vol. 20, no. 1, 1992, pp. 105–39; Will Kymlicka, 'The Rights of Minority Cultures', ibid., pp. 140–6; Chandran Kukathas, 'Cultural Rights Again', *Political Theory*, vol. 20, no. 4, 1992, pp. 674–80.

65. John Rawls, *Political Liberalism*, pp. 37, 41–2, 226.

66. To approach the question of toleration in relation to reasonable pluralism, and hence to the mutual acceptance of difference, indicates that it should be approached politically and not ethically. It has, in other words, to be discussed from the point of view of the political as free-standing *vis-à-vis* comprehensive doctrines. Says Laclau: '[t]oleration only starts when I morally disapprove of something and, however, I accept it. The very condition of approaching the question of toleration is to start realizing that it is not an ethical question at all.' The ground of toleration is, he continues, 'the need for society to function in a way which is compatible with a certain degree of internal differentiation.' Ernesto Laclau, 'Deconstruction, Pragmatism, Hegemony', pp. 9–10. Reasonable pluralism, acceptance of difference, and like terms, are *political* specifications of this 'certain degree of internal differentiation'.

67. See John Rawls, *Political Liberalism*, p. 157.

68. Slavoj Žižek, *The Sublime Object of Ideology*, p. 6.

69. Ernesto Laclau and Chantal Mouffe, *Hegemony and Socialist Strategy*, p. 188.

70. Cf. Henrik Paul Bang and Torben Bech Dyrberg, 'Hegemony and Democracy', p. 28.

Postscript on Conceptualizing Power

1. There are two points that should be clarified here: First, the subject as metaphor is prior to the dualisms of subject/object, agency/structure, individual/system and voluntarism/determinism. Structure, for example, is, metaphorically speaking, subject in so far as power (ability, capacity) is located in the structure. Second, the circular structure of power is overarching in relation to what Morris has termed the 'vehicle fallacy' and the 'exercise fallacy'. Power, he says, 'as a dispositional concept, is neither a *thing* (a resource or vehicle) nor an *event* (an exercise of power): it is a *capacity*.' Peter Morris, *Power: A Philosophical Analysis*, Manchester: Manchester University Press 1987, p. 19.

2. For Bhaskar the central question is, 'what properties do societies and people possess that might make them possible objects of knowledge for us?' Roy Bhaskar, *The Possibility of Naturalism*, 2nd edn. New York: Harvester Wheatsheaf 1989, p. 13 (italics in original). This approach presupposes a strict separation between epistemology and ontology. Science is conditioned by and studies 'intransitive' objects, meaning that 'for science to be possible or intelligible, the world must be made up of real things and structures', that is, 'there must be intransitive objects of scientific inquiry which exist and act in

certain ways.' William Outwaite, *New Philosophies of Social Science*, Houndmills: Macmillan 1987, pp. 31, 38.

3. Michel Foucault, *The Order of Things*, London and New York: Tavistock Publications 1970, p. 332.

4. Cf. Slavoj Žižek, 'Beyond Discourse-Analysis', in Ernesto Laclau, *New Reflections on the Revolution of Our Time*, London: Verso 1990, p. 254.

5. Cf. Ernesto Laclau, *New reflections on the Revolution of Our Time*, pp. 30, 44, 60–4; Slavoj Žižek, *The Sublime Object of Ideology*, London: Verso 1989, p. 226; *For They Know Not What They Do*, London: Verso 1991, pp. 46, 190, 198–203; *Tarrying With the Negative*, Durham: Duke University Press 1993, pp. 33–5.

6. Cf. Gilles Deleuze and Félix Guattari, *What is Philosophy?*, New York: Columbia University Press 1994, pp. 37–8, 45–7, 58–9.

7. Cf. Roy Bhaskar, *The Possibility of Naturalism*, pp. 9–13, 25–44; William Outhwaite, *New Philosophies of Social Science*, ch. 2; Andrew Sayer, *Method in Social Science*, London: Routledge 1992, ch. 3.

8. 'Every movement passes through the whole of the plane by immediately turning back on and folding itself and also by folding other movements or allowing itself to be folded by them, giving rise to retroactions, connections, and proliferations in the fractalization of this infinitely folded up infinity.' Gilles Deleuze and Félix Guattari, *What is Philosophy?*, pp. 38–9.

9. Michel Foucault, *The History of Sexuality*, vol. 1, Harmondsworth: Penguin Books 1981, p. 93

10. Cf. Gilles Deleuze, *Foucault*, Paris: Les Éditions de Minuit, pp. 37–8; Michel Foucault, 'Governmentality', *Ideology and Consciousness*, no. 6, 1979, pp. 13, 18, 20–1; Michel Foucault, 'Truth and Power', in Michel Foucault, Colin Gordon (ed.), *Power/Knowledge: Selected Interviews and Other Writings 1972–1977*, New York: Pantheon Books 1980, pp. 120–3; Slavoj Žižek, *For They Know Not What They Do*, pp. 33–4, 40–1, 203–6.

11. For a discussion of Derrida's notion of the supplement, see ch. 4, nt. 23.

12. Cf. Henry Staten, *Wittgenstein and Derrida*, Oxford: Basil Blackwell 1984, pp. 16–9.

13. Gilles Deleuze and Félix Guattari, *What is Philosophy?*, p. 59.

14. Ibid., p. 42.

15. Michel Haar, 'Nietzsche and Metaphysical Language', in David B. Allison (ed.), *The New Nietzsche*, Cambridge, Massachusetts: MIT Press 1985, p. 11.

16. Ibid., p. 12.

Index

NOTE: All entries refer to power unless otherwise stated.

ability 90–1, 116, 174
- and conceptualization 241–5
- dispensing with constituent subject 88, 93
- identity and political authority 95–8, 105

agency
- causality and responsibility 71, 72, 73, 74, 76, 78, 82, 83
- common good: individual and public interests 208
- identity and politics of subjective and real interests 167, 174
- political representation 192–3
- power as influence term and decision making 21
- presuppositionless conception of power 137, 141, 145
- 'third face of power' 66, 67, 68, 69

agency/structure 16
- causality and political agency in community power debate 63, 75, 80–1
- dualism 3–7
- identity and political authority 89, 90
- non-derivative conceptualization of power 9, 10
- power as influence term and decision making 25–6, 28, 29, 30, 33, 34, 35, 36, 39
- presuppositionless conception of power 140

Althusser, L. 123–4, 130

antagonism xi, 180
- democratic political community and the common good 194–8
- and identity 144–55

anticipating reactions 38–49, 51, 52, 55, 62, 67, 159

Archimides 83, 157, 226

Arendt, H. x, 27, 30

Aristotle 185

authority 15
- common good: individual and public interests 208, 209, 211, 216
- common good: political and social 204, 205, 206, 207
- democratic political community and the common good 197, 199
- hegemony and democracy 236
- non-derivative conceptualization of power 13
- political and politics 186–7, 188, 191, 193, 250
- power as influence term and decision making 27, 28
- presuppositionless conception of power 124, 143
- value pluralism and liberal democracy 228
- *see also* identity and political authority; politics-power-authority triangle

auto-negativity 133, 134, 135, 149, 151, 152
- common good 213, 218
- identity and politics of subjective and real interests 168, 172, 173, 174, 180
- order as reality effect 249
- origin and power 253, 255
- political ordering of power 250, 252

autonomy
- causality and political agency in community power debate 66, 68, 69, 71, 73, 74, 75–6, 77, 82–3

common good 205, 206, 219
identity and political authority 86, 96, 100, 101
identity and politics of subjective and real interests 160, 161, 165, 166–7, 168, 169–70, 175
order as reality effect 246
political and politics 186, 251
presuppositionless conception of power 150, 151, 155
and real interests 178–82
and reason versus causation and power 30–8
retroactive causation 241
value pluralism and liberal democracy 223

Bachrach, P. 49, 50, 129, 204, 240
causality and resposibility in power relations 71–2, 78
decision making and the 'two faces of power' 51–2, 53, 54, 55–7, 59
'third face of power' 63, 64, 66, 68
Ball, T. 26
Baratz, M.S. 49, 50, 129, 204, 240
causality and responsibility in power relations 71–2, 78
'third face of power' 63, 64, 66, 68
'two faces of power' 51–2, 53, 54, 55–7, 59
Barthes, R. 97, 182
basis and nature of power 1–2, 4, 6
behaviourism 21–30, 33, 51, 64, 81, 82, 240
Benn, S. 31
Benton, T. 3
Bradshaw, A. 72–3

Capra, F. 160
causality
means-ends 38
and overdetermination 130–2
and political agency in community power debate 50–84
causality and responsibility in power relations 70–84
decision making and 'two faces of power' 51–63
'third face of power' 63–70
presuppositionless conception of power 130, 147
and responsibility in power relations 70–84
causation 83–4
and behaviourist conception 21–30
order as reality effect 248
and power versus reason and autonomy 30–8
retroactive 238–41
social 39
cause and effect 104, 213–4, 243
characteristics of power 1–2, 6
Clegg, S.R. 33
coercion and consent 35, 38, 39
common good 18–19
political and social 200–8
see also under democracy
community power debate see causality and political agency in community power debate
conception 13–4
conceptualising power 20–1, 238–56
ability 241–5
non-derivative 7–13
order as reality-effect 245–9
origin and power 252–6
political ordering of power 249–52
power as influence term and decision making 26, 30
retroactive causation 238–41
conflict
causality and political agency in community power debate 50, 52–4, 56, 58, 60, 64–6, 78, 81
common good 215, 218
identity and politics of subjective and real interests 158–9
power as influence term and decision making 30, 40
presuppositionless conception of power 143, 144
value pluralism and liberal democracy 225–6
Connolly, W.E. 14, 22, 70, 73, 149, 241
conceptualization of real interests 163–70
identity and the politics of subjective and real interests 158, 159, 160–1, 178, 180–1
consensus 51, 58, 60, 64, 66, 218, 240
constituent subject, dispensing with 88–93
contextualization 14–5, 23, 25, 194–6
counterfactuals 24, 25, 28, 160, 168
causality and political agency in community power debate 62, 65–6, 75, 81, 82
Cousins, M. 102

Crenson, M.A. 50, 53, 60–2

Dahl, R.A. 50, 240
- democracy and the politics of interests and the common good 202–4, 206, 216, 219, 223
- power as influence term and decision making 20, 22, 40, 43–4, 45, 47–8
- 'third face of power' 65, 67
- 'two faces of power' 51, 52, 55, 58, 60, 62

Debnam, G. 41
decision making 51–63, 72
definition of power 86, 89
Deleuze, G. 103
democracy 18–9, 251
democracy and politics of interests and common good 183–237
- common good: individual interests and public interests 208–21
- common good: political community 194–200
- common good: political and social 200–8
- hegemony 234–7
- political and politics 184–94
- value pluralism and liberal democracy 221–34

Denmark 121–2
Derrida, J. 37, 131, 251
Descartes, R. 6
difference 90, 92, 98–9, 179, 180
- democratic political community and the common good 198–9
- logic 118–23
- value pluralism and liberal democracy 223

disciplinary power 105–11, 109
displacement/metonymy 125–7
domination 32, 79, 127, 218
double conditioning rule 106, 124
Dyrberg, T. x–xi, xii

Easton, D. 184
elites x, 42, 45, 47, 58, 60, 202
emancipatory interests 69, 165
equivalence 118–23, 179
ethico-political decisions 186, 199, 206, 212, 234
event causation 81, 82, 90, 142
exercise of power
- causality and responsibility 71, 72, 73, 74, 75, 76, 77–8, 80, 83
- identity and political authority 89, 104
- identity and politics of subjective and real interests 174, 177, 179, 182
- power as influence term and decision making 24, 25
- presuppositionless conception of power 124, 140, 141–2, 144, 146
- 'third face of power' 63, 64, 65, 67
- 'two faces of power' 51, 52, 57, 59, 60, 61, 62

'first face of power' 63, 67
Foucault, M. x–xi, 6, 8, 12, 84
- conceptualising power 240, 242, 244, 249, 253
- democracy and the politics of interests and the common good 185, 187, 215, 234
- identity and the politics of subjective and real interests 175–6, 178, 181
- power analytics 85–8
- power as influence term and decision making 14–5, 16, 17
- presuppositionless conception of power 116–7, 124, 132, 133, 134–5, 140, 148

Freud, S. 120, 138, 152, 153
Frey, F.W. 57, 58
fundamental reversal 96, 113, 132

Giddens, A. 4
governmentalization 108–9
Gray, J. 226

Haar, M. 96
Habermas, J. xi, 6, 37, 69–70, 103, 149, 165
hegemony xi, 18–9, 123–30, 184, 234–7
- common good 203, 208, 209, 210, 212, 213, 214
- democratic political community and the common good 195, 196
- political and politics 188, 190

Heidegger, M. 154, 171–2
Held, D. 6
Hobbes, T. 5, 184–5, 238
- power, identity and political authority 85, 89, 99, 104, 105
- power as influence term and decision making 23, 25, 38
- presuppositionless conception of power 119–20, 138, 139–40

Hoffman, J. 58
Hume, D. 23, 25
Hussain, A. 102

identity xi, 15, 16, 17
ability and its conceptualization 243
circular structure 93–9
common good 208, 211, 218
democratic political community and the common good 194
negativity 132, 133, 135, 140, 143, 144
non-derivative conceptualization of power 9, 11, 13
order as reality effect 248, 249
origin and power 255
political representation 192, 193
power as influence term and decision making 22, 26, 28, 35
presuppositionless conception of power 116–8
social reality 119, 120, 121, 122, 128–9, 131
see also under negativity
identity and political authority 85–115
ability 88–93
circular structure 93–9
Foucault's power analytics 85–8
political authorization 105–11
representation, politics of 99–105
identity and politics of subjective and real interests 156–82
autonomy and real interests 178–82
great gift of real interests 158–63
Luke and Connolly: conceptualization of real interests 163–70
relation between real interests and power 173–8
self-representation of real interests 170–2
indirect influence 38–49, 51, 67, 74
individual interests 207, 208–21
influence term and decision making 20–49
behaviourist conception of power as causation 21–30
indirect influence and anticipating reactions 38–49
reason and autonomy versus causation and power 30–8
interests *see* identity and politics of subjective and real interests
interpretation 175, 219, 220
Isaac, J.C. 3

Jameson, F. 212
juridico-discursive representation 85, 91, 98, 99, 102, 105–11, 133, 242
political and politics 185, 186, 187, 250
value pluralism and liberal democracy 225

justice 222, 228, 231

Kant, I. 36, 90, 107
Kaplan, A. 29
Keane, J. 6
Kierkegaard, S. 154, 173, 256
knowledge 78–9, 81, 83, 98
ability and its conceptualization 244
common good 211
identity and political authority 87, 90
identity and politics of subjective and real interests 160, 161, 169
order as reality-effect 247
retroactive causation 241
value pluralism and liberal democracy 223

Lacan, J. xi, 149
Laclau, E. 12, 17, 37, 53, 118, 128, 132, 234–5, 240, 242
Lasswell, H.D. 29
Lefort, C. 113, 122, 157, 226
legitimacy xi, 73
common good 205, 216
identity and political authority 99–106, 108, 110
non-derivative conceptualization of power 13
political and politics 186, 187
liberalism 6, 162, 186, 221–34
hegemony and democracy 234
political and politics 188, 189, 191, 251
presuppositionless conception of power 150
limits, reflection of 93–9
linearity 242, 247, 252–3
Locke, J. 105, 119
Lukes, S. 14, 49, 204, 240
causality and responsibility in power relations 70–84
conceptualization of real interests 163–70
identity and the politics of subjective and real interests 158, 160, 178, 180–1

power as an influence term and decision making 22, 27, 28, 33, 36
power, causality and political agency in community power debate 50, 58
presuppositionless conception of power 129, 145, 149
'third face of power' theory 63–70

McFarland, A.S. 30, 38–9
Machiavelli, N. 89, 209
March, J.G. 231
Marxism 6, 27, 68, 105, 162, 164
hegemony and democracy 234
political ordering of power 251
political and politics 186, 188, 189, 191
power as influence term and decision making 29
Merelman, R.M. 50, 57
Mills, C.W. 69, 70
Mitchell, T. 97
mobilization of bias
causality and political agency in community power debate 52–3, 55–60, 63–6, 72, 81
identity and politics of subjective and real interests 165
Morriss, P. 24, 26
Mouffe, C. x–xii, 12, 17, 118, 128, 132, 234–5, 240, 242

negativity 17, 116–55
causality and political agency in community power debate 55
and identity 132–55
antagonism and imaginary nature of identity 145–55
constitution 136–45
political authority 99
politics of subjective and real in terests 171
origin and power 256
presuppositionless concept of power 116–8
see also auto-negativity
neo-pluralism 45
Nietzsche, F.W. 172
no-decisions 50, 63, 64, 73, 174
nondecisions 58, 174
causality and political agency in community power debate 53–5, 57, 59, 62–4, 68–9, 71–2, 78

objectivity 68, 93, 116, 117, 246, 252

Olsen, J.P. 231
order 252–6
/disorder dichotomy 76
political 249–52
as reality effect 245–9
origin and power 252–6
Otherness 145–8, 151–5, 177, 180
overdetermination 123–30
and kind of causality 130–2

Parenti, M. 45
Parsons, T. x, 3, 27, 30
particularism 216–7, 222, 232
particularity 212–3, 214, 217
pluralism x
causality and political agency in community power debate 51–2, 54, 56–60, 64–5, 67, 69, 71
common good 217
democratic political community and the common good 197–8
power as influence term and decision making 29, 31, 40–8
presuppositionless conception of power 142
value 221–34
see also Bachrach; Baratz
politics-power-authority triangle 12, 16
politics/political x, 105–11
agency *see* causality
authority *see* identity and political authority
community 194–200
interests *see* democracy
non-derivative conceptualization of power 10
ordering 249–52
power 5–7, 12, 15
power as influence term and decision making 21, 31, 40–4, 47–8
presuppositionless conception of power 141–2, 143, 144, 145
social relations 14
theory 13
see also identity and politics; representation
Polsby, N. 22, 50, 51–2, 56, 60–2
Poulantzas, N. 29, 45
power analytics 85–8, 116, 117, 132, 134–5, 242
'power over' 2–3, 22, 83
ability 244
causality and political agency in com-

munity power debate 50, 59, 64, 81
common good 215, 216
identity and political authority 85, 88, 89, 99, 102, 104
identity and politics of subjective and real interests 165
political ordering of power 250
'power over' (continued)
power as influence term and decision making 34
value pluralism and liberal democracy 231
power relations 142, 144, 146, 188, 206
identity and politics of subjective and real interests 164, 165, 170, 173, 177, 181, 182
power struggles 104, 122, 141, 142, 143, 241
common good 203, 204, 205, 208, 210, 212
democratic political community and the common good 195, 197
identity and politics of subjective and real interests 175, 177, 178
presuppositionless conception of power 144, 147, 148, 150, 152, 153, 154, 155
'power to' x, 2–3
ability 244
identity and political authority 89, 99
identity and politics of subjective and real interests 165
political ordering of power 251
value pluralism and liberal democracy 231
presuppositionless concept of power 116–8
public interest 18–9, 207, 208–21, 230
public reason 224, 227, 228–9, 233
punishment 138–9

racism 121–2, 149
rationality 31–7, 83, 96, 169
identity and political authority 100
order as reality effect 246
political ordering of power 251
political and politics 186, 187
Rawls, J. 197, 222, 224, 227–8, 230, 231–2
real interests 68, 69, 81, 83, 241
see also identity and politics of subjective and real interests
reality effect 97, 245–9
reason and autonomy versus causation and power 30–8
reasonableness 230–1
see also public reason
recognition 169, 176
representation
common good 208, 209, 210
common good: political and social 205
order as reality effect 247
origin and power 252
political 99–105, 191–4
see also juridico-discursive representation
repressive hypothesis 87, 91–2, 96, 101, 133–4, 176
order as reality effect 246
political and politics 189
presuppositionless conception of power 153
retroactive causation 240
resistance 177–8
responsibility 205, 209–10
and causality 70–84
retroactive causation 238–41
rights 225–6
Rousseau, J.-J. 69
Rushdie, S. 198
Russell, B. 38, 80

Sartori, G. 185
Schattschneider, E.E. 52–3, 54, 64, 142, 165
Schmitt, C. 126
Schumpeter, J. 201–4, 206

'second face of power' 54, 57–8, 59, 60, 63, 67
causality and political agency in community power debate 56, 78
and decision making 51–63
self 167, 168, 240
self-determination 180, 227, 228, 240
value pluralism and liberal democracy 233, 234, 236
self-reflection 169, 171, 172, 178
signifier/signification 119, 126–8, 130, 133
social entities 116–7
social orders 120–1, 185
social reality, discursive structuring of 118–32
difference and equivalence, logics of 118–23

overdetermination and hegemonic power struggles 123–30
overdetermination and kind of causality 130–2
sovereignty 86, 88, 184
common good 200
hegemony and democracy 236
identity and political authority 96, 100, 103, 104, 114
order as reality effect 248
political and politics 187, 191
presuppositionless conception of power 139
value pluralism and liberal democracy 226, 227, 228, 233, 234
sovereignty-discipline-government triangle 109, 111
space 90, 107, 252
Spinoza, B. 130
Spivak, G. 155
Staten, H. 152
strategies 93, 98, 104, 192, 208, 210, 211, 213
subjectivity/subjectification 17–8, 68, 86, 91, 116
subordination 127, 165, 218
Swanton, C. 168
systemic bias 59, 60, 68, 165
causality and political agency in community power debate 63–4, 72, 80, 82
systemic power 66, 164
causality and political agency in community power debate 63–8, 71, 73–7, 79, 80–1, 83

telos 104, 253, 254–5
'third face of power' 63–70, 74, 76, 83, 164, 204
time 90, 107, 158, 160, 252
Tocqueville, A. de 226
transparency 151, 166, 169, 176, 178
'two faces of power' *see* 'second face of power'

United States 20, 44, 58, 62
unity 94, 95, 96, 98, 103
universality 12, 214, 217, 222, 232

value pluralism 221–34
violations 141, 142, 143

Watkins, G.W.N. 66
Weber, M. 23, 38, 209
Wittgenstein, L. 90
Wolfinger, R.E. 22, 41, 50, 57, 58, 65, 67, 68, 83
Wrong, D.H. 38

Žižek, S. 17, 118, 128, 155, 174, 243